# FRENCH AIRCRAFT CARRIERS
1910–2000

# FRENCH AIRCRAFT CARRIERS 1910–2000

John Jordan & Jean Moulin

Naval Institute Press
Annapolis, Maryland

**Overleaf:** The Milhaud finger piers at Toulon between November 1960 and January 1961, with the recently arrived *Clemenceau* in the foreground, *Arromanches* in the centre, and *La Fayette* on the left of the picture. Note the comparatively large size of *Clemenceau* and her fully angled deck.



First published in Great Britain in 2025 by
Seaforth Publishing
a division of Pen & Sword Books Ltd,
George House, Beevor Street, Barnsley, S71 1HN

www.seaforthpublishing.com
Email info@seaforthpublishing.com

Published and distributed in the United States of America and Canada by the Naval Institute Press,
291 Wood Road, Annapolis, Maryland 21402-5043
www.usni.org/press/books

Library of Congress Cataloging Number: 2025940350 (hardcover)

ISBN 978 1 68247 790 8 (hardcover)
ISBN 979 8 89241 007 6 (e-book)



Typeset and designed by Stephen Dent

# CONTENTS

# ACRONYMS & ABBREVIATIONS

|  |  |
|---|---|
| AA | *antiaérien*<br>anti-aircraft |
| ACAD | *automatique contre-avions double*<br>automatic twin AA mounting |
| AIDCOMER | *système d'aide au commandement à la mer*<br>digital decision-making system for CO |
| AEW | Airborne Early Warning |
| ALAE | *amiral aviation embarquée*<br>senior officer naval avaiation |
| ALAT | *Aviation légère de l'armée de terre*<br>Army Light Aviation |
| ALFAN | *amiral force d'action navale*<br>senior officer FAN |
| ALH | *Alizé mis à hauteur*<br>Alizé modified for AEW |
| ALM | *Alizé modernisé*<br>upgraded Alizé |
| ALPA | *amiral groupe des porte-avions et aviation embarquée*<br>senior officer for carriers and embarked aviation |
| AM | *air-mer*<br>air-to-surface |
| AN | *arme nucléaire*<br>nuclear weapon |
| AOF | *Afrique Occidentale Française*<br>French West Africa |
| ASM | *anti sous-marin*<br>anti-submarine |
| ASMP | *air sol moyenne portée*<br>medium-range air-to-ground missile |
| AWACS | Airborne Warning And Control System |
| BAN | *base d'Aéronautique navale*<br>naval aviation base |
| CA | *Contre-amiral*<br>Rear Admiral |
| CAM | Catapult Aircraft Merchant (ship) |
| CAS | Close Air Support |
| CATOBAR | Catapult Assisted Take-Off But Arrested Recovery |
| CCA | Carrier Controlled Approach |
| CEF | *Centre d'entraînement de la flotte*<br>Fleet Training Centre |
| CEL | *Centre d'essais des Landes*<br>Trials Centre in the Landes *département* |
| CEP | *Centre d'expérimentations du Pacifique*<br>French Pacific Nuclear Test Centre |
| CG | *Groupe de chasseurs*<br>Fighter Group |
| CI | *Central information*<br>Combat Information Centre |
| CO | *Central opérations*<br>Operations Centre |
| CSM | *Conseil supérieur de la Marine*<br>[consultative body for Navy] |
| DAGAIE | *dispositif d'autodéfense pour la guerre antimissile infrarouge et électromagnétique*<br>chaff launcher using infrared and electromagnetic decoys |
| DCA | *défense contre avions*<br>anti-aircraft defence |
| DCN | *Direction des constructions navales*<br>Directorate for Naval Construction |
| DCAN | *Direction des constructions et armes navales*<br>Directorate for Naval Construction & Weapons |
| DRBC | fire control radar |
| DRBI | height-finding radar |
| DRBN | navigation radar |
| DRBV | surveillance radar |
| DSM | *Dispositif spécial en Méditerranée*<br>special force based in Mediterranean |
| FAN | *Force d'action navale*<br>Naval Action Force |
| FBA | Franco-British Aviation [Company] |
| FNFL | *Forces navales françaises libres*<br>Free French Naval Forces |
| FNI | *Force navale d'intervention*<br>Naval Intervention Force |
| GASM | *Groupe d'action sous-marine*<br>Antisubmarine Action Group |
| GATAC | *groupement aérien tactique*<br>Tactical Air Group |
| GL | Gourdou-Leseurre [company] |
| HF/DF | high-frequency direction finding |
| HP | high pressure [turbine] |
| IE | *indisponibilité pour entretien*<br>maintenance period |
| IFF | Identification Friend or Foe |
| Inmarsat | International Maritime Satellite |
| IP | intermediate pressure [turbine] |
| IPER | *indisponibilité périodique pour entretien et réparation*<br>major refit period |
| LN | Loire-Nieuport [company] |
| LP | low pressure [turbine] |
| Mistral | *missile transportable aérien léger*<br>light portable surface-to-air missile |
| Mle | *Modèle*<br>Model |
| MN | *Marine Nationale*<br>French Navy |
| nm | nautical mile (1,852 metres) |
| OA | *Officier d'appontage*<br>Landing Officer |

OEA — *obus explosif en acier*
HE shell

OP — *optique d'appontage*
landing mirror sight

PA — *porte-avions*
aircraft carrier

PAN — *porte-avions (à propulsion) nucléaire*
nuclear-powered aircraft carrier

PC — *poste de commandement*
Command Post

PC ops — *poste de commandement opérations*
Command Post (operations)

PEI — *période d'entretien intermédiaire*
intermediate maintenance period

PH — *porte-hélicoptères*
helicopter carrier

PL — Pierre Levasseur [company]

QF — quick firing

RANAE — *remise à niveau après essais*
post-trials refit

RATOG — Rocket-assisted Take-off Gear

REM — *roquettes électromagnétiques*
electronmagnetic rockets

RHC — *régiment d'hélicoptères de combat*
Regiment of Combat Helicopters

RIR — *roquettes infrarouge*
infrared rockets

SAAM — *surface-air anti-missile*
anti-missile SAM

SADRAL — *système d'autodéfense rapprochée anti-aérien léger*
light missile point defence system

SAGAIE — *système d'autodéfense pour la guerre anti-missile infrarouge et électromagnétique*
infrared and electromagnetic anti-missile point defence system

SDC — *système de combat*
combat system

SEM — *Super Etendard modernisé*
modernised Super Etendard

SENIT — *système d'exploitation numérique des informations tactiques*
tactical data system

SIRPA — *Service d'informations et de relations publiques des Armées*
public information and relations service for defence

SNCASE — Société Nationale de Constructions Aéronautiques du Sud-Est

STCAN — *Service technique des constructions et armes navales*
Technical Service for Naval Construction & Weapons (post-war)

STCN — *Service technique des constructions navales*
Technical Service for Naval Construction (prewar)

SUE — Super Etendard (unmodernised)

SYLVER — *système de lancement vertical*
vertical launch (missile) system

SYRACUSE — *système de radiocommunication utilisant un satellite*
French naval satcom system

TCD — *transport de chalands de débarquement*
Landing Transport Dock

TF — Task Force

TG — Task Group

TLD — *traversée de longue durée*
long-distance cruise (to conclude trials)

TR — *télépointeur radar*
radar director

TRA — *télépointeur radar artillerie*
radar director for guns

TT — *tourelle de télépointage optique et radar*
optical and radar director

VAE — *Vice-amiral d'Escadre*
Fleet Vice Admiral

VHF — very high frequency

V/STOL — Vertical and/or Short Take-off and Landing

# PREFACE

THE PRESENT BOOK IS A NATURAL SEQUEL to the author's earlier series on the French Navy, written in collaboration with a variety of French co-authors, but is very different in nature and composition. The earlier books traced the development of French battleships, cruisers and destroyers over one of two distinct periods: the interwar period, and the period leading up to the First World War. There was continuity in the development of the various categories of warship during each of these two periods, which made it easier to present a coherent narrative. Outlining the developmental history of the French aircraft carrier has been more challenging, as it extends from the stumbling first steps of the second decade of the twentieth century, through the 'experimental' period of the 1920s and 1930s, a post-war era marked by loans and purchases of carriers from Britain and the USA and the first attempt at a 'modern' carrier design, the PA 54 *Clemenceau*, to the adoption of a 'mature' carrier with nuclear propulsion, the *Charles de Gaulle*. Finally, the authors have endeavoured to bring the story up to the present day with a brief review of developments since the year 2000.

Whereas histories of British and US carrier development have as their primary focus the ships that were completed, many of which served in the Second World War and in post-war conflicts around the globe, a study of carrier development in France necessarily embraces a host of serious, but ultimately abortive 'paper' projects that were never realised due either to 'conceptual' opposition, to the intervention of war in 1939, or to funding issues affecting both the authorisation/ construction of the ships and the provision of suitable embarked aircraft. The aircraft carrier is a very expensive item of naval hardware, and the realisation of such a major project in the modern era requires the careful planning of resources and associated programmes. Neither the British nor the French have had the advantage of 'scale', which has long been a feature of US Navy procurement of ships and aircraft, and this has made it difficult to provide suitable air groups at reasonable cost. French politicians have naturally had a preference for nationally developed aircraft, avionics and weaponry, and the purchase of aircraft from abroad, at least since 1960, has been strictly limited. This has frequently resulted in delays and compromise solutions.

The chapters of the book follow a broadly chronological sequence, covering the years 1910 to 2000. For each of the carriers completed (or loaned/purchased) there is a comprehensive service history that focuses on the principal activities (participation in exercises and conflicts, refits and modernisation) and aircraft operations (in-service dates of individual types, incidents). The cut-off date of 2000 means that for *Charles de Gaulle* there is an account of development and construction plus a detailed technical description, but no service history.

## ACKNOWLEDGEMENTS

A huge debt is owed to my co-author, Jean Moulin, who has written or co-authored a number of books on the French carriers. Jean supplied his own drawings and photos from his personal collection, and also read through my English-language text, much of which is derived from his own work, and suggested a number of corrections and amendments.

The book would not have been possible without the assistance of the Service Historique de la Défense (Marine section at Vincennes and the Centre d'Archives de l'Armement at Châtellerault) and of the Association pour la Recherche et Documentation sur l'Histoire de l'Aéronautique Navale (ARDHAN, Paris), and in particular Robert Feuilloy, former General Secretary, and Xavier Paitard, the current president of the Association. Many of the photographs reproduced here are from the ARDHAN collection, by kind permission of Jacques Alhéritière; other photos were supplied by Lars Ahlberg, Conrad Waters, and David Hobbs, who also kindly read through the opening chapter. Images from known sources have been credited; for photographs from private collections or of unknown origin (credited 'DR') all rights are reserved. Finally, sincere thanks are extended to Rob Gardiner of Seaforth Publishing, who has offered his customary support and advice throughout the project, and to Stephen Dent, whose well designed layouts have used the authors' material to best advantage.

**John Jordan**
January 2025

CHAPTER 1

# FIRST STEPS

EVERY NATION HAD ITS AVIATION PIONEERS. In France, Clément Ader was the first to achieve a motorised flight over 50 metres, which took place on 9 October 1890. In a subsequent memoir, written in 1895, he provided a strikingly accurate description of the aircraft-carrying ships that would materialise twenty-five years later.

In the United States of America, on the dunes of Kitty Hawk, North Carolina, the Wright Brothers made their first motorised flight on 17 December 1903; it lasted twelve seconds.

A decisive threshold was crossed on 13 January 1908 when a Voisin biplane piloted by Henri Farman flew a circuit at Issy-les-Moulineaux, and on 25 January 1909 Louis Blériot crossed the Channel in a Blériot XI. The first seaplane, piloted by Henri Fabre, took off from the Berre Pond (25km northwest of Marseille) on 28 March 1910.

These developments did not go unnoticed by the military. The first wartime mission was undertaken in Libya on 22 October 1911 by the Italian Captain Piazza, who flew a Blériot on a reconnaissance mission from Tripoli. The rapid development of aircraft from a first flight in 1908 to an operational weapon of war in 1914 is remarkable.

In France, the Navy hesitated between the airship, the seaplane and wheeled aircraft. A commission under Rear Admiral Le Pord was set up on 2 April 1910 to study the possibility of using airships to detect submarines. In July it decided in favour of a conventional aircraft; a Farman wheeled biplane was ordered on 12 July, and five officers were assigned to a school for pilots.

In March 1911, Commander (*Capitaine de frégate* or CF) René Daveluy was charged with setting up an embryonic naval aviation organisation. Voisin's Canard was purchased in the same year, and Daveluy requested the establishment of an aerodrome at Fréjus (near Saint-Raphaël in the south of France) and the modification of the former torpedo boat carrier *Foudre*

**Left:** Eugene B Ely takes off from the light cruiser USS *Birmingham* (CL-2) on 14 November 1910. *(Naval History and Heritage Command, NH-77545)*

to serve as a mobile base for seaplanes. Frustrated by the inertia of the ministerial bureaucracy, he resigned in December, but his successor, CF Louis Fatou, managed to obtain everything that Daveluy had requested, and on 12 March 1912 the *Aviation maritime* was set up by presidential decree. A second decree dated 10 July 1914 established the *Aéronautique maritime*, to comprise a Central Bureau and two groupings:

- the air stations (*aérostations*) for balloons and dirigibles
- the naval air bases (*centres d'aviation maritime*), to comprise an HQ at Saint-Raphaël, the seaplane carrier *Foudre*, and the aircraft squadrons, which were yet to be formed.

On 14 November 1910, in the USA, civil aviator Eugene Ely was the first to take off from a ship. Flying a Curtiss Pusher, Ely took off from a temporary platform erected over the bow of the light cruiser USS *Birmingham* (CL-2); the plane plunged downwards as soon as it cleared the 83-foot platform runway, and the aircraft dipped its wheels into the water before rising. Two months later, on 18 January 1911, Ely landed on and then took off from a platform mounted on the armoured cruiser *Pennsylvania* (CA-4), which was anchored in San Francisco Bay. The US Navy then shifted its interest to the seaplane.

Similar developments were taking place in the British Royal Navy. On 10 January 1912, Commander Charles Samson took off in a Short S27 using a pair of guide rails fitted to the forecastle of the battleship *Africa*. And on 2 May 1912, the first take-offs from a ship underway were undertaken using Short S27 and T5 planes from a platform fitted to the forward turret of the battleship *Hibernia*. The platform was subsequently transferred to the battleship *London*.

Next up was the elderly protected cruiser *Hermes*, which in early 1913 was fitted with a tracked platform forward backed by a canvas hangar, with a second hangar aft; trials were conducted with a Short Folder seaplane and a French Caudron amphibian.

## THE SEAPLANE CARRIER *FOUDRE*

*Foudre* was completed as a 'torpedo cruiser', the rationale for which chimed with the thinking of the

**Right:** Eugene B Ely takes off from a platform 120ft x 32ft (36.5m x 9.75m) fitted above the stern of the armoured cruiser USS *Pennsylvania* (CA-4) in San Francisco Bay on 18 January 1911. *(NHHC, UA 450.07)*

**Below:** The 'pre-dreadnought' battleship *Hibernia*, the first ship to launch an aircraft while underway. The forward-facing boom on the foremast was fitted to lift the aircraft into place on the take-off platform. The latter was a temporary structure, and prevented the foremost gun turret from training. *(Courtesy of David Hobbs)*

**Right:** *Foudre* between September 1911 and February 1913, before the bridge was moved aft to a position just forward of the first funnel. *(ARDHAN collection)*

**Right:** *Foudre* with a seaplane beneath the after derrick; the photo was taken before February 1913. *(ARDHAN collection)*

**Left:** A Voisin Canard floatplane on *Foudre* in July 1912, in front of the canvas hangar located between the funnels and the mainmast. *(ARDHAN collection)*

*Jeune Ecole*, which favoured the small torpedo boat over the traditional large and costly battleship. She was built by Chantiers et Ateliers de la Gironde, Bordeaux, the contract being signed on 9 June 1892. Launched on 20 October 1895, she was manned for trials on 1 February 1896. She left Bordeaux on 16 February, arriving at Toulon for sea trials on 6 March.

*Foudre* commissioned (*armement définitif*) on 24 October 1897. She was designed to embark small torpedo boats, but trials quickly demonstrated the limitations of the concept. The torpedo boats were too small to operate successfully at sea, and could be launched and recovered only in calm waters, or in a harbour or anchorage. The ship was placed in Reserve on 1 January 1902. She was subsequently reactivated to transport four torpedo boats plus the submarines *Protée* and *Lynx* to Saigon in June 1904, then the submarines *Perle* and *Esturgeon* in October 1905.

The role of torpedo cruiser was abandoned in 1907 and *Foudre* became first a repair ship then, in 1910, a minelayer. She was recommissioned for the fleet manoeuvres that took place from 15 April to 1 July 1910. Decommissioned, she was modified to conduct trials with aircraft. The gantries used for launch and recovery of the torpedo boats were landed, a hangar was installed between the mainmast and the funnel, and an aircraft handling derrick fitted to the mast. The ship retained her repair machinery, forge and foundry. She recommissioned on 1 September 1911; her commanding officer was CF Paris de Boisrouvray.

On 15 April 1912, CF Louis Fatou was appointed CO and the ship received a temporary canvas hangar. She sailed between Toulon, Saint-Raphaël and Corsica and served as a floating base for seaplanes, which were lowered to the surface for take-off and recovered by the derrick. *Foudre* would be further modified at Toulon from 1 February to 28 August 1913, when the bridge structure and conning tower were moved 12.40 metres farther aft, the funnels were raised, and the foremast moved aft by 14 metres and fitted with a derrick. In March/April 1914, a platform was fitted above the forecastle by the Chantiers et Ateliers de Provence, Marseille. The first take-off by a French wheeled aircraft, a Caudron C.2, a seaplane powered by an 80cv engine that had wheels housed in the floats, took place on 8 May 1914; the pilot was René Caudron himself. Two aircraft, a Caudron C.2 and a Voisin V.6, were embarked for the fleet manoeuvres of 14–30 May 1914. They were successful in determining the composition of the two squadrons engaged in the exercise.

On 9 June, *Lieutenant de vaisseau* (LV) Jean de Laborde attempted a second take-off from the platform, but his C1 aircraft plunged into the sea and he had to be rescued. The platform was then removed, probably in July.

On 1 August, uncertainty regarding the attitude of Italy led the Navy to despatch a flotilla to Bonifacio (Corsica) and a second to Nice. *Foudre* joined the *Armée navale* at the end of August with two Voisin seaplanes embarked. On 6 September, the two aircraft were lowered onto the water and tasked with reconnoitring the route to be taken by the *Armée navale*, but the first flipped over when attempting to take off; the second landed successfully at Antivari (Montenegro), making a few further flights before breaking down. She was then destroyed by a squall.

On 17 September, two Nieuport seaplanes were embarked. *Foudre* was again attached to the *Armée*

**Right:** Take-off from *Foudre's* forecastle platform of a Caudron J 80hp C2 piloted by René Caudron on 8 May 1914. *(Musée de la Marine)*

*navale* and her planes arrived at Antivari on 17 October, operating from Lake Scutari; however, one then suffered a breakdown and could not be repaired. On 3 November, *Foudre* embarked a second pair of Nieuport seaplanes at Malta; they arrived safely at Antivari, but were immediately withdrawn as the location proved to be unusable.

Admiral Augustin Boué de Lapeyrère, Commander-in-Chief (C-in-C) of the *Armée navale*, decided he wanted to have nothing more to do with the seaplanes, which he judged to be of no military value, but the British requested they be transferred to Port Said, where they were expecting a Turkish offensive against the Suez Canal. Nieuport seaplanes were duly disembarked by *Foudre* at Port Said on 30 November 1914, and the ship left again on 7 December. This would be her last mission as a seaplane carrier; she resumed her role as repair ship for the *Armée navale* and became indispensable in this role. Placed in Special Reserve on 15 March 1920, she was stricken

**Right:** An attempted take-off from *Foudre* of a Caudron J 100hp C1 piloted by LV Jean de Laborde on 9 June 1914; the aircraft flipped over as it left the platform and de Laborde had to be rescued. *(ARDHAN collection)*

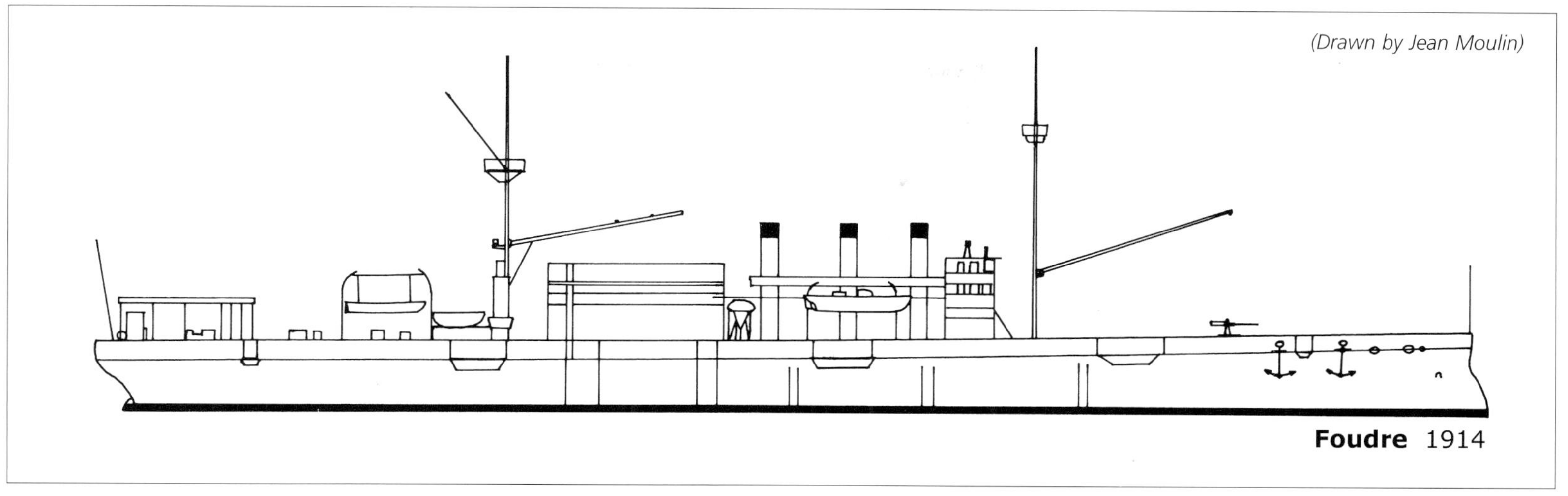

**Left:** *Foudre* with a small platform on the lengthened forecastle; the photo was probably taken at Argostoli, Kefalonia, between April 1916 and February 1917. *(ARDHAN collection)*

**Left:** The port of Argostoli, probably between April 1916 and February 1917. *Foudre* is on the left and *Campinas* on the right. A Nieuport VI.H, powered by an 80/100hp Gnome, Rhône or Clerget engine, is in the process of landing. *(ARDHAN collection)*

on 1 December 1921 and sold for scrap at Toulon on 27 May 1922.

## FRENCH SEAPLANE OPERATIONS 1914–18

War for the French began on 3 August 1914. Naval aviation comprised *Foudre* and fourteen aircraft. The latter figure increased to 24 on 1 January 1915, 66 on 1 January 1916, 168 on 1 January 1917, 521 on 1 January 1918 and 1,135 on 11 November 1918, the day the Armistice was signed. The commencement of unrestricted submarine warfare on 1 February 1917 brought about a major expansion of naval aviation with a multiplication of bases (*centres d'aviation maritime* or CAM) and command centres (*postes de combat* or PC, which constituted an annexe of the CAM) located around the French coasts. Seaplanes also operated for a time from modified seaplane carriers. The German submarines off the French coasts operated under a constant threat from both seaplanes and airships. Compelled to dive when sighting an aircraft, the submarines thereby lost much of their mobility and consequently their effectiveness.

**Below:** A Nieuport Clerget 80cv N16 is lowered onto the water at Port Said in July 1915. *(ARDHAN collection)*

The Nieuport seaplanes ferried by *Foudre* to Port Said were monoplanes powered by engines rated at 80cv and 100cv, and were easily adapted for land operations. They would play a decisive role in the failure of the Turks to capture the Suez Canal, conducting numerous reconnaissance missions. French seaplanes were also operated from a number of other vessels during the Great War.

### *RABENFELS*

*Rabenfels* was a former German cargo ship of 4750grt laid down by Swan, Hunter & Wigham Richardson Ltd at Wallsend for the Hansa Line (Bremen) and completed in December 1903. She was seized at Port Said in August 1914 by the British.

*Rabenfels* was subsequently requisitioned under the Red Ensign in January 1915 to operate seaplanes; no modifications were made to the ship. She departed Port Said on 18 March of the same year with the last three operational Nieuport VI.H floatplanes remaining at Port Said; the planes were flown by French pilots with British observers. After operating with the French squadron in the Eastern Mediterranean, she arrived at Mudros on 21 March, and the three aircraft were placed under the command of Vice Admiral John de Robeck. They found a Turkish torpedo boat north of Smyrna on the 26th. The three Nieuport floatplanes returned to Port Said on 31 March.

*Rabenfels* was commissioned into the Royal Navy on 12 June and renamed *Raven II* on 5 August 1915, operating British models of seaplane. She was transferred to the Merchant Navy in January 1918, renamed *Ravenrock*, and employed as a collier for Graham & Co until the end of the war. She was sold in 1923 to the Dominions Steamship Co, then in 1924 to Karfuto Kisen Kabushiki Kaisha (KKK) and renamed *Heiyei Maru No 7*. She was sold again in 1935 to Inui KKK and renamed *Kenei Maru*, and was sunk in the Pacific in January 1945 by aircraft from Task Force 38 (Vice Admiral John S McCain).

### *ÄNNE-RICKMERS*

The *Änne-Rickmers* was a German cargo ship of 4080grt, completed at Bremerhaven in 1911 by Rickmers Reismühlen, Rhederei & Schiffbau AG, and likewise seized at Alexandria in early August 1914 by the British. Still under the Red Ensign, she was employed as a seaplane carrier from early 1915. No modification was necessary; the aircraft were stowed on the after hatch covers and handled by her cargo booms.

On 24 February 1915, she left for the Dardanelles with two Nieuport VI.H floatplanes, which were flown by French pilots with British observers. During the night of 10/11 March she was torpedoed in the Smyrna anchorage by a Turkish torpedo boat, and was beached at Mudros. Damage to the ship was moderate, but both aircraft were put out of action. The vessel was patched up by the repair ship HMS *Reliance*, then returned to Port Said for repairs in May/June. She was commissioned under the White Ensign in August and rechristened *Anne*. She proved indispensable during the coming months, conducting aerial reconnaissance for the fleet from January to March 1916.

*Anne* was taken over by the Merchant Navy on 8 August 1917 and would serve as a collier under the management of F C Strick & Co from 29 January 1918

**Left:** The former German cargo ship *Rabenfels*, seized by the Royal Navy and renamed *Raven II* on 5 August 1915, is seen here at Castellorizo. *(ARDHAN collection)*

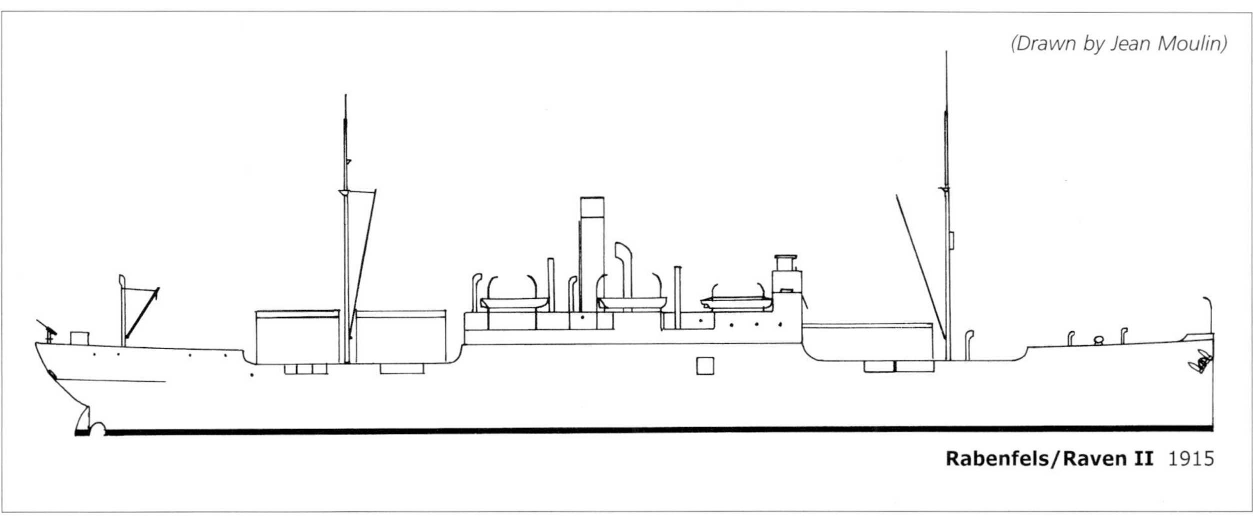

*(Drawn by Jean Moulin)*

**Rabenfels/Raven II** 1915

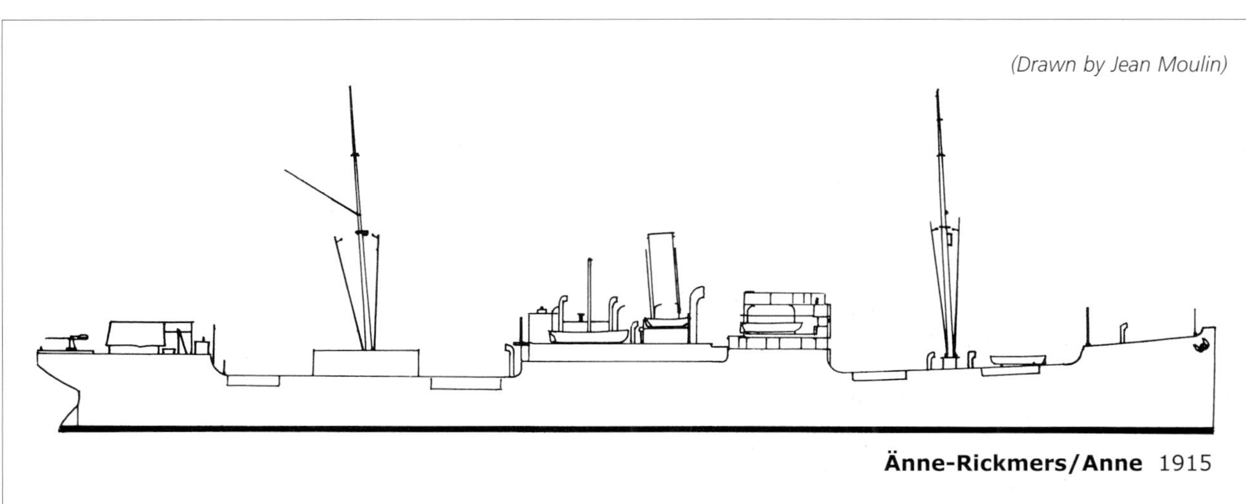

*(Drawn by Jean Moulin)*

**Änne-Rickmers/Anne** 1915

Right: The former German cargo ship *Änne-Rickmers*, which was employed as a seaplane carrier by the Royal Navy and renamed *Anne* in August 1915. Note the White Ensign flying at the mainmast, and the two seaplanes with wings folded atop the after hatches. *(ARDHAN collection)*

Above:: The seaplane carrier *Änne-Rickmers* under repair at Mudros after she had been torpedoed by a Turkish torpedo boat at Smyrna during the night of 10/11 March 1915. *(ARDHAN collection)*

until the end of the war. In 1922 she was sold to S N Vlassopoulos and became *Ithaki*, sailing under the Greek flag. She was sold on to Romania in 1939 and renamed *Moldova*. Transferred to Panama in 1942, she was sold in 1949 to Wallem & Co and became *Jagrahat* in 1954. She reverted to the name *Moldova* in 1955, and arrived in Hong Kong to be broken up on 8 November 1958.

## PAS-DE-CALAIS

*Pas-de-Calais* was a paddle-wheel cross-Channel train ferry built by Ateliers et Chantiers de la Loire at Saint-Nazaire for the Chemins de Fer du Nord company. Launched in 1898, she entered service in April 1899. She was requisitioned at Cherbourg on 3 August 1914 as an auxiliary scout for the 2nd Light Squadron (*2e Escadre légère*).

She was employed for trials with seaplanes with a view to bombing the canal and port of Zeebrugge. A trial took place at Dunkirk with an FBA 110cv Clerget on 22 June 1915. The fragility of the machine led the French to abandon the idea of a raid. In early 1916 *Pas de Calais* was modified to operate four FBA 110cv Clerget aircraft, the modification being completed on 4 April. She would embark only two planes, but operated between La Hague and La Pallice until October 1916. Her mission was to scout for minesweepers, to conduct reconnaissance of the zones to be swept, and to maintain surveillance of the channels. It was hoped that her seaplanes would also be able to locate enemy U-boats, but the aircraft proved too slow and the waters too opaque, and there was concern regarding mistaken identity given that French submarines were operating in the area. After October 1916 the mission was abandoned, and she was broken up in 1923.

## CAMPINAS

*Campinas* was a passenger liner laid down in 1895 by Chantiers et Ateliers de la Loire at Saint-Nazaire. Launched on 16 November 1895, she was operated by the Chargeurs Réunis company on the Bordeaux–Matadi–Dakar route.

Requisitioned on 8 March 1915 at Pauillac, she served as a troop transport for the *Armée d'Orient*, as a depot ship at Salonika, and even as a netlayer at the same port.

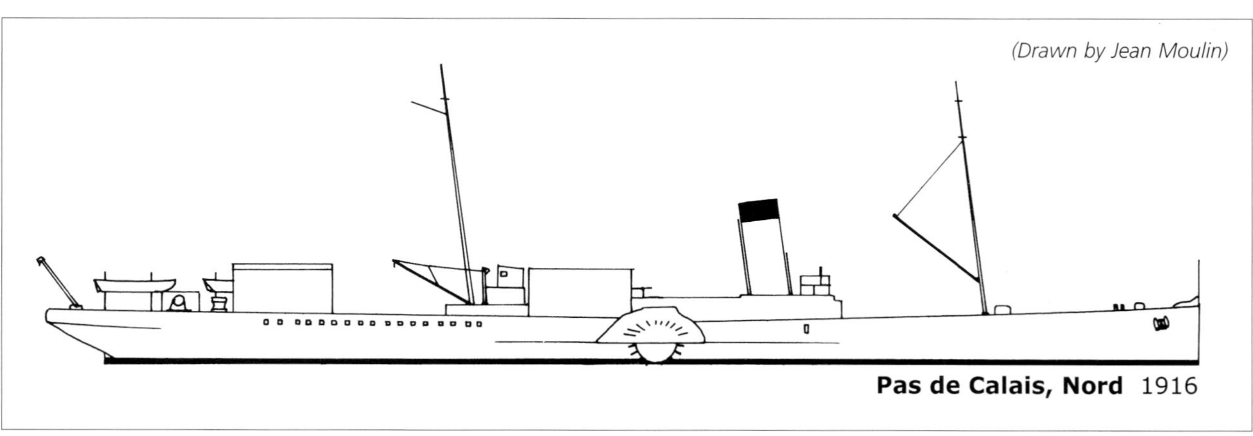

*(Drawn by Jean Moulin)*

**Pas de Calais, Nord** 1916

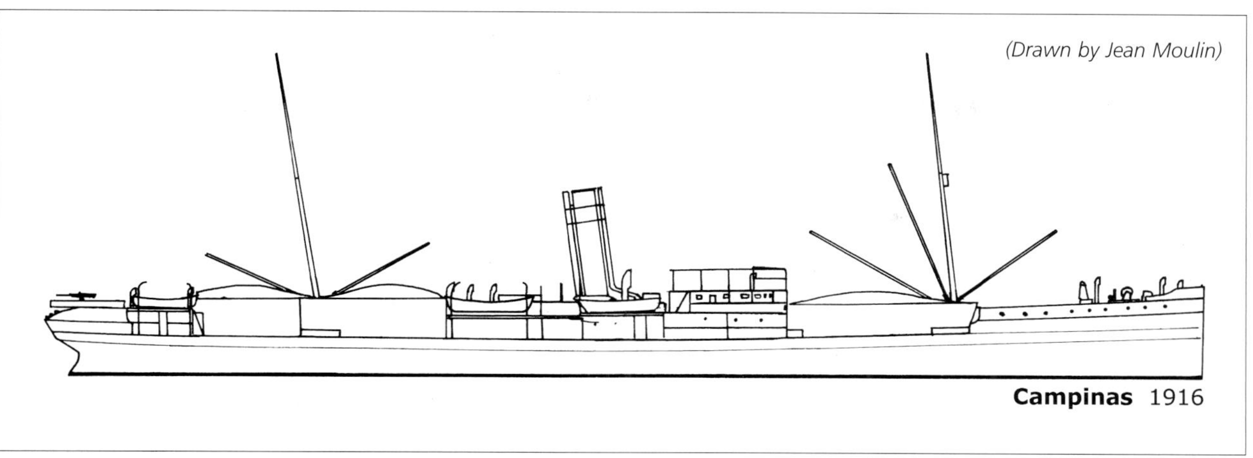


*Campinas* was converted into a seaplane carrier at Port Said between 29 January and 16 March 1916. She could embark four to six seaplanes (Nieuport 80/100cv, then FBA 110/130cv), and she recovered the Nieuport machines deployed to Port Said. She was at Malta on 14 April for repairs and relieved the Royal Navy's *Anne* on 22 April, operating out of Argostoli (Kefalonia). A passage to Toulon around 7 July allowed her to embark four FBA 100cv Clerget with folding wings; they would later be superseded by the FBA 130cv Clerget model. *Campinas* then operated in the Milos-Argostoli zone.

From early 1917 she was used to train new pilots and, following the disembarkation of her aircraft, for the transport of coal briquettes for isolated bases and ships. In June 1917, during the hostilities with Greece, seaplanes from *Campinas* reconnoitred the Corinth Canal and the Plain of Athens. She grounded in the Gulf of Patras on 15 October, but damage was limited. Several minefields were located, notably in the Milos area. The ship, considered unsuitable to operate with the fleet, continued her surveillance missions. A submarine discovered at Santorini could not be attacked because the swell prevented her seaplanes from taking off. On 20 July 1918 they were unable to catch an overflying Zeppelin.

The last mine reconnaissance mission was undertaken off Alexandretta (now Iskenderun) on 9 November. *Campinas* arrived at Corfu on the 14th, and her nine FBA 130cv Clerget seaplanes were disembarked on the 23rd. *Campinas*, which had been employed as a seaplane carrier for two years despite certain limitations (speed, habitability), had proved her value and had allowed the Navy to acquire experience in operating aircraft at sea. Efficiency in handling had progressed to a point where an FBA could be lowered into the water within one minute and recovered in only four.

**Left:** The former cargo ship *Campinas*, employed as a seaplane carrier from 16 March 1916. *(ARDHAN collection)*

*Campinas* was discharged from naval service in 1919 and returned to her owners, Chargeurs Réunis. She would be employed for coastal navigation in Indochina from 1925 before being sold for scrap in August 1929.

## NORD

*Nord* was a cross-Channel paddle steamer and a sister ship to *Pas-de-Calais*. Built by Ateliers et Chantiers de la Loire at Saint-Nazaire, she was laid down in 1897, launched in 1898 and entered service in April 1899.

She was hired by the British Red Cross in October 1914, then requisitioned at Calais on 22 November 1915 to serve as an auxiliary scout for the 2nd Light Squadron based at Cherbourg. Like her sister, she was modified to operate seaplanes, recommissioning on 5 April 1916 and embarking the FBA 110cv. Mine and submarine hunting was developed from August to October, but significant results were not forthcoming due to the fragility of the aircraft and the lack of any means of detection. *Nord* was at Saint-Nazaire in late August and early September, but only a single flight was possible due to unfavourable weather.

*Nord* arrived in Brest on 11 September, but operations were halted on 22 September due to a shortage of castor oil. The aircraft were disembarked at Dunkirk between 17 and 28 October. Although still viewed as an 'occasional' seaplane carrier, *Nord* would serve as a minesweeper until the end of the war. She would be lost in 1923, when she foundered.

## ROUEN

*Rouen* was a cross-Channel ferry built by Forges et Chantiers de la Méditerranée at Le Havre. Launched 18 May 1912, she was completed in September 1912 and entered service with the Chemins de Fer de l'Ouest company.

She was requisitioned in August 1914, initially serving as an auxiliary at Cherbourg. In October 1916 she was modified as a seaplane carrier with a hangar for two aircraft. Flights seem to have been paused in November due to the poor winter weather conditions in the Channel. On 29 December 1916 she was torpedoed by a U-boat and lost her bow. Although repaired at Cherbourg, she never again embarked seaplanes. She was returned to her owners in 1919 and resumed service as a ferry on 5 July 1920.

*Rouen* would be recommissioned for a second time

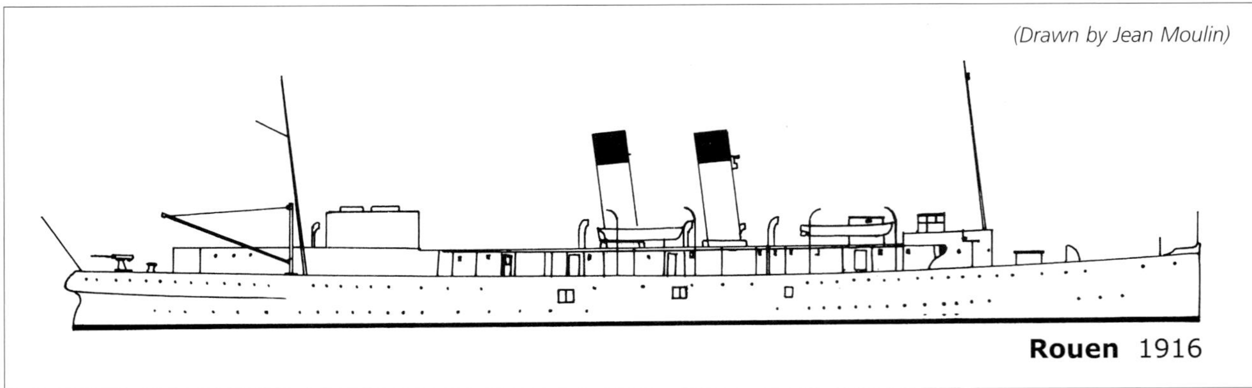
(Drawn by Jean Moulin)

**Rouen** 1916

on 14 March 1940. She transported troops to Vlissingen (Netherlands) on 11 May, but had to return to Dieppe to change one of her propellers. Engaged in the evacuation of Dunkirk, she brought 420 wounded men back to Cherbourg on 26 May. On 31 May she embarked 951 who had been landed at Dover that same evening.

On 2 June she embarked 1,000 men but, obstructed as she cast off, grounded and had to disembark her passengers. She was refloated at 1100 and took on board 1,286 men, disembarking them at Dover in the late afternoon of the following day. She subsequently took part in the evacuations from Cherbourg, Brest, Le Havre and La Pallice, disembarking the men from La Pallice at Saint-Jean-de-Luz near the Spanish border. She was at Bayonne when the Armistice entered force, and was seized by the Germans on 30 August 1940. She became the minelayer *Schiff 50* on 24 March 1941, and was renamed *Wullenwever* on 18 November 1941, serving as a trials ship in the Baltic. She was sunk on 25 April 1943 when she struck a mine, but was refloated in August and put back into service. At the end of the war she would be found heavily damaged at Kiel. She was recovered on 22 March 1946 and broken up at Dieppe in 1949.

### *DORADE*

*Dorade* was a former German river patrol boat, *Kuka*, built in 1905 by Vegesack Bremer Vulkan at Bremen. She was seized by the Royal Navy in Cameroon in 1914, being renamed *Sir Hugh*, then placed at the disposition of the French Navy at Dakar on 29 September 1916. She sailed for Rochefort via Bordeaux, arriving on 20 December 1916, to be modified as a seaplane carrier and netlayer, capable of handling anchors, marker buoys and nets and replenishing the Moroccan patrol boats with water and fuel oil. *Dorade* left for Gibraltar on 26 February 1917. She embarked an FBA 130cv Clerget and operated from Morocco from 7 May. On the 18th she pursued a U-boat in heavy seas, rolling to such an extent (30 degrees) that the hangar was stove in and the embarked seaplane damaged. Following this, her employment as a seaplane carrier was ended, apparently definitively in December 1917. She was finally stricken in 1922.

### *NORMANDIE*

*Normandie* was a large trawler belonging to the Pêcheries de Fécamp. She was laid down in 1912 by JT Eltringham & Co at Southfield and entered service in January 1914.

She was requisitioned at Fécamp on 30 November 1915 and assigned to the Algerian-Tunisian patrol division, serving with the 3rd trawler flotilla at Bizerte. She was modified at Bizerte in the winter of 1916/17 and embarked two FBA 110cv Clerget seaplanes with folding wings with a view to conducting surveillance of U-boats transiting to their patrol areas, with rest points at Bône, Gagliari, Marsala, La Galite, Tabarka and Kelibia. Normally only a single seaplane was embarked. The last flight took place on 29 July, being halted by an engine failure. The mission was formally terminated on 12 October 1917.

The operations of this ship highlighted the problems with operating seaplanes from an anchorage: they were difficult to launch and recovery could not be guaranteed, particularly in adverse weather. If the planes were left in the open they malfunctioned and sometimes suffered serious damage. The only bomb available was a 22kg model that was practically useless against a submarine. *Normandie* was returned to her owners in 1919.

## FOREIGN DEVELOPMENTS

The Great War served to accelerate the evolution of aviation. If the French led the way in land-based aircraft, it was the British who were largely responsible for the development of aircraft at sea.

### The British Royal Navy

The British were in the forefront when it came to the modification of mercantile hulls as seaplane carriers. On 10 December 1914 they commissioned *Ark Royal*, a collier taken over on the stocks in May of the same year. She was completely rebuilt: her machinery was moved aft to make space for a large 'aeroplane hold' 150ft x 45ft x 15ft (45.7m x 13.7m x 4.6m) that took up the most of the forward part of the ship and was capable of accommodating seven aircraft, which could be launched directly from on board using trolleys. A sliding hatch 40ft x 30ft (12.2m x 9.1m) gave access to the upper deck and the aircraft were hoisted in and out by two powerful 3-ton steam cranes. *Ark Royal* deployed to the Dardanelles in February 1915 to provide much-needed reconnaissance of the Turkish forts.

The old cruiser *Hermes*, modified with a take-off ramp forward and hangars fore and aft, was torpedoed and sunk by a German U-boat on 31 October 1914, but the experiment had proved successful, and just prior to the outbreak of war three fast ferries were requisitioned and modified as seaplane carriers. These were:

**Left:** HMS *Ark Royal*, the world's first purpose-built seaplane carrier. She had a long flat deck forward (which was never used for launching aircraft as intended), a capacious hold/hangar capable of accommodating seven seaplanes, and two 3-ton steam-powered cranes. She proved particularly useful off the Dardanelles, where her aircraft conducted regular reconnaissance missions over the Turkish forts. *(Courtesy of David Hobbs)*

- *Engadine*, which recommissioned on 1 September 1914
- *Riviera*, recommissioned on 6 September
- *Empress*, recommissioned on 25 August.

Each could carry three aircraft in a large canvas hangar aft. These three vessels launched the first naval air raid in history on 25 September 1914, when nine seaplanes attacked the Zeppelin hangars at Cuxhaven. Seven aircraft took off, but they failed to find the hangars and only three were recovered. At the Battle of Jutland, on 31 May 1916, a Short 184 from *Engadine* spotted the German Fleet but Vice Admiral Beatty, commanding the battlecruisers, never received the report.

The fleet would subsequently be reinforced by the following:

- *Ben-my-Chree* (23 March 1915)
- *Campania* (17 April 1915)
- *Vindex* (ex *Viking*, 11 October 1915)
- *Manxman* (17 April 1916)
- *Nairana* (25 August 1917)
- *Pegasus* (14 August 1917).

The British were particularly concerned about the

**Left:**The converted cross-channel ferry *Engadine*, which would accompany the Battle Cruiser Fleet under Vice Admiral David Beatty at Jutland. *(Courtesy of David Hobbs)*

possible bombing of the UK by Zeppelins, and only land-based fighters were capable of intercepting these. Fighters were also required to pursue Zeppelins conducting reconnaissance for the High Seas Fleet. It was found that the ability to operate aircraft from ships was limited, and was impossible in adverse weather conditions. The vessel needed to heave to in order to launch or recover her seaplanes, which exposed her to attacks by U-boats. The North Sea proved to be a particularly hostile operating environment. Aircraft flying from land bases, which were generally also capable of superior performance, held a decisive advantage.

*Ben-my-Chree*, *Vindex*, *Manxman*, *Nairana* and *Pegasus* were fitted with take-off platforms 20–26 metres long and were able to launch light aircraft. The first take-off took place on 3 November 1915 from *Vindex*. *Campania* had her bridge and funnel moved aft in early 1916 to enable a flying-off deck some 50 metres in length for wheeled aircraft to be fitted; her hold could accommodate seven seaplanes.

The small number of seaplanes available and their limited performance led to the fitting of one or two platforms atop the main turrets in major combat vessels, enabling a fighter to take off into the wind over a few metres. If the aircraft was launched too far from the coast to land on a friendly airfield, the plane would ditch and the pilot would be recovered by a destroyer. On 21 August 1917, Zeppelin *L 23* was shot down by Flight Lieutenant BA Smart, DSO, RNAS in a Sopwith Pup N 6430, which took off from a small platform fitted forward of the bridge of the cruiser *Yarmouth*.

The first major unit to be fitted with a turret platform was the battlecruiser *Repulse*, which had a platform fitted atop 'B' turret in October 1917. All the battlecruisers would subsequently be fitted with a platform for a two-seater aircraft forward plus a platform aft for a fighter. By the end of the war a total of 103 aircraft were embarked on platforms fitted to the battleships, battlecruisers and light cruisers of the Grand Fleet.

The British also used lighters that were towed into range of their targets by destroyers; each of the barges carried an aircraft that could take off with the destroyer towing at high speed. The first Zeppelin downed by an 'embarked' fighter was *L 53*, on 11 August 1918, which was shot down by a Sopwith 2F.1 Camel piloted by Lieutenant Stuart Culley, which took off from barge *H3* towed by the destroyer *Redoubt*.

The 'light battlecruiser' *Furious* was completed with a flight deck similar in length to the one on *Campania* forward in place of one of her 18in gun turrets and conventional superstructures. She was still expected to recover her planes, however, and landing on having negotiated the superstructures proved to be extremely hazardous. After a fatal accident on 4 August 1917, it was decided to replace the after turret with a second platform. Although some in the Admiralty thought it a good idea that could be achieved quickly, the ship's own pilots had predicted that it would be dangerous and unfit for purpose, as aircraft landing on would be adversely affected by the air turbulence generated by

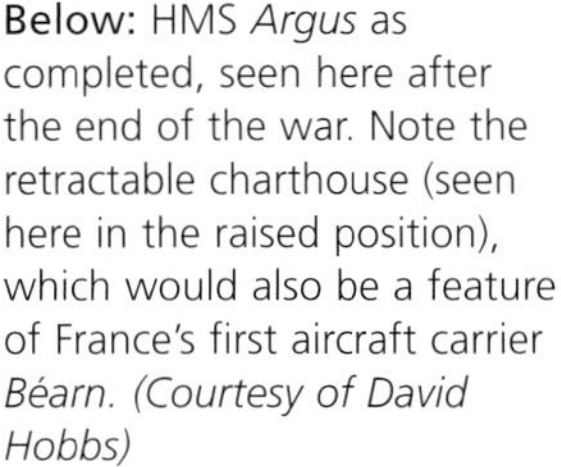

**Below:** HMS *Argus* as completed, seen here after the end of the war. Note the retractable charthouse (seen here in the raised position), which would also be a feature of France's first aircraft carrier *Béarn*. *(Courtesy of David Hobbs)*

**Left:** The 'large light cruiser' *Furious* as completed in July 1917, with her forward 18in gun turret replaced by a flight deck 228ft long and between 57ft and 36ft wide (70m x 17.5/11m), supported by a latticework structure of girders, with a hangar beneath. *(Courtesy of David Hobbs)*

the superstructures and the hot funnel gases. This proved to be the case, and the modification was deemed to be a failure.

The obvious solution was to eliminate all superstructures above the level of the flight deck. Studies to complete other vessels as aircraft carriers were modified in accordance with this, and the first 'flush-deck' carrier, *Argus*, laid down as the Italian passenger liner *Conte Rosso*, was completed on 14 September 1918. At the same time it was decided to modify *Furious* as a flush-deck carrier, but she would recommission in this guise only in September 1925.

The *Hawkins*-class cruiser *Vindictive* followed the pattern set by *Furious*, being completed with decks fore and aft of the superstructures on 1 October 1918. And the Royal Navy's commitment to naval aviation was reaffirmed with the conversion of the hull of a battleship building for Chile, *Almirante Cochrane*, as the through-deck carrier *Eagle* (initial trials April 1920, in service 1923) and the construction of the first aircraft carrier built from the keel up, *Hermes* (completed February 1924). These two ships introduced the island superstructure, offset to starboard.

### Other Nations

Developments in the other major navies followed a similar pattern to that of the Royal Navy.

The Japanese transformed a cargo ship completed in 1901, *Lethington*, as a seaplane carrier to operate four aircraft. Renamed *Wakamiya*, she recommissioned on 17 August 1914 and took part in the siege of Tsingtao in September/October 1914. In December 1919, the Imperial Japanese Navy laid down a flush-

**Left:** The Russian converted seaplane carrier *Nikolai 1* in the Black Sea in 1915–16. *(NHHC, NH-94397)*.

deck carrier, the 7,500-ton *Hōshō*, designed from the keel up and the first true carrier to be completed.

The US Navy, following the trials conducted by Eugene Ely, adopted the British procedure of fitting take-off platforms to the turrets of its battleships. The first platform was installed on *Texas* (BB-35), but the first take-off had to wait until 9 March 1919.

The Germans modified a number of ships to serve as seaplane tenders: the cruiser *Stuttgart*, and the mercantile *Adeline Hugo Stinnes 3*, *Answald*, *Santa Elena*, *Glyndwr* and *Oswald*. A proposal to convert the armoured cruiser *Roon* came to nothing.

The Russians employed a number of modified seaplane carriers in the Black Sea: *Imperator Aleksandr I*, *Imperator Nikolaï I*, *Almaz*, *Regele Carol I*, *Rumyanya*, *Imperator Trajan*, *Dakia* and *Korol Karl*. A single unit, *Orlitsa*, served in the Baltic.

Finally, in Italy, the protected cruiser *Elba* served as a seaplane tender in 1914–15. In the Adriatic, the Italians employed *Europa* (ex-mercantile *Quarto*, ex-*Salacia*, ex-British *Manila*) as a seaplane carrier and submarine depot ship from late 1915 to November 1918.

## DEVOPMENTS POST-WAR

France remained faithful to the concept of the seaplane, although from 1917 these were operated principally from land bases on the coast.

A new organisation, christened the *Aviation d'escadre* (Fleet Air Arm), was created on 1 October 1918 under the leadership of LV Paul Teste, and it was decided to renew experiments with embarked aircraft.

The Naval General Staff was inclined towards the British practice of fitting take-off platforms to turrets. Two were fitted in the battleship *Paris*, which was in the final stages of a major refit at Toulon. On 26 October 1918 LV Georges Guierre succeeded in taking off from the platform on turret II with a Hanriot biplane off Toulon, but a further trial on 7 November, in which the aircraft was piloted by Teste himself, was a failure, and the platforms were subsequently disem-

**Left:** The battleship *Lorraine* would be fitted experimentally with a gantry structure on her tripod foremast from which a fighter aircraft was suspended. The experiment was a failure as, once released, the aircraft failed to generate sufficient momentum to keep it clear of the surface. On 25 February 1924 at Toulon, the Hanriot H.29 of Paul Teste struck the water and flipped over during an attempted launch. Fortunately, Teste was rescued. *(ARDHAN collection)*

## PAUL TESTE

Paul-Marcel Teste was born at Lorient on 2 October 1892. He entered the *Ecole Navale* in October 1909 and served successively on board the transport sloop *Vaucluse* and the 800-tonne destroyer *Magon*, which operated first in the Mediterranean and then off Flanders. He transferred to naval aviation in March 1917 and served as an observer. He was captured and imprisoned on 26 May 1917 but managed to escape in 1918. He then qualified as a pilot and was promoted to lieutenant (*Lieutenant de vaisseau* or LV) in September 1918. The *Aviation d'escadre* was formed on 1 October 1918 under his command. In 1920, at Saint-Raphaël, he was appointed head of what would become Naval Aviation. He made the first of several take-offs from the sloop *Bapaume* on 12 March 1920 and made the first landings on a platform installed on the incomplete hull of *Béarn* on 20 October 1920.

Promoted Lieutenant-Commander (*Capitaine de corvette* or CC) in July 1921, he was appointed head of the *Bureau des études du service central aéronautique* (Naval Aviation Trials Unit) then, in 1924, attached to the Ministry. In 1925, with Lieutenant Jean Amanrich, he prepared a raid on Karachi as a prelude to a crossing of the North Atlantic in an Amiot 120. On 13 June 1925, at Villacoublay, the undercarriage of their aircraft collapsed on landing following a trial fully loaded, and the Amiot caught fire. Amanrich managed to get out but Teste was consumed by the flames. He died the following day and was posthumously promoted to Commander (*Capitaine de frégate* or CF). The aviation transport *Commandant Teste* (laid down September 1927 – see Chapter 3) would be named after him.

Lieutenant (LV) Paul Teste, who was instrumental in laying the foundations for the French Fleet Air Arm. The photo was taken at Saint-Raphaël in 1922. *(ARDHAN collection)*

barked. In order to explore a different technique, the battleship *Lorraine* was fitted with a prominent lattice gantry projecting from her tripod foremast from which a Hanriot H.29 was suspended (see photographs). The experiment was a failure and would not be repeated.

Teste's *Aviation d'escadre* was charged with trials which, while not openly admitted, closely followed British developments. It appears that shortly after the Armistice, the General Staff received a proposal from Lieutenant-Commander (CC) Henri de l'Escaille for an

**Right:** Photo of a Nieuport 21 being readied on the take-off ramp of the modified sloop *Bapaume* in 1920. *(ARDHAN collection)*

**Right:** Two images of a take-off of a Nieuport 21 from *Bapaume* in 1920. *(ARDHAN collection)*

air-capable ship with a flush deck, and in early 1920 there was a visit to the British carrier *Argus* by a commission headed by LV Henri Latham, who would subsequently propose the conversion of one of the incomplete battleships of the *Normandie* class. It should be noted that Projet 171, the naval programme put forward by the Minister of Marine, Georges Leygues, on 13 January 1920, had proposed the construction as a matter of urgency of six cruisers, twelve large destroyers for scouting (which became the

**Left:** A Hanriot HD.12 on the platform of *Bapaume* in 1921. *(ARDHAN collection)*

**Left:** Take-off of a Hanriot HD.12 from the platform of *Bapaume* in 1921. *(ARDHAN collection)*

**Right:** Take-off of a Nieuport 32 from *Bapaume* in 1922. *(ARDHAN collection)*

*contre-torpilleurs*), and the conversion of one of the incomplete battleships of the *Normandie* class as an aircraft carrier.

In 1920, take-offs from a ship underway were practised and perfected aboard *Bapaume* (see below). Studies for precise landings-on were undertaken using a concreted area shaped like a champagne cork (hence its nickname *bouchon de champagne*) at the Saint-Raphaël air base, but the decisive step was taken only with the availability of the hull of *Béarn* (see Chapter 2).

## *BAPAUME*

*Bapaume* was a 1st class sloop of the *Arras* class, one of a multitude of sloops, patrol boats and other escorts ordered from foreign shipyards or from France, where the workforce of even the naval dockyards was almost fully occupied with the demands of the Army. The *Arras* was the most numerous class of sloop. A total of forty-three units were initially envisaged, and thirty were laid down in 1917–18 and completed between 1918 and 1921, of which, eleven remained in service in 1940; the orders for the remaining thirteen were cancelled at the end of the war.

*Bapaume* was built at Lorient, together with her sisters *Bar-le-Duc* and *Belfort*. Laid down in 1917, she was launched on 8 August 1918 and completed in 1919. She arrived at Toulon on 1 July 1920. Equipped with a 13-metre platform forward, she was placed at the disposition of the air base of Saint-Raphaël. The first take-off took place on 12 March 1920.

*Bapaume* allowed pilots to practise taking off from a ship pending the availability of *Béarn*. The aircraft employed for the trials were the Hanriot HD.2, the Nieuport 21, the Hanriot HD.12 and the Nieuport 32. The last take-off took place on 24 June 1924. The *Aviation d'escadre* had no further use for the sloop, and her decommissioning would be requested on 6 August 1924 by the head of the 3rd Bureau. On 17 May 1926, the NGS would request the dismantling of the take-off platform and the restoration of the ship to her original configuration.

In 1930, *Bapaume* would be assigned to the training establishment for the indigenous population at Algiers, serving in a static role from 1 January 1934. In August 1935 she would be transferred to Bizerte, and was placed in Special Reserve at the end of the year. She was stricken on 31 July 1936.

## CHAPTER 2

# BÉARN

THE WASHINGTON TREATY, SIGNED ON 6 February 1922, prescribed the wholesale scrapping of battleships and battlecruisers currently in build, while at the same time permitting a substantial tonnage that could be allocated to aircraft carriers: 135,000 tons for Britain and the USA, 81,000 tons for Japan, and 60,000 tons for France and Italy. The carrier allocations for the three major powers were based on a theoretical unit displacement of 27,000 tons using a 5:5:3 ratio, those for France and Italy on three ships of about 20,000 tons. These figures, however, related to new purpose-built construction which, it was anticipated, would take place in the 1930s alongside the next generation of 35,000-ton battleships laid down after the ten-year 'holiday'. The conversion of incomplete capital ship hulls as an interim measure, given that the aircraft carrier as a type was still in its infancy, was not only assumed but was actively encouraged, both as an incentive for the major naval powers to accept the draconian prohibitions on new capital ship construction that were under discussion, and as a means of securing a return on the investment made in existing hulls, many of which were complete up to the armoured deck.

The British Royal Navy had already begun the reconstruction of two such ships, the former Chilean battleship *Almirante Cochrane* – rechristened *Eagle* – and the 'light battlecruiser' *Furious*, and in July 1921 had approved the conversion of one of *Furious*'s two half-sisters, *Glorious*. At around the same time, in the run-up to the Washington Conference, the US Navy embarked on studies for the reconstruction of two of the incomplete battlecruisers of the *Lexington* class.

France showed a keen interest in these developments. In early 1920 a French commission visited Britain and was given a tour of the first 'through-deck' carrier conversion, HMS *Argus*, to observe aircraft handling and flying operations. According to David Hobbs,[1] drawings of *Eagle*'s aviation and island arrangements were also made available. Out of this visit came a proposal for the conversion of one of the incomplete battleships of the *Normandie* class, and this was duly incorporated into the new building programme designated Project 171. Staff requirements included:

- the embarkation of the maximum number of wheeled aircraft, and the ability to operate seaplanes in harbour
- a continuous wooden flight deck at least 150m long, with the maximum possible width and no obstructions
- a hangar connected to the flight deck by two lifts, of which the larger should be 12m (L) by 20m (W)
- an access bay 20m wide for seaplanes at the after end of the hangar
- speed and endurance comparable to the battleships of the *Bretagne* class (*ie* 21 knots, 6000nm at 10 knots)

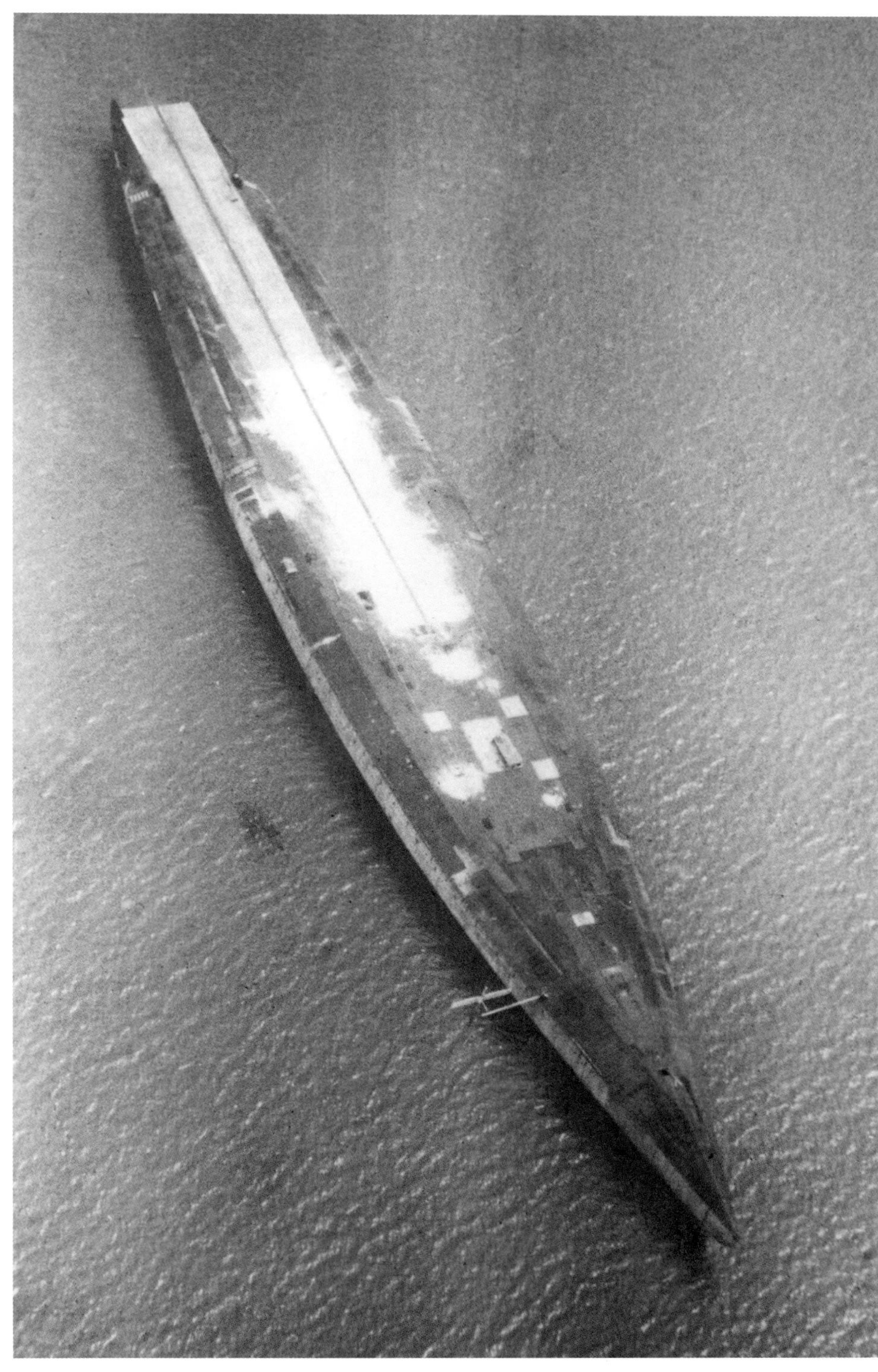

**Above:** The hull of *Béarn* in the Bay of Saint-Raphaël between May and August 1921. *(ARDHAN collection)*

[1] *British Aircraft Carriers*, Seaforth Publishing (Barnsley 2013), 66.

**Above:** Landing of a Hanriot HD.2 on the hull of *Béarn* on 20 October 1920. In the background can be seen the battleship *France*. *(Musée national de la Marine)*

– light vertical armour plating and protection against mines and torpedoes.

The hull of *Béarn*, which had been launched without ceremony to clear the slipway on 15 April 1920 and was complete up to the lower armoured deck, was selected for trials. Initial modifications involved a wooden platform 43 metres by 9 metres with an access ramp constructed directly on top of the lower armoured deck. The improvised arrester system used for the trials was based on transverse cables raised on circular pieces of cork and weighted with bags of sand (see photo). It was initially envisaged that trials would take place in the anchorage at Hyères, but the budget for towing did not allow this and the ship had to be moored in the busier Toulon roads. The hull was moored to Buoy No 7.

Prior to the trials Paul Teste and his team of pilots were drilled in precision landings using the concreted area (*bouchon de champagne*) at Saint-Raphaël, 60km to the northeast of Toulon. On 20 October 1920, Teste took off in a Hanriot HD.2. He succeeded with an arrested landing at the first attempt, rolling less than 30 metres. He took off again and landed three more times. The operation was repeated the following day with Teste, Sub-lieutenants Jean Reynaud and François d'Autheville and Petty Officer Georges Bougault. On the 24th, Teste landed a Sopwith 1½ Strutter with Lieutenant Etienne Levesque as passenger in the presence of the Minister of Marine. The only incident in this series of landings was a broken tailhook on a Hanriot piloted by Bougault.

Following this successful series of trials it was decided to complete *Béarn* as a carrier. A second series took place between May and August 1921, this time in the Bay of Saint-Raphaël, using a slightly longer platform. Seven new pilots qualified in landings.

The Washington Conference then intervened. Following its conclusion, the *Marine Nationale* decided to proceed with the proposed conversion of *Béarn*, and this decision was formalised in the 1922 Naval Programme. *Béarn* was selected rather than one of her sisters because she was the least complete; she would therefore be easier to modify without having to dismantle much of the existing steelwork, while at the same time having access to the machinery and other components already assembled for the other ships. Detailed plans were drawn up – although they would subsequently be subject to numerous modifications – and the contract for completion by the builder, Forges

**Right:** A Sopwith 1½ Strutter on the temporary platform fitted to the hull of *Béarn* on 24 October 1920. *(ARDHAN collection)*

***Normandie* Class: Profile & Plan**

**Note:** Adapted from plans dated Paris 31 October 1912.

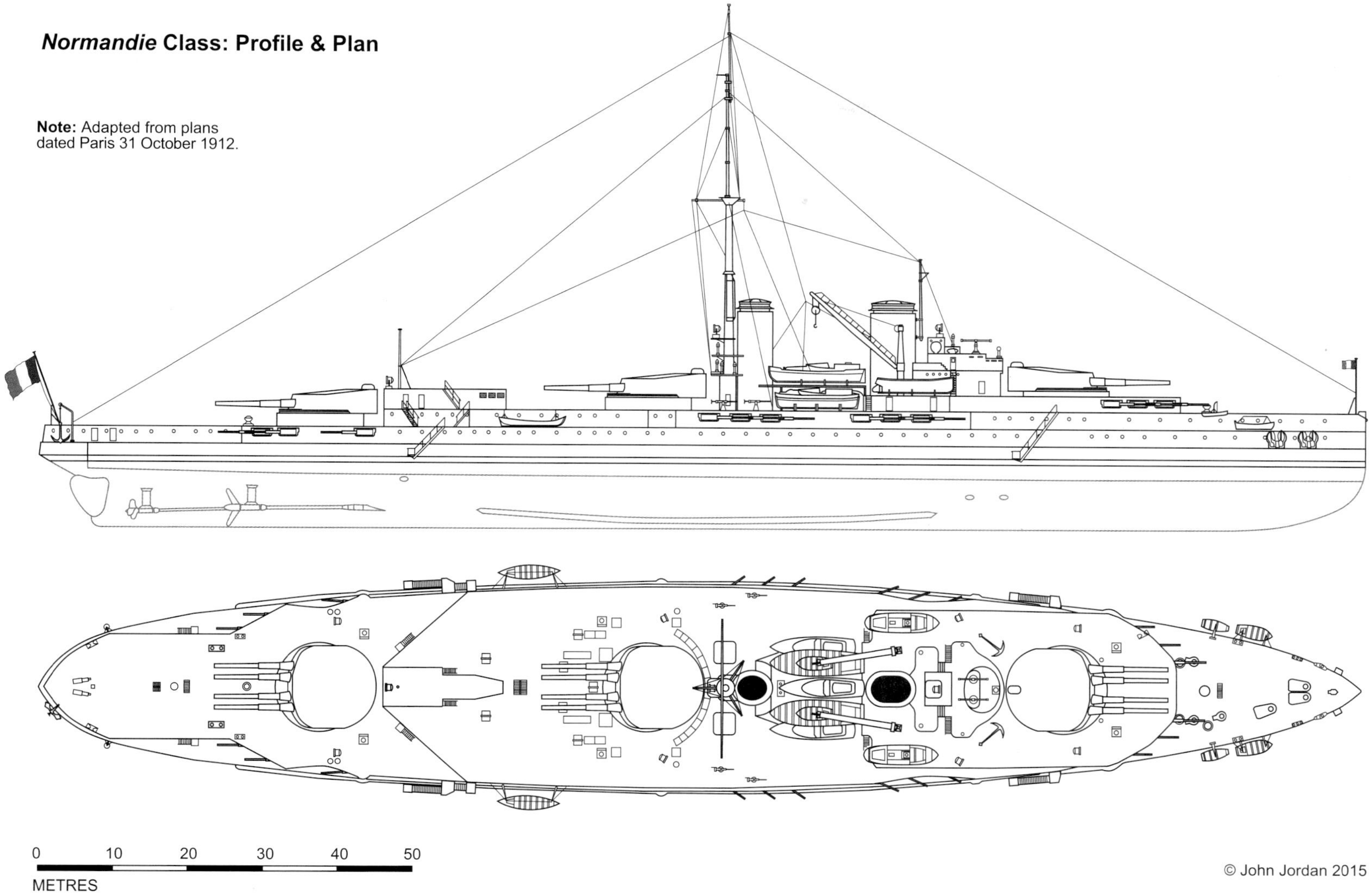

0 10 20 30 40 50
METRES

© John Jordan 2015

**Above:** *Béarn* as she would have looked had she been completed to the original plans. The design was dominated by its three quadruple turrets for 34cm guns.

**Left:** A Hanriot HD.3 is readied for take-off on the ramp fitted to the hull of *Béarn* during trials in the Saint-Raphaël anchorage in May 1921. *(ARDHAN collection)*

**Above:** A poor-quality image of a Sopwith following an arrested landing on the hull of *Béarn*, which nevertheless shows the arrester cables weighted by bags of sand. *(SHM-A collection)*

et Chantiers de la Méditerranée, was signed on 4 August 1923. The anticipated cost was 66.33 million French francs, of which 190,000FF were for the demolition of existing structures (452 tonnes).

### A TACTICAL FRAMEWORK

The influence of Britain's Royal Navy, rightly regarded as being at the forefront of naval aviation, went far beyond the technical and the operational. The Royal Navy of 1918 saw the aircraft carrier as key to providing scouting for the battle fleet in three dimensions, so reconnaissance aircraft were initially to be the key component of the air group. The air space over the battle fleet would also need to be denied to the enemy, hence the need for fighters. These ideas would subsequently be developed: it became clear that aircraft would be equally useful for spotting for the big guns, given ever-increasing ranges of engagement, for torpedo attack, which had the potential to slow an enemy fleet attempting to escape, and for anti-submarine patrol.

The air group initially envisaged for *Béarn* was to comprise two squadrons each of twelve reconnaissance aircraft plus a single squadron of eight fighters, for a total of thirty-two aircraft. The second reconnaissance squadron would subsequently be replaced by a squadron of torpedo attack aircraft. This conformed to RN theory and practice.

Royal Navy thinking around 1920 favoured two different types of aircraft carrier: one designed to operate in company with the battle fleet, with an air group comprising fighters, spotters and torpedo attack aircraft, the other intended to operate with the strategic scouting forces in the van, the air group being biased towards fighters and reconnaissance aircraft. Both types would need a small speed margin over the ships they would accompany, so the slower carriers (initially *Argus* and *Eagle*) would operate with the battle fleet, while the converted light battlecruisers, which were capable of top speeds in excess of 30 knots, would operate with the battlecruisers and light cruisers in the van.

The French had no battlecruisers, and the armoured cruisers that had survived the war were little faster than the 20/21-knot dreadnoughts, hence the staff requirement for speed and endurance comparable to the battleships of the *Bretagne* class. It would, in any case, have proved difficult to increase the top speed of *Béarn* beyond that of the original *Normandie* design given that a proportion of the hull volume occupied by machinery in the original plans would have to be reallocated to provide air ordnance magazines, aircraft spares and aviation fuel under armour. Nevertheless, the lack of any speed margin over the battleships showed a lack of appreciation of the need for an aircraft carrier to manoeuvre independently in order to launch and land aircraft into the wind.

## A: TECHNICAL DESCRIPTION

### MACHINERY AND LOWER HULL

When *Béarn* was launched in 1920 she was complete only to the lower armoured deck; neither the armour belt nor the propulsion machinery was in place.

As designed, the first four ships of the *Normandie* class were to have a composite propulsion plant, with turbines (for high speed) on the inner shafts, and reciprocating engines (for cruising/endurance) on the wing shafts. *Béarn*, on the other hand, would have had turbines throughout, to make it easier for her to operate in company with the three earlier ships of the *Bretagne* class.

Steam for the reciprocating engines and the turbines was to be supplied either by twenty-one Guyot–du Temple–Normand boilers, or twenty-eight Belleville boilers, both models being rated at 20kg/cm²; the Belleville boiler was of the traditional large watertube type, while the Guyot–du Temple–Normand boiler was a small-tube, three-drum model derived from the boilers fitted in contemporary destroyers. The boilers were disposed either as seven rows of three or seven rows of four in three boiler rooms. Both types burned coal, for which there was extensive bunkerage outboard of the boiler rooms (see Machinery plan).

The reversion to a composite propulsion plant in the *Normandie* class was the result of experience with direct drive turbines in the battleships of the *Danton* class. When the latter ships entered service in 1911, it quickly became apparent that coal consumption at moderate speeds was extraordinarily heavy. Since ships spent most of their active service lives steaming at cruise speed, even in time of war, this was a major concern. There was a cost in endurance, a financial cost, and a heavy price to pay for the crews: coaling was a tedious, dirty and back-breaking task which with high fuel consumption had to be performed with even greater frequency. It was anticipated that the reciprocating engines on the outer shafts would provide a range of 3375nm at 16 knots and 6500–6600nm at 12 knots (almost twice the radius of the *Bretagne* class).

For *Béarn* as a carrier it was decided to adopt the composite plant planned for her sisters, and to use the reciprocating engines and turbines intended for the first ship of the class, *Normandie*. Each of the vertical triple expansion (VTE) engines in the wing compartments, built by A C Loire at their Saint-Denis factory, had four cylinders (HP, IP and two LP), and drove a four-bladed propeller with a diameter of 5.2 metres; shaft revolutions were 115rpm. Quite apart from their greater efficiency at low and moderate speeds, the reciprocating engines had the advantage of being

**Left:** *Béarn* conducting take-off and landing trials with a Gourdou-Leseurre GL.22 trainer during landing trials in April–June 1927. Note that the forward 155mm casemate guns have yet to be embarked. *(Private collection, courtesy of Philippe Caresse)*

## Machinery Layouts

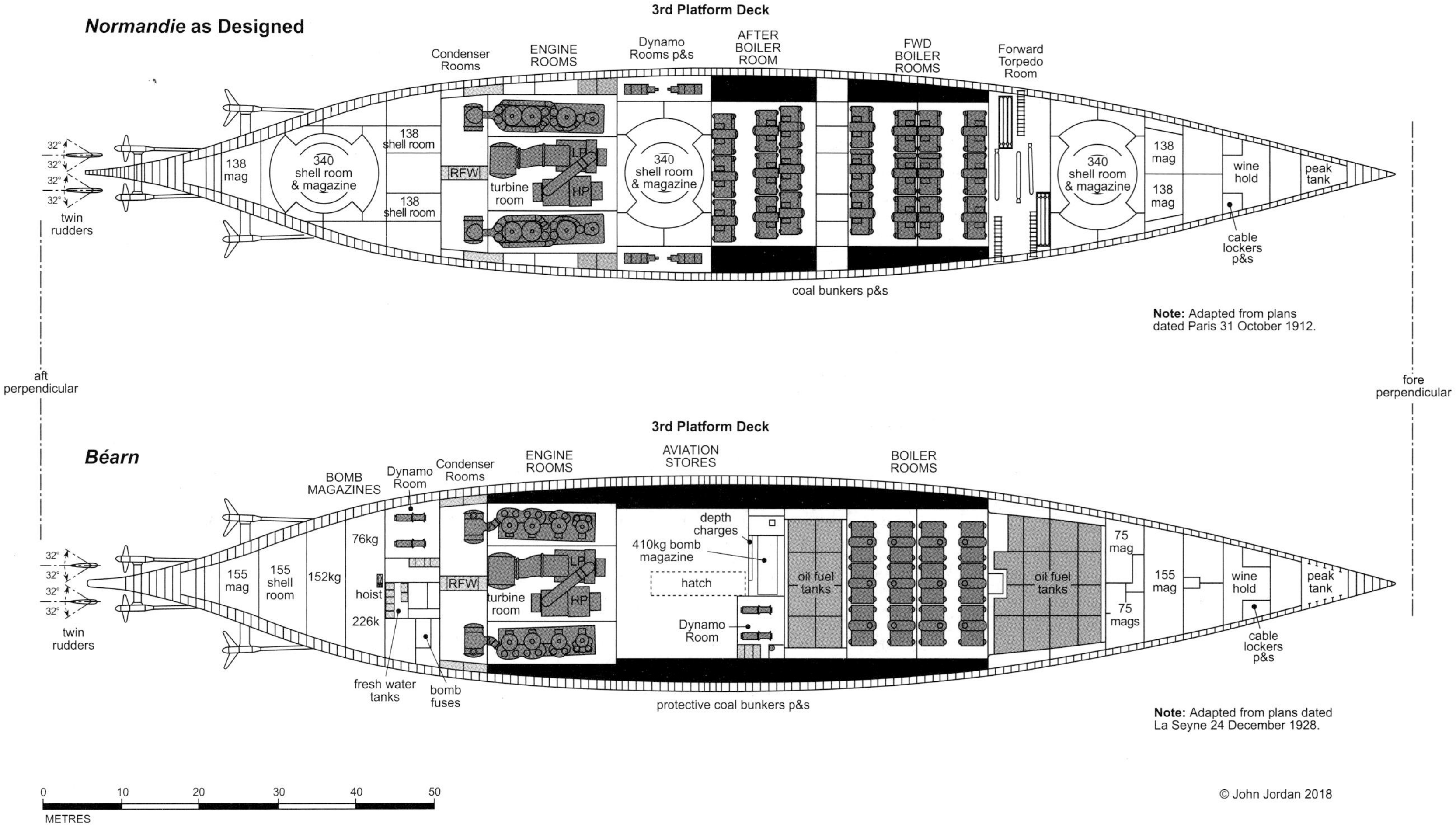

### *Normandie* as Designed

3rd Platform Deck

32° 32° 32° 32°
twin rudders
138 mag
340 shell room & magazine
138 shell room
138 shell room
RFW
Condenser Rooms
ENGINE ROOMS
turbine room
LP
HP
Dynamo Rooms p&s
340 shell room & magazine
AFTER BOILER ROOM
FWD BOILER ROOMS
Forward Torpedo Room
340 shell room & magazine
138 mag
138 mag
wine hold
peak tank
cable lockers p&s
coal bunkers p&s

**Note:** Adapted from plans dated Paris 31 October 1912.

aft perpendicular

fore perpendicular

### *Béarn*

3rd Platform Deck

32° 32° 32° 32°
twin rudders
155 mag
155 shell room
152kg
BOMB MAGAZINES
76kg
hoist
226k
Dynamo Room
fresh water tanks
bomb fuses
Condenser Rooms
RFW
ENGINE ROOMS
turbine room
LP
HP
AVIATION STORES
depth charges
410kg bomb magazine
hatch
Dynamo Room
oil fuel tanks
BOILER ROOMS
oil fuel tanks
75 mag
75 mags
155 mag
wine hold
peak tank
cable lockers p&s
protective coal bunkers p&s

**Note:** Adapted from plans dated La Seyne 24 December 1928.

0 10 20 30 40 50
METRES

**Right:** Another image of *Béarn* conducting take-off and landing trials with a Gourdou-Leseurre GL.22 trainer during landing trials in April–June 1927. The after section of the flight deck was sloped down at 10 degrees when the ship was first completed. *(Private collection, courtesy of Philippe Caresse)*

able to be reversed to drive the ship when going astern.

The turbines in the inner compartment comprised a single HP turbine (to starboard) feeding into a single LP turbine (to port), both of the Parsons type and likewise built by A C Loire. The turbines were ahead-only, and the adoption of a composite power plant meant that there was no need for separate cruise turbines. The propellers driven by the turbines on the inner shafts were of high-resistance bronze; they had three blades and a diameter of 3.44m; shaft revolutions at full speed were 280rpm. The twin balanced rudders were directly abaft the centre shafts; each had a surface area of 20.7m$^2$.

The main condenser for the turbines was located in the centre engine room just forward of (and above) the LP turbine. The condenser rooms for the reciprocating engines were directly abaft the outer engine rooms, and were separated by feed water tanks disposed along the ship's axis.

By the time the reconstruction of *Béarn* had been authorised, oil firing had been adopted for all new construction. Oil not only had a higher calorific value than coal, but it could be pumped on board and around the ship, thereby easing the task of the stokers and enabling their numbers to be reduced. It was decided to replace the original boilers with a new type of Normand small watertube oil-fired boiler. Only twelve were needed to supply the necessary steam for the 40,000cv propulsion machinery, and these were accommodated in the forward pair of boiler rooms and disposed in four rows of three (see plans). The fuel oil was stowed not in the original coal bunkers outboard of the boiler rooms, but in two groups of tanks fore and aft of the two surviving boiler rooms, the coal bunkers being retained for protection (see below). The forward group of tanks occupied the spaces formerly allocated to the forward torpedo flat and the magazine, shell room and handing room for the forward quadruple 34cm gun turret; the after grouping replaced the midship 14cm magazine and part of the original after boiler room.

Once the arrangement of the main propulsion machinery had been fixed it was possible to decide how to reallocate the remaining volume in the lower hull. In general terms this involved the suppression of the magazines, shell rooms and handing rooms for the three 34cm quadruple mountings, together with the magazines and handing rooms for the secondary 14cm battery. The original third boiler room was combined with the ammunition stowage and handling spaces

**Below:** An unusual overhead view of *Béarn* on her power trials, steaming at 19.7 knots. *(SHM)*

beneath the midship turret to create a capacious aviation store that included a magazine for the largest 410kg bombs, and there were further magazines for aircraft ordnance in place of the 34cm magazine and shell room aft. The magazines for the revised armament (see below) were located at the fore and after extremities of the 2nd and 3rd Platform Decks.

Electrical power for the ship was supplied by steam-powered turbo-dynamos, each with an output of 400kW feeding a 230V circuit. The four units installed in *Béarn* were those built for her uncompleted sister *Flandre*. In the original plans they were to have been mounted in wing compartments outboard of the midship 34cm turret; however, in *Béarn* they occupied two compartments offset to port and to starboard abaft and forward of the engine rooms respectively, within the protective 'box'. They would be supplemented by two 150W diesel generators higher up in the ship, located on either side of the Main Deck, for use when the ship was alongside.

## PROTECTION AGAINST ENEMY VESSELS

### Main guns

It was recognised that independent manoeuvre could potentially expose an aircraft carrier to the enemy's advanced scouting forces. The British *Argus* was an experimental mercantile conversion, and was fitted with neither low-angle guns nor protection. However, the carriers *Hermes* and *Eagle* featured not only a battery of low-angle (LA) guns comparable to that of a contemporary light cruiser, together with a massive control top to direct low-angle fire, but side and deck armour for the hull capable of withstanding cruiser shell. As originally designed, both ships were to have mounted nine 6in (152mm) guns;[2] *Hermes* was given a 3in (76mm) belt and a 1in (25mm) deck, *Eagle* a 4.5in (114mm) belt and a 1.5in (38mm) deck.

*Béarn* was completed with eight 155mm LA guns in casemates, mounted in pairs at the four corners of the ship. The forward two pairs had a command of 10.06 metres, the after guns 6.84 metres. The end guns were capable of axial fire and had arcs of 120 degrees; the inner guns could fire within 15 degrees of the ship's axis and had slightly reduced arcs of 110 degrees (see drawing).

The 155mm Mle 1920 was a 50-calibre weapon developed for the French Navy's light cruisers of the

**Table 1: CHARACTERISTICS (1928)**

| | |
|---|---|
| Displacement: | 25,335 tonnes normal |
| Dimensions: | |
| length | 175.00m pp, 182.50m oa |
| beam | 27.17m wl |
| draught | 8.86m aft |
| Aviation: | |
| flight deck | 180m x 27m |
| height above w/l | 15.65m |
| upper hangar | 124m x 19.5m x 6.5/5m |
| lower hangar | 108m x 15m (approx) x 5.4m |
| lifts (LxW) | F (fwd): 8m x 12m |
| | R (ctr): 10m x 15m |
| | T (aft): 15m x 15m |
| air group | nine fighters |
| | nine recce bombers |
| | nine torpedo attack |
| Machinery: | |
| boilers | twelve Normand small watertube, 20kg/cm$^2$ |
| engines | four-shaft mixed propulsion: |
| | two 4-cylinder VTE engines on wing shafts |
| | Parsons HP and LP turbines on centre shafts |
| propellers | two 5.20m diameter on wing shafts |
| | two 3.44m diameter on centre shafts |
| horsepower | 40,000cv |
| speed | 21.5 knots |
| oil fuel | 2100 tonnes |
| endurance | 6500nm at 10 knots |
| generators | four turbo-generators each 400kW |
| Protection: | |
| main belt | 83mm |
| decks | 24mm PBS + 28/70mm PBI |
| casemates | 50mm |
| Armament: | |
| LA guns | eight 155mm/50 Mle 1922 in single casemate mountings |
| HA guns | six 75mm/50 Mle 1924 in single mountings |
| light AA | eight 37mm/50 Mle 1925 in single mountings |
| | twelve 8mm Hotchkiss MG Mle 1914 |
| torpedo tubes | four a/w tubes for 550mm torpedoes |
| | eight torpedoes Mle 1923D |
| Boats: | one 10-metre steam pinnace |
| | one 13-metre motor boat |
| | one 11-metre motor boat |
| | one 9-metre motor boat |
| | one 13-metre pulling pinnace |
| | two 11-metre pulling pinnaces |
| | two 9-metre pulling cutters |
| | two 8.5-metre whalers |
| | two 5-metre dinghies |
| Complement: | |
| private ship | 45 officers, 830 men (includes air group) |

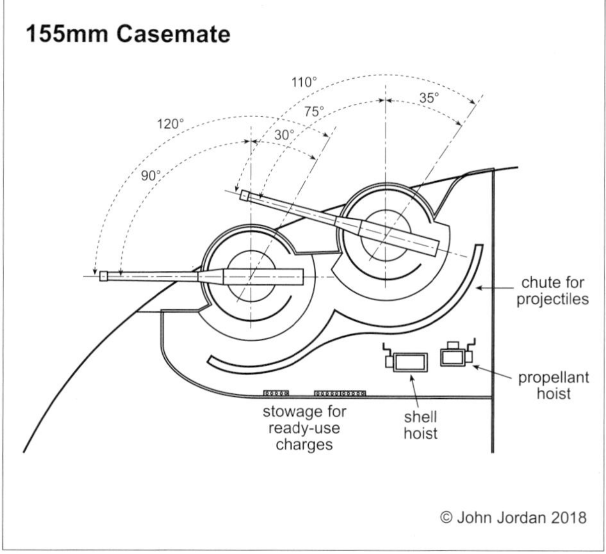


[2] The 6in guns for *Hermes* were subsequently replaced by 5.5in (140mm) guns from the discarded cruiser *Birkenhead*, and the three quarterdeck mountings were suppressed to enable the ship to operate seaplanes.

[3] The figure of 70mm given by Campbell in *Naval Weapons of World War Two* probably includes a double layer of 10mm steel to which the 50mm special steel plating would have been secured.

## Table 2: LOW-ANGLE GUNS

**155mm/50 Mle 1920**

| | |
|---|---|
| *Gun Data* | |
| Construction | autofretted 'A' tube with jacket & liner |
| Breech mechanism | upward-opening Welin screw |
| Weight of gun | 8763kg (incl breech) |
| Ammunition type | separate |
| Projectiles | OPf Mle 1927 (14.95kg) |
| Propellant | 19.81kg BM11 in two bags |
| Muzzle velocity | 850m/s |
| Range | 26,100m at 40° |
| *Mounting* | |
| Designation | Mle 1922 |
| Protection | 50mm shield |
| Weight of mounting | 37,400kg |
| Elevation | -3° / +40° |
| Firing cycle | 3–4rpm |

**Notes:**

| | | |
|---|---|---|
| Mle | Modèle | Model |
| OPf | Obus de Perforation | Semi-Armour Piercing (SAP) |

*Duguay-Trouin* class, the first major new ships to be authorised after the Great War. It fired an SAP shell weighing 56.5kg with a muzzle velocity of 850m/s using a 19.81kg propellant charge of BM11 in two bags. The projectile, which had a bursting charge of 2.9kg of *mélinite* (picric acid), had a ballistic cap (for increased range) and two driving bands.

In *Béarn* each of the guns was mounted within a cylindrical shield with 50mm sides[3] and a 24mm roof. The mountings allowed a maximum elevation of +40 degrees, giving a theoretical range of 25,000 metres, and the guns could be depressed to -3 degrees. There were separate hoists for projectiles and propellant charges for each pair of guns. These were from *Béarn*'s uncompleted sister *Flandre* and were capable of supplying twelve complete rounds per minute; the projectiles were lifted in cases of three, the half-charges in cases of six. There were chutes behind the guns that could hold eighteen ready-use projectiles; the corresponding propellant charges were stowed vertically in racks against the rear wall of each casemate. The standard ammunition provision for the LA guns totalled 2,000 shells, including 500 tracer for night fire, and 4,200 half-charges, equivalent to 250 combat rounds per gun.

Below: *Béarn* docked at Brest in December 1932. During this refit the mainmast would be landed and replaced by aerial spreaders on the funnel. Note the casemates for the 155mm low-angle guns on either side and the shielded 75mm HA guns above. *(ARDHAN collection)*

Mounting the 155mm guns in paired casemates at the four corners of the ship meant that they were fore and aft of the hangar, which could therefore occupy the full width of the hull. This meant that hangar volume was significantly greater than in *Hermes* and *Eagle*, which had their LA guns mounted in open shields on either side of the ship. However, it also precluded the operation of seaplanes from the quarter-deck, as initially envisaged, because of the location and height of command of the after casemate guns.

**Torpedoes**

The original plans featured no fewer than twelve above-water tubes for the new 550mm Mle 1923 D torpedo, as in the contemporary light cruisers of the *Duguay-Trouin* class. However, the number of torpedo tubes was progressively reduced from twelve to six and finally, following an amendment to the contract dated 12 August 1925, to four. The tubes, which were on the Main Deck with a command of 3.8 metres, ran on semi-circular tracks that permitted an angle of train of 30 degrees either side of the beam. When not in use they could be retracted within the hull. Eight torpedoes – two per tube – were stowed, complete with warheads, on racks close to the tubes fixed to the side bulkheads of the aircraft assembly and repair area beneath the hangar (see below).

**Fire control**

Range data for both the main guns and the torpedoes were supplied by four 3-metre coincidence rangefinders mounted on sponsons to port and starboard of the flight deck amidships and aft. The rangefinder arms were given a 0.5-metre clearance above the flight deck to ensure all-round coverage, except where they were masked by the island. The *Postes centraux*, divided into a lower steering position on the centre-line and a transmitting station to port, were located at the forward end of the 2nd Platform Deck. As originally conceived they were considered too small and cramped, and were extended while the

**Above:** Close-up of the after 155mm casemate guns to starboard. The cylindrical shields were protected by 50mm armour plating. *(Musée national de la Marine)*

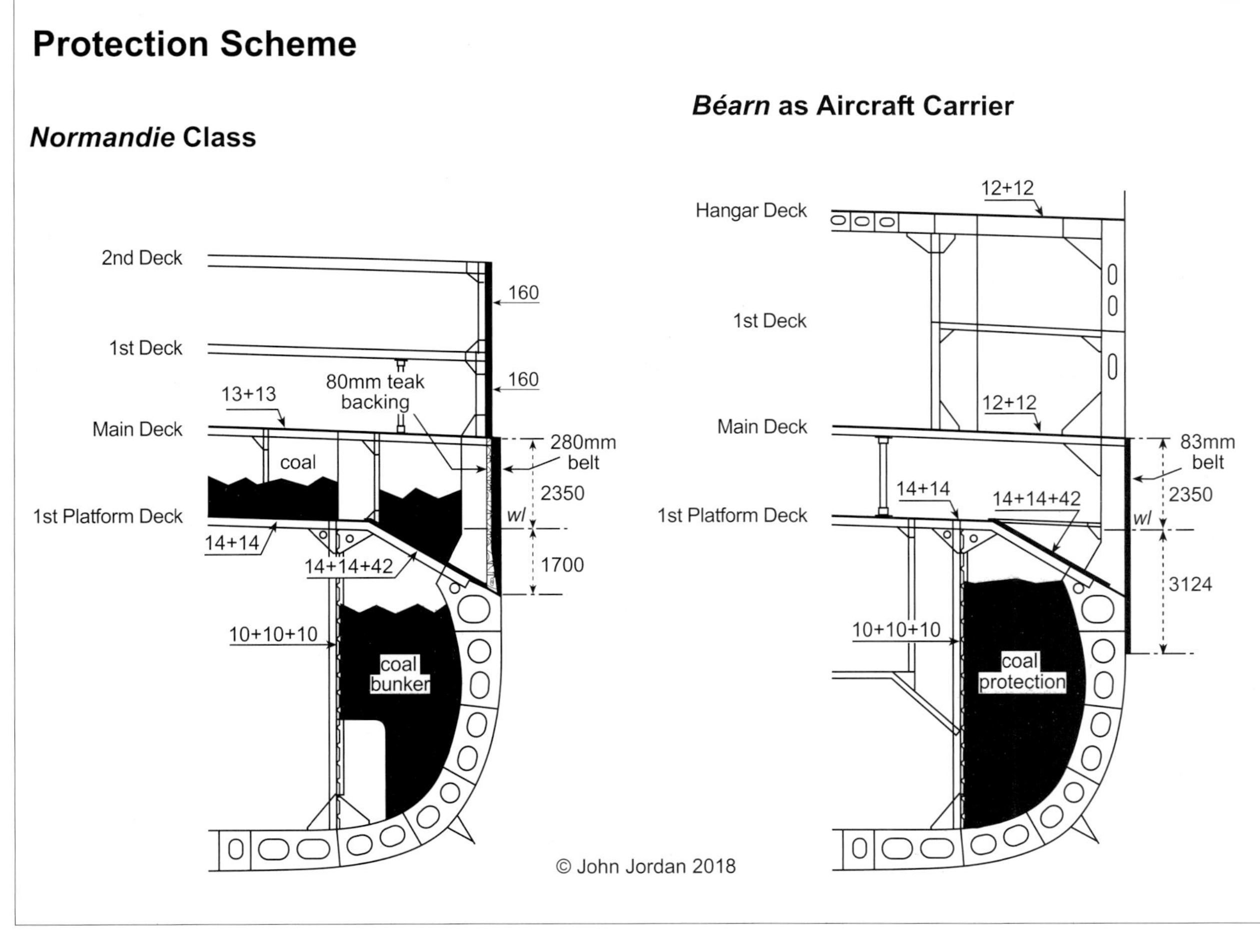

**Right:** A fine study of *Béarn* probably dating from 1930–31. The forward section of the flight deck is now sloped at 4.5 degrees forward, but the mainmast for the W/T aerials remains in place. The 'lamp base' beneath the funnel, with its rows of rectangular air intakes, is particularly prominent in this view. *(DR)*

ship was fitting out by adjusting the position of the bulkheads separating them from the forward 155mm magazines. The ship was completed with two Mle 1923 B mechanical computers to handle two separate targets, both housed within the fire control position. However, some of the fire control equipment was delivered late and was fitted only after completion.

**Protection**

The *Normandie* class as designed had the classic protection system associated with the distinguished naval architect Emile Bertin: a high, deep belt, with upper and lower armoured decks and a tightly divided cellular layer between. The main belt, which was of face-hardened steel, would have had a maximum thickness of 280mm, reducing at the ends and tapering

below the waterline; it was seated on a teak backing and secured by armour bolts to the shell. The upper armoured deck (PBS) comprised two layers of 13mm steel plating, and the lower armoured deck (PBI) two layers of 14mm steel, with reinforcing plates of special steel 42mm thick on the slopes for a total thickness of 70mm. The cellular layer comprised an outer cofferdam subdivided into watertight cells, each a single frame in length, with coal bunkers inboard to provide additional protection against shells that succeeded in penetrating the belt or the upper armoured deck. The system was designed to prevent large-calibre shell (305mm/12in and above) from reaching the ship's vitals. There would also have been an upper belt of 160mm extending for most of the length of the hull to protect the 14cm casemate battery (see Protection plan).

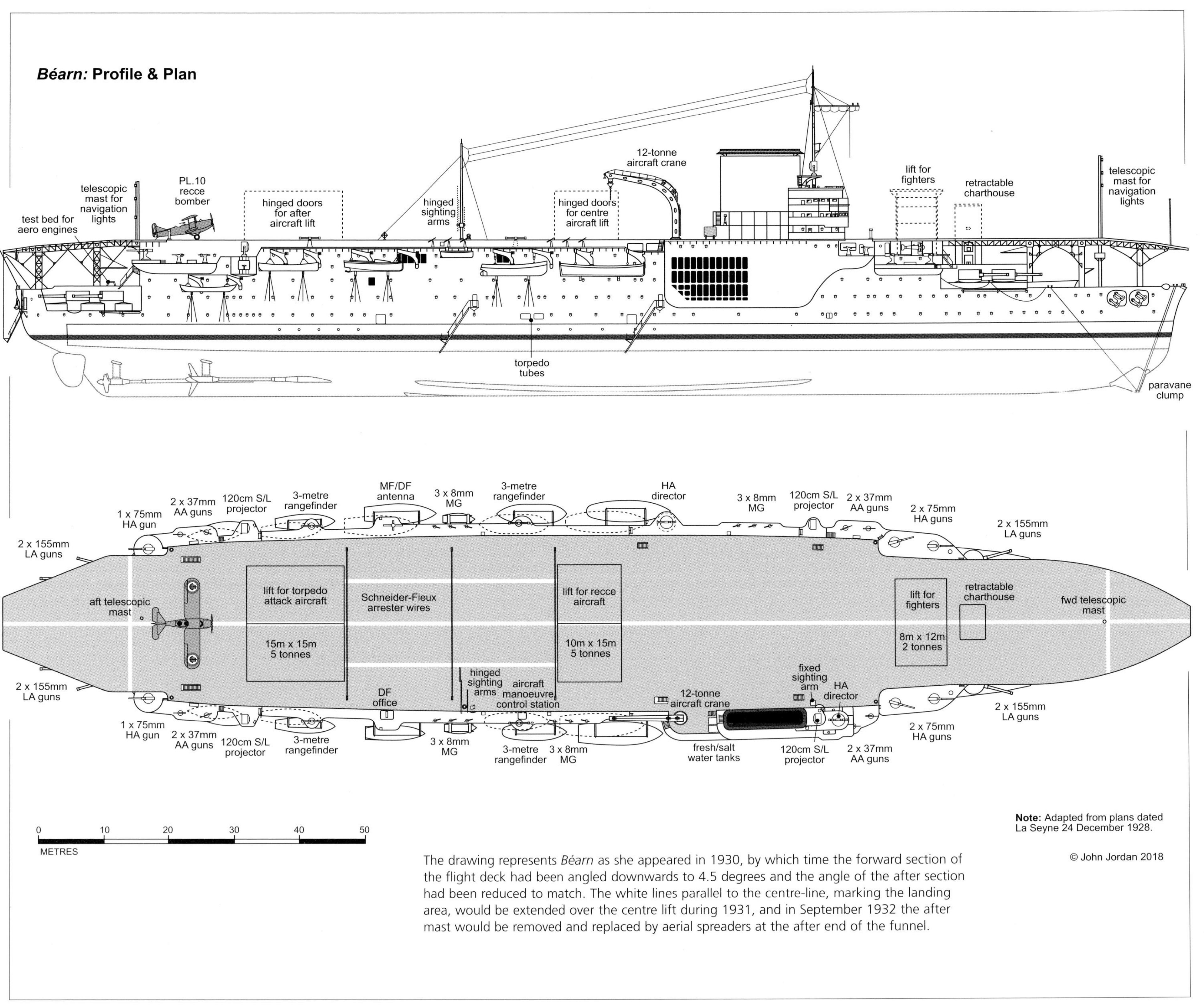


The drawing represents *Béarn* as she appeared in 1930, by which time the forward section of the flight deck had been angled downwards to 4.5 degrees and the angle of the after section had been reduced to match. The white lines parallel to the centre-line, marking the landing area, would be extended over the centre lift during 1931, and in September 1932 the after mast would be removed and replaced by aerial spreaders at the after end of the funnel.

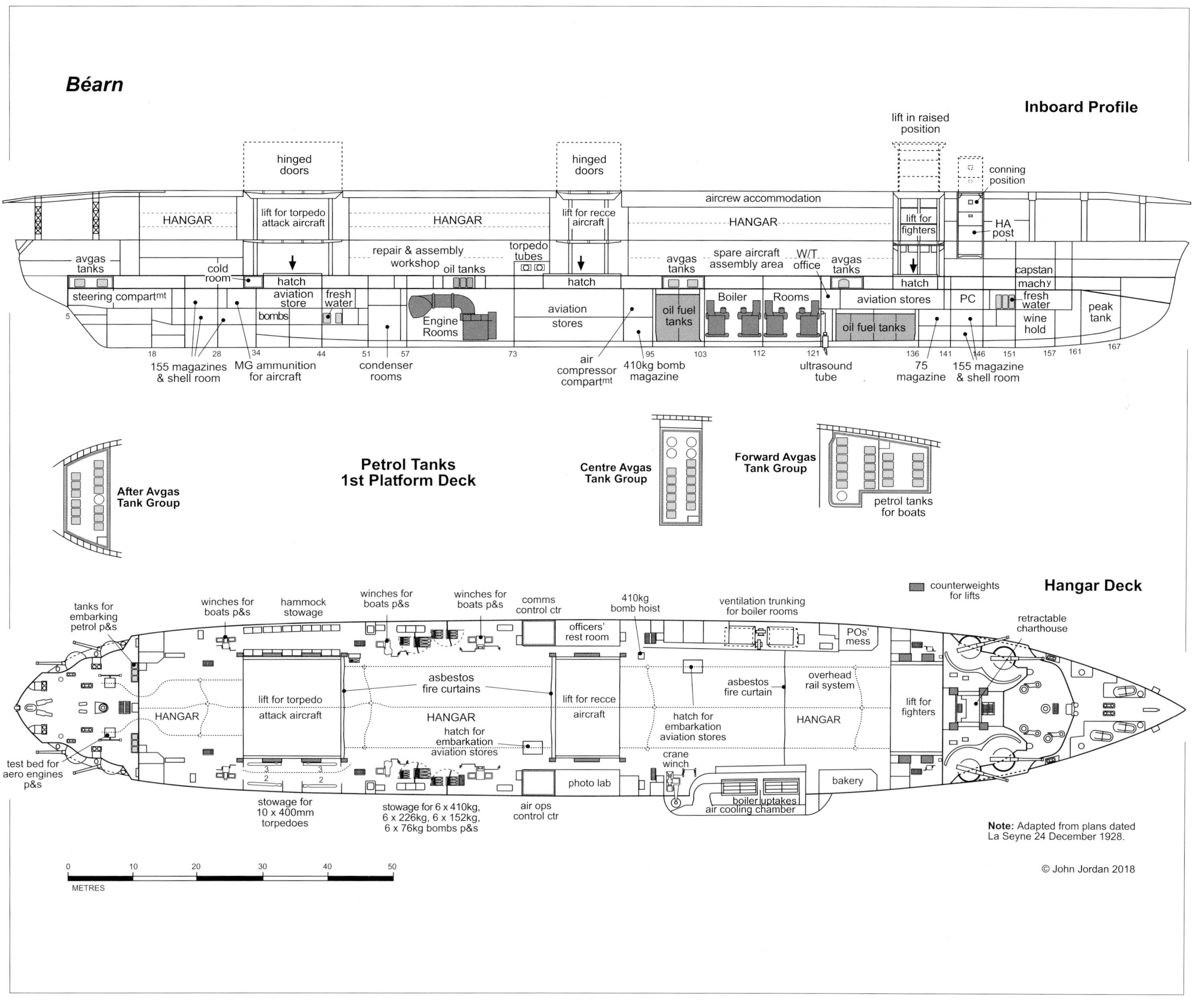
Béarn
Inboard Profile
hinged doors
hinged doors
lift in raised position
conning position
HANGAR
lift for torpedo attack aircraft
HANGAR
lift for recce aircraft
aircrew accommodation
HANGAR
lift for fighters
HA post
avgas tanks
cold room
repair & assembly workshop
oil tanks
torpedo tubes
avgas tanks
spare aircraft assembly area
W/T office
avgas tanks
capstan machy
hatch
hatch
hatch
steering compart^mt
aviation store
bombs
fresh water
Engine Rooms
aviation stores
oil fuel tanks
Boiler Rooms
aviation stores
PC
fresh water
oil fuel tanks
wine hold
peak tank
5
18
28
34
44
51
57
73
95
103
112
121
136
141
146
151
157
161
167
155 magazines & shell room
MG ammunition for aircraft
condenser rooms
air compressor compart^mt
410kg bomb magazine
ultrasound tube
75 magazine
155 magazine & shell room
Petrol Tanks 1st Platform Deck
After Avgas Tank Group
Centre Avgas Tank Group
Forward Avgas Tank Group
petrol tanks for boats
Hangar Deck
counterweights for lifts
tanks for embarking petrol p&s
winches for boats p&s
hammock stowage
winches for boats p&s
winches for boats p&s
comms control ctr
officers' rest room
410kg bomb hoist
ventilation trunking for boiler rooms
POs' mess
retractable charthouse
asbestos fire curtains
asbestos fire curtain
overhead rail system
HANGAR
lift for torpedo attack aircraft
HANGAR
lift for recce aircraft
hatch for embarkation aviation stores
HANGAR
lift for fighters
hatch for embarkation aviation stores
crane winch
test bed for aero engines p&s
photo lab
bakery
boiler uptakes
air cooling chamber
stowage for 10 x 400mm torpedoes
stowage for 6 x 410kg, 6 x 226kg, 6 x 152kg, 6 x 76kg bombs p&s
air ops control ctr
Note: Adapted from plans dated La Seyne 24 December 1928.
© John Jordan 2018
0
10
20
30
40
50
METRES

Such a system was not only unnecessary in a ship designed to resist cruiser and destroyer shell, but it was heavy, accounting for some 30 per cent of displacement, and face-hardened armour was costly. When *Béarn* was taken in hand for conversion, the hull was complete only to the lower armoured deck. This was retained in its original form, but the thickness of the plates that made up the Main Deck was reduced from 13mm to 12mm, for a total thickness of 24mm. The main armoured belt was replaced by plates of armour-quality ('special') homogeneous steel with a uniform thickness of 83mm, secured directly to the hull plating as in contemporary cruisers. It comprised three strakes, not two, and extended from the Main Deck (PBS) to 3.12 metres beneath the waterline. The original coal bunkers were retained, but were extended aft so as to provide protection not only for the boiler rooms but for the engine rooms (see GA plans). They were filled with coal that remained in place and was not consumed. As in the original *Normandie* design, there was an inner torpedo bulkhead of 20mm nickel steel (two layers each with a thickness of 10mm) lined on the outside by flexible corrugated plating of 10mm mild steel that was designed to act as a spring when exposed to a pressure wave. At its widest point this underwater protection system had a depth of 4.3 metres. However, it was feared that this would be insufficient to protect against the increasingly large warheads of modern torpedoes, and British-style bulges would later be proposed (see below).

The total weight of protection, including the coal, was 5,000 tonnes, which was an impressive figure for an aircraft carrier – the corresponding figure for the battleships of the *Bretagne* class was 7,070 tonnes, although this did not include the 2,000 tonnes of coal in the side bunkers, which would have been burned in the boilers.

## AVIATION

Having made a detailed study of British carrier developments during the visit in the summer of 1920, the French opted for a large two-tier hangar topped by a broad flight deck served by three aircraft lifts, with a narrow island to starboard incorporating a large single funnel. The weight of the island had to be compensated by solid ballast comprising 872 tonnes of cemented pig iron in the double bottom to port; this had the additional effect of lowering the centre of gravity and improving stability.

**Below:** Overhead of the flight deck of *Béarn* at her moorings in 1929. The distinctive clamshell doors of the lifts are in the open position, and the platforms of the lifts can be seen just below the level of the flight deck. Forward of the centre lift can be seen a Lévy-Biche LB.2 fighter aircraft. *(ARDHAN collection)*

Above: *Béarn* during 1932–34, following the removal of the W/T mast abaft the island, replaced by aerial spreaders secured to the after end of the funnel. The retractable charthouse is in the raised position, and the two-tier aircraft lift immediately abaft it is partially raised. *(Musée national de la Marine)*

Due to concerns regarding the conning of the ship from the low bridge at the forward end of the island, particularly at night, the design incorporated a retractable charthouse at the forward end of the flight deck, as in the British carriers *Argus* and *Furious*. This could be raised to a height of 5.4 metres above the deck using electric motors – a procedure that took two minutes. There was a *Poste de navigation* on the upper level with a hinged magnetic compass set into the roof, and a sea cabin for the commanding officer directly below; the third level housed the calculating position for the HA guns, the fourth the lift machinery. Only the upper two levels were ever above deck, and when the lift was in the lowered position there were views forward and to the sides beneath the flight deck. As flying operations at night were not envisaged, there were also retractable masts carrying the main navigation lights on (or close to) the middle line fore and aft.

The concept of an island was the subject of intense debate in all the major navies during this period. The aviation community generally preferred a clear deck free of any obstruction that might limit wingspan, or fixed structures that might create air turbulence. However, this then posed the problem of how to dispose of the large volume of hot funnel gases generated when the ship was steaming at high speed. It also precluded locating the command spaces necessary for conning the ship and supervising flight operations above the flight deck, hence the adoption of a retractable charthouse in some carriers with a flush deck. As early as October 1918, a narrow island superstructure of wood and canvas had been built at Rosyth and installed to starboard on *Argus*. Trials showed that the island structure produced little turbulence in itself, and that its presence actually helped pilots to orientate themselves when landing on. It was subsequently removed from *Argus* in order to maximise the width of the flight deck, but the decision was taken to complete *Hermes* and *Eagle* with islands to starboard, and plans of the latter ship were made available to the French commission in early 1920. In appearance the island adopted for *Béarn* bore a marked visual resemblance to the wood-and-canvas model fitted experimentally in *Argus*, with a single large narrow funnel.

The adoption of an island structure did not erase concerns about the potential turbulence over the flight deck caused by the hot funnel gases, and for *Béarn* the French devised a novel solution. A large streamlined housing (generally referred to in the French Navy as the *cul de lampe* or 'lamp base') was constructed beneath the funnel on the starboard side with rows of large, rectangular air intakes that were connected by ducting to the boiler uptakes. The hot combustion gases were mixed with cold air from outside the ship, thereby reducing the temperature of the gases that emanated from the funnel[4] and were drawn down onto the after part of the flight deck. This seems to have been reasonably effective, as a second bank of intakes was fitted when the ship was re-boilered in 1934–35 (see below).

### Flight deck

The flight deck was approximately 15.5 metres above the waterline at normal load and was supported on the walls of the hangar amidships and by pillars above the

4 Similar measures were adopted by some navies during the late twentieth century to prevent surface-to-surface missiles with infrared guidance from locking onto the hot funnel gases of ships powered by gas turbines.

**Right:** A Wibault 74 of 7C1 Squadron is brought up to the flight deck by the forward aircraft lift in 1933. The forward lift was unusual in having two platforms, and when raised protruded above the flight deck. *(DR)*

open forecastle and quarterdeck, which were used primarily for line handling and refuelling. It comprised two layers of 12mm steel plating with overlapping plates, topped by wooden planking of African teak (Iroko) with a thickness that varied between 50mm and 70mm. The flight deck was 180 metres long and had a maximum width of 27 metres. The forward section was horizontal when the ship was first completed in 1927, and the after section was angled down at 10 degrees. Following early manoeuvres in which it became clear that it was difficult for the carrier to maintain her station with the fleet when she had to turn into the wind to land aircraft (see below), in December 1928 the forward end of the flight deck was angled down at 4.5 degrees to permit landings over the bow, and in a short refit at the end of the following year the after end of the flight deck was raised to a similar angle. Aircraft used only the horizontal central section of the flight deck for take-off and landing, so the two 'breaks' in the deck were clearly marked by broad transverse white lines. Galleries ran on either side of the flight deck; they were 1.5 metres wide, increasing to 2 metres where the machine guns were located, and punctuated by broader sponsons for the HA guns and rangefinders.

**Below:** An aerial view of *Béarn* probably dating from 1930–31, prior to the removal of the W/T mast abaft the island. A Levasseur PL.4 reconnaissance aircraft is suspended from the crane. *(Musée national de la Marine)*

The flight deck and hangar were served by no fewer than three aircraft lifts, each of which was sized for a specific type of aircraft. This was a significant departure from contemporary British practice, which was characterised by a large 'T'-shaped or cruciform lift at the forward end of the hangar able to strike down the largest aircraft with wings deployed, and a narrower lift with a rectangular (or cruciform) configuration aft that could raise aircraft, normally with wings folded, from the hangar ready to be spotted for take-off. Operational doctrine in both navies was to strike down an aircraft immediately on landing before the next aircraft landed on, a process that generally took five or six minutes, as the landing interval was dictated by the speed of operation of the lifts; neither navy operated a deck park. For similar reasons the maximum strike that could be spotted for take-off, leaving sufficient length of deck for take-off, was six aircraft, and the Royal Navy 'flight' – the standard unit of organisation – was sized accordingly. French naval air squadrons were generally embarked as two or three sections each of three aircraft, so take-off and landing operations were generally by two sections.

The forward lift on *Béarn*, which was 8 metres long and 12 metres wide, was sized for fighters and had a 2-tonne capacity; on the 1928 plans of the ship it is labelled 'Ascenseur des A.C.' (A.C. = *avions chasseurs*). Unusually, it was a two-tier lift with the platforms separated by the height of the hangar. In the lowered position the lower platform was at the level of the hangar deck and the upper platform at the level of the flight deck. When the lift was raised to bring up aircraft from the hangar the upper platform was 7.5 metres above the flight deck.[5] A 1931 proposal to extend this lift on its after side by adding a rectangular section 1.5 metres long and 5 metres wide was not implemented.

The centre lift was 10 metres long and 15 metres wide, and could therefore accommodate the largest scout bombers of the day (A.R. = *avions de reconnaissance*) with wings deployed. It was complemented by an even larger after lift 15 metres square for torpedo bombers (A.T. = *avions torpilleurs*); both these lifts had a capacity of 5 tonnes. Because these two lifts occupied the centre of the flight deck and were relatively slow in operation – three minutes per complete cycle for the centre lift, a full five minutes for the after lift – the open lift shafts were closed by heavy clamshell doors when the lift was at hangar deck level to enable flying operations to continue. Despite the technical ingenuity of this solution, it was costly in terms of topweight and the power required to operate the doors, which required their own electric motors. It was also more vulnerable to breakdown and action damage – although three lifts did offer greater redundancy than two.

All three aircraft lifts and the retractable charthouse were powered by electric motors; large counterweights running in vertical shafts on either side of each lift meant that the power needed to raise the lift was reduced to a minimum. The lifts were designed to operate with a permanent list of 10 degrees, and with a ten-second roll of 5 degrees. The after lift and the charthouse were specified for six manoeuvres per hour indefinitely, the other two lifts for seventeen consecutive manoeuvres with a 24-hour break, or fourteen consecutive manoeuvres followed by six per hour.

Originally there was to have been a palisade similar to those fitted in the early British carriers to prevent the light wood-and-canvas aircraft of the day from being blown over the side on landing. However, this was suppressed by a directive dated 22 April 1925. Instead the French experimented with increasingly sophisticated arrester systems, which by the early 1930s were fully developed.

The first experiments were with five transverse cables strung across the flight deck at intervals of approximately 16 metres, the first of which was 31 metres forward of the 'round-down' across the after lift. The cables were raised 10cm above the deck by circular pieces of cork and weighted down by bags of sand with a total weight of 2400kg. These were replaced during the first refit of 1928–29 by prototype arrester systems developed by Schneider and Saint-Chamond. The Fieux system manufactured by Schneider worked by friction using restraining drums; the competing Saint-Chamond system used hydraulics. Three cables (two Schneider-Fieux aft, one Saint-Chamond forward) were sited between the after two main aircraft lifts, again at 16-metre intervals (see Profile & Plan). At the same time, white stripes were painted 6.5m on either side of the centre-line between the two lifts to mark out the area in which the arrester wires were located; they were later extended forward over the centre lift. The Schneider-Fieux system proved superior, and in a refit in late 1932, the Saint-Chamond arrester cable was replaced by a third Schneider model. The pilots who proposed that the forward end of the flight deck be inclined downwards also wanted three additional arrester wires between the forward and centre lifts be installed at frames 90, 105 and 120 to permit landings over the bow; however, this measure was not implemented, probably on grounds of cost.[6]

**Above:** A Levasseur PL.4 reconnaissance aircraft on the flight deck of *Béarn* during the late 1920s. The large 12-tonne crane, which was capable of lifting seaplanes on board, can be seen on the right of the picture. *(DR)*

5 The after lift in the IJN carriers *Akagi* and *Kaga* was similar.

6 Forward arresting gear was fitted in all US carriers during the 1930s.

**Right:** Landing of a Levasseur PL.4 on *Béarn*. The arrow-shaped sight of the after mast is being lowered. *(SHD-A)*

There was no deck landing officer. The landing procedure initially adopted was one pioneered by Paul Teste. This involved a horizontal approach between 50cm and 1 metre above the flight deck. The pilot used a pylon-mounted sighting arm plus the horizon – or sighting arms fore and aft in conditions of poor visibility – to line up his approach. This required considerable skill and nerve on the part of the pilot, particularly when the aircraft passed directly through turbulence abaft the flight deck.

**Right:** Landing of a PL 10; the arrester wire has been engaged. The French were the first to develop effective arrester systems. The Schneider-Fieux arrester cable was subsequently manufactured under licence by the Imperial Japanese Navy. *(SHD-A)*

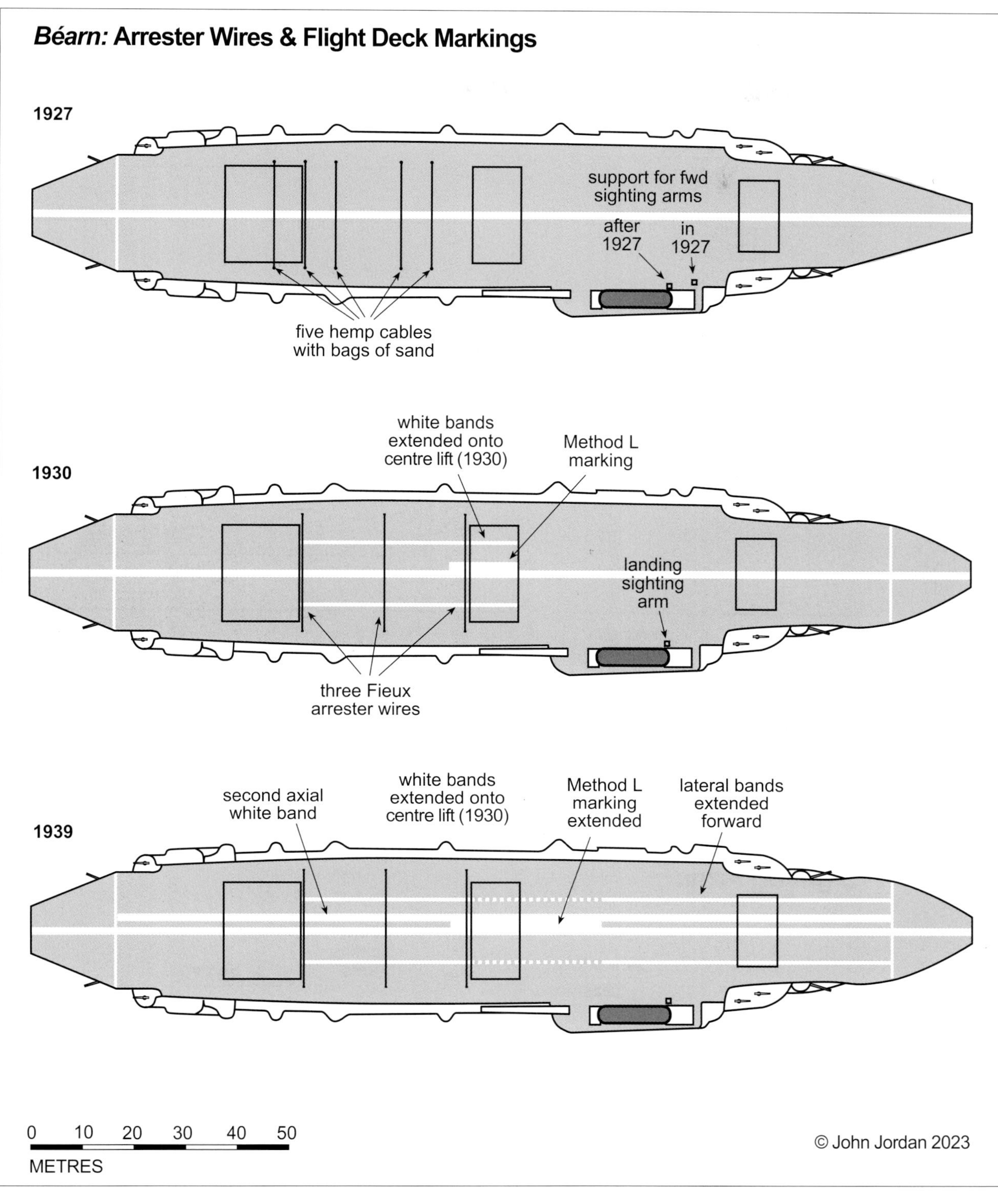


The French experimented with a variety of sighting arms. The first was installed to port of the island and had to be used in conjunction with the horizon. A second sighting arm, mounted first on a mast, then on a retractable pylon, was fitted between the centre and after lifts after the suppression of the mainmast in 1932. The pilot needed to align his approach using the two sighting arms, the positioning of which also allowed aircraft to land over the bow. The configuration adopted for the sighting arms varied, with both rectangles and arrows being used (see drawing).

In 1937, Method 'T' (for Teste) was superseded by Method 'L' (for Lartigue). The landing method pioneered by Jean-Julien-Pierre Lartigue, formerly a naval pilot and captain of *Béarn* from 1934, involved an angle of descent of 5–6 degrees, even 10–15 degrees. A single sight comprising a red and white hoop 75cm in diameter, mounted atop a manually operated hinged mast on the centre-line, had to be aligned with a white rectangle 6m by 2m painted on the flight deck 50 metres farther forward, where the wheels were due to touch down. The angle of approach ensured that the pilot came in above the turbulence and could better assess the pitching of the flight deck. The new procedure, adopted from 1937, reduced landing intervals from six minutes to two/three minutes, although the slow speed of operation of the lifts meant that there was little overall benefit.

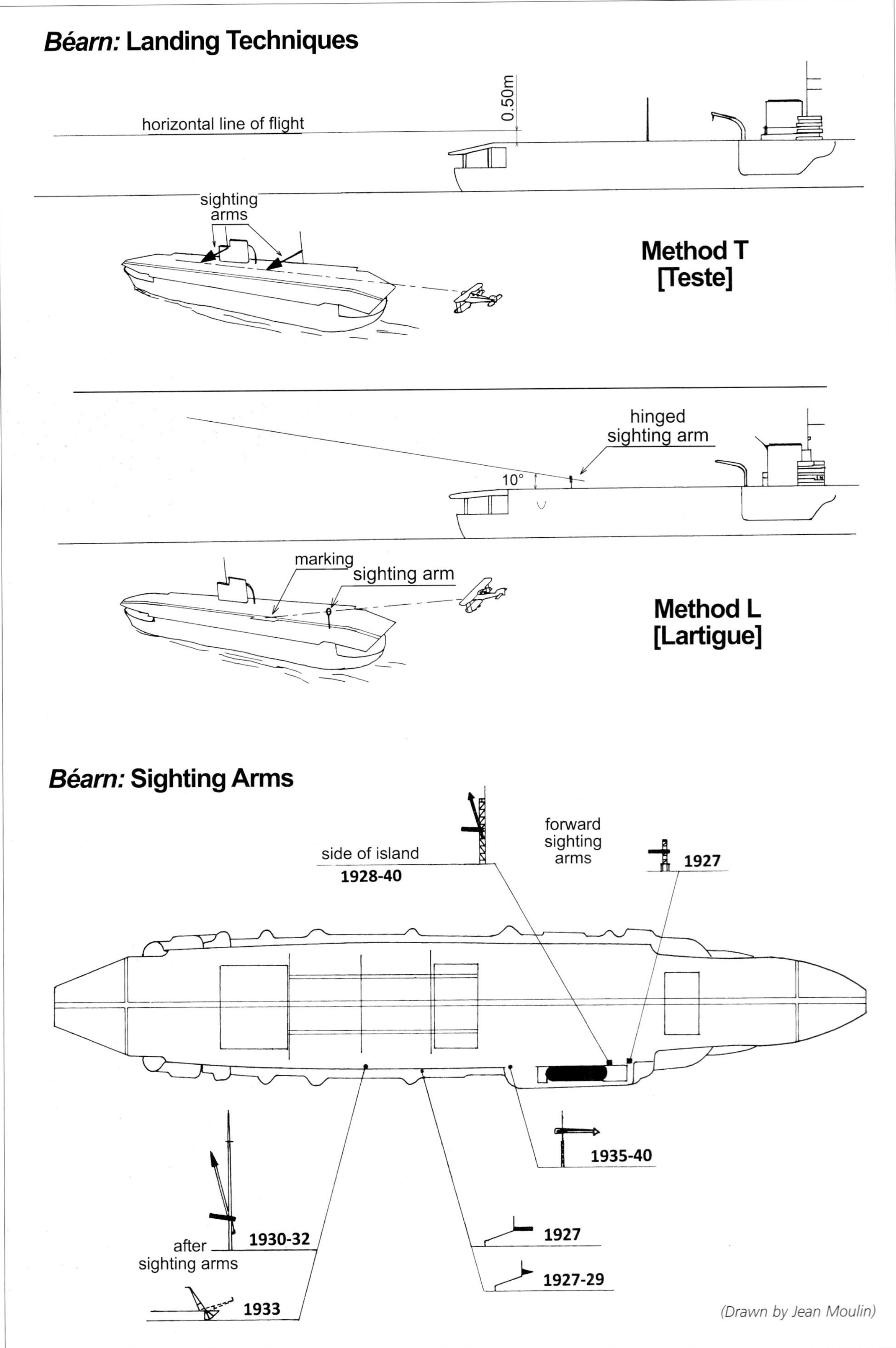
Béarn: Landing Techniques
0.50m
horizontal line of flight
sighting arms
Method T [Teste]
hinged sighting arm
10°
marking
sighting arm
Method L [Lartigue]
Béarn: Sighting Arms
side of island
1928-40
forward sighting arms
1927
1935-40
after sighting arms
1930-32
1933
1927
1927-29
(Drawn by Jean Moulin)

A further advantage of Method 'L' was that it could be used at night using deck lighting, the white rectangle being replaced by a 'luminous porthole'.

Finally, abaft the island, there was a large gooseneck crane. Its 12-tonne capacity enabled it to be used not only for embarking and disembarking aircraft when *Béarn* was alongside or from lighters when moored in an anchorage, but to lower and raise seaplanes used for long-range reconnaissance when the ship was in harbour. During the early part of her career, *Béarn* generally operated two CAMS 37A seaplanes in addition to her complement of wheeled aircraft.

**Hangar**

Although the French opted for a two-tier hangar on the British model, as in the contemporary *Furious*, *Courageous* and *Glorious*, only the upper hangar, originally referred to as the *entrepont aviation*, was employed for operational aircraft. The lower hangar was divided into two spaces: a repair and assembly workshop aft, and a space for the stowage and assembly of reserve aircraft forward.

The upper hangar extended from frame 16 to frame 140, with the smaller lift for fighters at its forward end. It was divided into two for the purpose of aircraft stowage, and into four for damage control. The forward section, from F90 (centre lift) to F132, had a gallery deck above to accommodate the air crews. Overhead clearance was thereby reduced to 5 metres, which meant that this section could accommodate fighters and reconnaissance aircraft only; usable length was approximately 42 metres. The after section, from F16 to F80 (centre lift), had 6.5 metres clearance and could therefore accommodate the larger torpedo bombers. Taking into account the after lift, this gave a usable length of 49 metres. The upper hangar had a nominal width of 19.5 metres, but this was reduced to 15 metres – the same width as the centre and after lifts – once the funnel trunking and ventilation, the winches for boat handling and the ready-use racks for air ordnance were taken into account (see Hangar Deck plan, page 41).

There were three asbestos fire curtains: one just forward of the after lift, one just abaft the centre lift, and one between the forward and centre lifts. These divided the hangar into four roughly equal sections and (in theory) prevented fire spreading through the hangar.

The aircraft of the day were generally armed and fuelled on the hangar deck, then raised to the flight deck for take-off. There was substantial ready-use stowage for air ordnance to the sides of the upper hangar: between the two after lifts (which handled the reconnaissance and the torpedo attack aircraft) and to starboard of the after lift. There were racks for six large 410kg bombs, six 226kg and six 152kg medium bombs, and six 76kg light bombs to port and to starboard, and for ten 400mm torpedoes to starboard of the lift.

The upper hangar was served by three parallel overhead rails in the form of an I-beam 152mm high and 127mm wide, secured to the underside of the flight deck or the gallery deck; these could accommodate cranes or block and tackle used to move aircraft parts (or even complete aircraft) within the hangar. The rails were broken at the lift shafts and/or the fire curtains.

**Above:** Landing sights on the side of the island of *Béarn* in 1932. *(ARDHAN collection)*

The outer pair of rails was extended aft above the quarterdeck to enable aero engines to be transferred from the hangar to one or other of the test beds above the open stern. The test bed to starboard was for in-line or 'V'-form water-cooled engines; the one to port was for radial air-cooled engines.

The lower hangar was shorter and had compartments to the sides, some of which were employed for accommodation. It extended from Frame 32 to Frame 140, and like the upper hangar had a usable width of approximately 15 metres. The aviation workshop occupied the after end; the remainder of the hangar was an assembly and stowage area for spare aircraft. The hangar was again divided into four by asbestos fire curtains, the location of which mirrored arrangements in the upper hangar. There were large rectangular hatches on the middle line at the base of each of the three lift shafts for the embarkation of aviation stores

**Right:** A deck-load of Levasseur PL.101s on *Béarn* during the late 1930s. The centre lift is in the raised position, as are the clamshell doors. *(Musée national de la Marine)*

## Centre Lift

### From Fwd

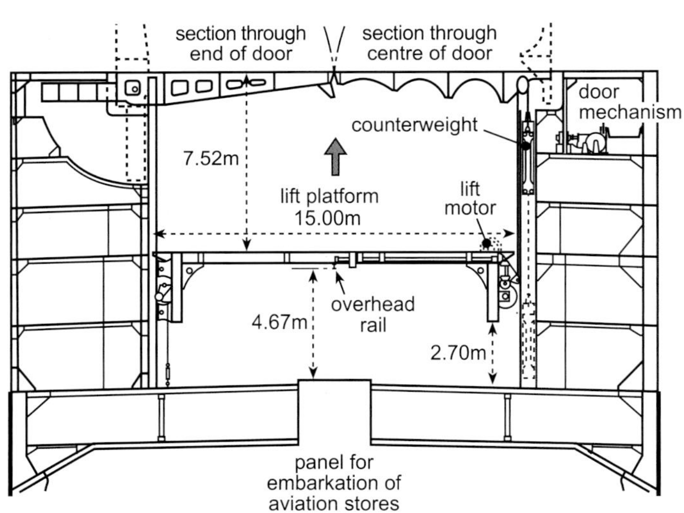


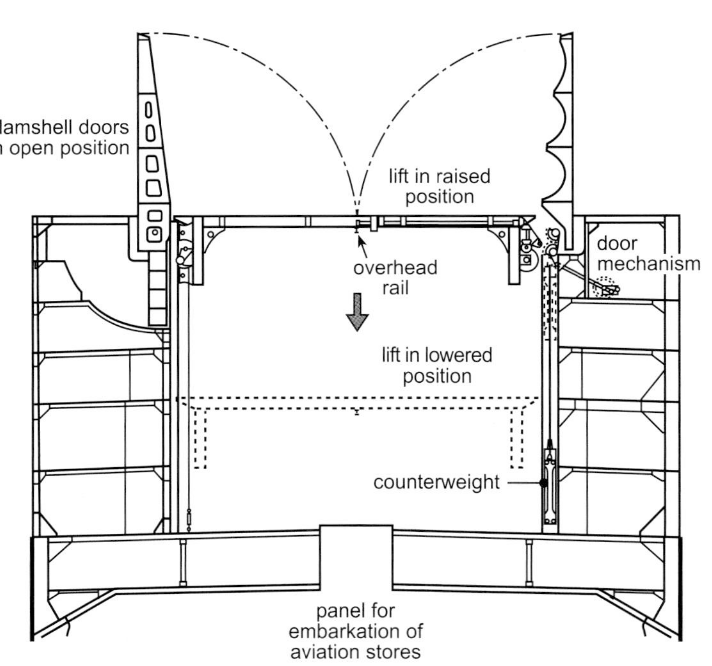


**Note:** Adapted from plans dated La Seyne 24 December 1928.



The official plans confirm that, contrary to what has been generally stated in secondary sources, the three aircraft lifts served only the upper hangar. When depicted at this level the lift platform is labelled '*plateforme de l'ascenseur au point bas*' (platform in its lowest position). Also, the run of cable for the counterweight is 7.52 metres, the distance between the hangar deck and the flight deck. The 'feet' at the corners of the lift, and the raised hatches for the embarkation of aviation stores, would in any case have prevented the lift from being lowered to the main deck.

and ordnance, and smaller hatches for the embarkation of lube oil and aviation fuel offset to port and to starboard, directly above their respective stowage compartments (see below).

Like the upper hangar, the lower hangar was equipped with three parallel overhead rails, secured to the underside of the deckhead. Despite claims in French (and English-language) secondary sources that the three aircraft lifts served both hangars, this was not the case, and in the lowered position the lifts were at the level of the (upper) hangar deck. A close study of the plans reveals that each of the lifts was fitted with a centre-line rail on its underside that lined up with the axial rails above each of the hangar decks. If an aircraft needed to be transferred between the assembly and repair areas in the lower hangar and the upper hangar, it was suspended from the underside of the lift and raised or lowered accordingly, then moved to the desired location using the overhead rails. This would have been an extremely laborious operation, and makes it clear why the French regarded the upper hangar as the only one capable of actively supporting air operations.

### Avgas and oil stowage

Aviation fuel, lubrication oil and petrol for the ship's boats was stored in individual tanks on the 1st Platform Deck. There were three groups of avgas and petrol tanks: the first two were located in the forward part of the ship and offset to port; the third was close to the stern, directly above the steering gear compartment (see GA plans). Total capacity for the air group was 100,000 litres.[7] These tanks of volatile fuel were all within the armoured citadel, being protected above by the 24mm plating of the main deck, and to the sides by the 83mm belt of nickel steel. Each of the three groups was surrounded by a protective box filled with inert nitrogen gas.

**Above:** A Dewoitine D1.C1 fighter belonging to 7C1 Squadron in 1931. The Dewoitine was the first of a series of high-wing monoplane fighters developed to operate from *Béarn*. *(ARDHAN collection)*

On the same deck level there were multiple tanks holding 15,000 litres of engine oil for the aero engines (aft of amidships, to starboard) and 39,000 litres for the diesel generators (amidships, on either side of the hatch for aviation stores).

The bomb magazines were amidships and aft and were grouped with the aviation store compartments for ease of access. The bomb magazine amidships could accommodate 60 of the large 410kg bombs, while the after magazine complex had stowage for 68 226kg bombs, 132 152kg bombs and 100 76kg bombs (see

**Left:** A Wibault 74 high-wing monoplane fighter of 7C1 at Hyères in 1932. The Wibault was well liked by the French pilots. *(ARDHAN collection)*

[7] By way of comparison, the French carrier *Clemenceau*, completed in 1961, could stow 1.6 million litres of aviation fuel.

**Right:** The first landing of a Dewoitine 373 of AC1 on *Béarn* in November 1938. A variant with folding wings, the Dewoitine 376, would enter service the following year. *(ARDHAN collection)*

Machinery plan). The total weight of air ordnance specified was 62 tonnes.

## AIR GROUP

A considerable amount of planning and preparation went into the formation of *Béarn*'s first air group under Paul Teste and his successors. Each of the three squadrons was to have a nominal strength of twelve aircraft organised as four three-plane sections. In 1928, *Béarn* generally deployed with six operational aircraft from each of the squadrons; in 1933 this figure was increased to nine, for a total air group of twenty-seven.

**Right:** A Levasseur PL.4 R3b belonging to SEBA on *Béarn* in 1932. The PL.4 was the first in a series of large biplanes used for reconnaissance. *(ARDHAN collection)*

**Left:** A Levasseur PL.10 R3b (7S1-5) landing on board in 1932. Note the tailhook extended to catch the arrester wire. The PL.10 and its later variant, the PL.101, were the standard surveillance aircraft operating from *Béarn* during the 1930s. *(ARDHAN collection)*

**Below:** Levasseur PL.7 T2B2b at Saint-Raphaël in 1926. The PL.7 was designed as a heavyweight torpedo bomber. When one of the machines broke up in flight in 1931, the aircraft was withdrawn and rebuilt; it then served until 1939. *(ARDHAN collection)*

**Right:** A Levasseur PL.14 (BA 25) belonging to SEBA in 1939. The PL.14 was initially developed as a torpedo bomber seaplane, but when the PL.7 was taken out of service some models had their floats replaced by a wheeled undercarriage to enable them to operate from *Béarn*. *(ARDHAN collection)*

By the time *Béarn* entered service in May 1928 the fighter squadron was designated 7C1 (C = *chasseur*). The first aircraft to serve with the squadron was the Dewoitine D.1, a small high-wing monoplane of metallic construction with a wingspan of 11.5 metres and a height of 2.75 metres. The D.1 proved to be robust; it was superseded in 1932 by the Wibault 74, which was similar in size and configuration and was well liked by the pilots who flew it. The Wibault 74 was to have been replaced by the Dewoitine 373: a prototype was trialled in 1936, but a series of accidents resulted in the aircraft being returned to the factory for

**Right:** Take-off of a Loire-Nieuport 40 of AB1 in July 1939. The LN.40, a gull-wing dive bomber, proved to be under-powered. *(ARDHAN collection)*

## Table 3: *BÉARN* AIR GROUP

**FighterSquadron [7C1 > AC1/2]**

| | Dewoitine D1.C1 | Wibault 74 | Dewoitine 373/376 |
|---|---|---|---|
| Type | high-wing monoplane | high-wing monoplane | high-wing monoplane |
| In service | 1925–32 | 1932–38 | 1938– |
| No ordered for MN | 40 | 24 | 20/25 |
| Length | 7.50m | 7.60m | 7.44m |
| Span | 11.50m | 10.95m | 11.22m |
| Height | 2.75m | 2.96m | 3.42m |
| Weight (empty) | 820kg | 1060kg | 1295kg |
| Weight (fl) | 1250kg | 1550kg | 1860kg |
| Power Unit | Hispano-Suiza<br>300hp | Gnome-Rhône<br>420hp | Gnome-Rhône<br>880hp |
| Max Speed | 250km/h | 220km/h | 340km/h |
| Ceiling | 8300m | 8200m | 10,000m |
| Armament | 2 x 7.7mm MG | 2 x 7.7mm MG | 4 x MAC 34 MG |

**Reconaissance Squadron [7S2 > AB2]**

| | Levasseur PL.4 | Levasseur PL.10 | Loire-Nieuport LN.401 |
|---|---|---|---|
| Type | 3-seat biplane | 3-seat biplane | single-seat dive bomber |
| In service | 1927–30 | 1931–33 | 1939– |
| No ordered for MN | 34 | 18 | 20 |
| Length | 9.67m | 9.75m | 9.75m |
| Span | 14.60m | 14.20m | 14.00m |
| Height | 3.85m | 3.75m | 3.50m |
| Weight (empty) | 1690kg | 1815kg | 2135kg |
| Weight (fl) | 2640kg | 2880kg | 2820kg |
| Power Unit | Lorraine<br>450hp | Hispano-Suiza<br>600hp | Gnome-Rhône<br>880hp |
| Max Speed | 180km/h | 200km/h | 380km/h |
| Ceiling | 5000m | 5500m | 9500m |
| Armament | 4 bomb hard-points<br>1 x 7.7mm MG | [as PL.4] | 1 x 225kg bomb<br>1 x 20mm cannon<br>2 x 7.5mm MG |

**Attack Squadron [7B1 > AB1]**

| | Levasseur PL.7 | Vought 156F |
|---|---|---|
| Type | 3-seat sesquiplane | 2-seat monoplane |
| In service | 1930–39 | 1939– |
| No ordered for MN | 30 | 40 |
| Length | 11.68m | 10.33m |
| Span | 16.50m | 12.80m |
| Height | 4.86m | 4.32m |
| Weight (empty) | 2800kg | 2138kg |
| Weight (fl) | 3950kg | 3300kg |
| Power Unit | Hispano-Suiza<br>600hp | Pratt & Whitney<br>825hp |
| Max Speed | 170km/h | 460km/h |
| Ceiling | 2900m | 8400m |
| Armament | 1 x Mle 26DA torpedo<br>4 bomb hard points | 3 hard points for bombs<br>2 x 7.5mm MG |

**Note:** The LN.401 and the 156F were to operate in both the reconnaissance and attack roles.

rebuilding, and it did not enter service until 1938. A folding-wing variant, the 376, was then introduced and replaced the 373 in first-line service; a second fighter squadron was formed with the older model shortly before the Second World War, the squadrons being designated AC1 and AC2 respectively.

The reconnaissance squadron embarked in May 1928 was 7S2 (S = *surveillance*). It was formed initially with the Levasseur PL.4, a single-engine, three-seat biplane with folding wings and a boat-shaped hull. The PL.4 had a wingspan of 14.6 metres, a height of 3.9 metres and a maximum weight of 2640kg, and was fitted with four bomb racks. It was superseded in 1931 by the Levasseur PL.10, which was similar in size, then by the PL.101, a modified PL.10 that served until 1939, when it was due to be replaced by the Loire-Nieuport 401, a single-engine gull-wing dive bomber that could carry a single 226kg bomb. The latter, however, proved to be underpowered and was never deployed operationally on *Béarn.* The reconnaissance squadron was rechristened AB2 (B = *bombardier*) in 1938.

The attack squadron was initially designated 7B1, and was initially formed with the same PL.4 aircraft that served with the reconnaissance squadron. In 1930, the PL.4 was replaced by the Levasseur PL.7, a large single-engine three-seat sesquiplane, the first French embarked aircraft capable of launching a torpedo. It had a wingspan of 16.5 metres (the upper wing had twice the surface area of the lower), a height of 4.86m, and an all-up weight of 3950kg. The PL.7 could carry either a Mle 26DA 400mm torpedo weighing 670kg, or a variable bomb load using the four

**Table 4: ANTI-AIRCRAFT GUNS**

| | 75mm/50 Mle 1922 | 37mm/50 Mle 1925 |
|---|---|---|
| *Gun Data* | | |
| Construction | autofretted barrel | |
| Breech mechanism | Schenider concentric ring | |
| Weight of gun | 1070kg (incl breech) | 158kg |
| Ammunition type | fixed | fixed |
| Projectiles | OEA Mle 1925 (5.93kg) | OEA Mle 1925 (0.73kg) |
| | OEcl Mle 1923 | OI Mle 1924 (0.73kg) |
| Propellant | 2.18kg BM5 in cartridge | 0.3kg BM2 in cartridge |
| Complete round: | | |
| weight | 12.01kg | 2.8kg |
| dimensions | 967mm x 110mm | 408mm x 61mm |
| Muzzle velocity | 850m/s | 810m/s |
| Range | 14,910m at 45° | 5000m |
| Ceiling | 7500m | |
| *Mounting* | | |
| Designation | CA Mle 1922 | CAS Mle 1925 |
| Weight of mounting | 5000kg | 470kg |
| Elevation | -10° / +90° | -15° / +85° |
| Firing cycle | 8–12rpm | 20rpm |

**Notes:**

| | | |
|---|---|---|
| Mle | *Modèle* | Model |
| OEA | *Obus Explosif en Acier* | High Explosive (HE) |
| OEcl | *Obus Eclairant* | Starshell |
| OI | *Obus Incendiaire* | Incendiary Shell |

hard points beneath the wings. A serious accident in 1931 that involved the aircraft breaking up in mid-air resulted in the PL.7s being returned to the factory for modification. The aircraft then served until 1939, when it was to have been replaced by the Vought 156F, an export version of the US Navy's SB2U Vindicator. The first of these were delivered in August 1939 and entered service the following month, but again the aircraft was never operational with *Béarn*. The attack squadron was rechristened AB1 in 1938.

Key data for all the aircraft described above can be found in the accompanying table (page 55).

## ANTI-AIRCRAFT GUNS

The anti-aircraft armament of *Béarn* was broadly comparable to that fitted in the contemporary 'treaty' cruisers of the *Duquesne* class.

There were four 75mm/50 Mle 1924 guns on sponsons port and starboard at the forward end of the flight deck, and two mountings aft. The 75mm Mle 1924 fired a 5.93kg HE time-fuzed shell designated OEA Mle 1925 or starshell Mle 1923. Provision was 450 fixed rounds per gun, and close to each mounting there was ready-use stowage for 36 rounds in cases of 3. Shields were fitted during the 1934–35 reconstruction (see below). Fire control was provided by two of the new high angle (HA) directors, each of which was fitted with a 3-metre stereo rangefinder from Optique

**Left:** Take-off of a Vought 156F (AB1-1) from *Béarn* in May 1940. The Vought 156F was an export variant of the US Navy's SB2U Vindicator scout bomber. An initial order for forty was placed, but the aircraft never deployed operationally from *Béarn*. *(ARDHAN collection)*

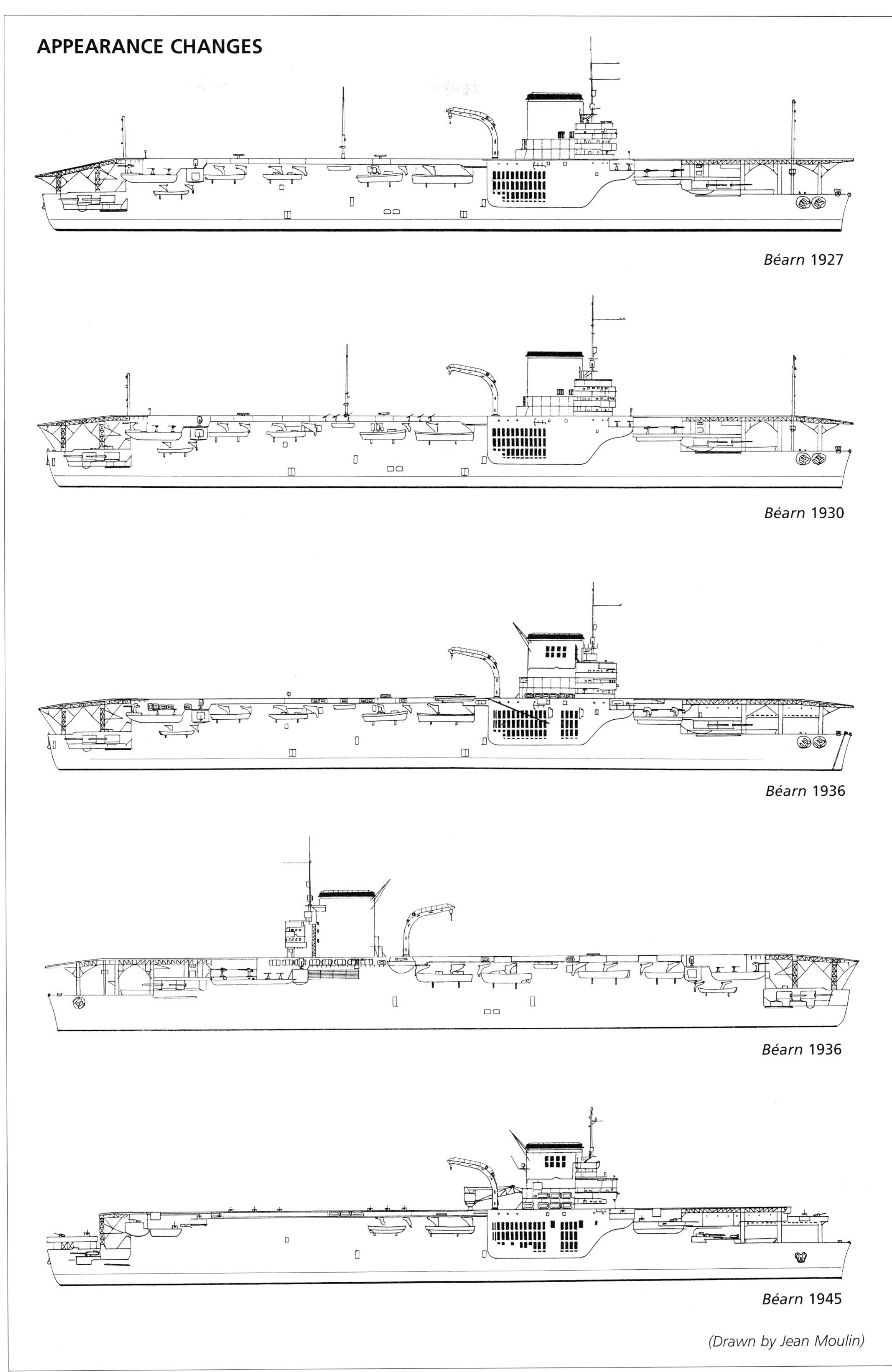

et précision de Levallois (OPL): one in the gallery to port and a second atop the forward end of the island. Due to delays in development and manufacture these were not in place until 1929. They were modified during the 1934–35 reconstruction, when the port-side director was relocated to starboard, beneath the crane.

The light AA initially comprised eight of the new semi-automatic 37mm/50 Mle 1925 guns and twelve 8mm Hotchkiss Mle 1914 machine guns. The 37mm guns, which were disposed in pairs fore and aft, used the same ammunition hoists as the 75mm HA guns. The forward magazine held 352 cases, each containing 6 fixed rounds, and the after magazine 147, for a total provision of 3,000 rounds (375rpg). There was stowage for ninety ready-use rounds close to each of the mountings.

The 8mm Hotchkiss MG, mounted as four sections of three in the gallery amidships to port and to starboard, proved to be ineffectual against modern aircraft; during the reconstruction of 1934–35 they would be replaced by the new Hotchkiss 13.2mm Mle 1929 gun in a twin mounting (see below).

### RECONSTRUCTION 1934–35

As soon as *Béarn* entered service with the fleet, it became apparent that her comparatively low speed would be an issue (see below).

In January 1931, less than three years after her entry into service, the ship was immobilised due to jamming of the clamshell doors of the centre lift and the poor state of her boilers, and in October the *Service Technique* was instructed to undertake a study for a major reconstruction to include:

- replacement of the boilers
- modifications to the forward lift
- replacement of the 75mm guns by the new 100/45 CA Mle 1927 being fitted in the aviation transport *Commandant Teste*.

Further studies were requested to determine the feasibility and cost of:

- replacement of the original propulsion machinery by geared turbines
- the fitting of anti-torpedo bulges
- enhanced protection of the decks to protect the ship against the increasing threat from land-based bombers.

Estimates were for immobilisation between twelve months and three/four years, depending on the extent of the works; the cost would be between 33 million and 125 million francs (possibly rising to FF200m). It was estimated that geared turbines would generate 60,000cv – an increase of 50 per cent – for a top speed of 23.4 knots. However, if bulges were fitted maximum speed would be reduced by more than one knot (22.3 knots),[8] and displacement would rise by about 500 tonnes.

The project was abandoned in part due to the age of the hull – twenty years from laying down by January 1934. Maximum speed would still have been only 22–23 knots – the new fast battleship *Dunkerque* had a designed speed of 29 knots – and it would not be possible to upgrade protection against aerial bombing. In the event, the Minister approved only a limited reconstruction costing 25 million francs, of which FF17m was for re-boilering. This took place at La Seyne and Toulon between February 1934 and November 1935, and included the following work:

- replacement of the original boilers by six of the new standard Navy-type du Temple three-drum boilers (three per boiler room)
- a second bank of vents in the *cul de lampe* (lamp base) that increased air volume by 50 per cent
- removal of the retractable charthouse and the 550mm torpedo tubes
- replacement of the 8mm machine guns by six twin 13.2mm Hotchkiss Mle 1929, mounted to port and to starboard on either side of the after aircraft lift
- modifications to the HA directors, and new-model rangefinders for the main and the light AA guns in the gallery to port and to starboard.

During her post-refit trials, on 26 August 1935 *Béarn* attained an average speed of 20.8 knots on the course off the Hyères islands (east of Toulon) with five boilers lit.

## B: SERVICE HISTORY

### TRIALS 1927–28

*Béarn* was manned for trials on 1 September 1926, when *Capitaine de vaisseau* (CV) Jean de Laborde took command of the ship. From 30 November she was moored in the Toulon anchorage and pilots from the training squadron at Hyères flying the Gourdou-Leseurre GL.22 practised approaches and wheeled touch-downs. On 9 December, Petty Officer (PO) Jacques Guillou was authorised by de Laborde to land on and made the first arrested landing on the deck of the carrier.

The ship was docked until 17 December to have her propellers fitted, then towed to La Seyne. On 18 February, the forward group of boilers was fired up, followed by the after group on 15 April. Static trials of the machinery took place on 2 March (port VTE), 4 March (turbines on centre shaft) and 5 March (starboard VTE). She returned to Toulon roads on 9 May.

*Béarn* put to sea for her first trials at 0700 on 10 May. At 1515, a problem with one of the boiler room ventilator fans led to the after boiler room being shut down and the trial was abandoned. The first arrested landings while underway began on the same day, 10 May, in the anchorage at Hyères and off the island of Porquerolles, with pilots representing the three air squadrons: 7R1 (reconnaissance), 7B1 (bombers), and 7C1 (fighters). These were generally successful.

**Table 5: BUILDING DATA**

| | |
|---|---|
| Builder: | F C Méditerranée, La Seyne |
| Laid down: | 5 January 1914 |
| Launched: | 15 April 1920 |
| Manned for trials: | 1 September 1926 |
| Commissioned: | 5 December 1927 |
| Entered service: | 1 May 1928 |

[8] The bulges would have had a depth of 2.70 metres on either side of the lower hull. They would have increased beam to 32.4 metres – the maximum that could be accommodated in the available dry docks.

Further arrested landings were made on 20, 21, 27 and 30 May with the ship moored in Toulon roads.

A second sortie took place on 31 May, when 32,000cv was maintained for thirty minutes and further arrested landings made. The ship was moored at the Milhaud finger piers on 8–23 June. She then embarked on her acceptance trial (*présentation en recette*), sustaining 36,000cv for seventy-five minutes and ending with almost 40,500cv. She was duly accepted, although various issues with the ventilation system would need to be addressed.

*Béarn* entered the dockyard on 1 July and was docked until the 21st. On 28 July she left for a ten-hour trial; she attained a speed of 21.7 knots before a problem with the low pressure (LP) cylinder of the port-side reciprocating engine halted proceedings. The

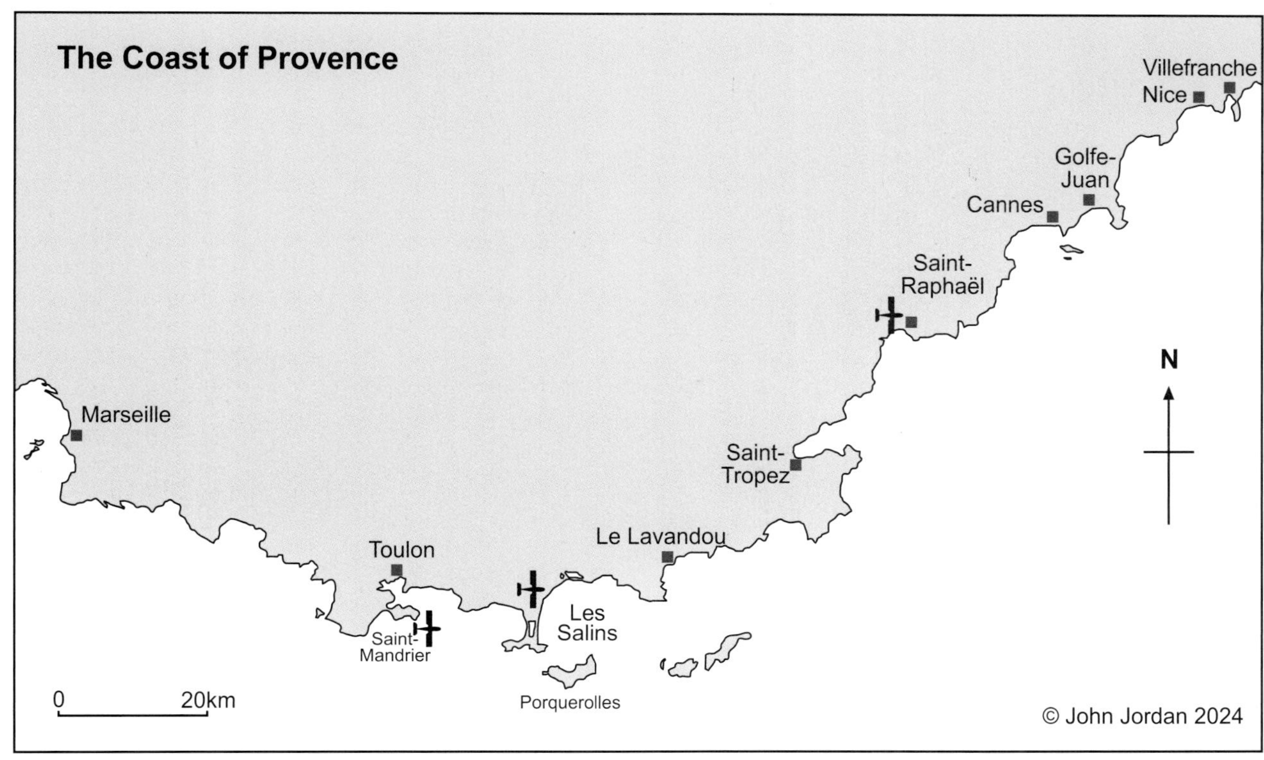


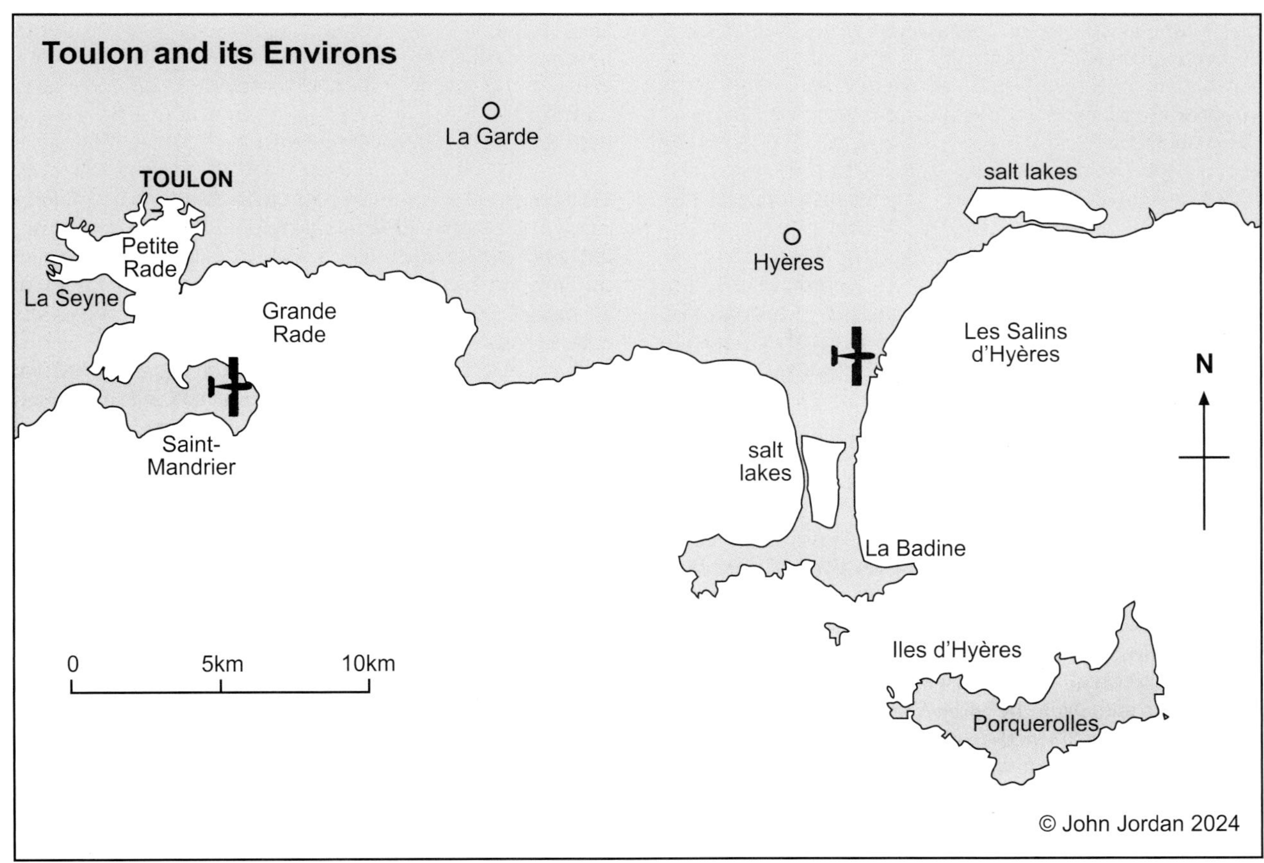

**Right:** *Béarn* steaming at high speed during her trials in late 1927. The hinged W/T masts to port are in the lowered position; the masts were suppressed in 1928 and replaced by a fixed mast to starboard, abaft the island. *(DR)*

same day saw the first arrested landing of a Levasseur PL.4 that had been delivered to 7R1 Squadron.

The ship was moored at the Milhaud piers from 30 July to 14 October, then docked, returning to Milhaud on the 19th before being moved to the anchorage on 25–27 October. She then repeated the ten-hour trial, attaining 21.5 knots with 40,250cv.

Machinery trials continued alongside arrested landings. On 14 November there was an accident with a Dewoitine D1.C1 fighter when the engine cut out during the final approach; the aircraft was lost but the pilot rescued. A series of landings with the PL.4 was successfully completed and the aircraft was formally accepted in November for service with 7B2 and 7R1. The first night landing, also in the anchorage, took place in the early evening of 24 November, with a Gourdou GL.22.

*Béarn* was commissioned on 5 December 1927, but machinery and deck landing trials continued. The 155mm guns were fired on 24 February 1928. The ship was accepted into service on 16 April. During the same month the first arrested landings of the Lévy-Biche LB.2 (7C1) took place.

A short first deployment (described in the trials report as *la traversée de longue durée*) was undertaken along the Côte d'Azur from 17 to 20 April 1928, when six Levasseur (three in 7B1, three in 7S1) and four Lévy-Biche LB.2 (7C1) were embarked; an FBA.17 seaplane was lifted on board using the crane on the morning of the 19th and took off again in the early afternoon. There were two incidents involving the Lévy-Biche fighters, one of which broke its tailhook on landing, struck the island and slid over the side. The final report praised the manoeuvrability of the ship and her robust and reliable machinery, but it was deemed too early to make a proper evaluation of her aviation capabilities.

After a further brief sortie on 26 April *Béarn* was incorporated into the 1st Squadron at Toulon.

## TOULON 1928–29

The 1st Squadron based at Toulon comprised the major combat units in service with the *Marine Nationale*: six battleships, three cruisers, four *contre-torpilleurs*, twenty-three fleet torpedo boats and nine submarines plus a small fleet train.

The missions of the aircraft carrier were clearly defined and dictated the composition of its air group:

- scouting for the naval forces at sea (7S1)
- attacking enemy ships with bombs and torpedoes (7B1)
- protecting friendly forces with its fighters (7C1).

*Béarn* put to sea on 8 May, embarking 7B1 and 7S1 then, at L'Estaque (NW of Marseille), a number of senators who were deposited in Corsica. She proceeded to the lake of Bizerte, where she was moored from 11 to 17 May. She returned to Toulon on 20 May, re-embarking the senators en route.

The activities of the ship, between regular spells of maintenance and repair in the dockyard, were focused on working up her air group and developing new procedures, using aircraft and associated equipment that were in a constant state of evolution. Outside these routine activities the ship took part in the major deployments undertaken by the Atlantic and Mediterranean Squadrons twice a year, with combined manoeuvres during the summer months.

The first major cruise with the Squadron based on Toulon took place from 27 May to 5 August 1928, when 7C1, 7S1 and 7B1 were embarked. The Squadron was at Casablanca from 3 to 12 June, joining up with the Atlantic Squadron between La Rochelle and Brest. Lorient was 'attacked' on 20 June, with a landing supported by *Béarn*'s aircraft pitted against the local aviation forces. Following the customary visits to the ports of Brittany and

Normandy, the ship took part in a major fleet review off Le Havre in which no fewer than seventy-four ships were assembled in lines stretching for 11 kilometres. The fleet was reviewed by President Gaston Doumergue in the brand-new *contre-torpilleur Jaguar.* After further port visits on the Cotentin Peninsula, *Béarn* and the Squadron returned to Toulon via Mers el-Kébir, arriving on 4 August. Her speed during the passage was limited to 16 knots, and the requirement to turn into the wind to launch or land aircraft meant a separation of seventy-five minutes from the Squadron before she could resume her station, even though the battleships were cruising at only 12 knots. This led to pressure from the pilots to modify the ship to permit landings over the bow; it was proposed to incline the forward section of the flight deck downwards by 4.5 degrees over a length of 15–20 metres to form a 'round-down', and to fit an additional three arrester cables at Frames 90, 105 and 120.

In October the ship embarked two Dewoitine of 7C1, three Levasseur of 7S1 and four of 7B1. She was at Saint-Raphaël until the 12th, then left for Bizerte via Corsica, returning to Toulon on 7 November. Over the course of October her aircraft made forty approaches and twenty-two arrested landings.

*Béarn* entered the dockyard in December. Work included the proposed modifications to the forward part of the flight deck and the installation of three Schneider-Fieux mechanical arrester systems in place of the cables weighted by sandbags.

The year 1929 would be relatively uneventful. *Béarn* took part in a cruise of the 1st Squadron from 27 May to 10 July 1929 with her three air squadrons on board. After calling in at Mers el-Kébir there was a joint exercise with the 2nd Squadron from Brest off the coast of Morocco, followed by a port visit to Casablanca. The only incident involved a Levasseur which failed to engage the arrester cable correctly and fell into the sea; the crew of the aircraft was rescued. The ship returned to Toulon on 10 July via Mers el-Kébir and Marseille.

*Béarn* also took part in the Squadron's autumn cruise from 10 October to 30 November. She landed her aircraft, which took part in joint exercises with the coastal aviation forces. When they returned to the carrier, fourteen aircraft conducted reconnaissance and suppression missions against the rebels in southern Morocco before the ship returned to the Mediterranean. She would be in dockyard hands from December to April 1930, when the after round-down of the flight deck was modified, the angle being adjusted from 10 to 4.5 degrees.

## TOULON 1930–31

*Béarn* left Toulon with the Squadron on 1 May and headed for Algiers. On the 10th there was a naval review to mark the centenary of the arrival of the French in Algeria. The fleet was reviewed by President Gaston Doumergue on board the cruiser *Duquesne.* After port visits along the coast of North Africa the Squadron returned to Toulon on 14 June. Following routine sorties to Les Salins d'Hyères and Golfe Juan, *Béarn* was again docked in late August. Delayed by repair and maintenance work, she was able to depart Toulon only on 22 October for the last part of the Squadron's autumn cruise. The 28th saw the first arrested landing by a PL.14, piloted by LV Paul Périès, at Les Salins d'Hyères.

*Béarn* again put to sea with the Squadron on 8–22 December. On the final day, a PL.4 of 7S1 flown by PO Guillaume struck the funnel of the ship and fell into the sea in the Hyères anchorage.The observer was

**Left:** *Béarn* in the Mediterranean in 1932 with a PL.7 on deck. *(ARDHAN collection)*

rescued but subsequently died; this was the first fatal accident on board.

On 10 January 1931, the Minister of Marine, Albert Sarraut, came on board. A sortie to Les Salins and Golfe Juan on 20–31 January with the sloop *Nancy* was interrupted by a machinery breakdown due to the poor state of *Béarn*'s boilers; the clamshell doors of the centre lift also jammed. Temporary repairs were carried out and the ship resumed her normal routines, taking part in a short cruise with the Squadron on 3–13 March.

She departed Toulon with the Squadron for the summer manoeuvres on 12 May 1931, and was at Casablanca from the 16th to the 27th. The six PL.4 of 7S1 were landed for five days, and on the 20th, four PL.7 were also flown ashore. On the same day, one of the PL.7s broke up in flight south of Meknes, resulting in the deaths of all four of the aircrew. As a result all the aircraft of this type were grounded. On the 27th, *Béarn* re-embarked the remainder of her air group, and made her way up the coast via Safi, passing through the Strait of Gibraltar on the 29th. She then headed for Bizerte via Mers el-Kébir and Algiers. The Squadron departed Bizerte on 22 June and entered Toulon on the 24th. After further routine local deployments, she entered the dockyard on 10 August for a major refit that would last almost six months.

On 5 September 1931, the Naval General Staff (NGS) asked the Director of *Constructions Navales* (CN) to undertake a study for a major refurbishment of *Béarn*. The study envisaged the complete renewal of the propulsion machinery, with the period in dockyard hands varying between twelve months and four years (see page 58). Cost and the time the ship would be out of service were considered prohibitive, and the work undertaken during the second half of 1931 was limited to the repair and maintenance of the current machinery.

## TOULON 1932–34

The work on *Béarn* was completed in early January 1932. A sortie to Les Salins on 11–22 January permitted the new PL.10 aircraft to acquire their landing qualifications, and the PL.7s returned to service following modification. A series of routine activities was marred by the loss of a Dewoitine D1.C1, which fell short of the flight deck when the pilot was attempting his first arrested landing and cut the supply of fuel to the engine prematurely.

On 3 April, the Minister of Defence came on board. Ten days later, *Béarn* departed Toulon with the Squadron for a cruise to the Eastern Mediterranean; only the PL.10s of 7 S1 were on board, one of which was lost, together with the pilot, on 14 April when the plane failed to engage the arrester wire and plunged into the sea. A joint exercise with the 2nd Squadron took place from 13 to 19 June, followed by a rest period at Bizerte. The sailing of *Béarn* on 22 June was delayed by a burst pipe for collector No 2 in boiler No 20. *Béarn* and *Commandant Teste* then played the part of a convoy hunted down by the remainder of the Squadron. The Squadron returned to Toulon on 25 June.

In late September the mainmast was landed and outriggers for the W/T aerials fitted to the funnel. Speed was now limited to 15 knots due to the poor state of the boilers, which had accumulated 6,000 hours of operation. During a routine sortie to Les Salins, an arrested landing by a PL.4 resulted in three casualties; the aircraft ended up in the water but was recovered. In December, the regulation strength of each of the squadrons was increased from six aircraft to nine – ten for the fighters of 7C1.

The year 1933 began with routine exercises and port visits. On 3 May, *Béarn* departed Toulon, together with the Squadron, for the summer manoeuvres, embarking the aircraft of 7B1, 7S1 and 7C1. She took

**Right:** *Béarn* and *Commandant Teste* at anchor with seven destroyers. The photo may have been taken at Suda Bay between 6 and 10 May 1932. *(SHAA)*

**Left:** The Milhaud finger piers at Toulon around 1933, with the old battleship *Patrie*, the *Commandant Teste*, three torpedo boats, *Béarn* and a *contre-torpilleur*. *(ARDHAN collection)*

part in a landing exercise off North Africa, then passed the Strait of Gibraltar for joint exercises with the 2nd Squadron. There were port visits to Casablanca, Cadiz, Mers el-Kébir and Palma de Mallorca before the ship returned to Toulon on 24 June.

On 10 July 1933, ministerial approval was given for the long-awaited modernisation of *Béarn*. It was estimated that the refit would take sixteen months and would cost 25m francs. Contract No 895 was signed on 4 October for the complete replacement of the boilers.

During manoeuvres that took place between the coasts of Provence and Corsica from 22 July to 5 August, Air Minister Pierre Cot embarked. The first arrested landing of a Levasseur PL.101 took place at Les Salins in November. There were further routine activities in late 1932 and early 1933, but a sortie scheduled for 13–18 March was cancelled due to the impending refit.

## MODERNISATION 1934–35

The refit officially began on 23 February 1934, and the ship remained at her moorings at Milhaud until 6 August. The new boilers were embarked in June. The hull was towed to the La Seyne shipyard on 6 August, returned to Milhaud from 13 August to 13 November, then was towed to the Repair Quay at La Seyne, replacing the battleship *Bretagne*. She recommissioned on 6 January 1935, and left La Seyne on the 15th to be docked at Toulon until 25 February. She returned to La Seyne, was docked again at Toulon (1–20 July) and returned to the Milhaud piers. The new boilers were first fired up on 30 July.

*Béarn* was in the anchorage 5–6 August, but then returned to Milhaud until 29 October to conduct trials of her machinery. On 13 August a preliminary trial was interrupted by a burst pipe on the exhaust of an air pump for the turbines. However, when the trial was repeated on the 16th, a power output of 27,300cv was registered. On 22 August, during the official trial with only the forward boilers lit, she attained 18.16 knots with 21,353cv. And on the 26th, with both boiler rooms online but only five of the six boilers fired up, she managed 20.38 knots against a 50km/h Mistral, and 21.25 knots in the opposite direction. Following the customary visual inspections of the machinery, she ran her final trials (*essais de bon fonctionnement*) from 15 to 17 October.

## TOULON 1935–36

*Béarn* rejoined the 1st Squadron on 25 October 1935, but the NGS now considered her too slow to work with the 1st class cruisers at Toulon, and confirmed that she would be transferred to the 2nd Squadron at Brest, where she would accompany the battleships of her generation.

A cruise from 7 May to 21 June took in the major ports and anchorages of North Africa, and there were further Mediterranean sorties in July, while the air base at Lanvéoc (Brittany) was prepared to receive her air group. On 22 September, two Potez 56E twin-engine aircraft landed on, and two days later a PL.10 piloted by Lieutenant Pierre de l'Orza de Montorzo attempted the first night landing using the Lartigue Method, in the Les Salins anchorage. De l'Orza made a successful landing, but when taking off again the tail-hook caught one of the arrester cables, the aircraft fell into the water and the pilot died.

## *BÉARN* IN THE ATLANTIC 1936–39

On 1 October 1936, the day of her incorporation into the Atlantic Squadron, *Béarn* left for Brest, arriving on the 7th. The air group, minus five planes that remained on board, had been flown directly to Querqueville, on the Cotentin Peninsula, the previous day. *Béarn* departed Brest for Cherbourg on the 13th; she would be based there temporarily to free up berths at Brest, with her air group at Querqueville. Returning to Brest on 28 November, she would undertake her first deployment with the Squadron from 3 to 5 December.

**Right:** A Levasseur PL.101 reconnaissance aircraft of 7S1 Squadron is brought up to the flight deck during the late 1930s using the centre lift. *(DR)*

*Béarn* recovered her air group off Cherbourg on 13 January 1937, then took part in the winter cruise to West Africa. On 3 February, two P.101s of 7S1 collided during a demonstration at Podor (Senegal); all six aircrew were lost. After a port visit to Casablanca, *Béarn* returned to Brest on 26 February and was docked from 22 March to 11 May.

On 19 May, in the Bay of Douarnenez, trials took

**Right:** A view of the flight deck in 1937, with aircraft being ranged for take-off. The three aircraft nearest the camera are Wibault 74 fighters of 7C1 Squadron; behind them are ranged the six Levasseur PL.7 torpedo bombers of 7B1. At the after end of the flight deck is a PL.101 reconnaissance biplane, probably the one assigned to the air group commander. *(DR)*

**Left:** PL.7 bombers of 7B1 being readied for take-off on *Béarn* in 1938. *(ARDHAN)*

place of the Lioré et Olivier C.30 autogiro. The first landing was successful, but the aircraft was then flipped over by the wind.

On 27 May 1937 the combined Atlantic and Mediterranean Squadrons were reviewed off Brest by the Minister of Marine, Alphonse Gasnier-Duparc, who was hosted by the new battleship *Dunkerque*. Following visits to the Atlantic ports, *Béarn* returned to Brest on 25 June. A total of 134 arrested landings had been made during June, of which 6 took place at night. There were further sorties with the Atlantic Squadron from 28 June to 7 July, and 19 to 22 July. No fewer than 600 arrested landings were recorded during the *année d'instruction* in 1936–37.

The ship remained alongside until 28 September due to problems with the port condenser. Air operations took place in the Bay of Douarnenez, which was relatively sheltered. The aircraft were then flown ashore to Guipavas pending the readiness of the new naval airbase at Lanvéoc.

During a sortie on 12 October, LV Guillaume Colas des Francs, the air commander of 7B1, died when the upper wing of his PL.7 struck the funnel. The ship was at Cherbourg from 12 to 25 October and put to sea with the Squadron on 10 December 1937. By this time the Lartigue Method of landing on had been definitively adopted.

After a short docking, *Béarn* left Brest with the Squadron from 1 to 11 February and 11–18 March 1938. The spring cruise began on 10 May, and there were visits to Lisbon, Madeira, the Azores and Morocco. The ships returned to Brest on 14 June. During this cruise *Enseigne de vaisseau* (EV) Louis Cassé successfully experimented with a new system of radio direction finding, which allowed him to relocate the carrier despite a heavy mist.

There were further sorties during July off Groix and Quiberon during July and September. On 20 July, during training for arrested landings, a PL.101 fell into the sea and the pilot was drowned. There were twenty-eight successful arrested landings during 28–30 September.

On 1 October 1938, *Béarn*'s air group became F1A, and the squadrons were redesignated AC1, AB1 and AB2. There were further brief sorties before the end of the year, including one with the Squadron from 8 to 18 October. Her Wibault fighters were replaced first by the Dewoitine 373 then, in early 1939, by the folding-wing 376 variant.

The ship was refitted from 20 January to 5 April

**Above:** A Lioré et Olivier C.30 autogyro on trials aboard *Béarn* on 19 May 1937. *(Musée national de la Marine)*

**Above:** *Béarn* follows in the wake of the three battleships of the *Bretagne* class, probably in 1938. *(SHM)*

1939, followed by routine activity between April and July. On 17 May, EV Carl Plaine-Lépine drowned when his PL.101 struck an antenna support and fell into the sea. A second accident involving a PL.101 took place on 24 May; the aircraft was lost but the pilot recovered. On 9 June, a PL.7 of AB1 failed to catch the arrester cable and went over the side, but the crew was recovered by the destroyer *Ouragan*.

On 10 and 11 July, *Béarn* was in the Bay of Douarnenez for the first landing trials of the Loire-Nieuport LN.40; the two aircraft involved were Nos 3 and 5 of F1A. There were further landing trials in August involving three LN.40s, a Vought 156F and a Potez 56E. She returned to Brest on 11 August.

## THE SECOND WORLD WAR

France declared war on Germany on 3 September 1939. *Béarn* was too slow to operate with the elite *Force de raid*, and on 4 September her CO was ordered to disembark her aircraft. She left for Lorient, then anchored off Quiberon from 11 to 27 September.

The presence of German commerce raiders in the North Atlantic, reported in early October, led to the formation of hunting groups with the Royal Navy. *Béarn* was provisionally assigned to Force 'L' based at Brest, comprising the fast battleship *Dunkerque* and three cruisers. However, this failed to materialise, and in October *Béarn* was fitted out to refuel large reconnaissance seaplanes of the Laté 523 and Bréguet Bizerte types. A 12-metre boom with a fuel line attached was installed aft.

*Béarn* was docked at Laninon (Brest) from 15 March to 3 April 1940. On 23 March the controlled explosion of two mines for the construction of a new dock resulted in two casualties, and the forward end of the flight deck was covered in rubble.

Following completion of her refit, the ship sailed for Toulon via Oran on 13 April and was assigned to the 3rd *Région maritime*. On 23 April she left for Les Salins for training with the Vought 156F aircraft from AB1 and the PL.101s of 2S3. Further training took place on 2–3 May, following a general repainting, and again from 6 May. On 10 May, AB1 was placed under the command of *Amiral Nord*; on the same day, the twelve Vought 156Fs of AB3 were all destroyed in their hangar at Alprecht. *Béarn* returned to Toulon the following day.

On 18 May, *Béarn* embarked 194 tonnes of gold at

Milhaud and cast off at 0100 on 19 May. She called in at Casablanca on 21–22 May, and three days later joined up with the cruisers *Jeanne d'Arc* and *Emile Bertin*. The group set course for Halifax, Nova Scotia, arriving on 1 June. The gold was landed, and from 3 June she embarked 44 Curtiss Helldiver SBC-4 scout bombers, 17 Curtiss H-75 Hawk and 25 Stinson 105 Voyager, together with six Brewster B-339 Buffalo intended for Belgium.

*Béarn* and *Jeanne d'Arc* left Halifax on 16 June and set course for Brest. However, the German *Wehrmacht* reached the latter port on 19 June, leading to an order to divert to Casablanca then, on 20 June, to go to the Antilles. Both ships arrived in Fort-de-France on 27 June; they were preceded by *Emile Bertin*, which had arrived on the 24th.

In principle, all three ships should have been immobilised under the terms of the Armistice, but *Jeanne d'Arc* was transferred to Pointe-à-Pitre, while *Béarn* and *Emile Bertin* remained at Fort-de-France. The aircraft were disembarked on 19 July.

The Antilles remained faithful to the government at Vichy. Agreements with the USA permitted them to maintain a status quo acceptable to all parties. French attempts to despatch the aircraft to Indochina were rejected by the Germans, and the Americans refused to allow them to be transferred to North and West Africa.

*Béarn* remained immobilised at Fort-de-France, occasionally shifting her moorings and making trips to Guadeloupe in May and August 1941. She lost her starboard propeller and was in care and maintenance from 27 January until mid-May 1942, keeping two boilers available to enable her to manoeuvre in the event of a hurricane.

**Above:** An aerial view of *Béarn* following in the wake of the three battleships of the *Bretagne* class, again probably in 1938. Note the parallel white lines straddling the arrester wires amidships, and the white rectangle associated with the Lartigue landing technique on the middle line. (SHM)

**Left:** *Béarn* at anchor off Louet Island in the Bay of Morlaix in 1939. The clamshell doors for the after aircraft lift are in the raised position. *(ARDHAN collection)*

Right: *Béarn* moored off Fort-de-France in December 1941. *(ARDHAN collection)*

Below: *Béarn* docked at Puerto Rico on 7 October 1943. *(ARDHAN collection)*

On 25 May, the US destroyer *Blakeley* (DD-150) was torpedoed by *U-156* and lost her bow. She managed to make Fort-de-France and came alongside *Béarn*, which tended to the wounded and supplied water.

In May 1943 the Vichy Government gave the order for the ships in the Antilles to be scuttled. *Béarn* was grounded by her captain on 19 May on the sandy bottom near the harbour entrance. The poor condition of her pipework led to the ship being placed in Special Reserve on 15 June 1943. A 'pretend' scuttling was effected in early July by filling the turbines and some of the boilers with seawater. Finally, on 14 July, the Antilles came under the authority of the *Comité français de Libération nationale* (CFLN) in Algiers.

*Béarn* was refloated on 8 September 1943. She had been cannibalised for spares for other vessels and had only a skeleton crew (eighty-seven men plus a handful of officers on 1 November). She left Fort-de-France under tow on 27 September and was docked at Ensenada Honda, Puerto Rico, from 30 September to 17 November, when a single boiler room was made operational. The ship ran trials on 18–19 November, and was then transferred to the Todd Shipyard in New Orleans, arriving on 3 December. The refurbishment of the ship, regarded by the Americans as no more than an aviation transport, was protracted, and she ran her first trial on the Mississippi on 17 December 1944. She was then docked at Portsmouth Navy Yard to correct a number of malfunctions. She left Portsmouth on 11 February 1945, sailed to Norfolk, Va, for work-up and was finally declared available for service on 26 February. She arrived in New York on 4 March and embarked 148 American passengers, 88 aircraft and other equipment.

*Béarn* left New York on 7 March with convoy CU 61, destined for the UK. During the night of 13 March she suffered a total power failure and, having lost her steering, collided with the US troop transport *JW McAndrew* (AP-47). A total of sixty-nine men died on the transport, and *Béarn* lost three with one missing. It was found that the fuse for the only working dynamo had tripped.

*Béarn* cruised off Ponta Delgada (Azores) from 17 to 22 March, arriving at Casablanca on 25 March. The damage to the starboard bow was repaired 25 March to 18 July. The ship was then docked at Gibraltar and arrived at Toulon on 3 August. She was employed as a transport between Toulon, Algiers and Oran, then docked at the latter port in late August, when her hawsepipes and anchors were replaced using materiel recovered from the old battleship *Océan* (ex-*Jean Bart*).

## FROM INDOCHINA TO THE GASM

*Béarn* left Oran on 10 September 1945, called in at Toulon, then left for Marseille. She would sail for Indochina on the 22nd with 408 passengers and a considerable quantity of materiel on board.

She moored at Saigon on 28 October. She made two trips to Singapore to pick up more equipment and took part in Operation 'Bentré', disembarking troops at Tonkin on 6 March. She then embarked Piper L-4 Grasshopper aircraft together with three Japanese Aichi E13 A-1 ('Jake') floatplanes. On 9 March the Piper L-4s took off from the flight deck and the floatplanes were lowered onto the water by crane in the La Noix anchorage. She returned to Saigon with wounded servicemen on 14 March, then rotated between Saigon and Manila, and brought the Aichi floatplanes back from Tonkin at the end of May. She departed Saigon on 10 June and, despite numerous problems with her boilers, re-entered Toulon on 23 July.

**Above:** *Béarn* at the La Noix anchorage in Ha Long Bay from 9 March 1946. An LST (*382* or *347*) is alongside with an Aichi E13A 'Jake' floatplane on the flight deck. *(ARDHAN collection)*

*Béarn* was placed in Special Reserve on 1 October 1946. She was then assigned to the submarine arm of the service on 9 December. Moored to the northern quay of the refuelling basin (*Darse des subsistances*), she served as a barracks and base for the *Groupe d'action sous-marine* (GASM), which was set up on 1 January 1949. She would be placed in Special Reserve A on 20 July 1949 and Special Reserve B on 9 September 1950.

Maintenance on board the ageing carrier was becoming more and more difficult, and a new barracks, named after Commandant Jean l'Herminier,[9] was built on the quay where *Béarn* was moored. The ship was finally towed from the quay on 1 November 1966 and moored at Milhaud. Stricken on 31 March 1967, she was redesignated Q 419. On 4 September she was sold to the Lotti viale San Bartolomeo company at La Spezia, and was then towed to Savone to be broken up.

[9] Jean l'Herminier was the intrepid CO of the French 1500-tonne submarine *Casabianca*, which escaped the scuttling of the French Fleet at Toulon on 27 November 1942, and undertook a number of important covert operations for the Allies during 1943.

**Above:** *Béarn* decommissioned at Toulon in 1947 or 1948. The battleship *Lorraine* can be seen beyond her. *(Musée national de la Marine)*

**Right:** *Béarn* in 1954, while serving as the base for the GASM in the Missiessy submarine basin, Toulon. *(Jean Moulin collection)*

CHAPTER 3

# *COMMANDANT TESTE*

WITH THE DECISION TO COMPLETE THE hull of the battleship *Béarn* as an aircraft carrier, attention turned to the other strand of French naval aviation thinking, the *centre mobile*, or 'mobile aviation base', which had been under consideration for some time. In 1923 the Naval General Staff (NGS) requested a second carrier with similar missions to those defined for *Béarn*. Ideally this ship would be a second *porte-avions d'escadre* (Fleet Carrier), but it was accepted that in the absence of a suitable hull for modification this would be an expensive solution.

The NGS was therefore prepared to accept a *transport d'aviation*, which would be cheaper to build and could be completed more quickly. Such a ship could serve as a mobile base for seaplane squadrons deployed overseas, and in wartime would have an auxiliary function, serving as a repair and replenishment vessel to support other warships equipped with aircraft. Initial requirements were for a ship equipped with two catapults capable of launching a 2500kg aircraft (such a catapult was already under development for the new 10,000-ton cruisers), an air complement of nine seaplanes for reconnaissance and six float fighters, a speed of 17 knots, and a minimum anti-aircraft armament of four single 75mm guns. It was thought that an ocean liner might prove suitable for conversion. However, this solution implied a displacement above 10,000 tons, which would then have to be counted as part of the 60,000-ton carrier allowance allocated to France under the terms of the Washington Treaty. Other possibilities were therefore considered, including:

- the conversion of a freighter such as the *Jacques Cartier* (judged too slow)
- the conversion of an armoured cruiser (a similar study of *Amiral Aube* had been undertaken in 1919)
- a purpose-built ship with a speed of 18–20 knots capable of operating nine seaplanes.

The limited capacity of contemporary catapults continued to be a problem. The standard land-based bomber of the period was a lumbering biplane built of wood and canvas with a take-off weight of between 4 and 6 tonnes. An early proposal, dated December 1923, was therefore for a transport capable of accommodating twelve Lioré et Olivier (LeO) H.10 scout seaplanes (launch weight: 2400kg) with folding wings, to be stowed in a hold and lowered three at a time into the water by crane from an open section of deck. The armament was to be four 14cm guns in casemates, four 75mm HA guns and 9–12 machine guns.

The *transport d'aviation* as a type was deemed promising, and in September 1924 the General Staff proposed that two such ships should feature in the *Statut Naval* (Naval Law), and that the *Service Technique* should begin technical studies. In November of the same year the *Service Technique* came up with a draft proposal for a 16-knot ship with the armament outlined above and able to accommodate twelve aircraft, of which the three largest would be carried fully assembled and ready for launch on deck. Operational radius was a mere 2000nm – *ie* sufficient only for transit to the French colonies in North Africa and the Middle East. The ship would have a dual role: as a mobile seaplane base, providing repair and maintenance facilities together with accommodation for the crews; and as a seaplane transport capable of forward deployment for a specific attack mission. It was subsequently decided that this would be a new-build ship, and would be ordered with a view to construction beginning in late 1925.

As the design evolved, further changes were made. The air complement was boosted to six large seaplane bombers of 5.5 tonnes, to be lowered into the water by crane, and fourteen float scouts and fighters, to be launched by catapult. The anti-surface armament was six or eight single 138.6mm guns, while the anti-aircraft armament was set at four 75mm HA guns, four 37mm, and twelve 8mm MG. On a displacement close to the 10,000 tons standard permitted by the Treaty, and with overall dimensions of 154 metres by 22.5 metres, the ship would have a maximum speed of 19 knots (17,000cv).

By July 1927, considerable emphasis was being placed on the independent base characteristics of the ship. The aviation complement had by now grown to twenty-four aircraft: eight float planes for reconnaissance and self-defence, launched from four 2500kg catapults and carried on the upper deck; and no fewer than sixteen giant Farman Goliath torpedo bombers, of which ten would be housed in a hangar 100 metres by 17 metres, with a further six broken down in crates carried in the hold.

Further studies of the propulsion system led to proposals F and G, presented by the *Service Technique* in November 1925: design F featured a unit propulsion layout with twin funnels outboard and *en echelon*, and a hangar for six 5.5-tonne bombers; design G had a conventional propulsion layout with the boiler rooms adjacent and a single centre-line funnel, and a shorter, broader hangar divided into two by the ventilation trunking and exhaust uptakes for the boiler rooms, capable of accommodating ten 5.5-tonne bombers. The NGS opted for an amalgam of these two designs, with the hangar of design G and the unit propulsion system of design F, the twin funnels being on the middle line – the boiler uptakes were later trunked together and led up into a single funnel amidships.

The final design was approved by the General Staff in December 1925. The new ship, which would later be christened *Commandant Teste* in memory of the man who had done so much to make French naval aviation a reality, was part of the 1925 tranche of the

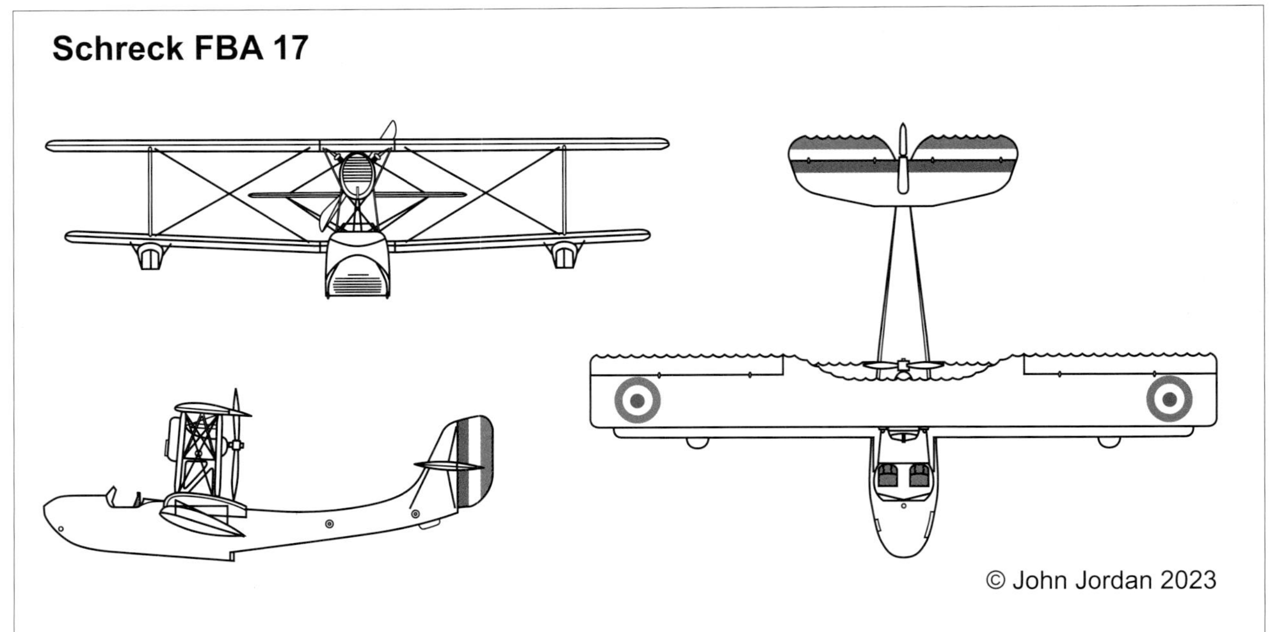


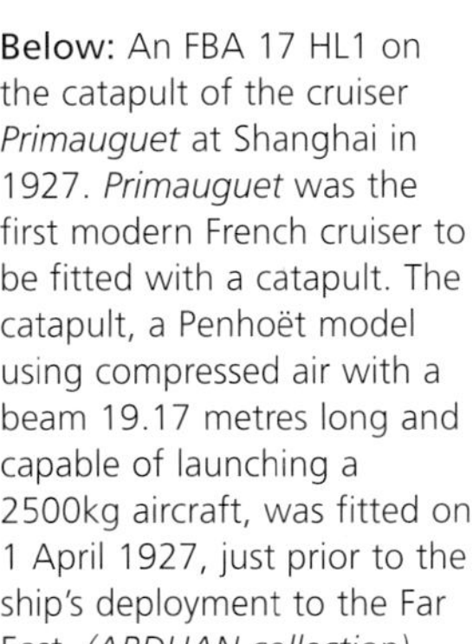

**Below:** An FBA 17 HL1 on the catapult of the cruiser *Primauguet* at Shanghai in 1927. *Primauguet* was the first modern French cruiser to be fitted with a catapult. The catapult, a Penhoët model using compressed air with a beam 19.17 metres long and capable of launching a 2500kg aircraft, was fitted on 1 April 1927, just prior to the ship's deployment to the Far East. *(ARDHAN collection)*

1924 Naval Programme, but construction was delayed for one year.

It was now envisaged that the air complement would comprise: ten Farman Goliath torpedo bombers, of which eight would be housed in the hangar and two broken down in crates in the hold; and twelve fighter/reconnaissance floatplanes, of which four would be readied on the catapults, four would be in the hangar (they replaced two Farman Goliath), and four broken down in crates in the hold. Twenty torpedoes were to be stowed in the hangar, the warheads and bombs (up to 700kg) being stowed in a magazine deep in the hull, and 80 tonnes of aviation fuel was to be provided. When employed as a transport, the ship would carry twelve Goliath, twelve recce floatplanes, and thirty-six aero engines.

The project was passed to the *Conseil Général* for approval in March 1926, by which time propulsive power had been increased to 20 knots by the adoption of a new superheated steam plant. It was felt that the *transport d'aviation* as a type had certain advantages over *Béarn*. It could operate large, long-range torpedo bombers; by keeping displacement to 10,000tW it escaped the Washington Treaty constraints, and cost was relatively low. On the other hand there were clear limitations in how the ship could be employed. Operations in adverse weather conditions were impossible (they were in any case marginal with fleet carriers given the aircraft and the technology of the day); and the ship could not operate at sea with the battle fleet due to her lack of stability.

# A: TECHNICAL DESCRIPTION

## HULL AND SUPERSTRUCTURES

The general configuration of *Commandant Teste* was essentially that of a broad cruiser hull topped by a massive box hangar, the forecastle being raised to the same height as the hangar roof. The lower hull housed the machinery spaces with a single deck above (Main Deck – see GA plan), which in the area of the hangar housed workshops, washrooms and messdecks. In a break with tradition, officers' accommodation was located forward. The broad bow section, which was five decks high, allowed a generous allocation of space to the crew; facilities included a recreation room and an eight-berth hospital.

At the after end of the forecastle was a raised structure incorporating an enclosed bridge, with a prominent pole foremast angled at 2.5 degrees, the forward high-angle (HA) guns being disposed forward and to the sides. The single funnel, which was broadly in the centre of the ship, was set into a two-deck structure with wing platforms extending almost to the ship's sides on which much of the light AA weaponry was mounted. There was a small built-up after structure atop the after end of the hangar to accommodate the after HA guns, surmounted by a second pole mast at an identical angle to the foremast, the main W/T aerials being slung between the two pole masts, and between the mainmast and the funnel.

The double hangar measured approximately 80 metres by 26.5 metres and was three decks (7m) high; it was divided into two by a longitudinal partition which incorporated the exhaust uptakes for the funnel and the ventilation trunking for the machinery rooms. The hangar was designed to accommodate ten large torpedo bombers with folding wings; two folding-wing reconnaissance floatplanes could be stowed in place of each of the bombers (see section drawing). Two additional large torpedo bombers and four reconnaissance seaplanes were carried broken down in cases stowed in a hold beneath the hangar. There was magazine space for twenty 400mm torpedoes, together with bombs ranging from 75kg to 700kg, and 75 tonnes of aviation fuel was provided in two tanks abaft the machinery spaces.

A system of Décauville rails extended through each

**Left:** *Commandant Teste* running her trials in 1931. Her armament has yet to be fitted. *(Musée national de la Marine)*

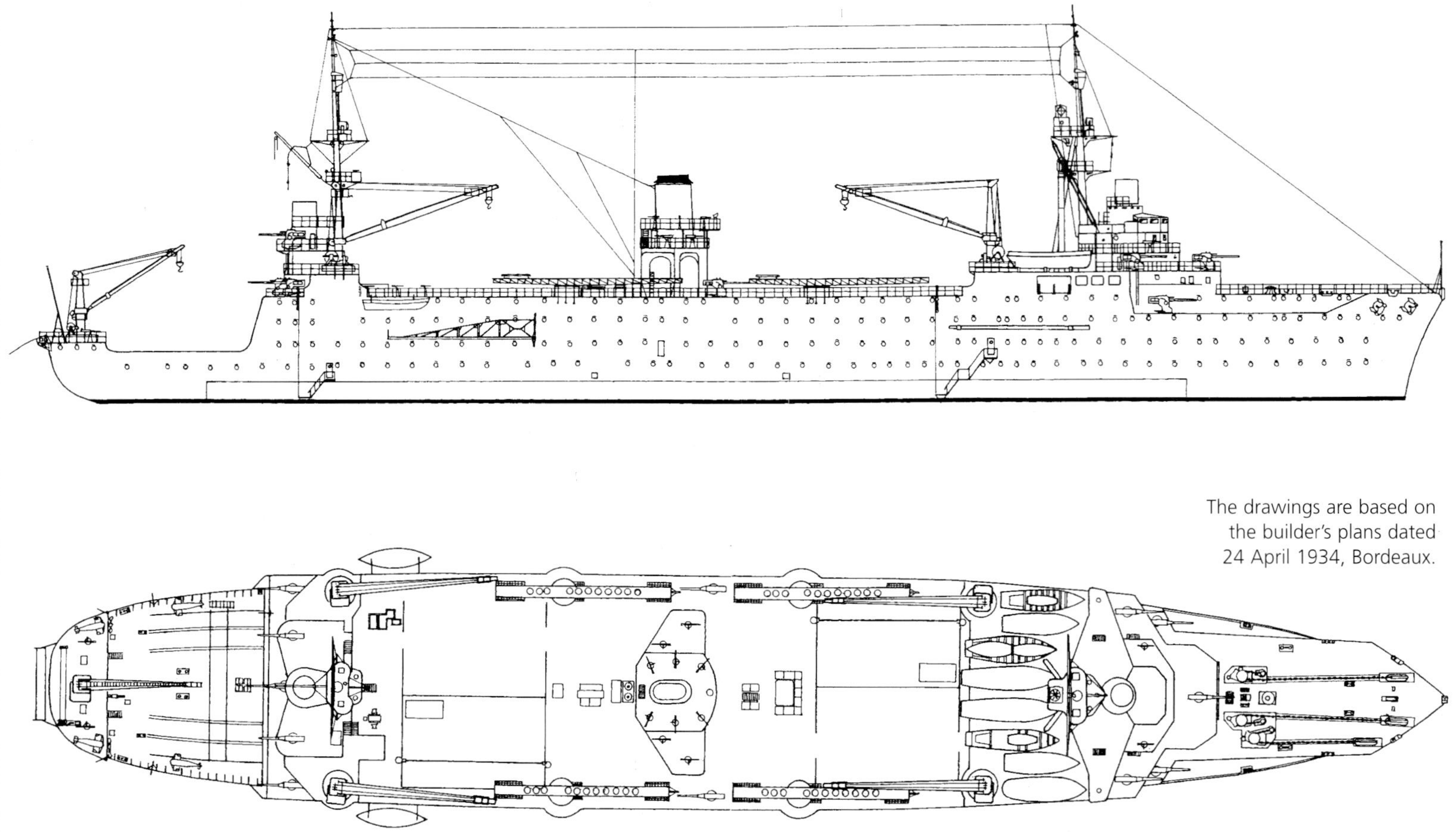

The drawings are based on the builder's plans dated 24 April 1934, Bordeaux.

© John Jordan 2001

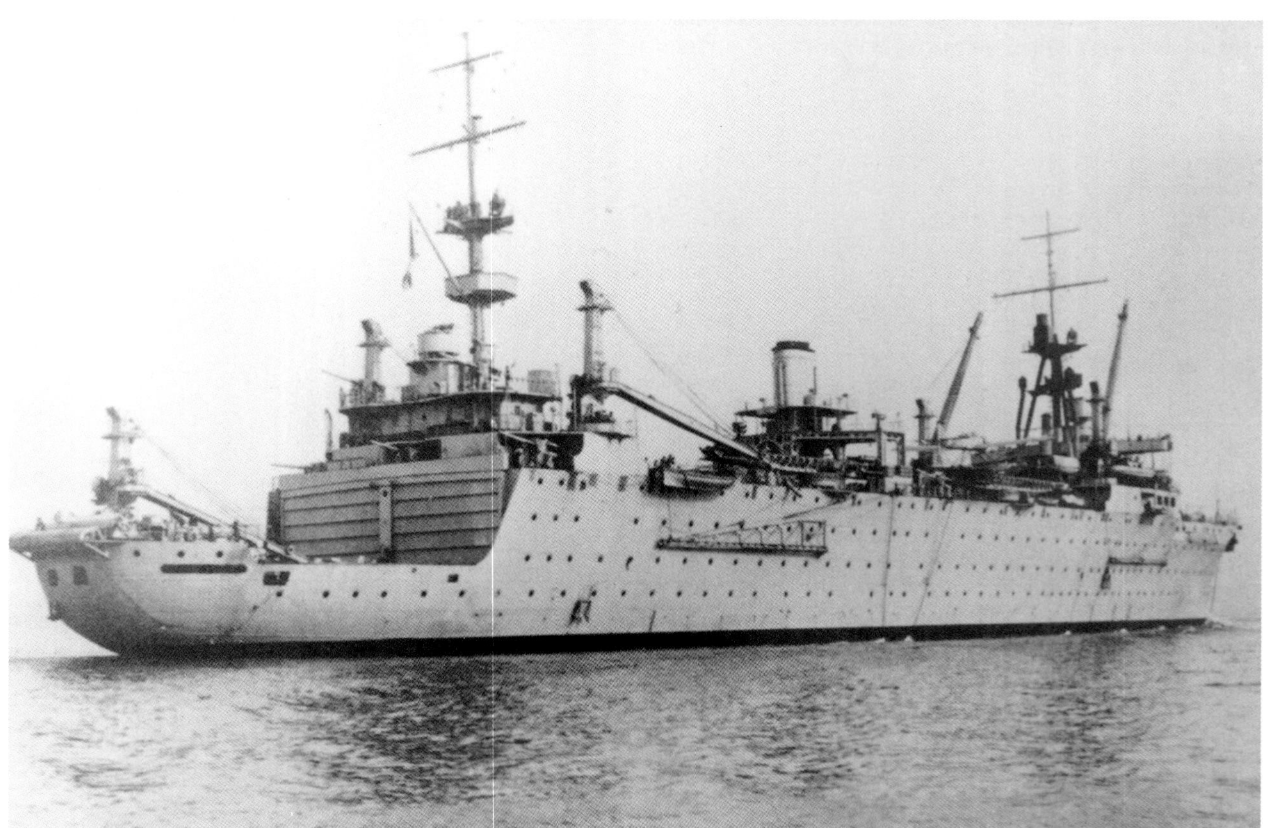

**Right:** *Commandant Teste* between October 1932 and November 1935 with her unshielded 100mm HA guns. Note the fitting on the stern for a Kiwull landing mat. *(Bernadac collection)*

## *Commandant Teste:* General Arrangement Plan

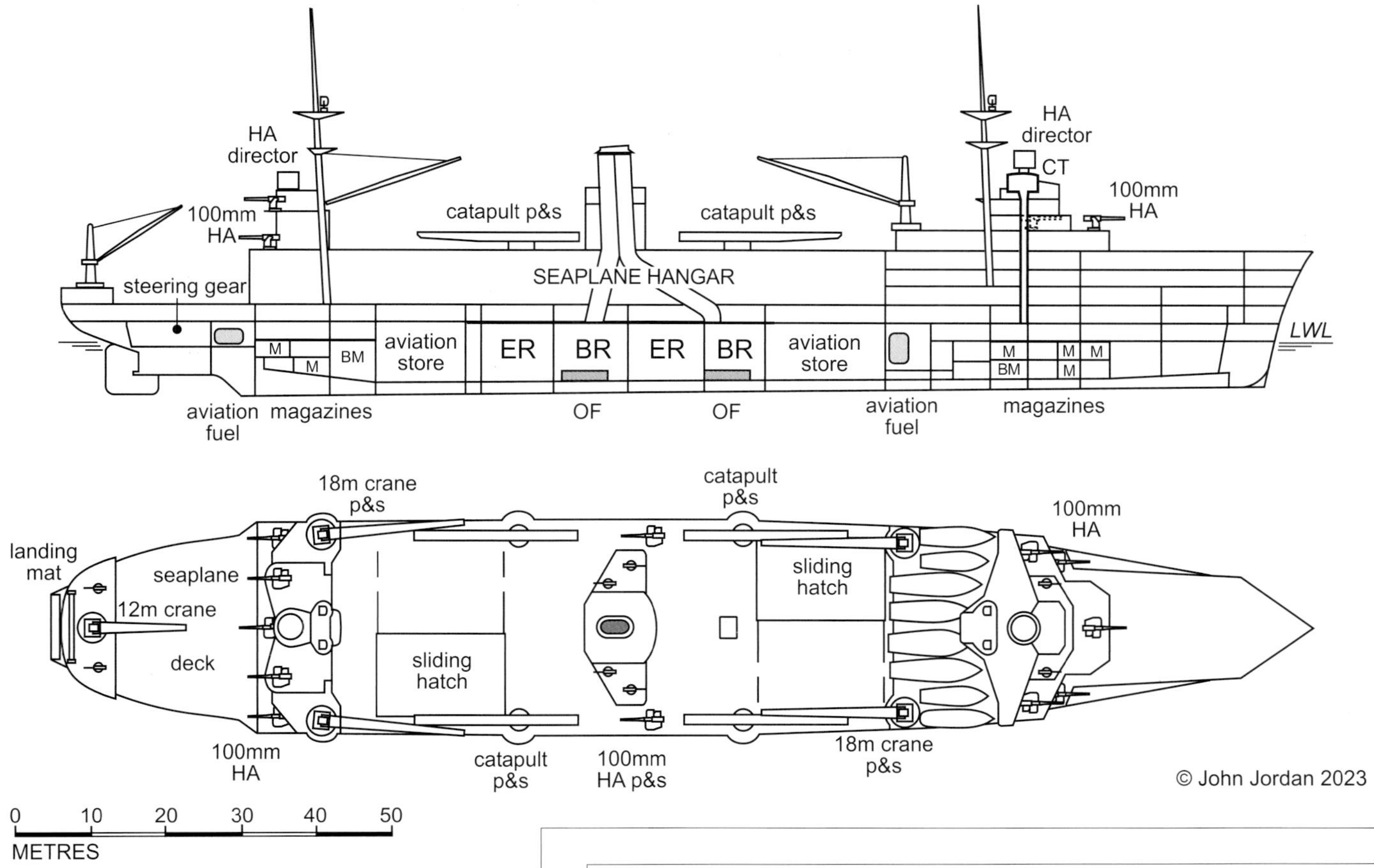

HA director
100mm HA
steering gear
catapult p&s
catapult p&s
SEAPLANE HANGAR
HA director
CT
100mm HA
LWL
M
M
BM
aviation store
ER
BR
ER
BR
aviation store
M
BM
M
M
M
aviation fuel
magazines
OF
OF
aviation fuel
magazines
18m crane p&s
catapult p&s
100mm HA
landing mat
seaplane
12m crane
deck
sliding hatch
sliding hatch
100mm HA
catapult p&s
100mm HA p&s
18m crane p&s
© John Jordan 2023
0 10 20 30 40 50
METRES

half-hangar onto the low quarterdeck, the floatplanes being moved on wheeled trolleys. Once the massive torpedo bombers had been prepared and wings deployed on the quarterdeck, they were lowered into the water by a 7-tonne crane with a reach of 5–12 metres located on the centre-line directly above the stern.

A prototype deployable 'landing mat' for seaplanes was trialled in the cruiser *Foch* during late 1931, then transferred to the *Commandant Teste* on the arrival of the cruiser at Toulon, and again trialled during May/June 1932. An order for a German Kiwull mat was duly placed in October 1934, and it was installed during February/March of the following year. The floating section of the mat measured 12 metres by 7.8 metres, while the upper section was 8.5 metres long. The mat was only partially successful, imposing serious constraints on the operation of the mother ship during recovery operations; speed was limited to 6 knots during the aircraft's approach, and embarkation then took a further twenty to thirty minutes. The mats, which were also fitted in the 7,600-ton cruisers of the *La Galissonnière* class, proved to be a serious maintenance problem: they were wet when stowed and the canvas tended to rot. They would eventually be removed from all ships.

Access to the hangar roof was via two large rectangular openings approximately 15 metres by 7 metres covered by sliding hatches. Access for the port-side half-hangar was forward, that for the starboard-side half-hangar aft (see plan drawing). Four Penhoët compressed air catapults 20.5 metres long with an

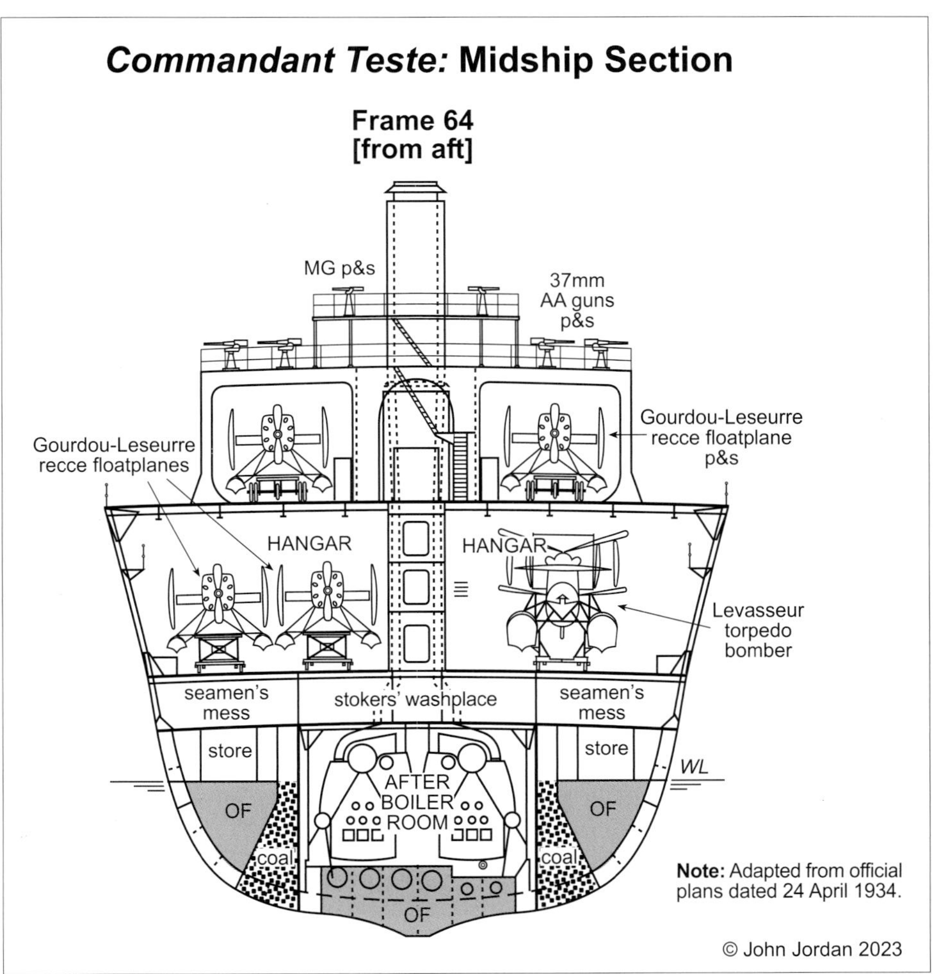

**Table 1: CHARACTERISTICS**

| | |
|---|---|
| **Displacement:** | 10,000 tons standard |
| | 11,500 tonnes full load |
| **Dimensions:** | |
| length | 156m pp, 167m oa |
| beam | 21.7m wl, 27m max |
| draught | 6.7m |
| **Aviation:** | |
| hangar | 80m x 25.5m x 7m |
| catapults | four Penhoët compressed air |
| cranes | four 12-tonne, one 7-tonne |
| air group | ten Levasseur PL.14 torpedo bombers |
| | fourteen Gourdou-Leseurre GL.811 recce floatplanes |
| **Machinery:** | |
| boilers | four Yarrow-Loire small watertube boilers with superheating |
| | (2 oil-fired, 2 mixed) 20kg/cm$^2$ (290°C) |
| wngines | two-shaft Schneider-Zoelly geared steam turbines |
| horsepower | 21,000cv |
| speed | 20.5 knots (designed) |
| fuel | 1163t oil, 700t coal |
| endurance | 2000nm at 18kts, 6000nm at 10kts |
| generators | two turbo-gens each 300kW |
| | three diesel-gens each 150kW |
| **Protection:** | |
| side belt | 36mm (50mm over machinery spaces) |
| main deck | 24mm over magazines & engine rooms |
| | 36mm over boiler rooms |
| magazines | box with 44/50mm sides, 16/20mm transverse b/heads |
| machinery | box with 40mm sides, 20mm transverse b/heads |
| steering gear | 26mm |
| conning tower | 80mm walls, 30mm roof |
| **Armament:** | |
| DP guns | twelve 100mm/45 Mle 1927 in single mountings |
| | (2760 rounds + 480 starshell + 120 tracer) |
| light AA | eight 37mm/50 Mle 1925 in single mountings (4,000 rounds) |
| | twelve 13.2mm/76 Mle 1929 Hotchkiss MG in twin mountings |
| **Boats:** | two 12-metre fast motor boats (aircrew rescue) |
| | two 9-metre motor boats (aircraft towing) |
| | one 10-metre steam pinnace |
| | one 11-metre pulling pinnace |
| | one 11-metre service motor launch |
| | one 10-metre service motor launch |
| | two 8.5-metre whalers |
| | two 5-metre dinghies |
| **Complement:** | 42 officers, 602 men |

initial launch capacity of 2500kg were fitted atop the hangar close to the deck edge. Used for launching the recce/fighter floatplanes, these proved particularly successful; in 1938 they were modified to permit the launch of the larger and heavier Loire 130, capacity being raised to 3500kg.

The hatches and catapults were served by four powerful cranes, mounted at the four corners of the hangar; each had a reach of 6–18 metres and could lift 12 tonnes (the forward cranes were also employed to handle the ship's boats). The cranes were judged robust but complex to operate and maintain. During trials in 1937 it took an estimated three hours to embark or disembark a flotilla of sixteen aircraft, seventeen minutes to embark a single GL.812 reconnaissance floatplane, and seven minutes to launch a section of four Gourdou floatplanes by catapult.

## MACHINERY

The propulsion plant selected for the *Commandant Teste* was a mix of the traditional and the ultra-modern. Two of the four small-tube Loire-Yarrow boilers, rated at 20kg/cm$^2$, had alternative coal-firing, while all four had superheaters rated at 290°C. The boilers were disposed in pairs in two boiler rooms separated by the forward engine room, the uptakes for the forward pair being angled aft to the single funnel amidships. The dual oil/coal-fired boilers were located in the after boiler room.

This was the first application of superheating in the *Marine Nationale*, the British and the Italians having recently adopted it for their latest destroyers. Unsurprisingly it was not a complete success, and modifications had to be made to the superheaters following trials, but it made possible a high power-to-weight ratio, and superheating would subsequently be extended to the later classes of *contre-torpilleur* and to the 7600-ton cruisers of the *La Galissonnière* class.

There were two sets of Schneider-Zoelly impulse turbines, each powering one of the two shafts via reduction gearing and completely independent in operation, so that action damage or breakdown in one engine room would have no effect on the other. Each set comprised an HP and an LP turbine; a cruise turbine was linked to the shaft powered by the HP turbine via reduction gearing, while the reversing turbine was incorporated into the casing for the LP turbine. The cruise turbine was declutched above 12 knots and steam admitted directly into the HP turbine.

Apart from the problems experienced with the superheaters the propulsion machinery was judged to be generally satisfactory, and the designed power loading and maximum speed were both exceeded on trials. On 23 July 1933, just over 22 knots were attained on one run, and the sustained speed of 20.5 knots over ten hours at normal power loading demanded in the contract was comfortably achieved.

Electrical supply was at 235V 'cruiser' standard. There were two turbo-generators in the Forward Engine Room, each rated at 300kW (400kW max), and three diesel generators – two in the After Engine Room with a third co-located with the auxiliary boiler at the base of the superstructures – each rated at 150kW (180kW max), primarily for use when alongside.

## PROTECTION

Protection for the machinery rooms and magazines was provided on a scale comparable to that of the cruiser *Suffren*, which was a close contemporary of *Commandant Teste*, and employed a combination of an outer 'citadel' and internal 'armoured boxes' over the vital spaces. A side belt 3.76 metres deep outboard of the boxes for the machinery spaces, magazines and aviation fuel tanks extended from Frame 14 aft to Frame 130 forward; it comprised two layers of 18mm plate, increasing in thickness to 20mm+30 mm amidships, abeam the machinery spaces. The Main Deck (*pont principal*), comprising two layers each of 12mm steel, rested on its top edge, and there was a double layer of 12mm on the 1st Deck (*premier pont*) above from Frame 46 to the bow. The machinery spaces were located inside an internal box formed by a longitudinal

**Left:** Recovery of a Loire 130 reconnaissance seaplane on a landing mat deployed from the stern of a cruiser. *(SHD-A)*

## *Commandant Teste:* Machinery, Avgas Tanks & Magazines

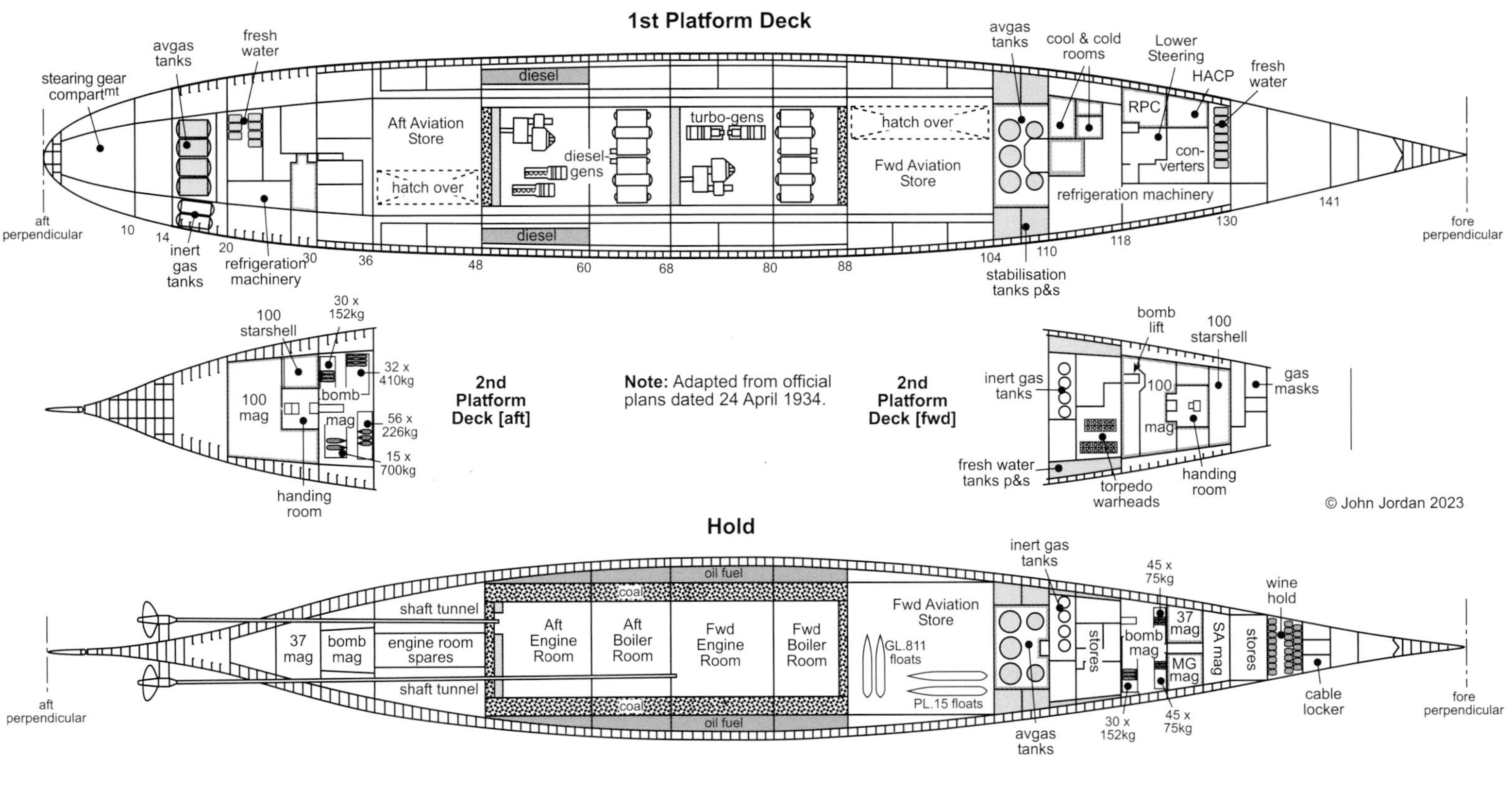

### 1st Platform Deck

stearing gear compart[mt]
avgas tanks
fresh water
Aft Aviation Store
hatch over
diesel
diesel-gens
turbo-gens
diesel
hatch over
Fwd Aviation Store
avgas tanks
cool & cold rooms
Lower Steering
RPC
HACP
fresh water
con-verters
refrigeration machinery
aft perpendicular
10
14
inert gas tanks
20
refrigeration machinery
30
36
48
60
68
80
88
104
110
stabilisation tanks p&s
118
130
141
fore perpendicular

### 2nd Platform Deck [aft]

100 starshell
30 x 152kg
32 x 410kg
100 mag
bomb
mag
56 x 226kg
15 x 700kg
handing room

**Note:** Adapted from official plans dated 24 April 1934.

### 2nd Platform Deck [fwd]

bomb lift
100 starshell
inert gas tanks
100
mag
gas masks
fresh water tanks p&s
torpedo warheads
handing room

© John Jordan 2023

### Hold

shaft tunnel
37 mag
bomb mag
engine room spares
shaft tunnel
oil fuel
coal
Aft Engine Room
Aft Boiler Room
Fwd Engine Room
Fwd Boiler Room
coal
oil fuel
Fwd Aviation Store
GL.811 floats
PL.15 floats
inert gas tanks
avgas tanks
stores
45 x 75kg
37 mag
bomb mag
MG mag
30 x 152kg
45 x 75kg
SA mag
stores
wine hold
cable locker
aft perpendicular
fore perpendicular

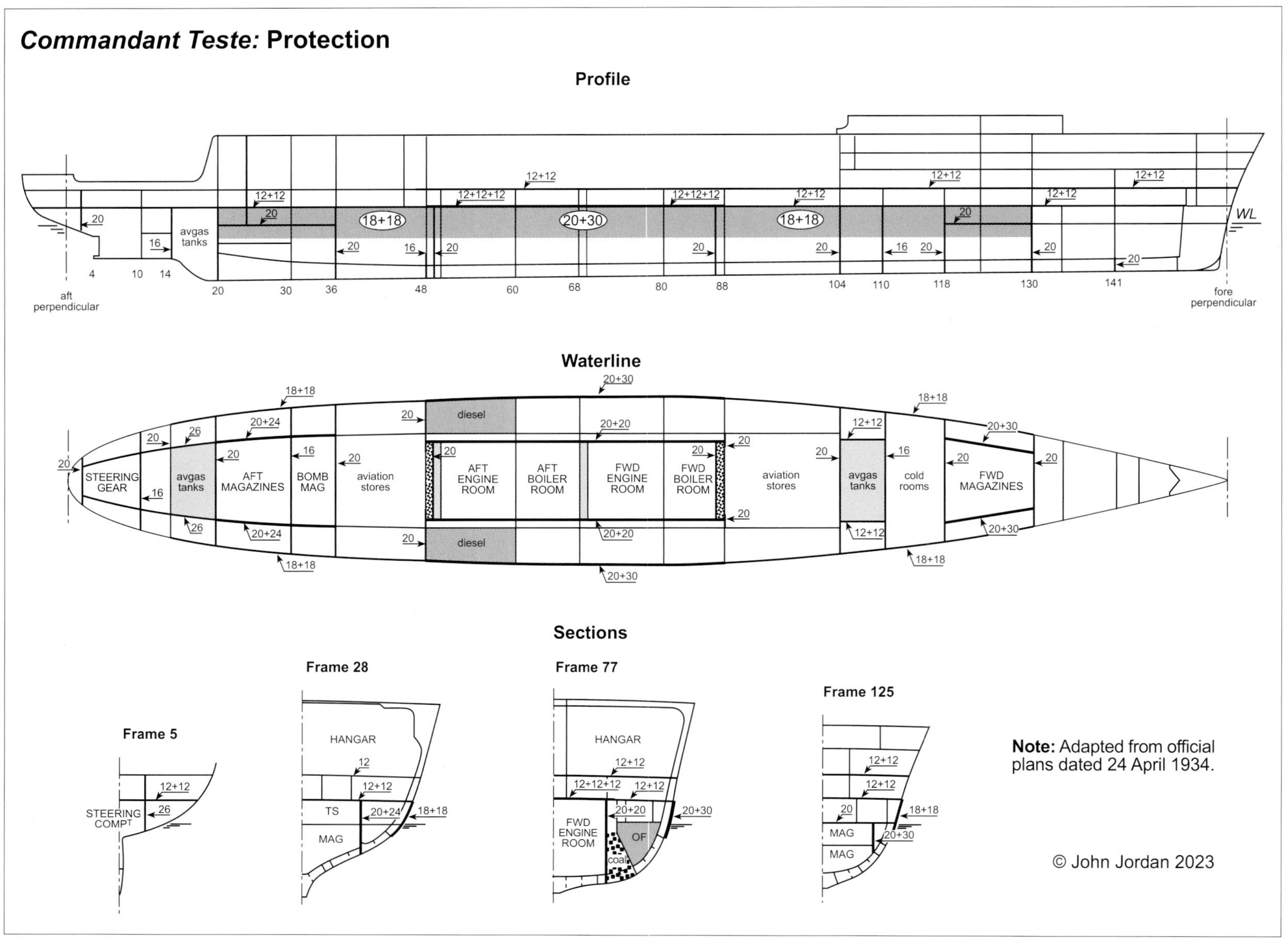


bulkhead comprising two 20mm plates from the keel to the Main Deck, enclosed at the ends by partial transverse bulkheads of 20mm; the Main Deck over the machinery spaces was reinforced by a third layer of 12mm steel for a total thickness of 36mm. The magazines had walls comprising two layers of 20–30mm steel, again with 20mm ends. The steering gear was protected by 26mm plating, while the conning tower had 80mm walls with a 30mm roof. All the armour was of 60kg 'special' steel except for the decks, steering gear and walls of the conning tower, which were of 50kg mild steel.

There was concern from the outset that such a high-sided vessel would prove to be unsteady in rougher sea conditions, the bulky hangar acting like a sail in high winds. The weight of armour and machinery in the lower part of the hull contributed to stability, but there was also a concentration of weights high in the ship in the form of catapults, heavy cranes and HA guns. It was therefore decided to fit a stabilisation system comprising two lateral tanks with a pressurised butterfly valve between. Trials in the long Atlantic swell off Morocco in 1933 were rated a complete success; the stabilisation system effectively deadened the roll of the ship by between 37 and 65 per cent. However, in the longer term the system was found to be difficult to maintain because of the difficulty of access to the tanks, and it was to remain experimental.

## ARMAMENT

In the early stages of the ship's design the *Conseil supérieur de la Marine* (CSM) was particularly anxious to provide *Commandant Teste* with an anti-surface armament capable of protecting the ship against destroyers, submarines and even small cruisers. Following a demand for the complement of 138.6mm guns to be raised from four to six, it requested that range for this weapon be increased to 24,000m. Both the heavyweight Mle 1910 and four of the latest 155mm Mle 1920 were considered, each involving a weight penalty of 60 tonnes. During this time the anti-aircraft armament remained at four 75mm plus four 37mm guns, although it was proposed in August 1926 that this be increased by two 75mm and four 37mm; rangefinders for AA fire were considered unnecessary for wartime operations, so none were to be provided!

By 1927, however, increasing recognition was being accorded to the aerial threat, and in August it was finally decided to suppress the anti-surface armament in its entirety, and to replace both the 138.6mm and the 75mm guns with a homogeneous battery of twelve single 100mm/45 Mle 1927 dual-purpose guns. *Commandant Teste* was the only ship to receive this model (the Mle 1932 was similar but had restricted elevation). The 100mm Mle 1927 was a modern weapon with a sliding breech and alternative electro-mechanical or mechanical firing. It could fire the OPf Mle 1927 semi-armour piercing (SAP) shell or the OEA Mle 1925S HE shell; 1,840 proximity-fuzed and 920 percussion-fuzed rounds were to be provided. There was also magazine space for 480 rounds of starshell and 120 rounds of incendiary tracer. The mounting had a maximum elevation of 85 degrees and was designed for remote power control (RPC) in elevation and bearing, with manual operation and optical sights for back-up.

The single 100mm mountings were disposed in three groupings, each of which was served by its own magazines and hoists; there were five mountings grouped around the forward superstructure, with a similar layout aft, and two mountings amidships atop the hangar, located at the deck edge between the catapults. Production delays resulted in late delivery of the mountings, which were installed only in October 1932. Protective shields with a thickness of 5mm were fitted during a refit in late 1935. The gun was generally successful in operation, but subsequently underwent a number of modifications to improve its performance against surface targets. The RPC also proved to be unreliable, as with other such French installations of the period.

The single 37mm/50 Mle 1925 guns, of which there were eight in the final design, were disposed as follows: two forward, two aft, and four on the wing platforms extending to port and starboard of the single funnel. They were installed during 1931. At the same time it was decided that the relatively ineffectual 8mm MG originally envisaged would be replaced by six of the new Hotchkiss twin 13.2mm mountings Mle 1929. These would eventually be fitted in the bridge wings forward, on the upper funnel platform amidships, and on either side of the centre-line crane above the stern.

There were fire control directors fore and aft, each equipped with a stereoscopic 3-metre rangefinder, for the 100mm guns. They provided control against both surface and aerial targets. It was later proposed that the rangefinders be upgraded to a model with a 5-metre base to improve performance against surface targets, but this modification was never implemented. There was a single 1-metre rangefinder forward of the single funnel for the midships 37mm mountings.

**Above:** A later view of *Commandant Teste*. The forward 100mm HA guns have now been fitted with shields. One of the starboard boat/aircraft handling booms is deployed. *(Bernadac collection)*

## Table 2: ANTI-AIRCRAFT GUNS

**100mm/45 Mle 1927**

| *Gun Data* | |
|---|---|
| Construction | monobloc, autofretted |
| Breech mechanism | horizontal sliding block |
| Weight of gun | 2010kg (incl breech) |
| Ammunition type | fixed |
| Projectiles | OPf Mle 1927 (14.95kg)<br>OEA Mle 1925S (13.47kg) |
| Propellant | 3.95kg BM7 |
| Total weight of round | OPf 26.15kg<br>OEA 22.67kg |
| Muzzle velocity | 770m/s |
| Range | OPf 16,300m at 45°<br>OEA 15,400m<br>(ceiling 10,200m) |
| *Mounting* | |
| Designation | Mle 1927 CA |
| Protection | 5mm shield |
| Weight of mounting | 7800kg |
| Elevation | -10° / +85° |
| Firing cycle | 6rpm |

**Notes:**

| | | |
|---|---|---|
| Mle | *Modèle* | Model |
| OPf | *Obus de Perforation* | Semi-Armour Piercing (SAP) |
| OEA | *Obus Explosif en Acier* | High Explosive (HE) |

## AIR GROUP

The air group, the *Flotille du Commandant Teste*, was formed on 1 September 1931. The lengthy gestation period of the ship meant that significant developments in naval aircraft had taken place in the interim. The scout floatplane to be carried was a folding-wing version of the Gourdou-Leseurre GL.810. The Farman Goliath was by this time obsolete, and would be replaced in the torpedo attack role by the Levasseur PL.14. No suitable float fighter had been developed by this time, so the first aviation complement would be built around these two types.

The scouting squadron, designated 7S2, was officially in service in October 1931. It was equipped as a temporary measure with the fixed-wing GL.810, which would be replaced by the folding-wing GL.811 variant in October 1933. An improved GL.813 model was embarked from early 1936. The Gourdou-Leseurre was a twin-float monoplane that proved very successful in service. Maximum take-off weight was just below the 2500kg limit of the Penhoët catapults, and the aircraft was to remain the standard French shipborne reconnaissance aircraft until the late 1930s, when it was replaced by the Loire 130. The latter was a much heavier aircraft, weighing in at 3500kg, and the catapults had to be modified in order to handle it. The Loire 130 replaced the GL.813 aboard the *Commandant Teste* from April 1938.

The torpedo bomber squadron, designated 7B2, was

**Right:** *Commandant Teste* at her moorings after 1936; note the Kiwull mat on its stern roller, and the shuttered rolling doors for the two half-hangars. The powerful after cranes are prominent in this view. *(René Bail collection)*

officially in service from January 1932, but did not receive its first aircraft until April. The Levasseur PL.14 was adapted from a land-based bomber and had a take-off weight of 4250kg. Twelve were built, but the type remained in service for only a short period as it proved too fragile for landing at sea, the engine cowling sustaining frequent damage. It was succeeded by the PL.15, which entered service in July/August 1934 and remained in service until shortly before the Second World War. The PL.15 was in its turn replaced by the first genuinely modern torpedo bomber to serve with the Marine Nationale, the Latécoère 298, which entered service in March/May 1939. With a top speed of 295km/h and a payload of a single 400mm torpedo or two 150kg bombs, this aircraft was highly regarded by all those who flew in it; 130 were built, and it was used extensively during the Battle for France in May/June 1940, albeit not in the role for which it was intended.

In peacetime a reduced aviation complement was embarked. In practice this meant two/three sections each of three aircraft for the GL.810 series, plus an additional aircraft for the officer commanding the flotilla (it was given a distinctive pennant marking on the sides of the fuselage), and two sections each of three torpedo bombers. On 1 October 1938, the scouting squadron was redesignated HS1 (*Hydravions de Surveillance*), and the bomber squadron HB1 (*Hydravions de Bombardement*); at the same time the *Flotille du Commandant Teste* became F1H.

The catapult fighter long planned to provide a self-defence capability for this and other ships finally became a reality with the entry into service of the Loire 210 in mid-1939. Under development for the *Marine Nationale* since 1933, this modern monoplane, which featured a single large float virtually the length of the fuselage with smaller floats beneath each wing, was so far outclassed by contemporary land-based fighters by the time it entered service as to be virtually ineffectual, and only twenty were built. A new squadron, desig-

**Below:** A Levasseur PL.15 of 7B2 at Saint-Mandrier in 1937. *(ARDHAN collection)*

## Table 3: AIR GROUP

**Reconnaissance [7S2 > HS1] & Fighter [HC1] Squadrons**

| | Gourdou-Leseurre GL.810/811/812/813 | Loire 130 | Loire 210 |
|---|---|---|---|
| Type | reconnaissance | reconnaissance | fighter |
| In service | 1931–44 | 1938–51 | 1939 |
| No ordered for MN | 86 | 124 | 20 |
| Length | 10.49m | 11.30m | 9.49m |
| Span | 16.00m | 16.00m | 11.79m |
| Height | 3.56m/3.86m | 3.85m | 3.79m |
| Weight (empty) | 1690kg | 2150kg | 1440kg |
| Weight (fl) | 2460kg | 3500kg | 2150kg |
| Power Unit | Gnome-Rhône 420hp | Hispano-Suiza 720hp | Hispano-Suiza 720hp |
| Max Speed | 200km/h | 225km/h | 345km/h |
| Ceiling | 6000m | 6000m | 8000m |
| Armament | 3 x 7.7mm MG<br>2 x 75kg bombs | 2 x 7.5mm M G<br>2 x 75kg bombs/DC | 4 x 7.5mm MG |

**Torpedo Bomber Squadron [7B2 > HB1]**

| | Levasseur PL.15 | Latécoère 298 |
|---|---|---|
| Type | torpedo bomber | torpedo attack |
| In service | 1934–38 | 1938–51 |
| No ordered for MN | 16 | 130 |
| Length | 12.85m | 12.56m |
| Span | 18.00m | 15.50m |
| Height | 5.10m | 5.24m |
| Weight (empty) | 2835kg | 3000kg |
| Weight (fl) | 4350kg | 4800kg |
| Power Unit | Hispano-Suiza 650hp | Hispano-Suiza 880hp |
| Max Speed | 210km/h | 295km/h |
| Ceiling | 4500m | 5500m |
| Armament | 400mm torpedo<br>or 700kg bombs<br>2 x 7.5mm MG | 400mm torpedo<br>or 2 x 150kg bombs<br>3 x 7.5mm MG |

**Right:** A Gourdou-Leseurre GL.810 of 7S2 leaves the catapult on *Commandant Teste* in 1932. *(ARDHAN collection)*

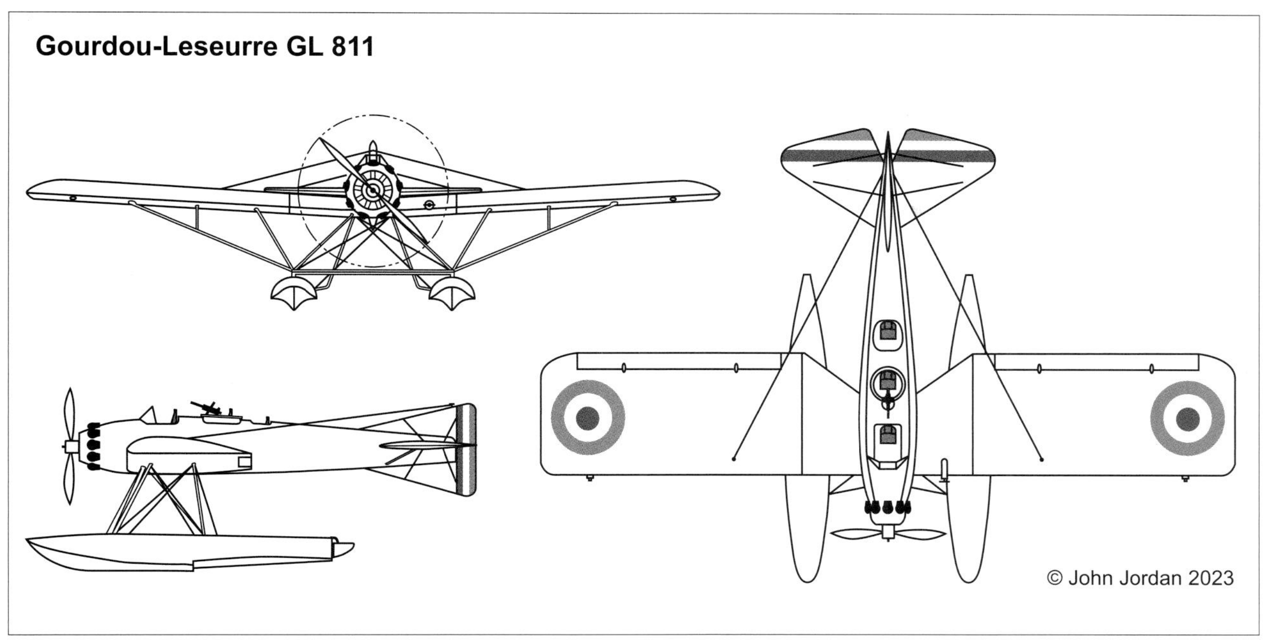


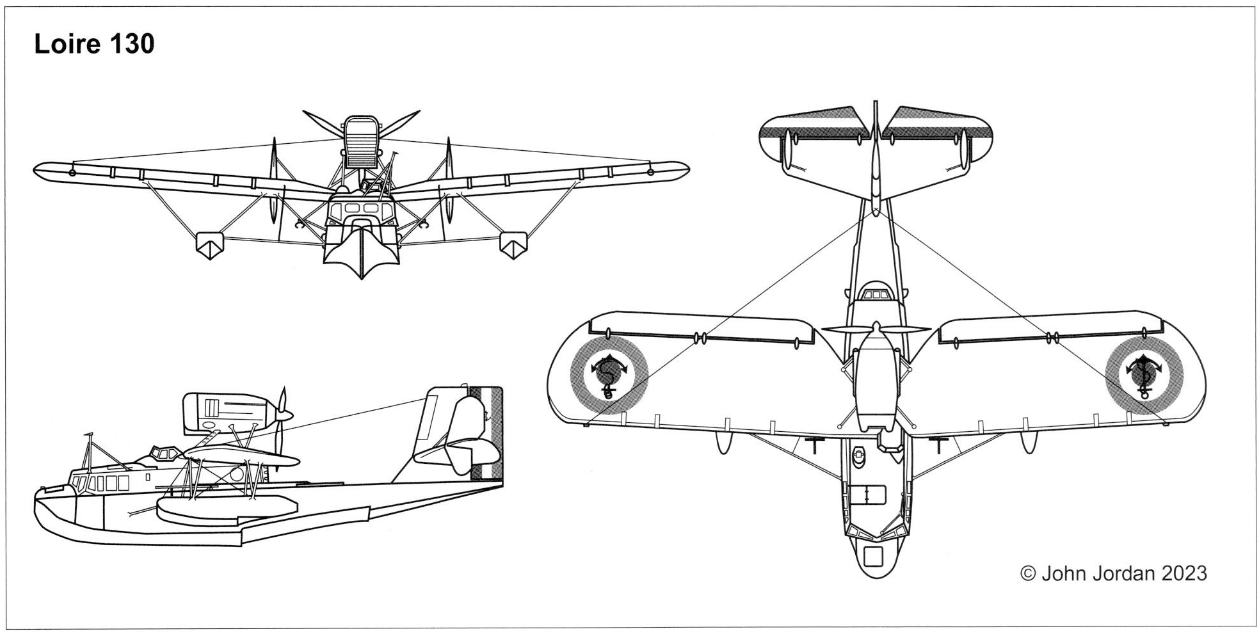

**Left:** A Loire 130 (7S3-18) reconnaissance seaplane is catapulted from the cruiser *Jean de Vienne* in 1938. *(ARDHAN collection)*

**Above:** A Loire 210 float fighter suspended from the crane of the battleship *Dunkerque* in 1939. *(ARDHAN collection)*

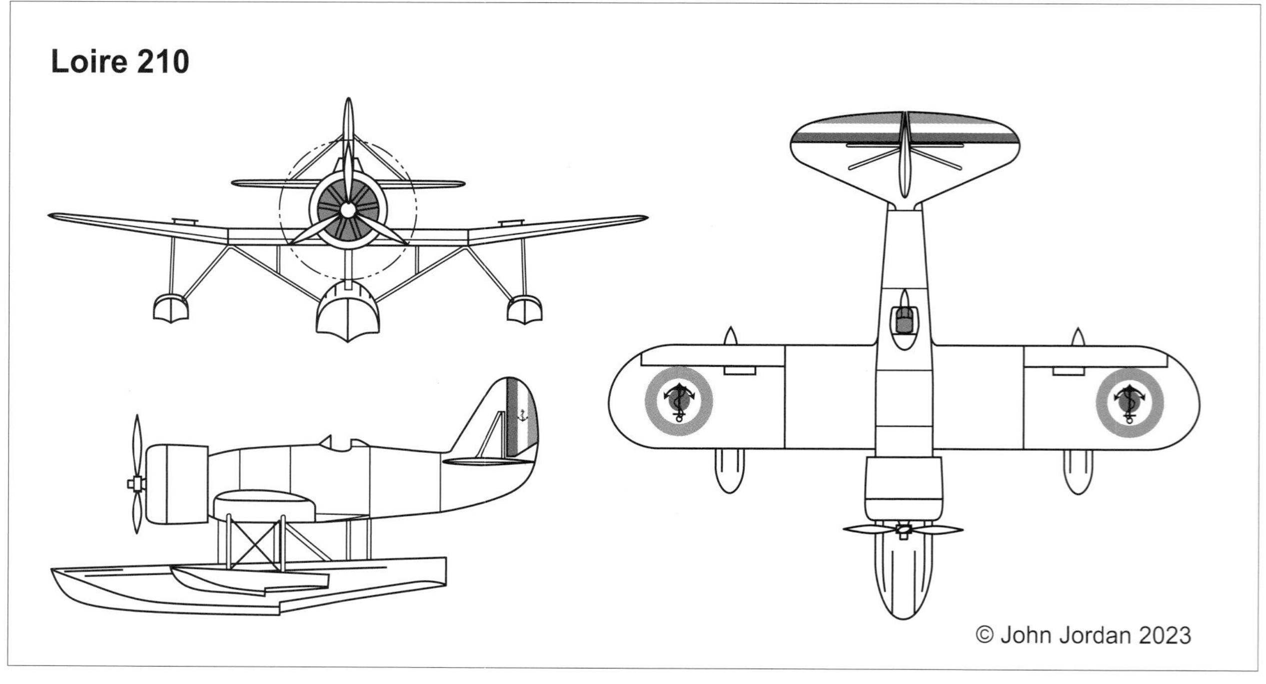

nated HC1 (*Hydravions de Chasse*), was formed at Saint-Mandrier on 1 July 1939, but although formally attached to F1H, the aircraft were never embarked.

# B: SERVICE HISTORY

## CONSTRUCTION AND TRIALS 1927–32

The aviation transport was authorised under the 1925 Estimates. However, her construction, together with that of the minelayer *Pluton*, was delayed by one year at the request of the Finance Minister. The contract, with the Chantiers de la Gironde of Bordeaux, was signed on 27 April 1927. The ship, designated PN72 by *Constructions Navales*, would subsequently be named *Commandant Teste* after CV Paul Teste, who had died while preparing for a raid in the Levant on 13 June 1925. (See page 25.) Laid down on 6 September 1927, she was launched on 12 April 1929. The installation of the machinery began on 20 July 1929 and *Commandant Teste* was manned for trials on 15 November 1930. Her first commanding officer was a former seaplane pilot, CV Victor Trucy.

The first sea trials took place on 22 April 1931, and the first seaplane handling trials took place during May: a Gourdou-Leseurre GL.810 reconnaissance floatplane on the 12th and a PL.7 torpedo bomber on the 21st.

*Commandant Teste* departed Bordeaux for Le Verdon on 16 June and ran her acceptance trial, which was interrupted by a problem with the turbines in the forward engine room. The ship returned to Bordeaux via Le Verdon, arriving on the 20th.

She left Bordeaux on 25 June for Toulon, her new home port, arriving on the 30th. The transit allowed a number of trials to take place en route. She was docked from 10 to 20 July and then resumed her sea trials. On 29 July, during her trial at maximum normal power, she attained 21.22 knots with 21,400cv. On a three-hour full power trial with forced draught on 31 July she achieved 21.77 knots with an estimated power output of 23,160cv. A total of eight trials were undertaken between 23 July and 12 August without any serious problems or machinery failures.

**Above:** Laté 298 torpedo bombers of 4T Squadron at Berre in 1941. *(ARDHAN collection)*

Table 4: **BUILDING DATA**

| | |
|---|---|
| Builder: | F C Gironde, Bordeaux |
| Laid down: | 6 September 1927 |
| Launched: | 12 April 1929 |
| Manned for trials: | 15 November 1930 |
| Commissioned: | 1 March 1932 |
| Entered service: | 12 April 1934 |

*Commandant Teste* was then docked on 14 August for the standard visual inspection of her machinery. Although still lacking her guns, she was commissioned (*armement définitif*) on 1 March 1932.

The final trial (*essai de bon fonctionnement après démontage*) took place on 5 March. She then embarked the GL.810s of 7S2 and departed Toulon on 30 March for her long-range transit (*traversée de longue durée*). She put in to Algiers, Bizerte, Djerba and Ajaccio and re-entered Toulon on 12 April.

**Left:** The launch of *Commandant Teste* on 12 April 1929 at Bordeaux. *(Musée national de la Marine)*

**Left:** *Commandant Teste* on trials. *(René Bail collection)*

**Far left:** A GL.811 of 7S2 Squadron is catapulted from *Commandant Teste* around 1933. *(Musée national de la Marine)*

Still lacking her guns, she was assigned to the 1st Squadron at Toulon on 18 April 1932. Her air group comprised two squadrons:

- 7S2 with six/nine Gourdou-Leseurre GL.810 reconnaissance floatplanes (two/three sections each of three aircraft
- 7B2 with six PL.15 torpedo bombers (two sections).

In principle, the ship would have embarked a supplementary aircraft for the flight commander, which was marked with a distinctive pennant on the sides of the fuselage. When not embarked the air group would be based at Saint-Mandrier.

*Commandant Teste* embarked her two squadrons and accompanied the 1st Squadron on a cruise in the Eastern Mediterranean, departing Toulon on 26 April. The ships called in at Bizerte on 1–3 May, then set course for Beirut via Suda Bay (Crete). On 19 May, a GL.810 flipped over following a catapult launch in the port of Beirut; the pilot, EV Maxime Vezon, was drowned. Returning via Tripoli and Eleusis, there was a longer stay at Bizerte from 8 to 22 June, which also saw joint manoeuvres with the 2nd (Atlantic) Squadron. The ships re-entered Toulon on 25 June. The performance of the floatplanes embarked was judged to be unimpressive; they were too slow, too vulnerable, and had insufficient endurance.

After a further sortie on 27 June, *Teste* was towed into the dockyard on 5 July and officially left the 1st Squadron on 15 July to resume her fitting out. She emerged from the dockyard on 17 October and put to sea for further trials and work-up on 20, 21 and 28 October and 10 November. The first firings from her new 100mm HA guns took place on the first two of these dates, and on 24 October the ship was finally declared fit for service.

## TOULON 1932–33

On 18 November, *Teste* left for Les Salins. During a training exercise that involved launching torpedoes, one of her PL.14s struck the surface in the Bay of Saint-Mandrier, with the loss of all three of the crew.

During the early part of 1933, *Teste* was immobilised in the Missiessy Basin due to problems with the superheaters and turbine corrosion. Her air squadrons, which were based temporarily at Saint-Mandrier, continued their work-up and took part in exercises with the fleet.

Following her repairs, *Commandant Teste* sortied on 3 March 1933 and rejoined the 1st Squadron on the 9th. She was docked from 19 to 22 March, then departed Toulon on the 26th, reportedly for Indochina. In reality she embarked four GL.810s and three Farman 168 Goliath heavy bombers belonging to 3B1 based at Berre, together with a company of Senegalese light infantry. The bombers and the light infantry were to reinforce French forces at Djibouti following incursions and border incidents involving Somalia. *Teste* called in at Beirut on 30–31 March, replenished at Port Said on 1 April and arrived at Djibouti on the 5th, being joined by the sloop *Ypres*. The Goliaths were disembarked. The arrival of the ships and the aerial patrols produced the desired effect, and a degree of calm returned. *Teste* then needed to replenish her stores before proceeding on to Saigon. She left Djibouti on 20 April, and returned to Toulon via Aden and Port Said on 6 May; the deployment to Indochina was then abandoned.

The ship departed Toulon for North Africa on 10 May with 7S2 and a three-plane section of 7B2. After a short stay at Arzew she headed for Casablanca, which she left on the 24th after exercising with the combined 1st and 2nd Squadrons. She then dropped anchor at Lanzarote, returning to Casablanca from 1 to 6 June; there was then a port visit to Lisbon from 9 to 15 June. Attached temporarily to the 2nd (Atlantic) Squadron, she arrived at Lorient on 17 June and moored in the Port Louis anchorage. During the night of 22/23 June, during a change of moorings in the Bay of Quiberon, she was struck by the *contre-torpilleur Maillé-Brézé*. The latter ship suffered virtually no damage but her bow tore away part of the side plating of *Teste* over a length of 4–5 metres above the waterline. She was repaired in Lorient Dockyard from 24 June to 10 July.

*Commandant Teste* was at Cherbourg from 12 to 14 July, where she embarked the Farman 168s of 1B1. These were subsequently disembarked at Bizerte during a stay from 19 to 23 June, when she embarked Nieuport NiD 622 fighters of 4C1. She ferried the fighters to Hyères, anchoring at Les Salins on 24–25 June. She then rejoined the 1st Squadron, taking part in a sail-past to the south of Carqueiranne on the 25th, and returned to Toulon.

Apart from a brief sortie to Golfe Juan 31 July to 4 August, *Teste* would not go to sea again before October. She underwent trials to test her anti-roll stabilisation system in the Toulon roads on the 12th and then at sea on the 17th. She left the following day to continue her stabilisation trials off Morocco, which was notorious for its Atlantic swell. She embarked eight GL.811s and a CAMS 37A. She called in at Casablanca, then moored off Rabat from 24 to 27 October, awaiting the swell. She changed her moorings several times. On 7 and 18 November, when off Casablanca, there was a 6-metre swell that prompted a roll measured at just over 20 degrees; the effectiveness of the stabilisation system was classified as 'remarkable'. The ship returned to Toulon on 1 December. After a further brief sortie with the Squadron on 18–20 December, she entered the dockyard for a refit that lasted more than four months.

## TOULON 1934–35

*Commandant Teste* left the dockyard on 11 April 1934. She was finally admitted to active service on 12 April, incorporated into the 1st Squadron and attached to the 2nd Battle Division.

She was at Les Salins from 11 to 16 April, and on the 16th practised embarking the CAMS 55 flying boat. She left Toulon for Bizerte on 17 April, leaving 7B2 at Saint-Mandrier, and was docked at Sidi-Abdallah from 29 April to 5 May. She departed Tunisia on 5 May and headed for the Atlantic, accompanied by the cruisers *Foch*, *Colbert*, *Dupleix* and *Tourville*. She took part in an exercise with the 2nd Squadron, then entered Brest on 12 May. After manoeuvres with the 2nd Squadron, she left Brest on the 22nd and anchored off several ports on the French Atlantic coast before heading for Casablanca, arriving for a three-day stay on 16 June. She then passed through the Strait of Gibraltar and returned to Toulon via Mers el-Kébir, arriving on 29 June. Deployments to Les Salins and Bizerte followed. She again left Toulon on 20 November, moored at Saint-Raphaël and was at Ajaccio from 22 to 27 November for exercises with 7B2, which had recently been equipped with the Levasseur PL.15 torpedo bomber. There was further routine activity in December before the ship was briefly docked over Christmas.

*Commandant Teste* was towed out of the dockyard on 12 January 1935. During a short cruise with the Squadron from 15 to 25 January, there were moorings at Les Salins and Golfe Juan, where she served as a mobile base. During a refit from 28 February to 20 March, a Kiwull landing mat was fitted and the stabilisation system modified. There was further work during late April. She was at Les Salins from 2 to 6 May and embarked twenty-eight Air Force Morane-Saulnier 225 fighters of 3FC, which she was to transport to Bizerte. She was in the Bizerte area on 8–23 May and returned to Toulon on the 29th.

On 6 June she departed Toulon with 7B2 and 7S2, called in at Oran then Mers el-Kébir and, after exercises between Oran and Morocco, entered Casablanca on the 14th. She conducted further stabilisation trials on 3–4 July, returning to Toulon via Mers el-Kébir on the 12th. Trials of the Kiwull landing mat took place in late July, and in August there were trials with the Lioré et Olivier H-43 and Loire 130 seaplanes.

Off the Hyères Islands on 16 October, one of the floats of a PL.15 struck the surface and the aircraft broke up; fortunately, the three crew suffered only slight injuries. Trials with the LeO H-43 concluded with two catapult launches on 22 October. The first catapult launch of the Loire 130 prototype (No 01) took place on 6 November in the Bay of Saint-Mandrier.

*Commandant Teste* began a long refit on 12 November 1935. Her air group continued its work-up from the air base at Saint-Mandrier.

## TOULON 1936–38

*Commandant Teste* was at sea on 23 June, 28–31 July and 4–7 August 1936 and was moored at Saint-

Raphaël and Le Lavandou, even though she was operating with reduced manning.

The Spanish Civil War began on 18 July. The *Marine Nationale* was initially engaged in evacuating French nationals and securing communications with the diplomats who had remained in post. On 10 August *Commandant Teste* left Toulon with no aircraft on board to relieve the *contre-torpilleur Albatros* at Barcelona and to embark Rear Admiral Marcel Gensoul. She was in turn relieved on the 19th by the cruiser *Colbert* and re-entered Toulon the following day.

Training for the air group was resumed with a sortie to the anchorages of Saint-Raphaël, Golfe Juan and Les Salins from 14 to 22 October. There were fifteen catapult take-offs, nine landings using the Kiwull mat and two torpedo drops.

On 30 October 1936, the 1st Squadron at Toulon was redesignated the Mediterranean Squadron (*Escadre de la Méditerranée*). *Teste* left with part of the Squadron on 17 November for exercises at Les Salins, and returned on the 27th with the port forward catapult out of action. From 6 to 22 December she took part in a cruise along the Spanish Mediterranean coast, leaving her air group at Saint-Mandrier. There were visits to Tarragona, Valencia, Barcelona and Palma de Mallorca. She arrived back in Toulon on 23 December and was briefly docked. A short cruise with the Mediterranean Squadron followed during 13–22 January 1937, with the ship mooring successively at Les Salins, the Gulf of Fos, Grau du Roi, Palavas and La Ciotat. At Grau du Roi the floatplanes attached to the cruisers were replenished by *Teste*.

On 2 February she left for further trials with her stabilisation tanks off Morocco, embarking a three-plane section of 7S2 and a CAMS 37. The transit took in Alicante and Almería on the Spanish coast; the ship then proceeded to Casablanca and Agadir. She took part in exercises with the Atlantic (ex-2nd) Squadron and was in company with *Béarn* for the last time. She

**Below:** *Commandant Teste* at anchor off Bougie in September 1937. *(SHD-A)*

returned to Toulon on 22 February via Tangier, Málaga, Alicante and Valencia. After a one-day sortie on 28 February, she joined the Squadron with her air group for a tour of the coast of Provence, adding Saint-Florent to the usual ports. On 10 March a premature catapult launch of a GL.811 occurred, fortunately with no injuries to the aircrew.

On 1 April, she landed 136 of her crew to man ships assigned to the naval patrol off the Spanish coasts. Despite her reduced complement she was able to take a limited part in a cruise by the Squadron from 13 to 24 April. She then departed Toulon on 5 May with her two air squadrons for Bizerte and Arzew via Les Salins, returning on the 22nd. During a further sortie to Arzew and Oran on 10–24 June she provided support for aircraft from squadrons E1, E4, E5 and E7, which had been tasked with attacking part of the Squadron between Oran and Algiers. She was then in maintenance until 15 September.

On 12 September, the Navy set up a force designated the *Dispositif spécial en Méditerranée* (DSM) for the protection of neutral shipping against 'piracy'. *Commandant Teste* was assigned to this force on 18 September and left Toulon the same day with four aircraft of 7B2 and four of 7S2. She dropped anchor in the outer harbour of Bougie (now Béjaïa) on the 20th, and began reconnaissance patrols the following day with the aircraft of 7S2. She left for Toulon on 26 October and remained there until 2 November. She then departed for Les Salins and transported twenty-eight fighters to Karouba air base, near Bizerte. She was at Bizerte from 4 to 8 November, returning to Bougie on the 9th. The adverse sea conditions precluded landings, but from 20 November her aircraft conducted patrols every other day. On 14 December, four aircraft of 7S2 were detached to Algiers, and on the 16th the ship departed Bougie for Toulon, arriving the following day to be docked.

*Commandant Teste* put to sea again on 12 January 1938 and headed for Bizerte via Hyères, returning to Bougie on the 20th. She had on board seven GL.811 (including one for the air group commander), three PL.15, plus a CAMS 37 Lia for the ship's CO. She left Bougie on 7 February for Algiers, where she remained until the 21st. On 12 February a strong gust of wind ruptured her moorings and she was driven onto the breakwater of the Mustapha Basin. She needed repairs to her hull plating and replacement of the starboard propeller. She re-entered Toulon on 24 February via Bizerte and Les Salins, and left the DSM.

*Teste* began a major refit on 1 March. The thirteen hull plates damaged at Algiers were replaced, the capacity of the catapults was increased to 3500kg to enable them to handle a fully loaded Loire 130, and the turbines were refurbished. The work was completed on 7 August 1938.

## TOULON 1938–39

*Commandant Teste* was at sea on 17 August and again on 6 September, when she undertook training for her air group in the anchorages of Brégançon and Les Salins. The first catapult launches of the Loire 130 took place from the 7th. She returned to Toulon on the 11th, embarked 7S2 on the 13th and headed for Oran, arriving on the 16th. The movement was prompted by the Czechoslovakia crisis, which was ended by the Munich Agreement of 30 September.

On 1 October 1938, the *Teste* air group became Flotilla F1H; Squadron 7B2 was redesignated HB1 and 7S2 became HS1. The ship departed Oran on 4 October and returned to Toulon via Arzew on the 8th. There were further sorties on 20–21 and 26–28

**Right:** *Commandant Teste* at Oran between September and December 1939. *(Alain Marchand)*

**Above:** On board *Commandant Teste* between 19 and 26 February 1940 at Beirut, where she disembarked Morane-Saulnier MS.406 fighters of GC I/7. *(ECPAD)*

October, and 2–4 November. On 19 November she left for Casablanca, arriving on the 22nd, and spent the next few days supporting the transit of three Bréguet Bizerte seaplanes of E1 Squadron from Berre to Dakar. She proceeded on to Dakar and returned to Toulon on 19 December. She was then in dockyard hands for the next thirty days.

*Commandant Teste* sailed again on 18 January 1939. She was at Bizerte from 19 to 21 January, Casablanca from 24 to 26 January, and Port Etienne on 30–31 January. Three Bréguet Bizerte seaplanes arrived at Dakar on 5 February to relieve E1. One of *Teste*'s condensers failed on the evening of 1 March and she was restricted to her port turbines for just over twenty-four hours. She returned to Port Etienne on 4–5 February, where she restocked the local supplies of aviation fuel. She was at Dakar on the 7th, leaving on the 9th with the cruisers *Marseillaise* and *La Galissonnière* for Conakry, where she was moored from the 12th to the 16th. She returned to Toulon via Dakar, arriving on 24 February.

*Teste* was then tasked with transporting nineteen Air Force Morane-Saulnier 406 intended for the future GC I/9 at Tunis, together with two trucks. She arrived at Bizerte on 2 March, and the aircraft were landed using barges. In preparation for a second ferrying mission, she embarked a further twenty fighters from the Le Palyvestre air base, but they had to be landed again on 7–8 January due to congestion in the port of Bizerte, where the Spanish Republican fleet had been interned, and she returned to Toulon on 10 March.

The first two Latécoère 298 torpedo bombers arrived on 12 March. *Teste* began a major scheduled refit on 17 March, but due to the deteriorating political situation the work was accelerated and was completed on 20 April. She left immediately for Oran and Arzew, returning to Toulon on 11 May. She was assigned to the Mediterranean Squadron on the same day. She took part in a short cruise by the Squadron along the coasts of Provence from 31 May to 9 June. The Mediterranean Squadron became the Mediterranean Fleet on 10 July 1939.

There were sorties to Les Salins and Saint-Raphaël in late July and early August. *Teste* returned to Toulon on 10 August and joined the old battleships *Provence*, *Bretagne* and *Lorraine*, which had arrived from Brest on 22 July. A general exercise took place on 10 August between the Balearics and the Gulf of Genoa.

*Commandant Teste* was at Toulon on 23–24 August and embarked HS1 with six Loire 130 reconnaissance aircraft and HB1 with eight Laté 298 torpedo bombers. She left Toulon on 24 August and arrived at Oran on the 27th. She was then incorporated into the 6th Squadron, which was based at Oran to complement the activities in the Western Mediterranean of the British at Gibraltar.

## THE SECOND WORLD WAR

*Commandant Teste* remained at Oran, but the exposure of the port to the wind meant that it was unsuited to seaplane operations. HB1 was flown to Arzew on 31 August. The ship remained at Oran until 18 December with HS1, which was likewise transferred to Arzew on the 13th. She then returned to Toulon, arriving on the 20th.

*Teste* would go on to serve as an aircraft transport between metropolitan France and North Africa. She departed Toulon on 30 December and headed for Les Salins to embark thirty-one aircraft. She arrived at Bizerte on 1 January, landed the planes and returned to Toulon on the 3rd. She left again on 11 January for Hyères and Brégançon, and embarked twenty-five trainers together with two Laté 298 for HB1. She was at Bizerte on 15–16 January 1940 and returned on the 18th. A third transport mission took place from 22 January to 3 February, when she embarked twenty-two wheeled aircraft and the last three Laté 298 intended for HB1 at Hyères and headed for Bizerte.

Air group F1H was officially disembarked on 1 February; HS1, HB1 and the newly formed HB2 were based at Karouba air base in Tunisia.

*Commandant Teste* left Toulon on 8 February for Hyères, where she embarked twenty-six Morane 406 for GC I/7 and a Caudron Simoun liaison aircraft intended for the Levant. She sailed on the 11th, called in at Bizerte on the 13th and arrived at Beirut on 19 February. She returned to Toulon on 5 March. She left again on the 15th for Les Salins and embarked eleven Dewoitine 501 and six Loire 46 fighter aircraft, which she disembarked at Algiers on 19–20 March. Returning to Hyères on the 21st, she embarked thirty Caproni 164 and twelve Morane 230 trainers, which she landed at Algiers on the 23rd. She then returned again to Hyères, and on the evening of the 24th embarked twenty-nine Morane, six Caproni, a Hanriot and two Dewoitine 501, which she landed at Algiers on the 26th. She was at Toulon from 27 April to 1 May, embarking thirteen Potez 63-11, two Loire 130 and eleven vehicles for Beirut then, on the 3rd, embarked six Potez 63-11 and a Morane 406 for Port Said at Hyères. She was at Bizerte on 4–5 May, Alexandria on the 8th, Port Said on 9–10 May, and Beirut from 11 to 14 May, returning to Algiers on the 18th. She then embarked thirty-eight vehicles for the 62nd Bomber Squadron (Glenn Martin 167F) and returned to Toulon on the 20th.

She left again on the 22nd, embarking forty Caudron Simoun that she landed at Algiers. She returned to Hyères on the 26th to embark twenty-three Morane 230, fifteen Simoun and two Bloch 81; these were landed at Algiers, where she embarked the forty vehicles belonging to the 2nd group of the 62nd Squadron on the 28th, returning to Toulon on the 30th.

On 10 June, *Teste* began to embark aircraft from Hyères, but the entry of Italy into the war interrupted the operation and she returned to Toulon on the 11th. She was there during the Italian bombing raid of 13 June, and was complimented on the density of the

**Right:** Another photo of *Commandant Teste* taken between 19 and 26 February 1940 at Beirut, where she disembarked Morane-Saulnier MS.406 fighters of GC I/7. *(ECPAD)*

barrage she put up from her anti-aircraft guns. She resumed the embarkation of aircraft at Hyères on 14 June, when she loaded forty trainers and five Potez 63 twin-engine multi-role aircraft. She left accompanied by the torpedo boats *Baliste* and *La Poursuivante*, was at Algiers from 16 to 18 June, and returned to Toulon on the 19th, the transit being marked by the sighting of two torpedo tracks which she manoeuvred to avoid.

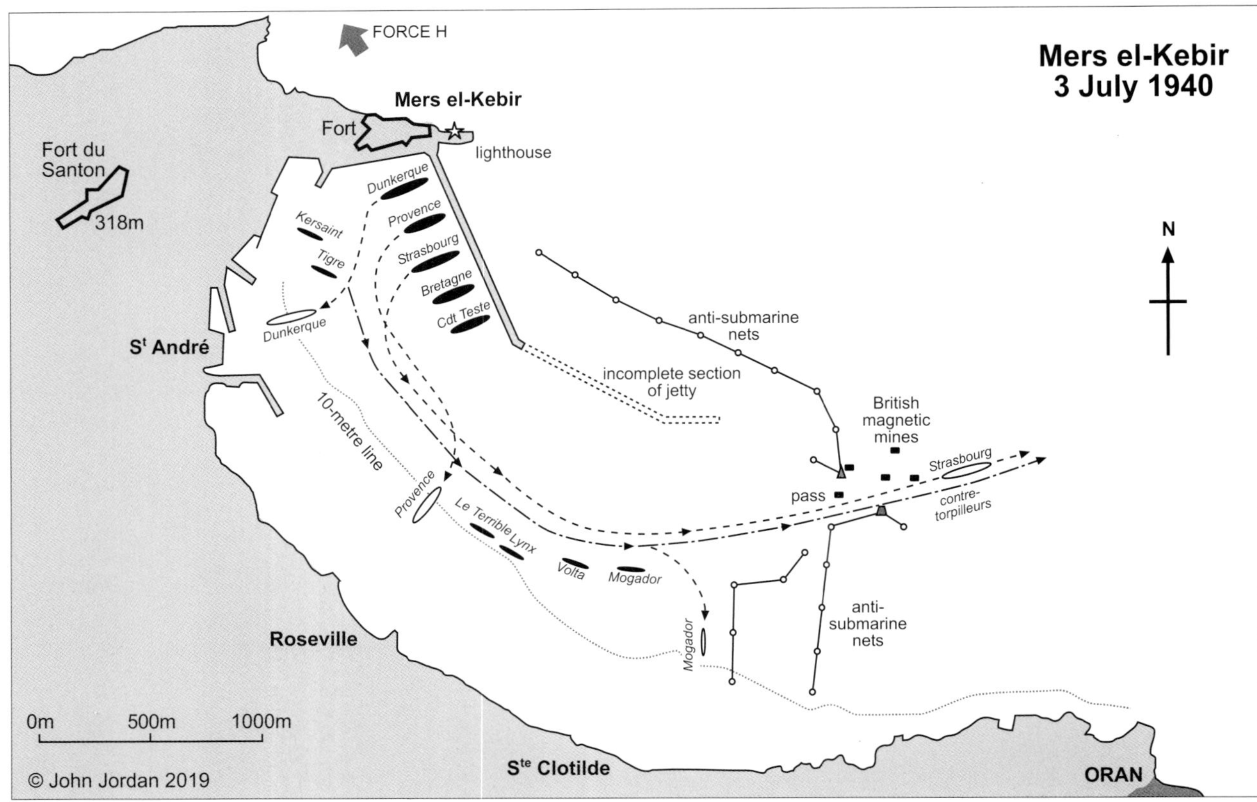

**Right:** The French squadron at Mers el-Kébir seen from the Santon heights shortly before the British attack on 3 July 1940. Moored with their sterns to the jetty are the battleships *Dunkerque*, *Provence*, *Strasbourg* and *Bretagne*, and beyond them *Commandant Teste*; in the foreground are the six *contre-torpilleurs* present in the anchorage. Note the darker 'Atlantic' grey of the two modern battleships. *(DR)*

On 20 June, the 3rd *Région maritime* began to evacuate materiel and *Teste* embarked Asdic A/S gear together with 251 personnel, 10 of whom were British. She left on the evening of the 20th, escorted by the *contre-torpilleur Kersaint* and by the *Baliste*. She arrived at Oran on the 22nd, unloaded and moved to Mers el-Kébir in order to free up space in the port of Oran. Immobilised following the Armistice, she was moored with her stern to the jetty, at Post No 9. To starboard were ranged the battleships *Bretagne*, *Strasbourg*, *Provence* and *Dunkerque*, the flagship of Vice Admiral Gensoul (see map and photo).

On 3 July 1940, the issuing of an ultimatum by the British was followed by discussions which concluded when Force 'H' opened fire on the immobilised French ships. The engagement lasted from 1656 to 1735. *Strasbourg* managed to cast off and escape to Toulon, *Bretagne* was sunk, and *Dunkerque* and *Provence* were hit several times by 15in (381mm) shell and had to be grounded. *Commandant Teste*, ironically the only unarmoured ship in the French squadron, received only light damage: she was struck by splinters that damaged her boats, penetrated bulkheads and passed through the upper part of her mainmast. Not a single member of her crew was wounded. She subsequently assisted with the rescue of survivors from the *Bretagne*, which had capsized only 150 metres away. Fifty men from *Bretagne* and the *contre-torpilleur Mogador*, which lost her stern to a 15in shell, were treated in the sick bay; six died. The ship had not been able to return fire due to the limited range of her guns.

*Teste* was moored in the anchorage of Oran during the evening. She sailed on the morning of the 4th, had a narrow escape from the British submarine *Proteus*, which was patrolling north of Cap de l'Aiguille, and moored off Arzew, leaving on the 6th for Bizerte, where she arrived on the evening of 7 July. She remained at Sidi-Abdallah, leaving on 16 October and arriving at Toulon on the 18th to be immobilised (*en gardiennage*) under the terms of the Armistice. She would be in dockyard hands for repair and maintenance during the early months of 1941.

## ARMISTICE 1940–42

The Franco-German protocol of 28 May 1941 allowed the French to reactivate a number of ships including *Commandant Teste*, which recommissioned 9 June 1941, in theory for the gunnery school. The aviation materiel was not put back on board and the catapults were disabled. The ship was assigned to the schools group of the 3rd *Région maritime* and was to be used to train apprentice gunners and rangefinder operators.

Below: *Commandant Teste* at Toulon following the Armistice, with her national recognition markings painted on the side of the hull. *(ARDHAN collection)*

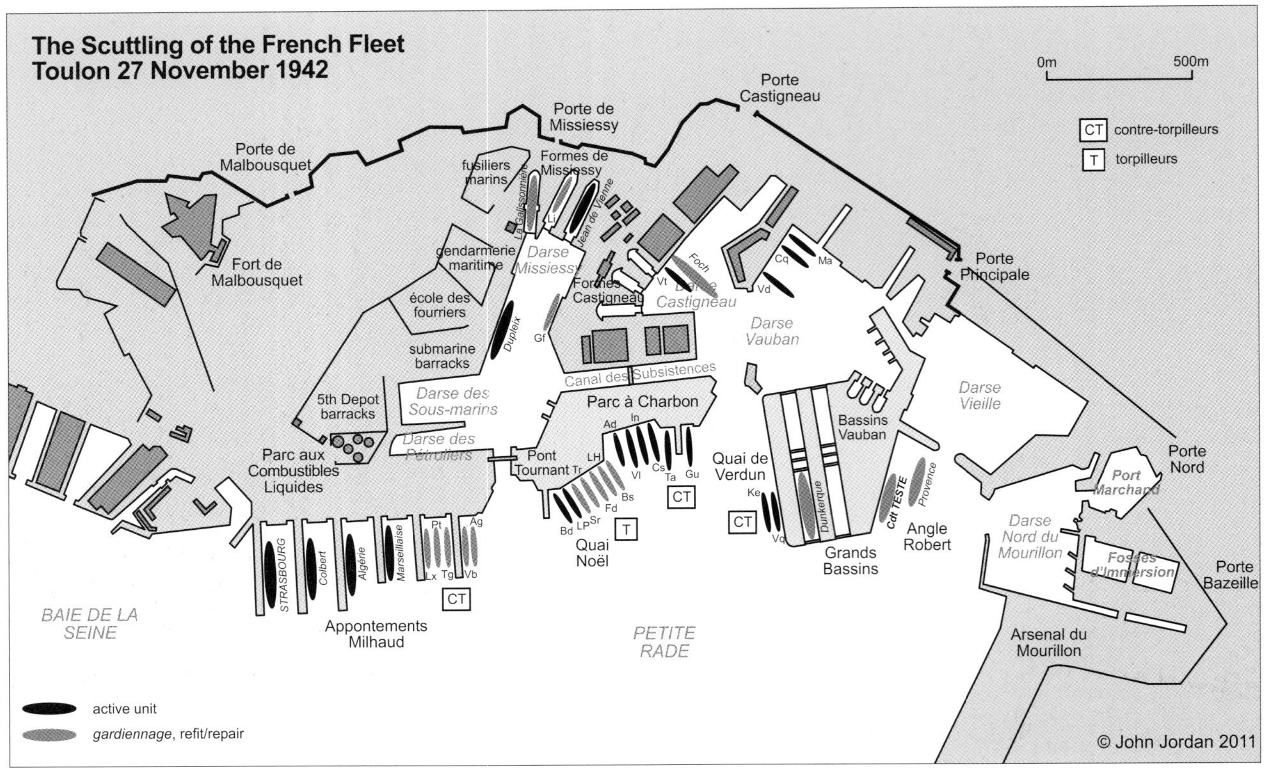


The first course began on 1 July, and there were sorties to Les Salins in November 1941, and January/February and April/May 1942. Following a short docking during July, she was again in the Les Salins anchorage from 1 to 11 August.

On 11 November, the Germans began their occupation of southern France and, on 26 November, a cohort of trainees was disembarked and sent to Cahors. The ship was at the Angle Robert to the east of the dockyard with her starboard side to the quay. At 0430 the following day there was an anti-aircraft alert. A battery of 13.2mm MG belonging to *Commandant Teste* fired to provide cover for the submarine *Le Glorieux*, which was attempting an escape from the Mourillon Basin with her engines in reverse. The volume of fire deterred the German air crews, notably a Ju-88 that was targeting *Le Glorieux*; a bomb fell some 70 metres from the submarine, which was the last to cast off and was able to make for Algiers.

At 0535, *Teste*'s crew received the order to prepare to

**Right:** *Commandant Teste* scuttled at the Angle Robert, Toulon. On the right of the picture is the battleship *Provence*. (SHD-M)

**Left:** *Commandant Teste* as Q113 in the Castigneau Basin in late 1954 when she was used as a store. The superstructures have been dismantled. *(Jean Moulin collection)*

scuttle the ship. The trainees had a hurried breakfast, then disembarked between 0545 and 0630. The order to scuttle was finally received at 0630 and operations began immediately. The seacocks were opened, and the ship quickly settled; everything was over by 0640. Four Germans came on board but the ship was soon evacuated in good order. At 0700, one of the Germans threatened to shoot the CO if the explosives were detonated. However, the ship was already resting on the bottom and now heeled first 10, then 15 degrees to port.

The Germans salvaged the anti-aircraft equipment that had not been sabotaged and the ship was stripped of everything of use. Work to raise the ship began on 26 March 1943. The 100mm HA guns were landed from 17 to 22 April and the ship was refloated on 11 May. She was in dock from 13 to 22 May without any work being undertaken, then towed to Milhaud and finally, on 3 January 1944, to Toulon roads.

Handed back to France on 15 May 1944, *Commandant Teste* was towed to Le Lazaret on the 19th and placed in care and maintenance. A team headed by Captain Emile Rosset, tasked with the conservation of the ships that had been handed over, placed a ring of barges around the ships at Le Lazaret to prevent the Germans from sinking them in the harbour narrows. The French were evacuated on 17 August, and the following day an Allied bombing raid sank the cruiser *La Galissonnière*. *Commandant Teste* was sunk on 19 August during a bombardment of Le Lazaret by the Allied fleet. She she emerged from the bombardment with with a list of 10 degrees to port.

She would be refloated a second time in February 1945. The hull and the machinery was judged to be 'in good condition'. Proposals to modify her as, first, an escort carrier, then as a trials ship for helicopters and missiles came to nothing due to lack of funds. The ship was mothballed during the fourth quarter of 1946. She was then moored quayside in the Castigneau Basin and used by the DCAN as a store for spares for ships of US Navy origin. She was stricken on 10 May 1950, becoming Q 113. She was sold on 14 November 1963 to the Société Navale du Midi and towed away on the 21st to be scrapped.

## CONCLUSION

Although the attack squadron of large sea-launched torpedo bombers represented something of a dead-end in naval warfare, the concept of a 'mobile aviation base' responded to French military requirements at a time when military facilities in the North African colonies were relatively underdeveloped, and *Commandant Teste* was to have an undeniable influence on the Japanese seaplane carriers of the *Chitose* and *Mizuho* classes built during the mid-1930s.

CHAPTER 4

# THE INTERWAR STUDIES PA1–15

UNDER THE TERMS OF THE WASHINGTON Treaty of February 1922, France was accorded 60,000 tons for the construction of aircraft carriers (Article VII). In order to give maximum flexibility in the use of the respective tonnage allocations, all aircraft carriers in existence or building on 21 November 1921 were to be considered 'experimental' and could be replaced at any time, regardless of age (Article VIII). The maximum displacement allowed was 27,000 long tons (Article IX); the largest-calibre gun permitted was 8in/203mm and the maximum number that could be mounted was ten (Article X).

The Imperial Japanese Navy would take full advantage of these provisions in their conversions of the battlecruisers *Akagi* and *Amagi* (the latter replaced by the battleship *Kaga* following the Tokyo earthquake of 1 September 1923). The US Navy was granted an exception to the tonnage limitation to enable it to complete the two battlecruisers *Lexington* and *Saratoga* as aircraft carriers of 33,000 tons, but kept close to the maximum armament allowed. However, the 'light battlecruisers' that the British opted to convert, *Courageous* and *Glorious*, belonged to an earlier generation of capital ships and would displace only 22,500 tons when completed as aircraft carriers, and it was decided that a heavy gun armament was out of the question; they mounted only HA guns for defence against aircraft, and would rely on other fleet units to protect them against enemy surface vessels larger than a destroyer.

The figure of 60,000 tons agreed for France and Italy during the Washington negotiations exceeded the 54,000 tons that might have been expected had the same 5:3:1.75 ratio that governed capital ship displacement been applied. The figures agreed for the two major contracting powers and Japan were multiples of the maximum unit displacement of 27,000 tons: 135,000 tons (= five units) for Britain and the USA, 81,000 tons (= three units) for Japan. The French delegation to the conference, supported by the Italians, argued that two aircraft carriers would not constitute a viable force, given that one ship would normally be in refit, and that building three hulls within the 54,000-ton allocation being proposed, while feasible, would mean that each unit would be significantly less capable than the 27,000-ton vessels likely to be built by the other powers. A compromise was reached that, in theory, permitted the two minor contracting powers three carriers each of 20,000 tons, without prejudice to the possibility that either might opt to build two ships of the maximum 27,000 tons or four ships each of 15,000 tons; given the embryonic nature of naval aviation, the latter course of action was considered eminently practicable. These arguments set the parameters for future planning once the *Marine Nationale* had realised its first 'experimental' conversion in the form of *Béarn*.

In the interim, the Navy looked into the feasibility of a hybrid cruiser-carrier of 10,000 tons. A Note of 10 December proposed the construction of a ship of 10,000 tons standard displacement armed with six 203mm guns mounted as a twin turret and four casemates, and capable of embarking fifteen aircraft; speed was to be 28–30 knots and there would be eight 75mm HA guns for defence against enemy aircraft. Under the terms of the Treaty such a vessel would not be counted as part of the tonnage allocation for aircraft carriers, so could be built in unlimited numbers – a loophole that would be exploited by the Japanese with the original design of the light carrier *Ryūjō* but which would subsequently be closed by the London Treaty of 1930.

In the aftermath of Washington the priority for the *Marine Nationale* was the construction of a new generation of fast, lightly protected cruisers, flotilla craft and submarines, which were ordered under the 1922 and 1924 programmes. These ambitious programmes, which aimed to completely rebuild the Navy as a modern, capable force able to hold its own against the combined navies of Italy and Germany, were not only costly and difficult to implement given the destruction of much of France's naval and industrial infrastructure during the Great War, but fully occupied the *Service Technique des Constructions Navales* (STCN), the directorate of construction and plans. It would be 1928, the year *Béarn* entered service, before the Navy again turned its attention to the issue of major fleet units, which were to include new capital ships and aircraft carriers.

With regard to aircraft carriers, a series of studies designated PA1–16 (PA = *porte-avions*) were undertaken between 1928 and 1938. These were generally 'paper' projects, exploring possible options without any likelihood that they would mature into firm proposals. Most were accompanied by sketches and technical data, but some were more developed than others. The documentation is patchy and much has not survived. However, a number of the plans were recovered from Potsdam in the early 1990s, with handwritten annotations in German and in Russian, and are currently held in the Centre d'Archives de l'Armement at Châtellerault. These have been used extensively in the preparation of this chapter.

What these studies tell us is that the French were exploring the same possibilities as the other major navies, that they were having to take into account the same considerations, and that they were facing the

**Left:** HMS *Eagle*, which influenced not only the overall configuration of *Béarn*, but the design of PA1 and her 'paper' successors. Note the cruciform lift at the forward end of the hangar, which enabled a fully deployed aircraft to be struck down, and the rectangular lift aft. *(David Hobbs collection)*

same constraints. The sketch plans for these projects feature carriers of the maximum 27,000 tons, intermediate ships of 18,000–20,000 tons, and small carriers of 13,000–15,000 tons. There were hybrids with a heavy anti-surface armament of 8in/203mm guns and a reduced complement of aircraft, ships with islands incorporating a large funnel, flush-deck types with either diesel propulsion or with the gases produced by their steam machinery evacuating, Japanese-fashion, from vents in the starboard side of the hull, ships with enclosed or 'open' bows, ships with varying degrees of protection, ships with single or multiple hangars, ships with aircraft lifts that were cruciform, 'T'-shaped or rectangular, and ships with innovative features such as an asymmetric flight deck and upper hangar.

## PA1–2: 1928–29

The two major preliminary designs studied during late 1928 and early 1929, designated PA1 and PA2, responded to an identical set of staff requirements: a displacement of 27,000 tons (the maximum permitted under Washington), a 'cruiser' armament of eight 8in guns comparable to the recently completed US and Japanese capital ship conversions (*Lexington*/*Saratoga* and *Akagi*/*Kaga*), a large battery of HA guns, protection for the hull, and a maximum speed of 27 knots; the carrier was to be able to operate an air group of forty planes with a dozen additional aircraft in reserve.

The resulting designs were similar in many respects, despite the categorisation of PA1 on the plans as an 'air-capable cruiser' (*croiseur d'aviation*) and her sister as an 'aircraft carrier' (*porte-avions*). However, there was one important difference that impacted on the configuration adopted: PA1 was powered by conventional geared steam turbines, whereas her 'half-sister' had a modern four-shaft diesel arrangement.

Diesels addressed a major concern with the aircraft carriers designed post-Washington: how to best dispose of the exhaust gases from the propulsion machinery. Combustion from the boilers associated with steam turbines generated huge quantities of funnel gases, and this was a particular issue for the battlecruiser hulls that the UK, the United States and Japan opted to convert. The British *Furious* and *Courageous* generated sufficient steam for 90,000shp; the figure for the IJN's *Kaga* was similar, while *Akagi* and the US Navy's *Lexingtons* had machinery delivering 130,000shp and 180,000shp respectively. For HMS *Furious* the Royal Navy opted for large-diameter horizontal exhaust trunking that emerged close to the stern of the ship, and this solution was also adopted for the Japanese *Kaga*; her battlecruiser counterpart *Akagi* had large funnel vents to starboard, which were inclined downwards to keep the hot exhaust gases clear of the flight deck. *Lexington* and *Saratoga* received a massive single funnel to starboard, while the British adopted a similar (albeit less extreme) arrangement for *Courageous* and *Glorious*, which were initially typed as 'funnel carriers'. A similar solution was adopted by the French for *Béarn*. However, the latter ship was converted from a battleship hull that had been designed for a maximum speed of only 21 knots, and the theoretical power output was a mere 40,000shp. It was estimated that the desired speed of 27 knots for the new ships would require double the power: 80,000shp (initially 60,000shp on three shafts was proposed, but this proved inadequate).

The pilots of the day found that landing on a ship generating large quantities of hot funnel gases was hazardous, as these were responsible for considerable air turbulence over the flight deck. Further turbulence was generated by an island offset to port or to starboard, hence the contemporary predilection in aviation circles for a flush deck. This was attempted in the purpose-built USS *Ranger* (CV-4), which had three small hinged funnels on either side of the flight deck that could be lowered to the horizontal position when conducting air operations. However, *Ranger* was a relatively small ship (13,800tW as designed) with propulsion machinery delivering only 53,000shp. Moreover, a flush deck made it difficult to con the ship, and an island had the advantage of being able to accommodate spaces for the control of flight deck operations and a mast on which fire control installations and searchlights could be mounted and from which signal halyards and W/T aerials could be suspended.

With the PA1 and PA2 designs the *Service Technique* attempted to evaluate both alternatives. In order to achieve the desired 80,000shp, PA1 was given a conventional four-shaft steam plant and the funnel gases evacuated through a tall, narrow funnel to port broadly similar in configuration to that of *Béarn*. For PA2, on the other hand, a more radical solution was adopted: the ship would have a completely flush deck, with power supplied by no fewer than sixteen diesel engines driving four shafts.

The diesel engine had long established itself as the main powerplant for submarines when operating on the surface. However, its employment in naval surface units was still in its infancy due to the limited horsepower available from a single engine and the difficulty of combining multiple engines on a single propeller shaft. From 1924, the *Marine Nationale* had embarked on a series of 'fleet' submarines of 1,500 tonnes displacement powered by large two-stroke diesels from the Swiss company Sulzer – some were built under licence by the French company Schneider – and was on the point of ordering a sub-group (M6 *Agosta* group, 1930 Estimates) that had a Sulzer diesel rated at 4000bhp on each of its two shafts. The Navy would undoubtedly also have been aware that the German *Reichsmarine* had just laid down (in February 1929) the first of a series of 'armoured ships' (*Panzerschiffe*) armed with six 28cm guns and powered by eight large diesels of a new type designed and manufactured by MAN. These revolutionary vessels caused a considerable stir: their diesel propulsion plant gave them not only exceptional endurance at cruise speeds, but could drive them at a maximum speed of 26 knots. These 9-cylinder, 2-stroke M9Z 42/58 MAN diesels had a theoretical unit power rating of 7100bhp for a total of 56,800hp, and four engines were combined via gearing and a Vulcan clutch to each of the two shafts. It was therefore not inconceivable that a 2-stroke diesel rated at 5000bhp could be developed to deliver 80,000bhp, employing four units on each of the four shafts envisaged for the carrier. A diesel propulsion plant gave PA2 a theoretical range of 4360nm at 18 knots, whereas the comparable figure for PA1 was 3750nm.

There was a downside to the main propulsion diesel that had yet to be fully appreciated. Rotary engines such as turbines, particularly when driving through reduction gearing, were very efficient at higher speeds, whereas the diesel engine, like the reciprocating engine that preceded it, disliked being run at maximum power for long periods due to vibration in the piston cylinders, and was prone to wear and breakdown if employed in this way. Moreover, diesels often failed to make their designed power rating in service: the total horsepower available to the German *Panzerschiff Deutschland* was subsequently reassessed as 41,500bhp (4200bhp per engine).[1] Submarines rarely ran their engines at more than 70 per cent of their power rating in order to reduce wear and tear; the main benefit of the diesel was the added range that enabled them to undertake lengthy transits and

## Table 1: FRENCH CARRIER PROJECTS 1928–29

| | PA1 | PA2 |
|---|---|---|
| **Displacement:** | | |
| standard | 27,400TW | 28,500TW |
| normal | 30,641t | n/a |
| **Dimensions:** | | |
| length pp | 236m | [as PA1] |
| beam wl | 29m | [as PA1] |
| depth of keel | 8m | [as PA1] |
| **Propulsion:** | | |
| type | steam turbines | diesel [x 16] |
| horsepower | 80,000cv | [as PA1] |
| max speed | 27 knots | [as PA1] |
| no of shafts | four | four |
| endurance | 3750nm at 18kts | 4360nm at 18kts |
| **Flight Deck:** | | |
| total length | 164m | 156m |
| horizontal section | 156m | 148m |
| max width | 27m | [as PA1] |
| **Hangars & cranes:** | | |
| cranes | one | two |
| catapults | one fixed, one trainable | [as PA1] |
| lifts (L x W) | two 12m x 11m | two 15m x 11m |
| upper hangar | 148m x 27m | [as PA1] |
| lower hangar | 96m x 12m | 92m x 15m |
| **Aircraft:** | | |
| upper hangar | 40 | [as PA1] |
| lower hangar | 12 | 14 |
| total | 52 | 54 |
| | [uniform type: 11.6m x 5m wings folded] | |
| **Armament:** | | |
| main guns | 8 – 203mm (4xII) | [as PA1] |
| HA guns | 12 – 100mm (12xI) | 14 – 100mm (14xI) |
| light AA | 8 – 37mm (8xI) | 4? – 37mm (4xI) |
| **Protection:** | | |
| side belt | – | 100mm |
| deck | 16+16/40 | [as PA1] |
| torpedo bulkhead | 40mm | [as PA1] |

**Note on displacements:**
TW long tons (Washington standard)
t metric tons (tonnes)

[1] For the figures cited here, see MJ Whitley, *German Capital Ships of World War Two* (Arms & Armour Press, 1989).

**Above:** A well-known photo of the Japanese *Kaga*, clearly showing the twin 20cm turrets on either side of the forecastle. Six Type 3 fighters (*kanjō sentōki*) can be seen on the lower flight deck, which was used for unassisted take-offs. Eight Type 13 attack planes (*kanjō kōgekiki*) can be seen on the upper flight deck, which was used both for launching and landing planes. The photo was taken in 1930. *(Lars Ahlberg collection)*

patrols. However, it would be some time before the limitations of the diesel engine became apparent, and the vision of ever larger and more powerful diesels capable of powering major surface vessels would continue to excite the imagination of European and Japanese naval engineers.[2]

### General Configuration

The PA1 and PA2 designs had a remarkably similar overall configuration, despite the differences in their propulsion machinery. Both had a hull with a length between perpendiculars of 236 metres and a beam at the waterline of 29 metres; draught was approximately 8 metres.

There were two capacious superimposed hangars, and these were intended to function as in *Béarn*: the upper hangar was intended to house the operational air group, and the lower was to be employed for maintenance and to accommodate reserve aircraft. The upper hangar had a length of 148 metres (including lifts) and was 26/27 metres wide; it could hold forty aircraft, the estimated dimensions of each individual plane being estimated at 11.60m by 6.00m (wings folded). The adoption of diesel propulsion for PA2 meant that the width of the lower hangar could be increased from 12 metres to 15 metres due to the reduced cross-section of the exhaust uptakes (see section drawings). In compensation it was shorter than the lower hangar in PA1: 92 metres *vice* 96 metres. It was estimated that PA1 would be able to accommodate twelve reserve aircraft, a figure that increased to fourteen in PA2.

Twin 203mm turrets were located in a four-square arrangement fore and aft of the hangar. The arrangement of the forward turrets reflected the layout adopted by the Japanese designers for *Akagi* and *Kaga*, but the French opted for a similar arrangement aft in preference to that of the IJN carriers, which had their after 20cm guns in casemates, thereby allowing the flight deck to be extended over the stern with the ships' boats stowed on platforms beneath. The upper hangar of PA1 and PA2 had doors that opened onto the forecastle and the quarterdeck. The doors gave access

2 The German *Schlachtschiff 'H'* of December 1936 was to have been propelled by twelve 9-cylinder 2-stroke MAN diesel engines, each rated at 13,500–16,100bhp on three shafts, for a total of 165,000bhp. The IJN 'super-battleships' of the *Yamato* class were likewise initially to have been powered by large diesel engines.

**Right:** *Akagi* at sea probably in 1928, with the 20cm twin turrets in place. The Type 13 torpedo bombers on her flight deck were undergoing launch training. The upper flight deck was 190m long and 30.5m wide, which was approximately 20m longer than *Kaga's* and is evidence of *Akagi's* battlecruiser origins. *(Lars Ahlberg collection)*

to a fixed catapult on the forecastle above the bow and a trainable catapult with a 22-metre beam (presumably the same model mounted in contemporary French cruisers) above the stern. At least one plan of a PA1 variant shows an aircraft crane mounted alongside the catapult aft on the port side, but the PA2 plans show a quarterdeck cut down to bring the catapult beam to the same level as the hangar floor, thereby enabling aircraft to be wheeled out on their launch trolleys directly onto the catapult; the plane would presumably have been recovered by one of the cranes mounted on either side of the flight deck and struck down in the hangar using one of the lifts.

The advantage of this arrangement was that a reconnaissance seaplane (a CAMS 37 is depicted in one of the PA1 plans) could be launched without interfering with operations involving wheeled aircraft on the flight deck and, in the case of the trainable catapult aft, without the carrier needing to steam directly into the wind (and possibly having to leave the main body of the fleet in order to undertake this manoeuvre).

The flight deck itself was 27 metres wide and extended beyond the hangar at its after end, the last 8 metres being inclined downwards as in *Béarn*. PA1 also had an 8-metre (horizontal) extension at its forward end, but this was not possible in PA2 because it would have obstructed the view from the navigation bridge, which due to the lack of an island needed to be accommodated above the forward end of the hangar, as in the flush-decked HMS *Furious*. Total length was therefore 164 metres in PA1 and 156 metres in PA2 – more than sufficient to launch or recover one of the wheeled aircraft of the day.

There were to be two aircraft lifts and, according to at least one of the plans, four arrester cables of the new Schneider-Fieux type (see drawing of PA1). The lifts in the early variants of PA1 were broadly square in configuration, 12 metres long and 11 metres wide. Those on later variants and on PA2 were significantly longer, approximately 15m x 11.5m, and could therefore have accommodated more advanced types of aircraft. Even the larger lifts, however, would have required the wings of all except fighters to be folded before the aircraft was struck down in the hangar, so moving the first lift farther forward in PA2 to clear the landing zone made considerable sense.

The plans show tanks for aviation fuel fore and aft in both PA1 and PA2. Beneath the lifts were large stores for aviation materiel. The lift platforms were presumably fitted with rails beneath (see *Béarn*) to enable them to move large items to the hangar decks using block and tackle. The bomb lifts were grouped with the magazines for the guns.

### Self-defence

In addition to the eight 203mm guns in twin turrets, which were intended for use against hostile surface units, there were to be twelve single 100mm Mle 1927 HA guns of the type that would arm *Commandant Teste* (see Chapter 3). These were mounted in pairs on either side of the flight deck fore and aft. The plans of the PA2 design show an additional pair of guns mounted on either side of the low quarterdeck, where they were less likely to be damaged by the blast of the after 203mm guns. PA1 would have also had eight single 37mm AA guns, divided between the forecastle and the quarterdeck. PA2, which had the additional pair of 100mm HA guns, appears to have had only four 37mm, but the mountings were more favourably positioned on either side of the flight deck amidships (see plans).

Fire control for the 100mm guns was provided by a single HA director on either side of the flight deck, and there was a single calculating position (forward in PA1, aft in PA2). PA1 also had a fully-fledged director control tower (DCT) for the main 203mm low angle

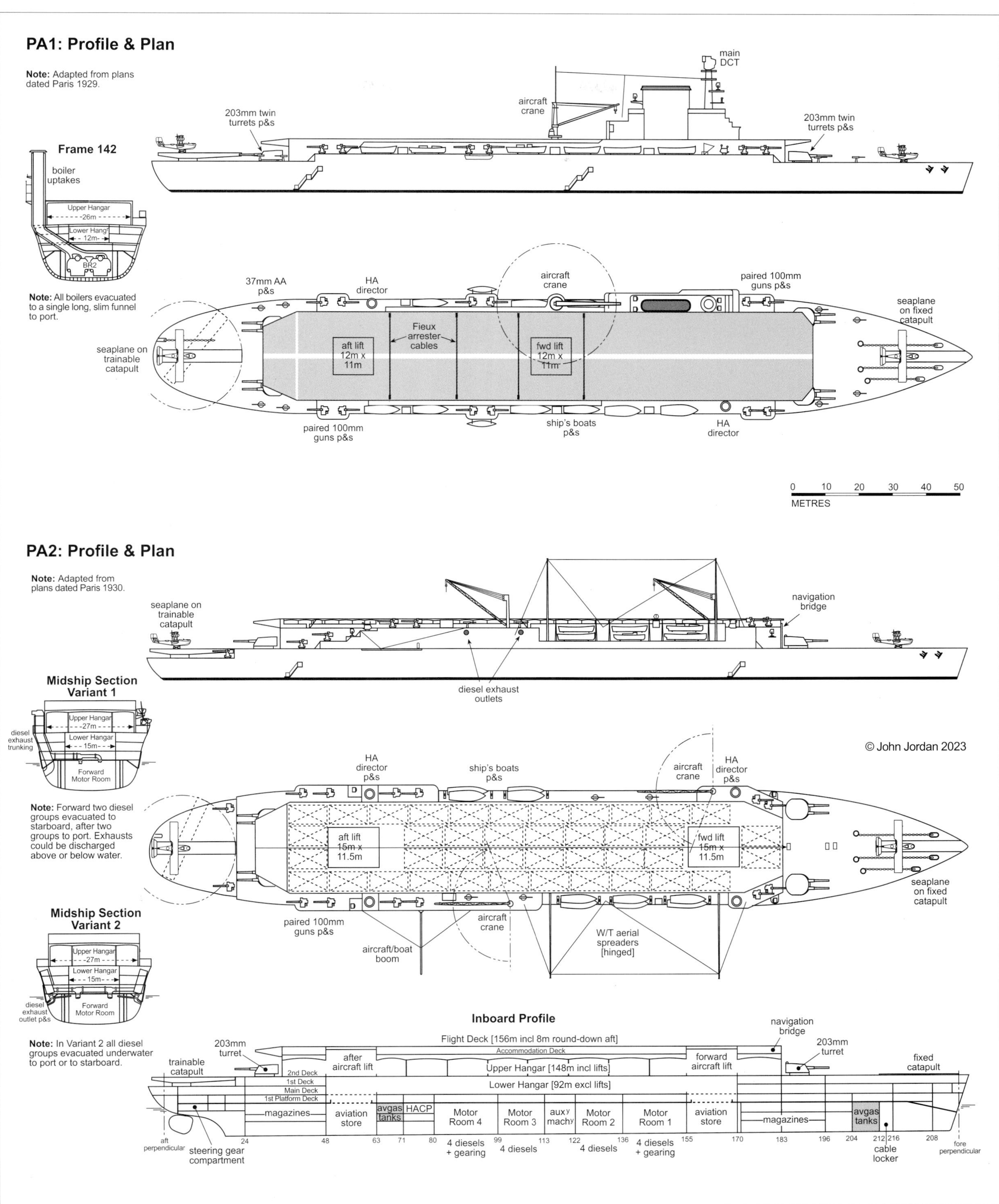
PA1: Profile & Plan
Note: Adapted from plans dated Paris 1929.
main DCT
aircraft crane
203mm twin turrets p&s
203mm twin turrets p&s
Frame 142
boiler uptakes
Upper Hangar
26m
Lower Hangar
12m
BR2
Note: All boilers evacuated to a single long, slim funnel to port.
37mm AA p&s
HA director
aircraft crane
paired 100mm guns p&s
seaplane on fixed catapult
seaplane on trainable catapult
aft lift 12m x 11m
Fieux arrester cables
fwd lift 12m x 11m
paired 100mm guns p&s
ship's boats p&s
HA director
0 10 20 30 40 50
METRES
PA2: Profile & Plan
Note: Adapted from plans dated Paris 1930.
seaplane on trainable catapult
navigation bridge
diesel exhaust outlets
Midship Section Variant 1
Upper Hangar
27m
Lower Hangar
15m
diesel exhaust trunking
Forward Motor Room
© John Jordan 2023
HA director p&s
ship's boats p&s
aircraft crane
HA director p&s
Note: Forward two diesel groups evacuated to starboard, after two groups to port. Exhausts could be discharged above or below water.
aft lift 15m x 11.5m
fwd lift 15m x 11.5m
seaplane on fixed catapult
Midship Section Variant 2
Upper Hangar
27m
Lower Hangar
15m
diesel exhaust outlet p&s
Forward Motor Room
paired 100mm guns p&s
aircraft/boat boom
aircraft crane
W/T aerial spreaders [hinged]
Inboard Profile
Note: In Variant 2 all diesel groups evacuated underwater to port or to starboard.
203mm turret
trainable catapult
Flight Deck [156m incl 8m round-down aft]
Accommodation Deck
after aircraft lift
Upper Hangar [148m incl lifts]
forward aircraft lift
navigation bridge
203mm turret
fixed catapult
2nd Deck
1st Deck
Main Deck
1st Platform Deck
Lower Hangar [92m excl lifts]
magazines
aviation store
avgas tanks
HACP
Motor Room 4
Motor Room 3
auxy machy
Motor Room 2
Motor Room 1
aviation store
magazines
avgas tanks
aft perpendicular
24
48
63
71
80
99
113
122
136
155
170
183
196
204
212
216
208
fore perpendicular
steering gear compartment
4 diesels + gearing
4 diesels
4 diesels
4 diesels + gearing
cable locker

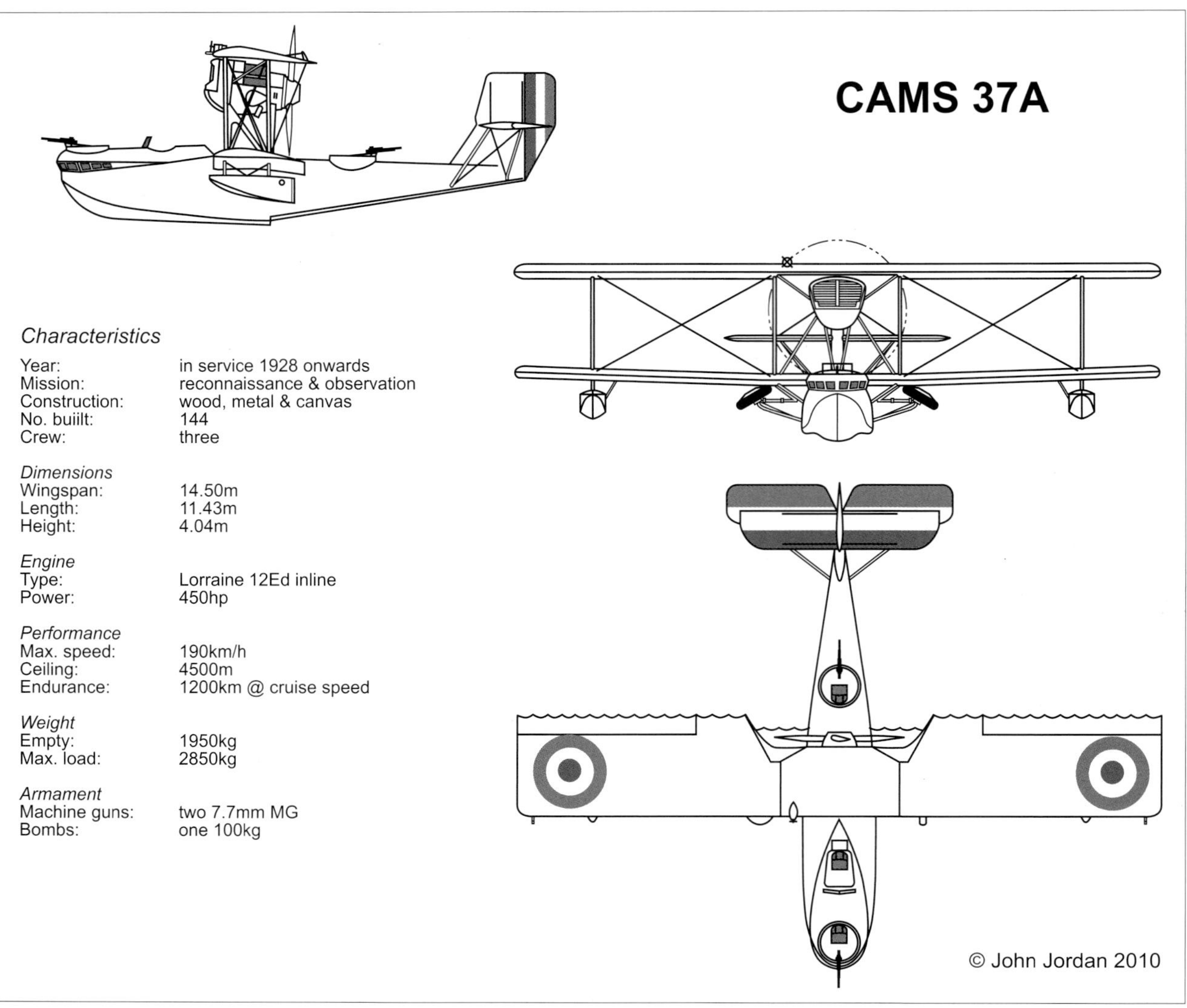


guns atop the foremast. This would have been the same model as that fitted in the latest treaty cruisers of the *Suffren* class, and it was paired with a transmitting station in the upper part of the island superstructure. This arrangement was problematic in the flush-decked PA2 design, and there is no evidence in the plans of either a DCT or a transmitting station, although the forward turrets appear to be fitted with rangefinders.

Passive protection for the magazines, avgas tanks and magazines against shell fire and the torpedo comprised a side belt combined with an armoured deck sloped downwards to meet the lower edge of the belt. The deck comprised two plates of 16mm steel on the flat, with the upper layer reinforced to 40mm (probably of special steel) on the slopes. The Main Deck and 2nd (Hangar) Deck above comprised a double layer of 12mm steel. The belt was of 100mm special steel, but is shown only in the plans of PA2. This may account for the higher displacement of the latter design, which is tabulated as 28,500 metric tons standard as compared with 27,400 long tons for PA1. It should be noted that the former figure is above the maximum displacement allowed under Washington, so weight savings in the final design might have been required.

In the event, neither of these ships was built, but the design process continued throughout the first half of the next decade.

## THE LONDON CONFERENCE OF 1930

The London Conference convened to review and amend the Washington Treaty took place between January and April 1930. Two key decisions regarding aircraft carriers emerged: the allocation of 60,000 tons of new tonnage for France and Italy was confirmed; and the possibility of building aircraft carriers up to 10,000 tons standard displacement outside treaty limitations was closed off, leaving Japan with a difficult decision to make regarding *Ryūjō*, which was already on the stocks.

The large French programme of flotilla craft and submarines was nearing completion, and France was now looking to build a new generation of capital ships, which would ideally be accompanied by aircraft carriers. The new battleships would be designed for high speed (29 knots for *Dunkerque* and *Strasbourg* as completed), so the carriers would need to be faster than PA1 and PA2 to enable them to manoeuvre while operating their aircraft in proximity to the fleet.

These considerations seem to have provided the rationale for the series of carrier designs requested from the STCN in 1930. PA3, which was presented for discussion as early as March (*ie* before the closure of the conference), had a displacement of 13,500–15,000 tons, allowing four ships to be built within the 60,000-ton allocation; her relatively small size was undoubtedly influenced by the contemporary USS *Ranger*, which had been authorised by Congress in February

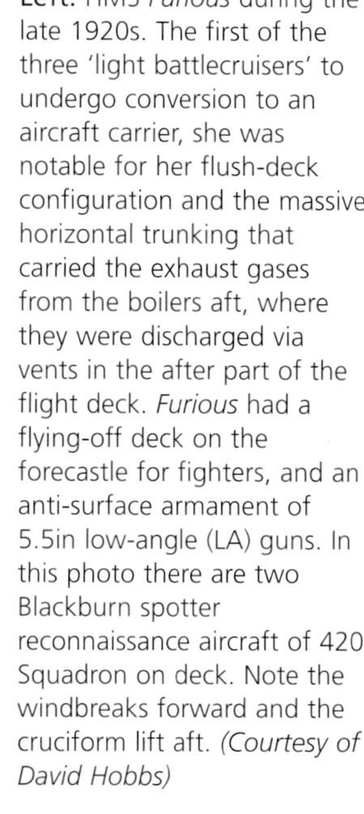

**Left:** HMS *Furious* during the late 1920s. The first of the three 'light battlecruisers' to undergo conversion to an aircraft carrier, she was notable for her flush-deck configuration and the massive horizontal trunking that carried the exhaust gases from the boilers aft, where they were discharged via vents in the after part of the flight deck. *Furious* had a flying-off deck on the forecastle for fighters, and an anti-surface armament of 5.5in low-angle (LA) guns. In this photo there are two Blackburn spotter reconnaissance aircraft of 420 Squadron on deck. Note the windbreaks forward and the cruciform lift aft. *(Courtesy of David Hobbs)*

**Left:** HMS *Courageous*, one of the three Royal Navy 'light battlecruisers' to undergo a carrier conversion during the 1920s. These ships had a major influence on the PA design series from about 1930. They retained the short flying-off deck of *Furious* forward of the upper hangar, but had a uniform HA armament of sixteen 4.7in (120mm) guns with no LA guns. Note the aircraft lifts, which were positioned at either end of the hangar. *(John Jordan collection)*

1929 but was yet to be laid down. PA4 was to have displaced 19,000–21,000 tons, which would have allowed three ships to be built, and PA5 was a ship of 24,500–27,000 tons (the maximum allowed under Washington), so only two ships of this size would have been permitted.

These three designs were strikingly similar in their general configuration, which appears to have been heavily influenced by the converted British carriers *Courageous* and *Glorious*, the first of which entered service in 1928. All were 'funnel carriers', with an island similar to that of *Béarn* to starboard, a uniform armament of HA guns, and a flight deck that ended well short of the bow with cruciform aircraft lifts at either end. The twin Mle 1931 mountings for the 100/45 guns were the same model as those fitted in the latest treaty cruiser, *Algérie*; four were to be fitted on the forecastle forward of the hangar and two at the stern.

PA4 and PA5 had two superimposed hangars, as in the British carriers, while for the smaller PA3 only a single hangar was possible (as in *Ranger*). This governed the size of the air group, which was 21 in PA3, 38 in PA4, and 52 in PA5. In the latter design fighter aircraft could be launched without catapult assistance from the forecastle as in the British and IJN carrier conversions; they were simply wheeled out of the forward end of the hangar and took off under their own power with the carrier steaming into the wind.

All three designs were powered by steam turbines. Total horsepower in PA3 was 80,000shp for 30 knots; in PA4 it was 105,000shp for 31 knots, and in PA5, 130,000shp for 31.5 knots. Endurance at 15 knots was 5000nm, 6000nm and 7000nm respectively. Protection was a 50mm belt with a 80/30mm deck in PA3, and a 100mm belt with a 100/40mm deck in the other two designs.

## PA6–7: 1930–31

The French Naval General Staff was clearly unhappy with the abandonment of low-angle guns in favour of a uniform HA armament, as the plans for PA6, dating from later in the year, and PA7 (early 1931) saw a reversion to the hybrid *croiseur d'aviation* type, and were almost certainly influenced by American proposals for a 'flying deck cruiser'. The latter had emerged from internal discussions among the US delegation to the London Conference concerning how best to utilise an allocation for light cruiser tonnage that the US Navy considered surplus to its requirements. The US Navy was interested in a 10,000-ton ship with three triple 6in (152mm) turrets forward, cruiser-scale protection for the hull, and a flight deck and hangar aft for twenty-four fighters and dive bombers. The advantage of a larger *croiseur d'aviation* for the French was that, while it would have to be counted under carrier tonnage, aircraft carriers were still permitted 8in guns, whereas this calibre was no longer available to cruisers under the London Treaty, so France would effectively gain an additional 'treaty cruiser' capable of operating aircraft. The displacement recorded on the sole plan to have survived was 19,230 metric tons standard; in the normal condition it was 21,000 metric tons.

Like the US Navy's Flying Deck Cruiser, PA6 had a relatively short flight deck (128m x 30m) that ended well short of the bow, with cruciform lifts 13m x 15m at the forward and after ends of the hangars as in the British *Courageous*. The lifts were sized to accommodate the latest torpedo bombers, which could be struck down with their wings deployed; the wings would be folded manually once the aircraft was lowered to the hangar, thereby speeding up the process of landing, securing and stowing the aircraft. Four of the new Schneider-Fieux arrester cables are shown in the

**Below:** USS *Ranger* (CV-4), designed and built from the keel up, was a revolutionary, if ultimately unsuccessful design. On a design displacement of only 13,800 tons, she could support an air group of no fewer than seventy-two fighters, scouts and dive bombers. Every 'ship' feature was subordinated to the operation of aircraft: a flush deck (although *Ranger* would be completed with a small island), a large, rectangular flight deck with no round-down (to maximise deck parking), and a capacious hangar below with exceptional overhead clearance, served by three large, rectangular aircraft lifts. The boiler exhausts were led up into six hinged funnels to the sides and there was a uniform dual-purpose armament of 5in (127mm) guns. *Ranger* is seen here at Guantanamo Bay, Cuba, in 1939. *(NHHC, 80-G-391559)*

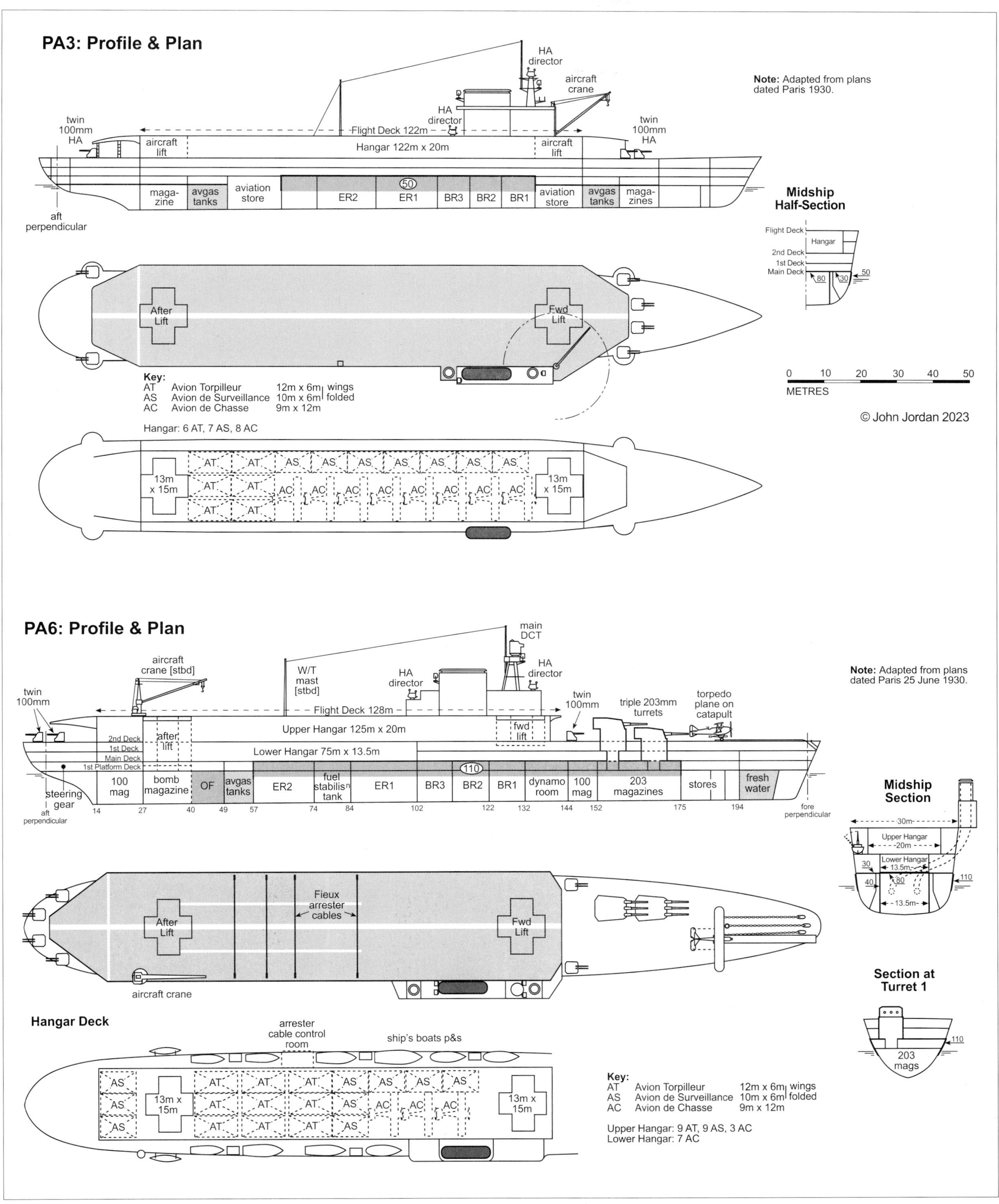
PA3: Profile & Plan
HA director
aircraft crane
Note: Adapted from plans dated Paris 1930.
twin 100mm HA
HA director
Flight Deck 122m
twin 100mm HA
aircraft lift
Hangar 122m x 20m
aircraft lift
maga-zine
avgas tanks
aviation store
50
ER2
ER1
BR3
BR2
BR1
aviation store
avgas tanks
maga-zines
aft perpendicular
Midship Half-Section
Flight Deck
Hangar
2nd Deck
1st Deck
Main Deck
80
30
50
After Lift
Fwd Lift
0 10 20 30 40 50
METRES
© John Jordan 2023
Key:
AT Avion Torpilleur 12m x 6m wings
AS Avion de Surveillance 10m x 6m folded
AC Avion de Chasse 9m x 12m
Hangar: 6 AT, 7 AS, 8 AC
13m x 15m
13m x 15m
PA6: Profile & Plan
main DCT
aircraft crane [stbd]
W/T mast [stbd]
HA director
HA director
Note: Adapted from plans dated Paris 25 June 1930.
twin 100mm
Flight Deck 128m
twin 100mm
triple 203mm turrets
torpedo plane on catapult
2nd Deck
1st Deck
Main Deck
1st Platform Deck
after lift
Upper Hangar 125m x 20m
fwd lift
Lower Hangar 75m x 13.5m
110
100 mag
bomb magazine
OF
avgas tanks
ER2
fuel stabilisn tank
ER1
BR3
BR2
BR1
dynamo room
100 mag
203 magazines
stores
fresh water
steering gear
aft perpendicular
14 27 40 49 57 74 84 102 122 132 144 152 175 194
fore perpendicular
Midship Section
30m
Upper Hangar
20m
Lower Hangar
13.5m
30
80
40
110
13.5m
Fieux arrester cables
After Lift
Fwd Lift
aircraft crane
Section at Turret 1
110
203 mags
Hangar Deck
arrester cable control room
ship's boats p&s
13m x 15m
13m x 15m
Key:
AT Avion Torpilleur 12m x 6m wings
AS Avion de Surveillance 10m x 6m folded
AC Avion de Chasse 9m x 12m
Upper Hangar: 9 AT, 9 AS, 3 AC
Lower Hangar: 7 AC

## Table 2: FRENCH CARRIER PROJECTS 1930–31

| | PA3 | PA4 | PA5 | PA6 | PA7 |
|---|---|---|---|---|---|
| Displacement: | | | | | |
| standard | 13,500tW | 19,000tW | 24,500tW | 19,230tW | 17,335tW |
| normal | 15,000t | 21,000t | 27,000t | 21,000t | n/a |
| Dimensions: | | | | | |
| length pp | 190m | 210m | 224m | 210m | 200m |
| beam wl | 23m | 26m | 27m | 26m | 24.5m |
| depth of keel | 6.6m | 7.5m | 8m | 7.5m | 7.1m |
| Propulsion: | | | | | |
| type | steam turbines | steam turbines | steam turbines | steam turbines | diesels [x 8] |
| horsepower | 80,000cv | 105,000cv | 130,000cv | 105,000cv | 96,000cv |
| max speed | 30 knots | 31 knots | 31.5 knots | 31 knots | 30 knots |
| no of shafts | four | four | four | four | four |
| endurance | 5000nm at 15kts | 6000nm at 15kts | 7000nm at 15kts | 7000nm at 15kts | 8000nm at 15kts |
| Flight Deck(s): | | | | | |
| total length | 148m | 156m | 168m + 58m | 141m | 134m |
| horizontal section | 122m | n/a | n/a | 128m | n/a |
| max width | 27.5m | n/a | n/a | 30m | n/a |
| Hangars & cranes: | | | | | |
| cranes | one | one | one | one | one |
| catapults | – | – | – | one fixed | – |
| lifts (L x W) | two 13m x 15m | two 13m x 15m | two 13m x 15m | two 13 x 15m | two 13m x 15m |
| upper hangar | 122m x 20m | 126m x 20m | 126m z 20m | 125m x 20m | 107m x 20m |
| lower hangar | – | 90m x 13,5m | 80m x 20m | 75m x 13.5m | – |
| Aircraft: | | | | | |
| upper hangar | 21 | n/a | n/a | 21 | 18 |
| lower hangar | – | n/a | n/a | 7 | – |
| total | 21 | 38 | 48/52 | 28 | 18 |
| Armament: | | | | | |
| main guns | – | – | – | 6 x 203mm (2xIII) | [as A6] |
| HA guns | 12 – 100mm (6xII) | [as PA3] | [as PA3] | [as PA3] | [as PA3] |
| light AA | 8 – 37mm (8xI) | [as PA3] | [as PA3] | [as PA3] | [as PA3] |
| Protection: | | | | | |
| side belt | 50mm | 100mm | [as PA4] | 110mm | 110mm |
| dccks | 80/30mm | 100/40mm | [as PA4] | 80/30mm | [as PA3/4] |
| torpedo bulkhead | 40mm | 40mm | [as PA4] | 40mm | 40mm |

plans, and these were controlled from a specially fitted space just below the flight deck, to port.

Forward of the upper hangar two triple 203mm turrets were mounted, superimposed and offset to port. This had two advantages: the starboard side of the forecastle was still available for use by aircraft, and the weight of the turrets, their hoists and their barbettes could be used to offset the weight of the island to starboard. There was a fixed catapult offset to starboard that was capable of launching a fully armed torpedo bomber (see the plans). The upper hangar measured 125m x 20m, and could house nine torpedo bombers and nine surveillance aircraft with wings folded, plus three fixed-wing fighters. The lower hangar (75m x 13.5m) could accommodate a further seven fighters. The lower hangar stopped just short of the island superstructure (see inboard profile) and was served by the after aircraft lift; the forward lift served only the upper hangar.

The HA armament comprised six twin 100/45 mountings as in PA3–5, but only two of these were forward of the hangar; the remaining four were located above the stern. Fire control comprised a cruiser-type director control tower atop the tripod foremast, and HA directors mounted at either end of the island.

The ship's boats were stowed on either side at the level of the hangar deck in order to maximise the width of the flight deck above. They were generally launched from powered davits, and there was a large-capacity crane capable of handling both boats and aircraft located to starboard towards the after end of the flight deck.

There were three boiler rooms, each housing two of the new high-pressure, small watertube, three-drum boilers, and two large engine rooms each housing two sets of turbines. The turbines in the forward engine room powered the two wing shafts, those in the after engine room drove the inboard shafts. Between the two engine rooms was a fuel tank used to stabilise the ship to ensure a steady platform for air operations.

Protection comprised a side belt of 110mm homogeneous 'special' steel that extended from the 203mm magazines to the after engine room, backed by a 40mm torpedo bulkhead. There were also protective decks: atop the armoured belt, at the level of the Main Deck (lower hangar) there was 80mm plating above the machinery and the magazines, reducing to 30mm outboard of the torpedo bulkhead.

Studies for a diesel variant, PA7, were initiated in October 1930 and the results presented in March 1931. PA7 had an identical gun armament to PA6, but was otherwise smaller and less capable; the displacement of the earliest variant was 15,800 tonnes, rising to 17,335 tonnes in later iterations of the design. One of the variants considered was powered by eight large diesel engines, each rated at 12,000bhp (total 96,000bhp), that would drive the ship at 30 knots; another variant was to mount sixteen diesels, each

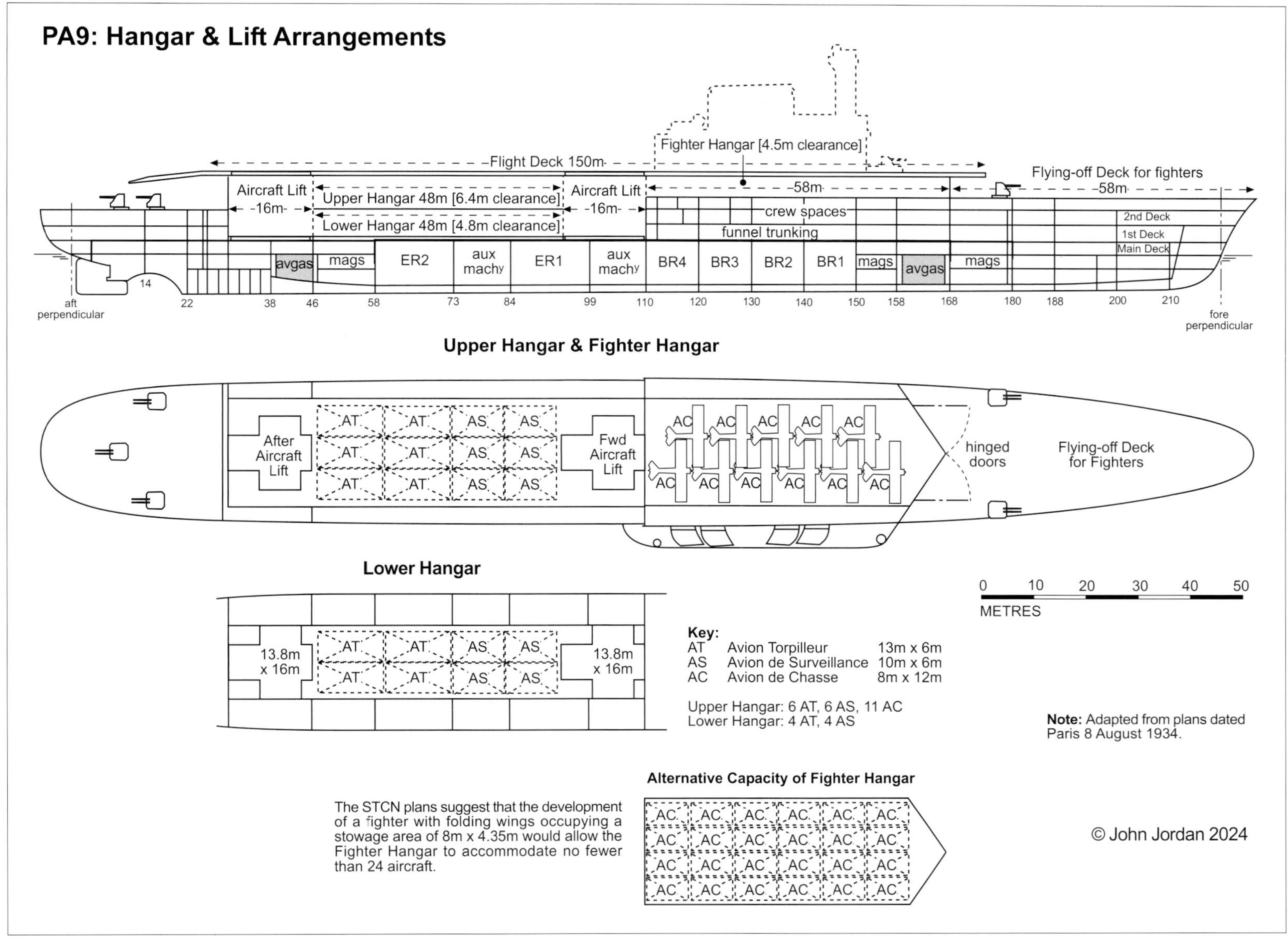


rated at a more modest 7500bhp (120,000bhp). The flight deck was 7 metres shorter than in PA6, and the smaller single hangar (107m x 20m) could accommodate only eighteen aircraft.

PA7 would be the last design in the series to be powered by diesels, which suggests that the technical difficulties involved in developing a reliable engine with such high power proved beyond the capabilities of French industry. However, there was a second problematic element in these two designs. The main armament of six 203mm guns, which was generally considered the minimum for fire control purposes, implied the development of a new triple turret, which would have been time-consuming and costly. All of the French treaty cruisers armed with guns of this calibre mounted them in a twin turret, and a triple 152mm turret designed for the new type of 'light' cruiser had yet to enter service.[3]

## PA9–11: 1933–34

No documentation for PA8 appears to have survived. After the flurry of projects undertaken in 1930–31 there was something of a hiatus, punctuated only by a handful of unofficial design proposals from serving naval officers: Captains Fromager and Lartigue, and the future Admiral Nomy, who would come to prominence in the post-war period (see Chapters 7–8). The Navy continued to plan for the construction of two carriers of around 18,000 tons (or possibly three of 13,000 tons) to serve alongside *Béarn* and to complete its Washington tonnage allocation of 60,000 tons. The *Conseil supérieur de la Marine* favoured a ship with speed and protection comparable to the treaty cruiser *Foch*, a low-angle armament of at least one 203mm or 152mm turret, a high-angle armament comprising twin 100mm guns and a flight deck with two fixed catapults. This suggests that a philosophical divide was already opening up between the more conservative institutions of the *Marine Nationale* and the naval aviation community represented by officers such as Lartigue and Nomy.

The next series of studies began with PA9, which was presented for discussion in March 1933. There were four variants, all displacing 18,900 metric tons, with a variety of internal hangar arrangements, a 110mm side belt, a maximum speed of 33 knots, and a uniform HA armament of six twin 100mm mount-

[3] The first ship with the triple 152mm turret, *Emile Bertin*, would enter service only in May 1934.

ings. The general configuration was similar to that of PA6, with an upper flight deck that terminated well aft of the bow, an island dominated by the now-standard long, narrow funnel to starboard, superimposed hangars, and a 58-metre forecastle. There were, however, no turrets for low-angle guns and no catapult. Instead, the short flight deck on the forecastle was to be used for unassisted take-off by fighters (as in the British and IJN carrier conversions). In the plans of the most developed variant, No 4, the first of the two cruciform lifts was moved aft and a separate 58-metre upper hangar with a clearance of 4.1m worked in between the lift and the forward end of the hangar structure. It could house eleven fixed-wing fighters, and had direct access to the forecastle via large hinged doors, which are shown on the plans.

The main body of the upper hangar between the lifts could accommodate six torpedo attack and six surveillance aircraft (three abreast with wings folded) and the lower hangar, which had a reduced width of 14 metres, four of each (two abreast), for a total of 30–31 aircraft (10–11 fighters, 10 surveillance, 10 torpedo attack).

PA9 was followed by a smaller, simpler design, PA10, which introduced a number of innovative features. Again there were four variants, all of which displaced around 14,000 tons. Two of these prioritised speed over protection: horsepower was 145,000cv for a maximum speed of 34 knots. The remaining two (designated *protégé*) had enhanced protection, but power was reduced to a more modest 115,000cv and speed to 32 knots. All four had a radically different hull to their predecessors.

PA10 was a flush-decked design with a single hangar and a flight deck that extended to the bow, where it was rounded off to secure good sea-keeping qualities. Propulsion was by four-shaft geared steam turbines, but instead of a tall funnel offset to port or to starboard there were two groups of exhaust vents to starboard with their outlets angled outboard; the air ventilation trunking for the boiler rooms was to port. This solution was the one favoured by the Imperial Japanese Navy for its own carriers, and it made possible a unit propulsion layout similar to that adopted for the French treaty cruisers (see drawing). Two boiler rooms, each housing two large 3-drum boilers, were followed by the forward engine room, which housed two turbo-generators in addition to the two sets of turbines for the wing shafts. This arrangement was then repeated for the two inboard shafts.

The diesel generators and auxiliary boilers that were standard on French major surface vessels of the period were located in compartments on the middle line forward of the machinery spaces; these were flanked by stabilisation tanks to ensure a steady aviation platform. The magazines for the HA guns and MGs (now boosted to eight of the new quad mountings for the 13.2mm Hotchkiss machine gun) and for the aircraft ordnance were fore and aft, and in the after part of the ship there was a tank for aviation fuel flanked by compartments filled with inert gas to minimise the fire hazard.

The ship was conned from a raised, fully glazed pilot house to starboard forward of the exhaust vents. This had good views of flight deck operations, but vision was restricted forward and to port by the flight deck itself. There were hinged masts to port and to starboard for the W/T aerials, and the forward pair of searchlights could be retracted into the flight deck, as in the IJN carriers.

The single, compact hangar could house a maximum of twenty aircraft: seven fighters, seven surveillance aircraft and six for torpedo attack. It was served by two cruciform lifts that effectively divided the hangar into three for damage control purposes. The lifts were flanked by control rooms, and at the forward end of the hangar there was a torpedo workshop to port and the command spaces for the ship, located directly beneath the pilot house, to starboard.

Protection for the two 'fast' variants was limited to a 40mm deck over the machinery and 30mm over the magazines, plus a 40mm torpedo bulkhead. In the 'protected' variants the thicknesses of the decks were increased to 80mm and 50mm respectively, but there was insufficient weight available for a side belt.

This was a neat, functional design and the study was developed in greater depth than many of the interwar projects. The plans that have survived are unusually detailed, showing even ladderways and hatches, and comprise external and inboard profile and plan views, the arrangement of the lower decks, a full set of section views and a 'master frame' with structural detail.

The downside was the relatively small air group of twenty aircraft, which barely justified the high cost of the ship given the size and power of her propulsion plant and the need to provide an adequate level of protection against aerial and underwater threats. The STCN therefore embarked on a version lengthened by 20 metres capable of embarking twenty-five aircraft, PA11, which would have had a standard displacement of 15,350 metric tons. Adding 20 metres to the length of the ship while retaining the 22.9-metre beam (which was largely dictated by the 20-metre width of the hangar), meant that there was no loss in speed or endurance, while judicious use of the additional 20 metres allowed the hangar to be lengthened to accommodate five more aircraft.

The solution adopted was to move the first aircraft lift forward of the first set of uptakes, thereby extending the length of the main body of the hangar. This allowed the incorporation of an additional hangar forward, 25.5 metres long and with the same 5-metre clearance but with the width reduced from 20 metres to 14 metres, to house three fixed-wing fighters. The short after hangar section was extended to the end of the cropped round-down, and was now 21.5 metres in length, although width had to be reduced to 14 metres, allowing only two of the larger aircraft to be stowed abreast, and there was reduced clearance at the after end. By rearranging these aircraft between the main body of the hangar and the after section, an additional two aircraft could be squeezed in, bringing the air complement up to twenty-five.

One unfortunate consequence of the new arrangements was that the floor of the new forward section of the hangar was approximately 2.5 metres lower than that of the main body due to the need for crew spaces on the 'gallery' deck above. As the fighters housed in this section could no longer simply be wheeled out onto the forecastle (as in PA9), this meant an extra 'stop' for the aircraft lift. The division of what was essentially a single hangar into three has led to some confusion when reviewing the STCN documentation about these designs, as the data tables often record

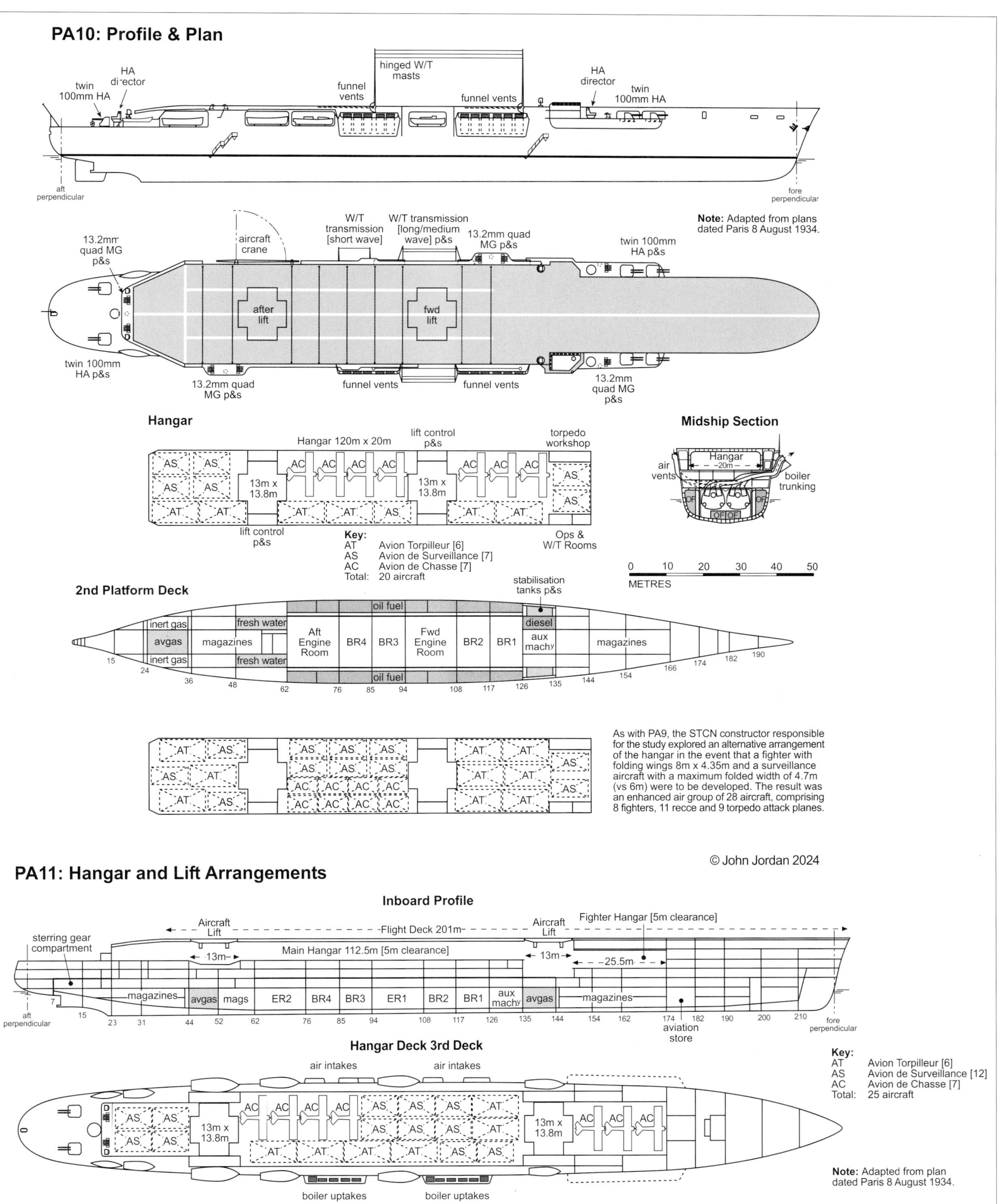
PA10: Profile & Plan
twin 100mm HA
HA director
funnel vents
hinged W/T masts
funnel vents
HA director
twin 100mm HA
aft perpendicular
fore perpendicular
Note: Adapted from plans dated Paris 8 August 1934.
13.2mm quad MG p&s
aircraft crane
W/T transmission [short wave]
W/T transmission [long/medium wave] p&s
13.2mm quad MG p&s
twin 100mm HA p&s
after lift
fwd lift
twin 100mm HA p&s
13.2mm quad MG p&s
funnel vents
funnel vents
13.2mm quad MG p&s
Hangar
Hangar 120m x 20m
lift control p&s
torpedo workshop
13m x 13.8m
13m x 13.8m
lift control p&s
Ops & W/T Rooms
Key:
AT Avion Torpilleur [6]
AS Avion de Surveillance [7]
AC Avion de Chasse [7]
Total: 20 aircraft
Midship Section
Hangar
20m
air vents
boiler trunking
OF
0 10 20 30 40 50
METRES
2nd Platform Deck
stabilisation tanks p&s
inert gas
avgas
inert gas
magazines
fresh water
fresh water
oil fuel
oil fuel
Aft Engine Room
BR4
BR3
Fwd Engine Room
BR2
BR1
diesel
aux machy
magazines
As with PA9, the STCN constructor responsible for the study explored an alternative arrangement of the hangar in the event that a fighter with folding wings 8m x 4.35m and a surveillance aircraft with a maximum folded width of 4.7m (vs 6m) were to be developed. The result was an enhanced air group of 28 aircraft, comprising 8 fighters, 11 recce and 9 torpedo attack planes.
© John Jordan 2024
PA11: Hangar and Lift Arrangements
Inboard Profile
sterring gear compartment
Aircraft Lift
Flight Deck 201m
Aircraft Lift
Fighter Hangar [5m clearance]
13m
Main Hangar 112.5m [5m clearance]
13m
25.5m
magazines
avgas
mags
ER2
BR4
BR3
ER1
BR2
BR1
aux machy
avgas
magazines
aft perpendicular
aviation store
fore perpendicular
Hangar Deck 3rd Deck
air intakes
air intakes
13m x 13.8m
13m x 13.8m
boiler uptakes
boiler uptakes
Key:
AT Avion Torpilleur [6]
AS Avion de Surveillance [12]
AC Avion de Chasse [7]
Total: 25 aircraft
Note: Adapted from plan dated Paris 8 August 1934.

## Table 3: FRENCH CARRIER PROJECTS 1933–34

| | PA9 | PA10 | PA10 Protégé | PA11 à protection renforcé | PA11 |
|---|---|---|---|---|---|
| **Displacement:** | | | | | |
| standard | 18,900tW | 14,000tW | [as PA10] | 15,350tW | 17,300tW |
| normal | 20,000t | 14,800t | [as PA10] | 16,250t | 18,500t |
| **Dimensions:** | | | | | |
| length pp | 220m | 200m | [as PA10] | 220m | [as PA11] |
| beam wl | 24.8m | 22.9m | [as PA10] | 22.9m | 23.25m |
| depth of keel | 7.2m | 6.4m | [as PA10] | 6.5m | 6.6m |
| **Propulsion:** | | | | | |
| horsepower | 145.000cv | 145,000cv | 115,000cv | 145,000cv | [as PA11] |
| max speed | 33 knots | 33.3 knots | 32 knots | 34 knots | 33.5 knots |
| no of shafts | four | four | four | four | four |
| endurance | 5700nm at 15kts | 5500nm at 15kts | 6000nm at 15kts | 5500nm at 15kts | 6000nm at 15kts |
| **Flight Deck(s):** | | | | | |
| total length | 164m + 58m | 186m | [as PA10] | 209m | [as PA11] |
| horizontal section | 150m | 172m | | 201m | |
| max width | 30m | 26.5m | [as PA10] | 26.5m | [as PA11] |
| **Hangars & cranes:** | | | | | |
| cranes | one | one | [as PA10] | one | [as PA11] |
| lifts (L x W) | two 13.8m x 16m | two 13m x 13.8m | [as PA10] | two 13m x 13.8m | [as PA11] |
| upper hangar | 126m x 20.5m x 6.4m | 120m x 20m x 5m | [as PA10] | 153m x 20m x 5m | [as PA11] |
| lower hangar | 50m x 19.3m x 4.1m | – | – | – | – |
| **Aircraft:** | | | | | |
| upper hangar | 11 AC, 6 AS, 6 AT | 7 AC, 7 AS, 6 AT | [as PA10] | 7 AC, 12 AS, 6AT | [as PA11] |
| lower hangar | 4 AS, 4 AT | – | – | – | |
| total | 31 | 20 | [as PA10] | 25 | [as PA11] |
| **Armament:** | | | | | |
| HA guns | 12 – 100mm (6xII) | 12 – 100mm (6xII) | [as PA10] | 12 – 100mm (6xII) | [as PA11] |
| light AA | n/a | 32 – 13.2mm (8xIV) | [as PA10] | 32 – 13.2mm (8xIV) | [as PA11] |
| **Protection:** | | | | | |
| side belt | 110mm | – | – | – | 110mm |
| dccks | 80/30mm | 40/20mm | 80/30mm | 40/20mm | 80/30mm |
| torpedo bulkhead | 40mm | 40mm | 40mm | 40mm | 60–40mm |

them as separate hangars with their own dimensions and suggest that there were three (or even four) hangars on the same level(!).

Like its immediate predecessor, design PA11 featured 'fast' (*ie* 34-knot) and 'protected' (32-knot) variants, together with a third variant with 'reinforced' protection. The base-line variant had protection on a par with the unprotected variants of PA10: 40mm over the machinery spaces and 30mm over the magazines with a 40mm torpedo bulkhead. In the 'protected' PA10 variant the thickness of the decks was again increased to 80mm and 50mm respectively. The variant with reinforced protection had a uniform deck thickness of 80mm over the machinery spaces and magazines, and incorporated a 110mm waterline belt of special steel; the torpedo bulkhead was reinforced to 60–40mm. The same horsepower was required as in the baseline design (145,000cv) for a reduced maximum speed of 33.5 knots, but displacement increased by some 2,000 tonnes to 17,300 tonnes.

PA12 was a supplementary variant of PA11 with enhanced protection and a larger air group. The ship would have displaced 17,000 metric tons, would have had a 220mm armour belt, and would have embarked thirty-three aircraft.

### PA13–14: 1934–35

One of the unintended consequences of the Washington Treaty was that while tonnage limitations were imposed on aircraft carriers, no such restrictions were imposed on the number of aircraft they could carry. If aircraft – as opposed to 8in guns – were regarded as the main armament of the carrier, it made sense to maximise the air group at the expense of other capabilities. The US Navy led the way, laying down the 13,800-ton *Ranger* with a nominal air group of 72 in 1931, having experimented with 'pulsed strikes' and large deck parks with the converted *Lexington* and *Saratoga* during a series of Fleet Problems that took place from the late 1920s.

The Royal Navy briefly considered a US Navy-style deck park during the early 1930s, but rejected it as impractical and fundamentally unsuited to naval air operations in the North Atlantic. Nevertheless, *Ark Royal*, the first RN aircraft carrier to be built from the keel up, was designed to operate sixty aircraft and to accommodate a total of seventy-two in two superimposed full-length hangars – the converted light battlecruisers *Furious*, *Courageous* and *Glorious*, which had a similar hangar arrangement, could operate only thirty-six to forty-two aircraft. Approved in June 1934, the design of *Ark Royal* had an undoubted influence on subsequent French studies, as the operational doctrine of the *Marine Nationale* was more closely aligned with Royal Navy thinking than with US concepts. Project PA13, reportedly developed from late 1934, had a number of features in common with *Ark Royal*, including a starboard-side island with anti-aircraft gun mountings at either end, superimposed hangars capable of accommodating sixty to seventy aircraft, and even a short round-down at the forward end of the flight deck.

**Left and below:** The British *Ark Royal* had a major influence on some of the later French interwar designs, which had superimposed hangars and were intended to operate between sixty and seventy-five aircraft. Note the three narrow lifts offset to port and to starboard, intended to facilitate the movement of aircraft at hangar deck level. This would also be a feature of the French PA-15 *n'*. *Ark Royal* also had twin fixed catapults (termed 'accelerators' by the Royal Navy), which the French also considered for some of their interwar designs. *(Jean Moulin collection/ NHHC NH-79167)*

The most innovative feature of the PA13 design was a flight deck and upper hangar that were offset to port, their middle line being 3 metres off the ship's axis (see drawing). This conferred a number of advantages: it provided weight compensation for the island to starboard, it enabled the full 30-metre width of the flight deck to be maintained throughout, and it permitted free fore and aft movement of wheeled aircraft in the upper hangar. In earlier French studies, the adoption of British-style cruciform lifts 15–16 metres wide precluded aircraft movement past the lift when the latter was in the raised position, as the hangar had a maximum width of only 19 metres. The lifts were therefore positioned at either end (PA3), or in such a way as to divide the hangar into distinct zones for damage control purposes (PA10).

In order to facilitate movement within the hangars of *Ark Royal*, the Royal Navy had adopted narrow rectangular lifts only 22–25ft (6.7–7.2m) wide, offset to port or to starboard so that aircraft with wings folded could move past them.[4] The lifts in PA13 were 'T'-shaped (not cruciform) and had a maximum width of 14 metres. However, moving the flight deck and hangar 3 metres to port while continuing to locate the lifts on the ship's axis opened up a passageway some 6 metres wide on the port side of the lift through which aircraft could be wheeled fore and aft. With this arrangement the lifts continued to serve the lower hangars, which were 14.6 metres wide and centred on the middle line. It is unclear from the plans how these lifts were raised and lowered; they appear to be open on three sides, so may have been powered by hydraulics (as in *Ark Royal*) rather than the classic system of guides and cables powered by electric motors.

Fitting two full-length superimposed hangars in *Ark Royal* had proved problematic in that the uptakes and ventilation trunking for the port-side and centre boiler rooms had to be run horizontally beneath the lower hangar before being angled upwards on the starboard side of the ship. This would contribute to the loss of the ship to a single German torpedo in November

4 Lifts with similar dimensions were retained in the armoured carriers, which were unable to strike down modern, high-performance fixed-wing monoplanes in the hangar when these were embarked from 1941.

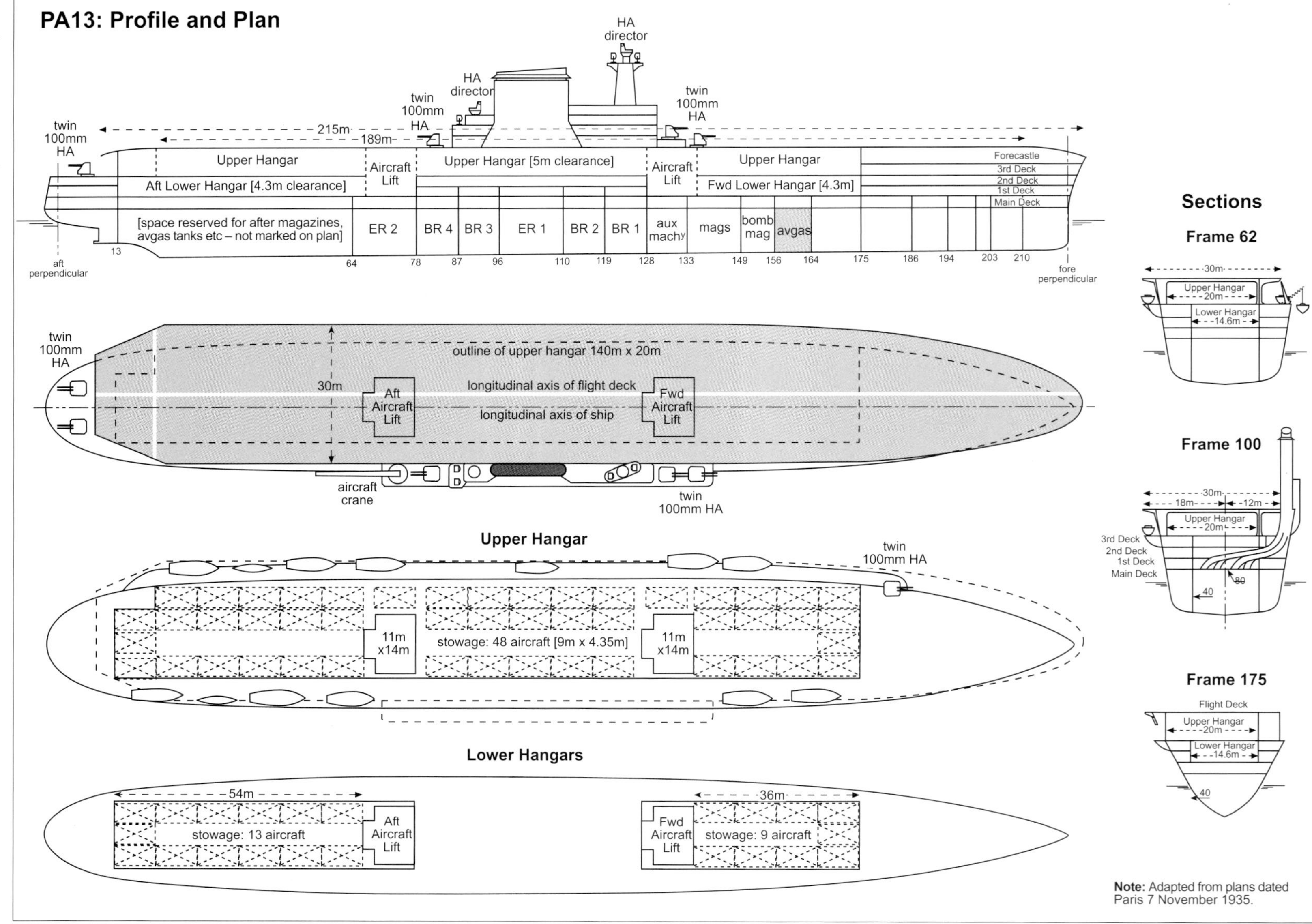


1941, when the flooding spread via the ventilation ducts to all three boiler rooms, causing the ship to lose lighting and power for the pumps. In PA13 the French resolved this problem by separating the lower hangar into two distinct and independent units fore and aft, thereby freeing up the midship part of the ship below the upper hangar for the boiler uptakes (see section drawing). Each of the lower hangars had one of the two aircraft lifts at its inboard end. The forward hangar was 36 metres long and could stow nine 'standard' (9m x 4.35m) aircraft; the after hangar was 54 metres long and could stow thirteen aircraft. The upper hangar could accommodate forty-eight aircraft, for a total air complement of seventy.

Unusually, the island superstructure of PA13 was amidships. It was characterised by a long, narrow funnel and a plated mast carrying a high-angle director and two searchlights. A second HA director and two further searchlights were mounted at the after end of the island. The HA armament comprised the now-standard six twin 100mm mountings, two of which were superimposed forward of the island with a third mounting aft. Two further mountings were located on the open quarterdeck, while the sixth was located beneath the flight deck forward, to port. This mounting had poor aerial arcs, an unwanted consequence of the asymmetric arrangement of the flight deck.

The plans show the same unit arrangement of the machinery adopted for the PA10–11 series. Each 'unit' comprised two boiler rooms, each with two 3-drum boilers side by side, followed by a large engine room. The transverse forward bulkhead of Boiler Room 1 was a downward continuation of the bulkhead which closed off the forward (lower) hangar, the after bulkhead of Boiler Room 4 a continuation of the transverse bulkhead that closed off the after lower hangar. This serves to explain the unusual choice of a central position for the island superstructure, which is related to the need to accommodate the uptakes for the boilers between these two hangars (see drawing), and is also responsible for the impressive length of the narrow funnel. No figures are available for the horsepower generated by the machinery, but the layout suggests that it was as in PA10–11, around 145,000cv, giving a maximum speed in excess of 32 knots.

PA13 had a length between perpendiculars of 220 metres, a waterline beam of 24.6 metres, and a displacement of 19,000 metric tons standard, 20,600 tonnes normal. The section views in the original plan do not show the level of protection (but see

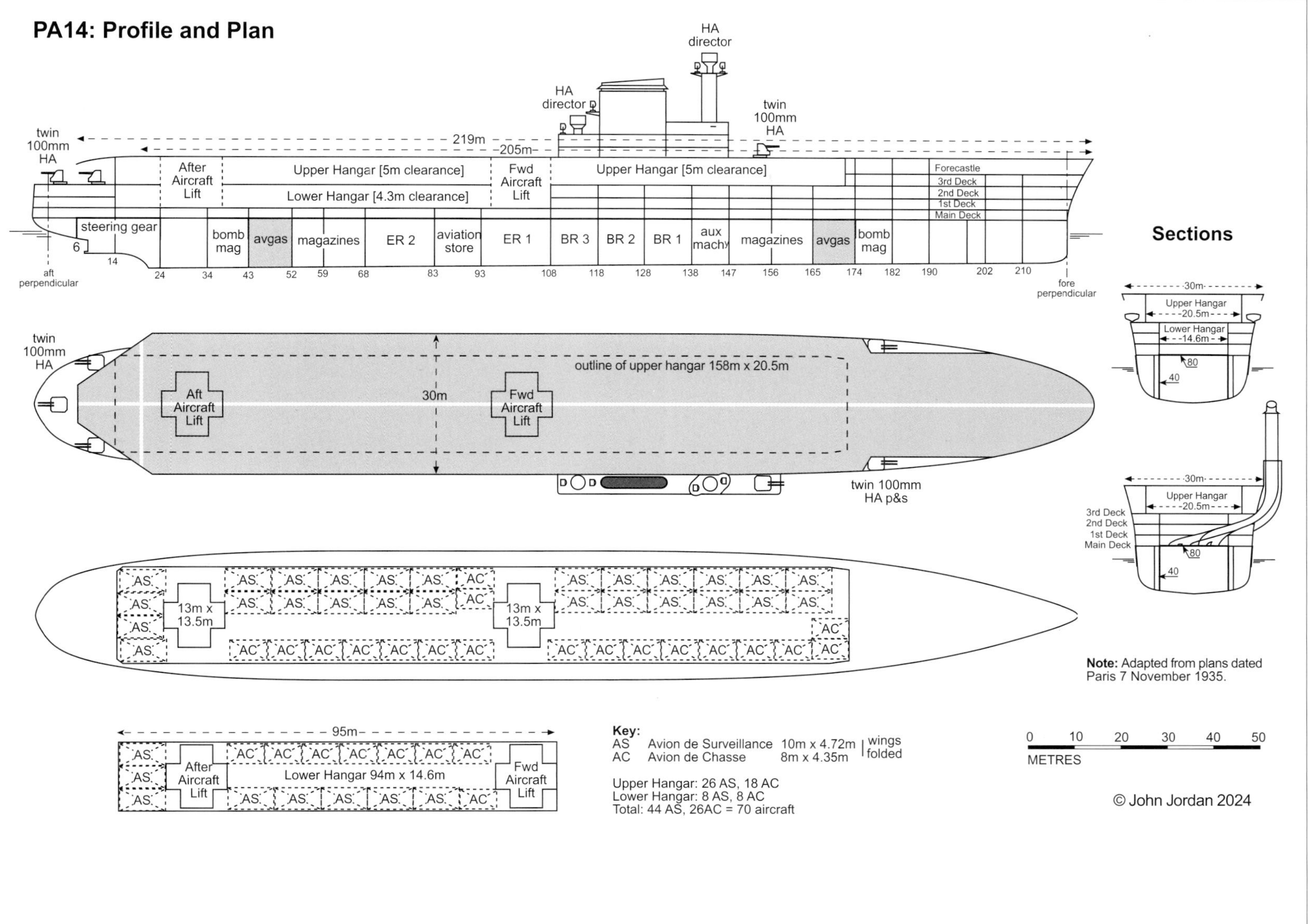


PA14 below). The single plan that has survived, which is dated Paris 7 November 1935, is essentially a feasibility study for a carrier with sixty-plus aircraft. It lacks detail, and the scheme does not appear to have been developed to the same extent as, for example, PA10, with multiple detailed plans. However, it clearly exerted an influence on later studies; PA16, laid down as *Joffre* (see Chapter 5), would have a similar asymmetric flight deck and upper hangar.

PA14 was effectively a reworking of PA13 with more conventional arrangements. The flight deck and upper hangar were realigned with the ship's axis, and there was a narrower, slightly shorter island to starboard. The flight deck was cut away on either side forward to accommodate two of the six 100mm mountings; the port-side mounting now had improved aerial arcs. There were a further three mountings on the quarterdeck, with the sixth forward of the island to starboard. The HA directors and searchlight projectors were similarly arranged to PA13.

The forward aircraft lift was now amidships, abaft the island, which was moved forward. This created the space for a single lower hangar 95 metres long and 14.6 metres wide served by both lifts. This was an undeniably superior arrangement to the two independent lower hangars each served by a single lift in PA13, and was made possible by reverting to the classic in-line arrangement of the boiler rooms, which were forward of the engine rooms. The plans show only three boiler rooms instead of the four required by the unit arrangement of the machinery in PA10–13, and this served to compress the longitudinal space occupied by the boiler uptakes. It also created more hull space for ordnance and bomb magazines and for avgas tanks and other aviation-related material in the after part of the ship. However, it is possible that horsepower was reduced to 115,000cv, as in the 'protected' PA10/11 variants.

Only two types of aircraft are shown: a reconnaissance aircraft with dimensions of 10 metres by 4.72 metres (wings folded), and a fighter 8 metres by 4.35 metres, suggesting the Dewoitine 376 (an improved variant of the 373 with folding wings), which would enter service from 1938.

The section plans show a deck over the machinery spaces of 80mm steel, a now-standard 40mm torpedo bulkhead, and a belt of indeterminate thickness. The protection of PA13 may have been similar, as overall characteristics (displacement, dimensions etc) were essentially unchanged.

## Table 4: **FRENCH CARRIER PROJECTS 1934–5**

| | **PA13** | **PA14** |
|---|---|---|
| Displacement: | | |
| standard | 19,000tW | [as PA13] |
| normal | 20,600t | [as PA13] |
| Dimensions: | | |
| length pp | 220m | [as PA13] |
| beam wl | 24.6m | [as PA13] |
| depth of keel | 7m | |
| Propulsion: | | |
| horsepower | 145,000cv | 115,000cv? |
| max speed | 32? knots | 31? knots |
| no of shafts | four | four |
| endurance | | |
| Flight Deck(s): | | |
| total length | 215m | 219m |
| horizontal section | 189m | 205m |
| max width | 30m | [as PA13] |
| Hangars & cranes: | | |
| cranes | one | [as PA13] |
| lifts (L x W) | two 11m x 14m | two 13m x 13.5m |
| upper hangar | 140m x 20m | 158m x 20.5m |
| lower hangar(s) | 36m+54m x 14.6m | 95m x 14.6m |
| Aircraft: | | |
| upper hangar | 48 | 44 |
| lower hangar(s) | 22 | 26 |
| total | 70 | 70 |
| Armament: | | |
| HA guns | 12 – 100mm (6xII) | [as PA13] |
| light AA | ?? – 13.2mm (? x IV) | [as PA13] |
| Protection: | | |
| side belt | ? | 105mm? |
| dccks | 80/30mm | [as PA13] |
| torpedo bulkhead | 40mm | [as PA13] |

### PA15

The penultimate study in the series, PA15, was initiated in September 1935 and comprised two variants: variant *n'* of 29,900 metric tons standard with a length of 242 metres, a speed of 34 knots and a capacity of seventy-five aircraft; and *gamma*, displacing 22,800 metric tons. Both were very much 'paper' projects, as the Navy's preference as previously expressed was for a carrier of 14,000–18,000 tonnes. The STCN was effectively being asked to explore what could be achieved on these higher displacements.

For *n'* only two significant plans appear to have survived: one of the 'master frame', the other a plan of the decks from the main deck to the 3rd Deck (upper hangar). The midship section shows the protection scheme, which would have comprised a 105mm waterline belt with a 40mm deck extending across the full beam of the ship above (main deck), and a 40mm torpedo bulkhead. More interesting are the plans of the two hangar decks, which like the midship section plan, are dated 25 April 1936.

The main body of the upper hangar was 17 metres wide, with side extensions to port fore and aft of the boat stowage (see drawing); these extensions had a maximum width of 5.95 metres (5.4m clear) and could accommodate a single row of aircraft with wings folded. The lower hangar was likewise 17 metres wide, reduced to 12 metres amidships abeam the boiler uptakes and ventilation trunking. Both hangars were divided into three sections by fire curtains and an air space for damage control purposes, with access between the sections being provided by doors 7.5 metres wide. All three sections in the upper hangar, and the after two sections of the lower hangar

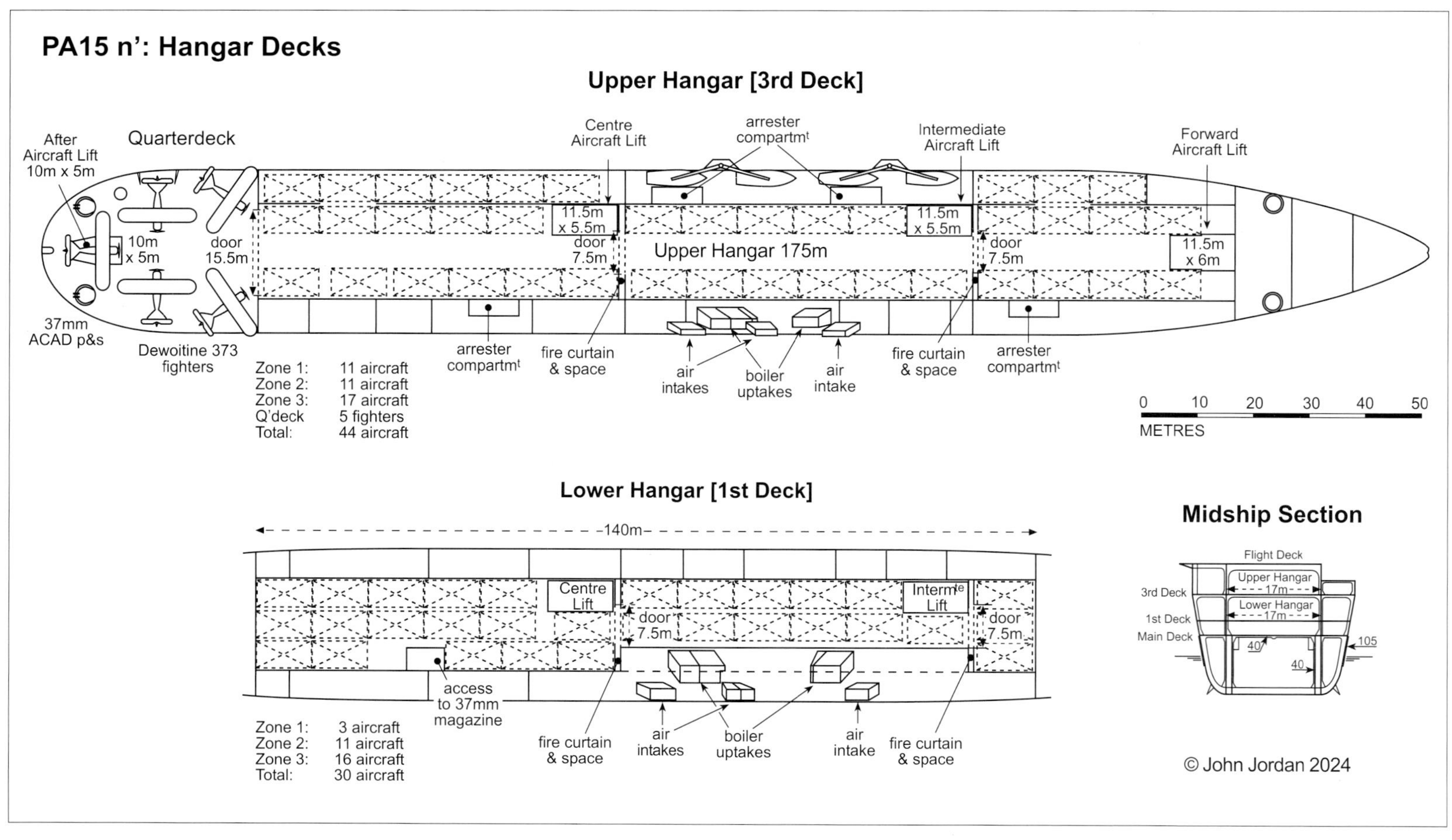

Above: The 'treaty' cruiser *Tourville* in the spring of 1939. As the first of their type, *Tourville* and her sister *Duquesne* were fast but had only very light protection. Their conversion to aircraft carriers was briefly considered in 1935 but came to nothing. *(Marc Saibène collection)*

were served by narrow British-style lifts 11.5m x 5m, which were almost certainly raised and lowered using hydraulics. The two lifts for the after sections, designated 'intermediate' and 'centre' respectively, were offset to port to enable aircraft to be wheeled past them. The lift for the forward section of the upper hangar was on the middle line.

At the after end of the upper hangar there was a door 15.5 metres wide giving access to an open quarterdeck. The plan shows five fighters with wings deployed, apparently of the Dewoitine 373/376 type, arranged around the quarterdeck. The last of these is shown atop a fourth narrow lift 10m x 5m tapered at its after end, similar to the after lift that would be adopted for *Joffre* in her final iteration. This would have been located at the after end of the flight deck (not shown on the plan), which must therefore have been horizontal (as in PA16) with no round-down.

The size of the air group was not notably greater than in the 19,000-ton PA13/14 (74 vs 70), and although the two hangars were more spacious they were clumsily arranged, with partition bulkheads separating the side extensions of the upper hangar from the main body, presumably for structural reasons. The only significant influence on the later PA16 design was the narrow, 'open' after lift connecting the quarterdeck with the flight deck.

## PROPOSED CONVERSION OF *DUQUESNE* AND *TOURVILLE*

When France's first 'treaty cruisers', *Duquesne* and *Tourville*, were completed in 1928 they were only marginally less well-protected than their foreign contemporaries. However, by the mid-1930s they had been outclassed by the latest construction abroad and were considered to have limited military value.

In 1935 there was a proposal to convert them into aircraft carriers, France's single fleet carrier *Béarn* having proved too slow to operate tactically with the *Marine Nationale*'s latest ships, and studies were duly commissioned. All except one of the four preliminary designs were for a carrier/cruiser hybrid, with either turret I or turret IV being retained. The flight deck would have been 139 metres long and 22 metres wide, with a hangar 98–102 metres long but only 14.2 metres wide. In the third sketch design all four turrets were to have been removed, giving a 176-metre flight deck and a 116.5-metre hangar. Exhaust gases were to have been discharged through horizontal funnels on the starboard quarter. There were to be six twin 100mm/45 HA mountings, as in the latest PA studies, and four single 37mm Mle 1925. Displacement would have increased to 12,000 tonnes, but the fine hull-form adopted for *Duquesne* and *Tourville* to secure high speed meant that the ships would have had a hangar capacity of only twelve to fourteen aircraft.

The small size of the air group compared with the relatively high cost of conversion resulted in the project being abandoned in favour of new carrier construction. The proposal to convert *Duquesne* and *Tourville* to aircraft carriers would resurface in 1945, by which time the hulls were twenty-seven years old, but was not pursued.

CHAPTER 5

# PA16 *JOFFRE* AND *PAINLEVÉ*

HISTORIES OF CARRIER DEVELOPMENT between the wars have tended to be skewed by what came afterwards. However, the 'pulsed' air operations employed by the two Pacific navies, and which had become the norm by 1945, were a long way from those envisaged by European navies during the 1930s. In Britain, the leading European power, the aircraft carrier continued to be seen simply as a 'force multiplier' for the battle fleet, which it was intended to accompany in close order. The Royal Navy, haunted by the escape of the German Fleet at Jutland, had wanted carrier-borne aircraft that could locate the enemy and monitor his course, aircraft that could spot fall of shot at the longer engagement ranges now possible, aircraft armed with torpedoes that might slow the enemy's speed and prevent his escape, and fighter aircraft that could shoot down the enemy's spotters and reconnaissance aircraft. During the mid-1930s, when the Americans and the Japanese were moving towards high-performance monoplanes each designed for a specific task (fighter, dive bomber, torpedo bomber) and with a primary attack function, the British were reaffirming their traditional carrier missions with the development of the Fairey Swordfish for the reconnaissance, spotter and torpedo attack (TSR) roles, and the Blackburn Skua for the fighter and dive bomber (FDB) roles. Multipurpose aircraft made sense given the comparatively small size of the British air groups, but even multipurpose aircraft could perform only one role at a time. Air operations from the British carriers therefore typically involved relatively small groups of aircraft taking off or landing, with the multi-role aircraft being rotated through their various missions (which included anti-submarine patrol), depending on the requirements of the situation. In contrast to the 'pulsed' strikes envisaged by the two Pacific powers, air operations from the British carriers were expected to be continuous and sustainable.

There were other factors that impacted on carrier development in Europe. A naval force operating in the North Sea, the Channel or the Mediterranean would be in striking range of numerous and powerful groupings of shore-based aircraft. A carrier operating at best fifteen to twenty fighters might be opposed by 'unsinkable' air bases ashore, each operating well over a hundred aircraft. And as the 1930s progressed, land-based aircraft became faster, longer-ranged and generally much more capable, while the performance of carrier aircraft was limited by take-off weight restrictions and landing speed requirements. The Mediterranean crisis of 1935, in which it initially appeared that Britain might find herself at war with Italy, was profoundly influential in the design of the British 'armoured carrier' of the late 1930s. For the Royal Navy at least, it appeared that carrier operations in theatres dominated by land-based air were possible only with ships able to resist multiple bomb hits. In the absence of early warning of strikes by land-based bombers and torpedo planes, it was envisaged that all aircraft (including fighters) would be struck down in the armoured hangar and the enemy aircraft engaged by the anti-aircraft guns of the carrier and her escorts, which would employ controlled barrage fire.[1]

When the French Naval General Staff, prompted by news of the projected construction of aircraft carriers by Nazi Germany, gave serious consideration to a new generation of carriers in 1936, strong reservations were expressed regarding the ability of such ships to operate in the Mediterranean and the Channel due to the proximity of hostile land bases. Only operations in the North Atlantic 'beyond the 400nm line' and overseas were considered viable and, in the view of the NGS, the North Atlantic was unfavourable to air operations due to the prevailing weather and the heavy swell.

## THE FRENCH NAVAL AIR ARM IN 1936

Until 1928, the *Marine Nationale* had full control over naval aviation, including training and deployment, although aircraft development was the responsibility of the Ministry of Transport. However, 1928 saw the formation of the *Ministère de l'Air*, modelled on the British Air Ministry and responsible for integrating all aspects of military aviation. Only embarked aircraft and their crews remained under the direct control of the Navy; aircraft development, training, shore bases and coastal aviation were taken over by the Air Ministry. One of the immediate consequences of this reorganisation was that no new aircraft types were developed for the Navy during the period 1928–32.

As in Britain, this political development encountered determined, often bitter opposition from the Navy. The Air Ministry's control over maritime air was progressively eroded between 1931 and February 1934, when a new law gave the Navy its own budget for embarked aircraft and for coastal aviation, now designated the *Forces aériennes de coopération navale*. Finally, in August 1936, these forces were returned to the full control of the Navy.[2]

[1] This doctrine was only reversed with the advent of long-range aerial detection using radar, which made it possible to vector fighter patrols out to intercept enemy bombers.

[2] Since 1931, they had been part of the *Direction des forces aériennes de mer*, a separate bureau within the air ministry set up as part of an initial compromise.

**Table 1: COMPARISON BETWEEN *JOFFRE* AND OTHER CONTEMPORARY EUROPEAN CARRIERS**

| Name of Ship | Displacement | Dimensions of Flight Deck | Dimensions of Hangars | Aircraft | Aviation Fuel |
|---|---|---|---|---|---|
| *Ark Royal* (GB) | 22,000tW | 244m x 29m* | *Upper*: 173m x 18m x 4.9m<br>*Lower*: 138m x 18m x 4.9m | 60 | 455,000 litres |
| *Graf Zeppelin* (Ger) | 23,200tW | 242m x 29m* | *Upper*: 180m x 16m x 5.7m<br>*Lower*: 172m x 16m x 5.3m | 42 | 245,000 litres |
| *Joffre* (Fr) | 18,000tW | 201m x 27m | *Upper*: 159m x 20.8m x 4.8m<br>*Lower*: 79m x 14.8m x 4.4m | 40 | 270,000 litres |

* Note that these are maximum dimensions. In *Ark Royal* and, more particularly *Graf Zeppelin*, the width of the flight deck abeam the island was significantly reduced whereas in *Joffre*, which had her flight deck offset to port, the usable width was constant throughout.

There was now a particular urgency to the renewal of France's naval air arm. The *Marine Nationale* was already firmly embarked on a new programme of fast battleships capable of speeds of 29–32 knots, and the 21-knot *Béarn* was simply too old and too slow to operate effectively with them. She underwent a major refit from 1934–35, but was subsequently transferred from the Mediterranean to the Atlantic, where she operated with the older dreadnought battleships and would be used increasingly for trials of new aircraft operating procedures and new, more advanced types of aircraft (see Chapter 2).

The French now also needed to take into account the resurgence of the German Navy, which in 1935 had placed orders for two new aircraft carriers with Deutsche Werke and Germaniawerft.[3] The *Marine Nationale*, as we have seen, had strong reservations about the viability of carrier operations in the Mediterranean and the Channel theatres. However, if the Germans were intending to support incursions by surface raiders into the North Atlantic with carrier-borne aircraft, the French Navy would need to respond by building carriers that could operate with its own battleships and cruisers, as there was no guarantee that France would have the support of the Royal Navy in this vast expanse of open water.

In 1935, a Note from the NGS requested the study of an aircraft carrier with a displacement of 12,000–15,000 tonnes. In response, on 26 November the *Service Technique*, possibly influenced by the laying down of USS *Wasp* (CV-7: 14,700 tons), proposed two ships of 15,000 tonnes with minimal protection. Protection was subsequently increased and the design, designated PA16, approved. The *Conseil supérieur de la Marine* was unhappy with the uniform high-angle armament of the more recent studies, and proposed that the twin 100mm mountings be replaced by eight 130mm in twin turrets of the same model currently being fitted in the fast battleships *Dunkerque* and *Strasbourg*, in order to provide a dual-purpose capability. These would be mounted at the forward and after ends of the island bridge, as in the US Navy's *Lexington* and *Saratoga* and the Italian proposal by Bonfiglietti dating from 1929,[4] of which the French were no doubt aware. The proposed aviation arrangements were presented by the STCN at meetings on 22 January, 11 June and 23 August 1937. The military capabilities were decided at a meeting on 23 April, and the principal characteristics approved by the Chief of the Naval General Staff on 19 June. Discussions regarding the configuration of the flight deck and the landing-on arrangements (which included the adoption of no fewer than nine arrester cable systems) continued, and the final plans were approved on 5 July 1938. By this time, displacement had increased to around 18,000 tons standard.

The design incorporated the lessons learned from operations with *Béarn*, and had many of the features of the later 'paper' plans of the PA1–15 series (see Chapter 4).

The construction of two new carriers built to these plans, to be named *Joffre* and *Painlevé*,[5] was approved under the 1938 Estimates. The ships were to be ordered from Penhoët (Saint-Nazaire), which would lay down each of the 236-metre ships in succession on the No 1 slipway, which had built the liner *Normandie* and the fast battleship *Strasbourg*. On completion their armament would be fitted at Brest.

## AN ASYMMETRIC FLIGHT DECK

The most striking feature of the PA16 design was its asymmetric flight deck and upper hangar – a feature that was introduced with the PA13 study (see Chapter 4). Rather than being aligned with the ship's axis, the flight deck was offset 6.83 metres to port. The attraction of this arrangement was that it counterbalanced the weight of the island to starboard, which was a particular issue with PA16 due to the location of the 130mm twin turrets at either end. It also meant that the flight deck could retain its full 27-metre width throughout.[6]

[3] Carrier 'B' was laid down on 30 September 1936; carrier 'A' (subsequently *Graf Zeppelin*) on 28 December 1936. When first unveiled, the Germans announced that the project was for a ship displacing 12,250 tons standard, despite the fact that by 1935, legend displacement was 24,000 tonnes.

[4] The Bonfiglietti design featured eight low-angle 152mm guns in twin turrets.

[5] General (later Marshal) Joseph-Jacques-Césaire Joffre (1852–1931) was Commander-in-Chief of French forces on the Western Front when war was declared in 1914; he is best known for regrouping the retreating Allied armies to defeat the Germans at the strategically decisive First Battle of the Marne. Paul Painlevé (1863–1933) was a French mathematician and statesman; he served twice as Prime Minister of the Third Republic (1917 and 1925).

[6] By contrast, the width of the flight deck of the German *Graf Zeppelin* was reduced from 29m to only 23m abeam her equally substantial island.

The downside of the asymmetric flight deck was that no major anti-aircraft weapons could be mounted to port. This was not considered desirable by either the Royal Navy or the US Navy, which continued to mount 4.5in and 5in guns respectively on sponsons just beneath the level of the flight deck on the port side. Both the latter navies emphasised the impracticality of firing the larger HA guns across the flight deck during air operations. However, the French attempted to circumvent this by locating all the major-calibre HA guns atop the island, where they could engage hostile aircraft to port or to starboard without impacting on air operations except at very low angles of elevation.

This solution made for an exceptionally long island, which increased air turbulence over the flight deck and also precluded locating many of the ship's boats to starboard. The solution adopted to the latter problem, which had been likewise adopted in the PA13 study, was to locate seven of the smaller boats on sponsons beneath the overhang of the flight deck to port, with access from the upper hangar. There was also a platform at the forward end for a quadruple light AA mounting and its rangefinder, to preclude strafing attacks below the level of the flight deck on the port side. As part compensation the flight deck stopped short of the bow and stern, as in US Navy carriers, thereby enabling light AA weapons to be mounted at the extremities of the ship.

The flight deck, which was of 16mm steel, had an overall length of 201 metres, and was tapered only at its forward end. This represented an increase of 21 metres over *Béarn* – some 38m if the after 'round-down' of the latter ship is taken into account. In contrast to *Béarn* there were only two lifts connecting the flight deck with the upper hangar, and these were at the fore and after ends of the flight deck. The forward lift had the 'T' configuration adopted for PA14; length was 13 metres and maximum width 17 metres, allowing it to accommodate the largest aircraft with wings deployed. The arrangement and configuration of the after lift was identical to the one devised for the PA15 *n'* study. It was aligned with the aftermost extremity of the flight deck and was open on three sides (see drawings). This enabled dimensions to be reduced without precluding the possibility of raising or lowering a fully deployed aircraft; length was 12.5 metres, while maximum width was only 6 metres, the lift being tapered at its after end to accommodate the tailplane of the aircraft.

The significance of the new lift arrangements for air operations was considerable. Both lifts could accommodate a fully deployed aircraft. This meant that in contrast to the contemporary British *Ark Royal*, whose unusually narrow lifts required the wings of an aircraft to be folded before it was struck down in the hangar, aircraft landing aboard *Joffre* could be struck down immediately in their fully deployed condition, the wings being folded for stowage once the aircraft was safely inside the hangar. This made for a faster recovery cycle. Moreover, the position and configuration of the lifts facilitated 'double-ended' operations similar to those envisaged in the US Navy, so that aircraft making a conventional landing over the stern would be struck down via the forward lift, while the after lift could be utilised for aircraft landing over the bow.

The layout of the arrester wires reflected these intended arrangements. Whereas *Béarn* had only four cables and these were located on the after part of the flight deck, where they straddled the two after lifts, in *Joffre* there were nine and they were located amid-

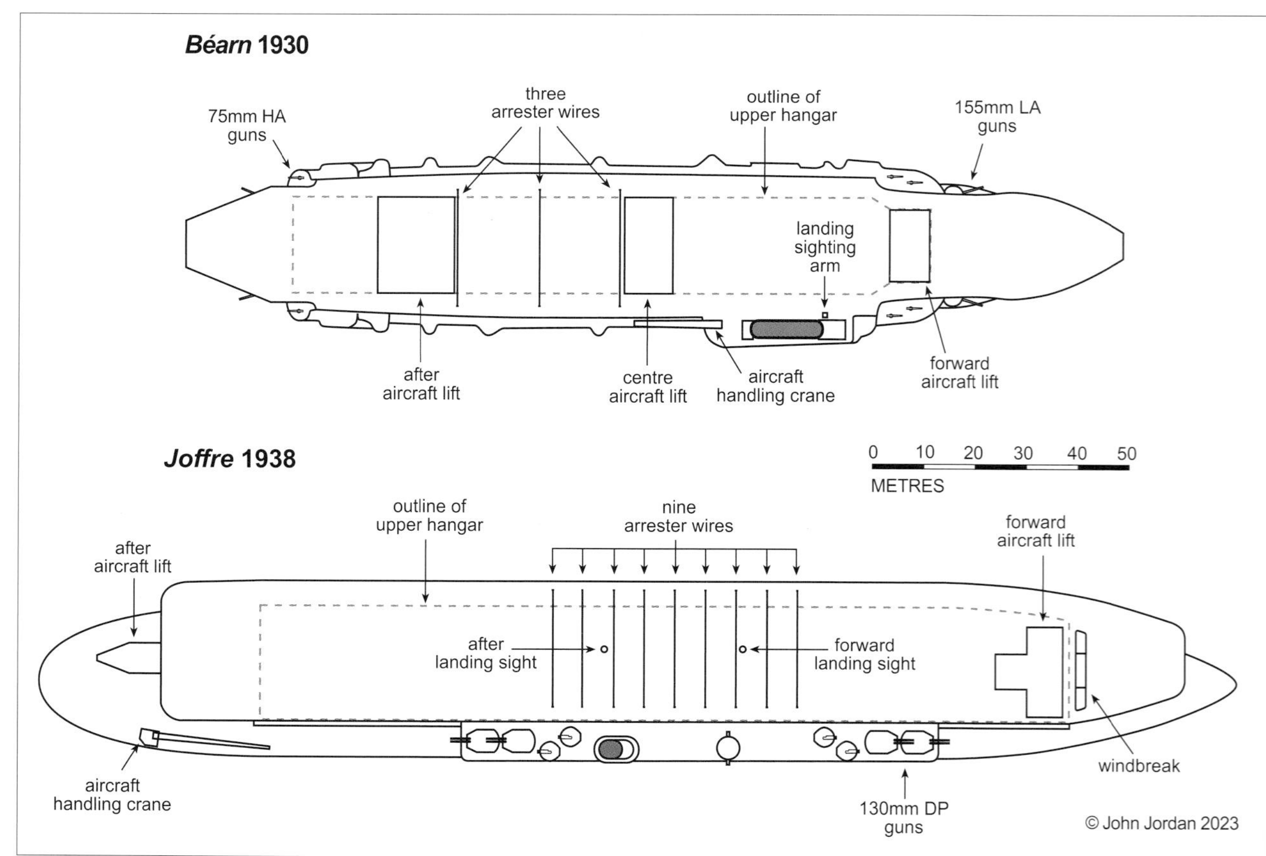

**PA16 *Joffre:* Profile & Plan 1938**

**Note:** Adapted from plans dated Paris 2 May 1938.

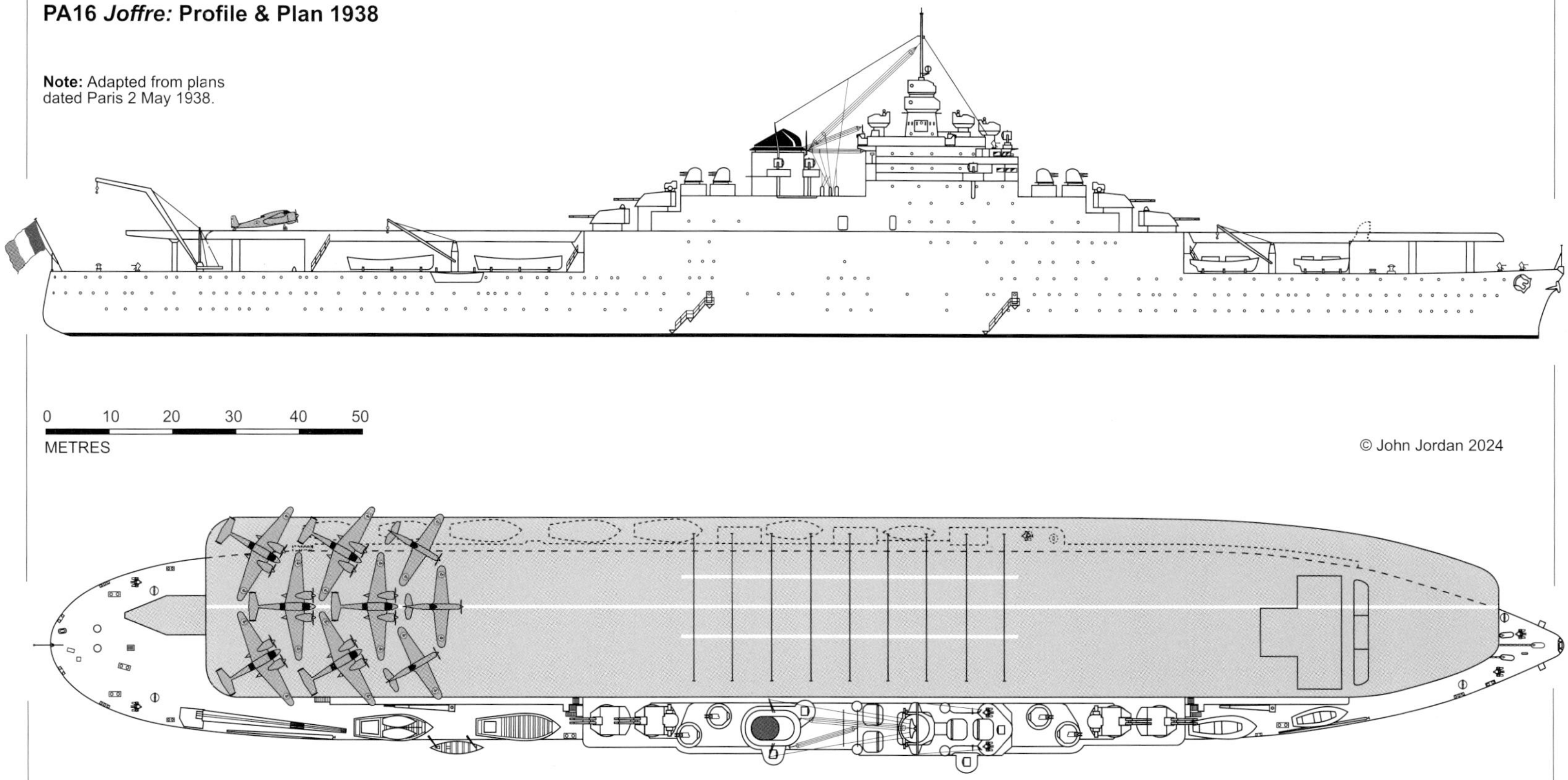

0 10 20 30 40 50
METRES

© John Jordan 2024

**PA16 *Joffre* 1938**

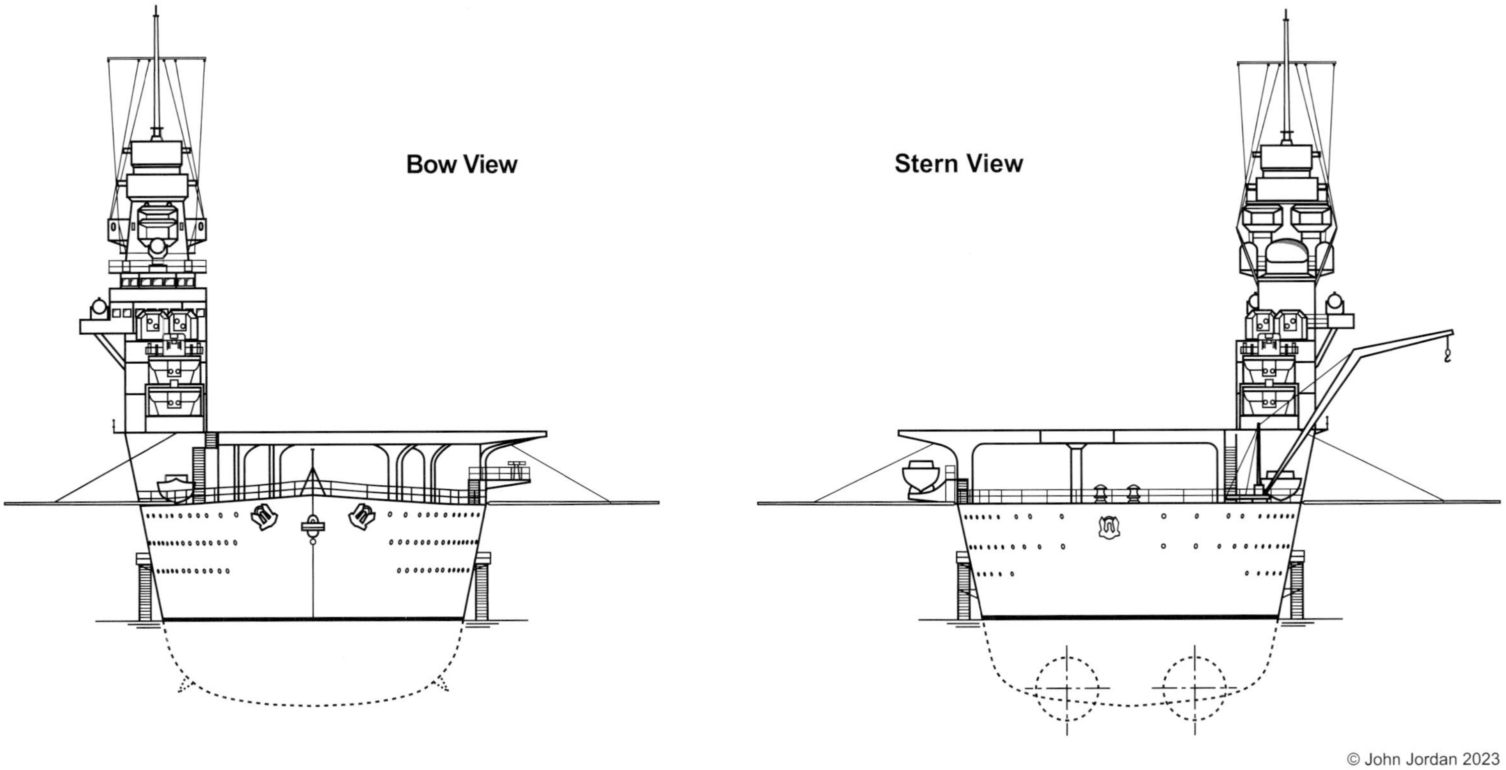

**Bow View**

**Stern View**

© John Jordan 2023

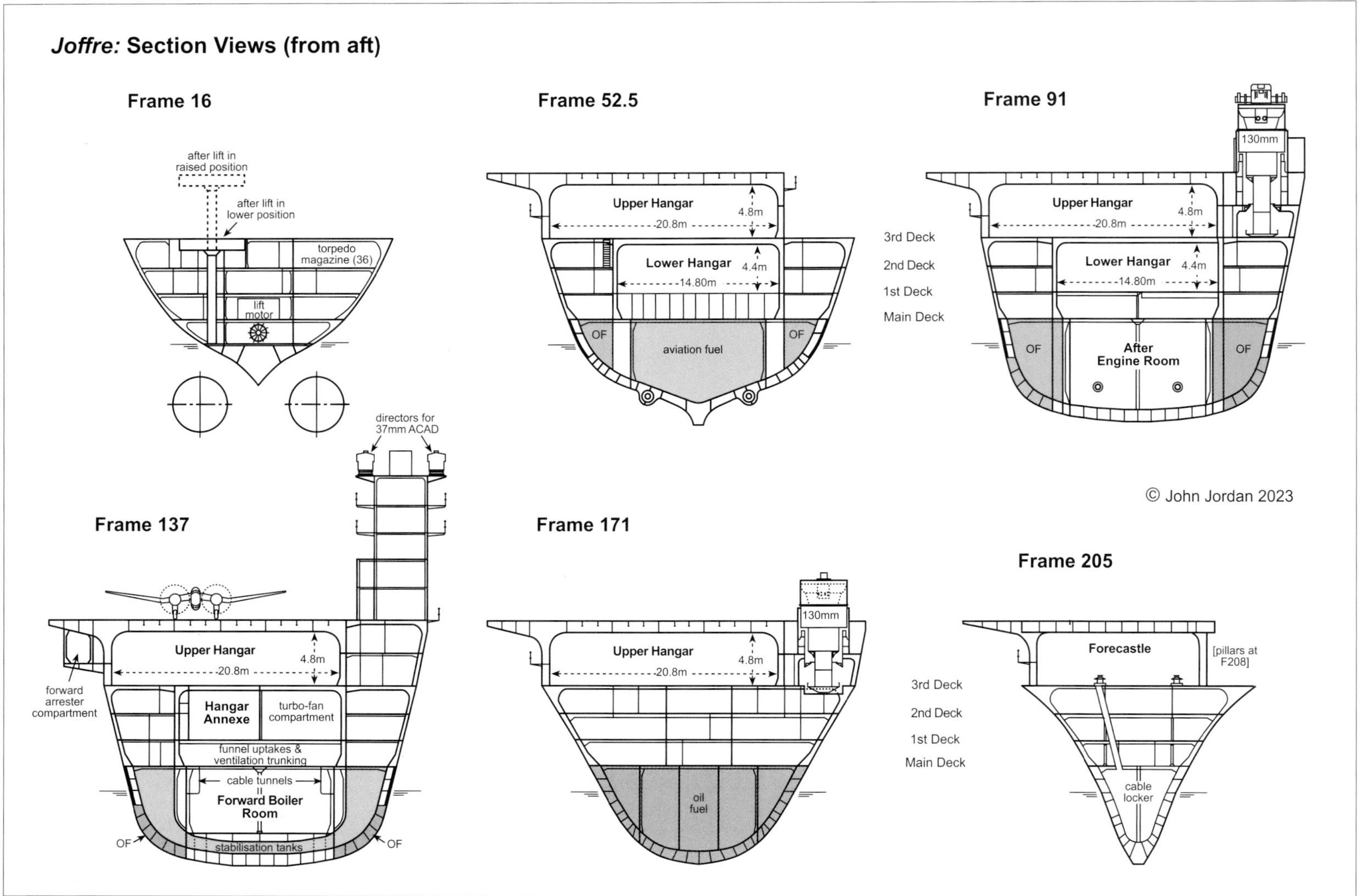


ships, abeam the island superstructure. Double-ended operations are evidenced by the provision of not one but two hooped landing sights, located between the second and third arresting cables at either end of the central landing section.

A major advantage of locating the arrester cables amidships was that this was the part of the flight deck least prone to pitching – a particular advantage in the heavy swells of the North Atlantic, which the *Marine Nationale* considered unfavourable to air operations. The configuration of the after end of the flight deck would also have made it difficult to locate the arrester cables close to the stern, as in the other major carrier navies, because of the danger that an aircraft approaching too low would crash into the after lift, with adverse consequences for subsequent air operations. On the other hand, air turbulence from the long, 'spiky' island superstructure would have been at its most intense and unpredictable over the midship section of the flight deck. US Navy-style flight deck operations using a permanent deck park were also precluded. No serious consideration appears to have been given to barrier nets, which are conspicuously absent from all the official plans,[7] so the flight deck would have to be kept clear during landing operations.

## HANGAR DECKS

In *Béarn*, the two superimposed hangars had different functions. The upper hangar, designated *entrepont aviation*, was reserved for the operational air group and was served by bomb and torpedo lifts and fuelling points. The lower hangar, designated *chambre de montage et de réserve*, was for aircraft assembly and for aircraft undergoing maintenance or in reserve. The aviation workshops were grouped around this lower hangar. The lower hangar was not served by the lifts, so movement between the lower hangar and the flight deck had to be executed in two phases using a system of overhead rails and pulleys (see Chapter 2).

This arrangement was taken a stage further in *Joffre*. The upper hangar, which was 158.5 metres long and 20.8 metres wide with a 4.8-metre overhead clearance, was designed to accommodate the entire air group of forty aircraft, which could be comfortably stowed three abreast. Like the flight deck, it was offset to port, with its starboard side aligned with the flight deck. The large 'T'-shaped lift serving the flight deck was at its forward end, and smaller lifts emerged at the level of the hangar floor for bombs, torpedoes, torpedo warheads, and aircraft parts. In line with British practice, aircraft were armed in the hangar before being raised to the flight deck.

[7] Crash barriers were a feature of the design of all the British carriers built during the 1930s, despite reservations on the part of the Royal Navy about the usefulness and viability of deck parks.

As in *Béarn*, the larger torpedo bombers were to be accommodated in the after section of the hangar, where the lifts for torpedoes and warheads were located, together with 'ready-use' lockers along the hangar walls for twenty torpedoes.[8] The smaller fighter aircraft would normally have been stowed in the forward section of the hangar, which could be closed off by a single fire curtain (see Flight and Hangar Decks drawing). The after end of the hangar incorporated a door giving access to a 'warm-up' area (*plage de réchauffement*) approximately 20 metres square, which allowed planes' engines to be started before they were moved to the flight deck to be spotted for take-off via the after aircraft lift. The latter was positioned abaft this warm-up area, its forward edge being some 20m from the after end of the hangar. This section of clear deck could also accommodate a large seaplane, which could be lifted on board using the heavy-lift crane located to starboard.

The two aircraft lifts were of unusual design, being operated by hydraulics rather than electrically driven cable systems. Each of the lift platforms was raised by a central pillar, which retracted into the hull of the ship when lowered, and there were roller guides at the forward end of the lift to prevent lateral movement (see drawings). One of the primary benefits of a hydraulically driven lift of this type was that it provided easy access from all sides. The comparatively narrow after lift of *Joffre* could be lowered flush with the deck. However, positioning the forward lift so close to the bow presented a serious structural problem in that a 17m-wide opening would have seriously weakened the hull girder. The solution was to seat only the 6m-wide central section fully into the deck, the outer 'wings' of the lift platform resting on the deck itself. This was recognised as an unsatisfactory solution – there is a constructor's note on one of the drawings stating that the depth of the upper platform needed to be reduced to the minimum as it necessitated an inclined ramp on the hangar floor up which the aircraft would have to be manhandled – although it was anticipated that most movements using this lift would, as we have seen previously, have been from the flight deck to the hangar.

The lower hangar, which was to be housed within the main hull, presented the customary problem of how best to run the funnel uptakes and ventilation trunking for the machinery spaces. The solution adopted was a half-hangar aft similar to that adopted in the PA14 study; dimensions were 79m by 14.8m with a slightly reduced 4.4-metre overhead clearance. The lower hangar was primarily for maintenance, and was not served by either of the main aircraft lifts; instead it was connected to the upper hangar by a conventional electrically powered 13m x 7m rectangular lift at its forward end. The lift was sufficiently wide to accommodate any current or projected aircraft with wings folded. It was offset to starboard, and the starboard sides of the upper and lower hangars aligned to permit fore-and-aft movement of aircraft to port of the lift. Forward of the lower hangar, and separated from it by a broad passageway, was a hangar annexe 42m by 6.6m with the same 4.4-metre clearance. This narrower hangar, which would presumably have been used for the stowage of aircraft parts, was offset to port to enable the uptakes and ventilation trunking for the machinery rooms to be run up to the island superstructure to starboard. Sliding doors in the lower hangar and the annexe were aligned on either side of the transverse passageway to facilitate movement of bulky items between the two.

[8] There was a magazine for a further thirty-six torpedoes aft (see section drawing at Frame 16).

## Table 2: CHARACTERISTICS

| | |
|---|---|
| **Displacement:** | 18,000 tons standard<br>25,335 tonnes normal |
| **Dimensions:** | |
| length | 228m pp, 236m oa |
| beam | 24.6m wl, 34.5m oa |
| draught | 6.6m aft |
| **Aviation:** | |
| flight deck | 201m x 27m |
| height above wl | 16.2m |
| upper hangar | 158.5m x 20.8m x 4.8m |
| lower hangar | 79m x 14.8m x 4.4m |
| lifts (LxW) | Fwd: 13m x 17m (max)<br>Aft: 12.5m x 6m |
| air group | 15 D.790 fighters<br>25 Br.810 recce bomber/torpedo attack |
| **Machinery:** | |
| boilers | 8 Indret small watertube, 20kg/cm$^2$ |
| engines | two-shaft Parsons geared turbines |
| horsepower | 120,000cv |
| speed | 33.5 knots |
| endurance | 7000nm at 20 knots, 3000nm at 33 knots |
| **Protection:** | |
| main belt | 105mm |
| main deck | 70mm |
| 130mm turrets | 20mm |
| **Armament:** | |
| DP guns | eight 130mm/45 Mle 1932 in twin DP mountings |
| light AA | eight 37mm/70 in ACAD twin mountings<br>twenty-eight 13.2mm Hotchkiss in quad mountings Mle 1929 |
| **Complement:** | n/a |

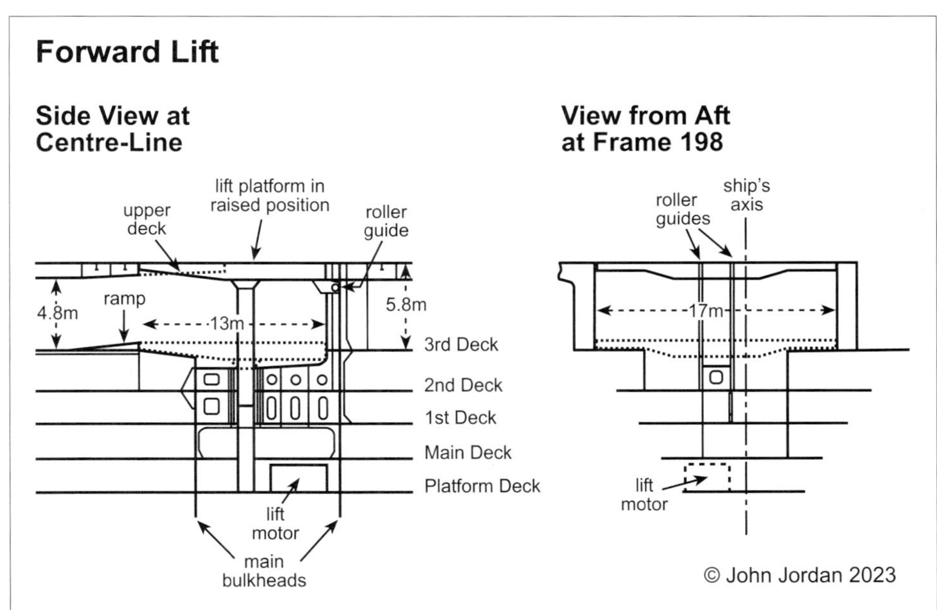

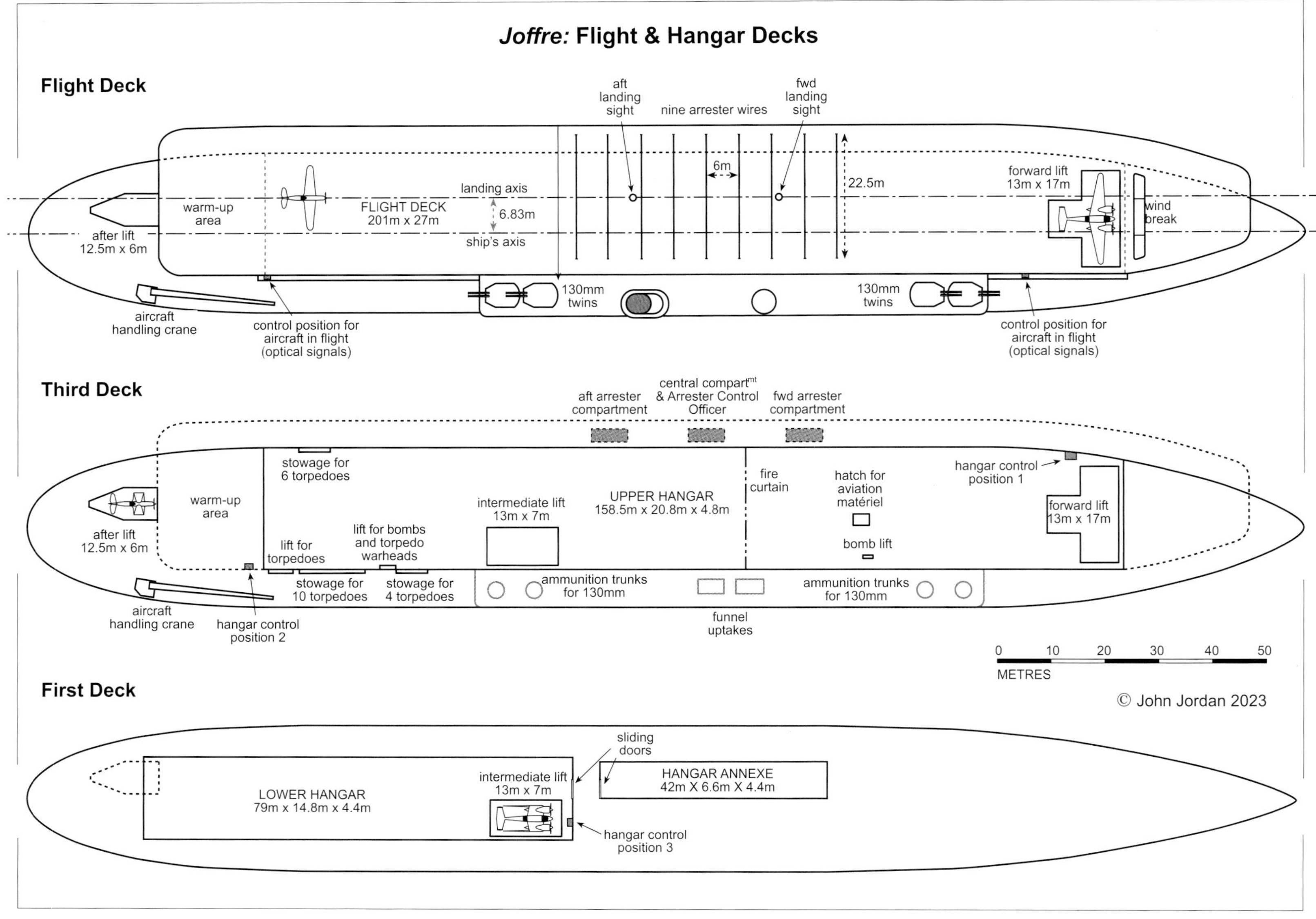


## AIR OPERATIONS

The proposed internal organisation of aviation personnel for *Joffre* is tabulated in an STCN plan dated 6 February 1940 entitled '*Tranmission d'ordres d'aviation*'. This is a particularly interesting document, revealing a well-thought-out command structure based on evolving French operational doctrine that reflects the aviation arrangements outlined above, and which shows a number of important differences from contemporary British and US Navy practice.

There were to be three key aviation officers: the *Chef de l'aviation*, the *Chef des manoeuvres-aviation* and the *Chef de l'arrimage* (see accompanying schematic, which has been translated into English from the original document). The *Chef de l'aviation*, translated here as 'Commander Air', exercised overall operational command of the air group in close liaison with the ship's captain and, where applicable, an onboard flag officer. His primary station was on the navigation bridge, where he had direct access to the Operations Room and the Transmissions Centre. His role was to plan and direct air missions, and besides the direct communications he shared with his two senior aviation officers there was a two-way intercom connection with two aircraft observers stationed at the forward and after ends of the Upper Bridge Platform, and with the ship's Meteorological Office at the base of the island (see Island drawing).

One deck level below, in a post corresponding to the RN/USN Flyco, to port immediately abaft the Admiral's Bridge, was the Flying Control Officer (*Chef des manoeuvres-aviation*). His area of responsibility extended beyond that of his counterpart in RN and USN carriers in that he was in charge not just of take-off and landing operations, but also of the movement of aircraft between the flight deck and the hangar via the lifts. This was entirely logical in the context of French operating procedures in that aircraft were generally brought up for ranging using the after lift and were lowered to the hangar using the forward lift immediately on landing and before the next aircraft made its final approach. The lifts were therefore an essential element of flying operations rather than constituting part of 'deck management', as was the case in the US Navy. The Flying Control Officer had under his direct command the Landing Sights Officer (stationed in the Aircraft Control Room in the after part of the island at flight deck level), the Arrester Control Officer (stationed in the Central Arrester Compartment on the port side), and had two-way communications with the Wind-break Station, the three air squadron offices (on the 2nd Deck to starboard between frames

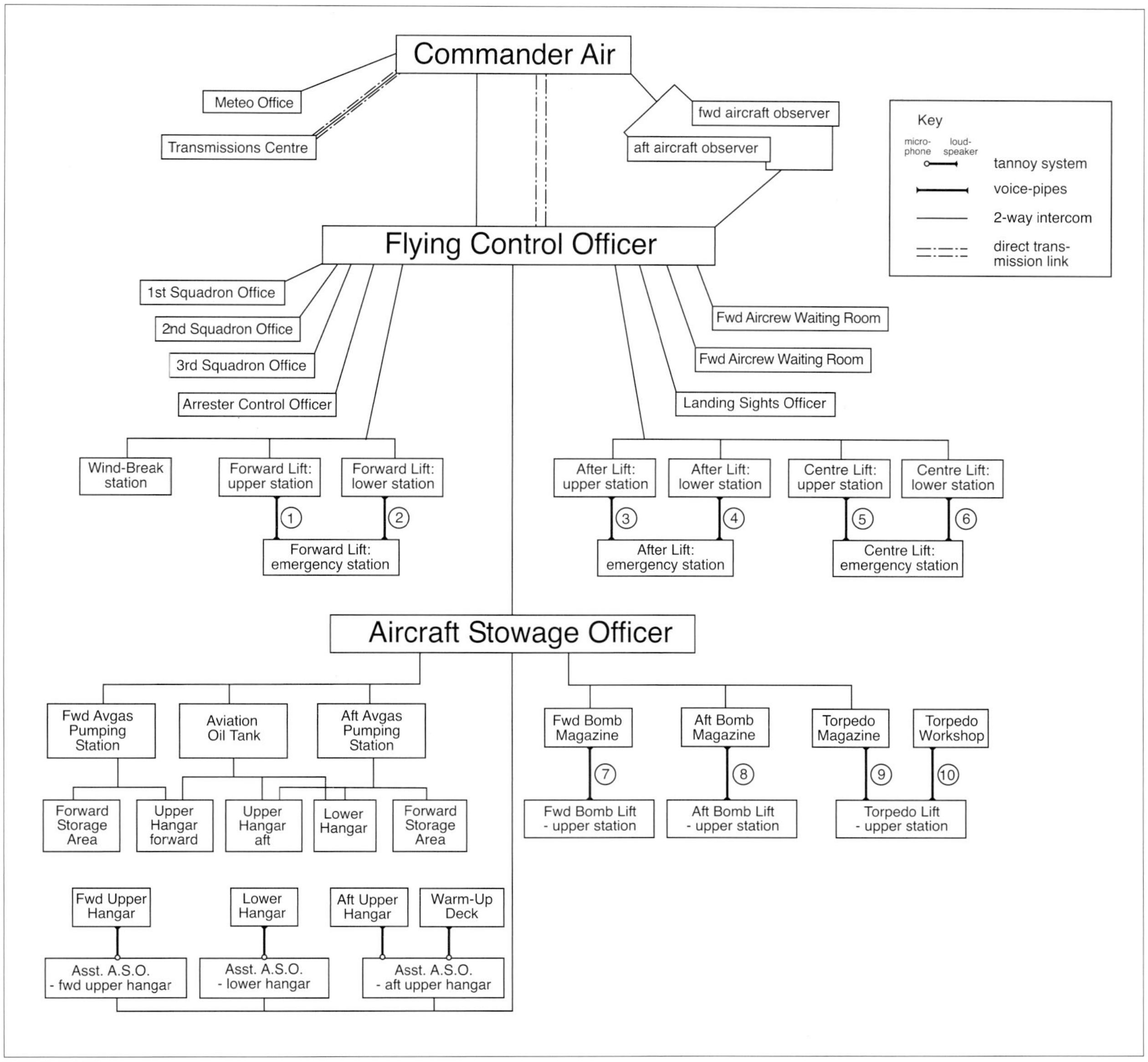

Commander Air

Meteo Office
Transmissions Centre
fwd aircraft observer
aft aircraft observer

Key
micro-phone
loud-speaker
tannoy system
voice-pipes
2-way intercom
direct trans-mission link

Flying Control Officer

1st Squadron Office
2nd Squadron Office
3rd Squadron Office
Arrester Control Officer
Fwd Aircrew Waiting Room
Fwd Aircrew Waiting Room
Landing Sights Officer

Wind-Break station
Forward Lift: upper station
Forward Lift: lower station
(1) (2)
Forward Lift: emergency station

After Lift: upper station
After Lift: lower station
(3) (4)
After Lift: emergency station

Centre Lift: upper station
Centre Lift: lower station
(5) (6)
Centre Lift: emergency station

Aircraft Stowage Officer

Fwd Avgas Pumping Station
Aviation Oil Tank
Aft Avgas Pumping Station
Forward Storage Area
Upper Hangar forward
Upper Hangar aft
Lower Hangar
Forward Storage Area

Fwd Bomb Magazine
(7)
Fwd Bomb Lift - upper station
Aft Bomb Magazine
(8)
Aft Bomb Lift - upper station
Torpedo Magazine
Torpedo Workshop
(9) (10)
Torpedo Lift - upper station

Fwd Upper Hangar
Asst. A.S.O. - fwd upper hangar
Lower Hangar
Asst. A.S.O. - lower hangar
Aft Upper Hangar
Warm-Up Deck
Asst. A.S.O. - aft upper hangar

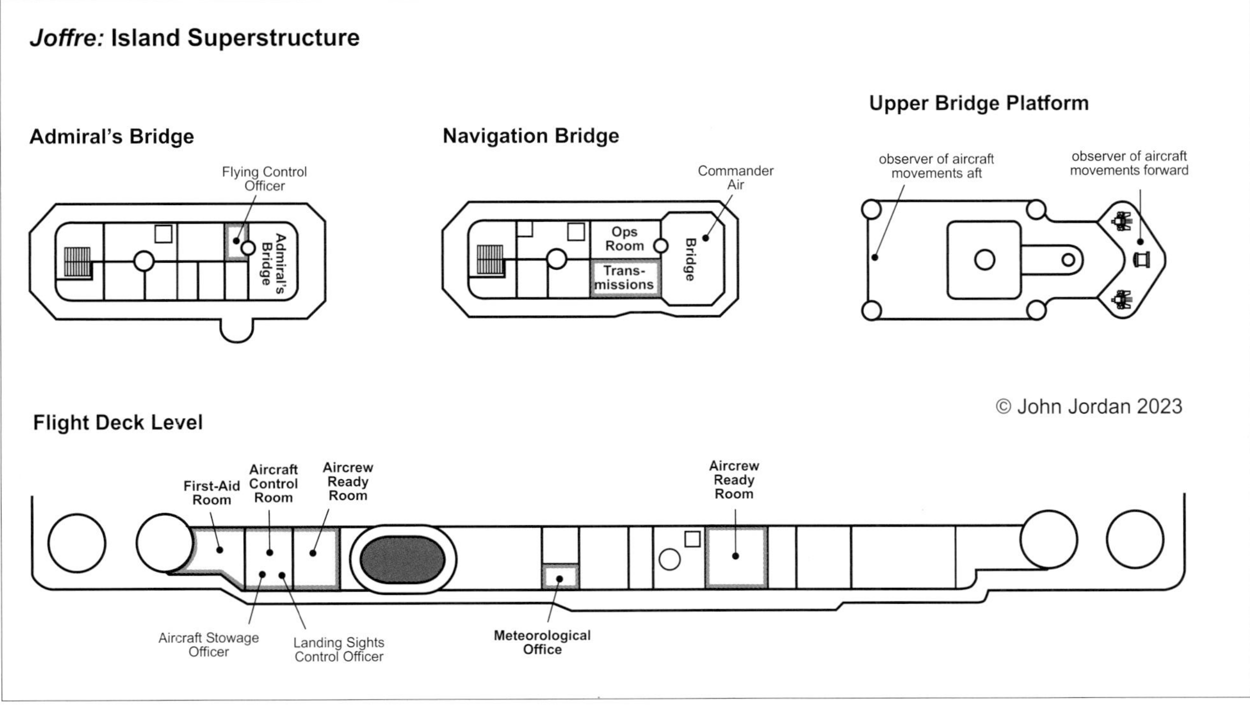

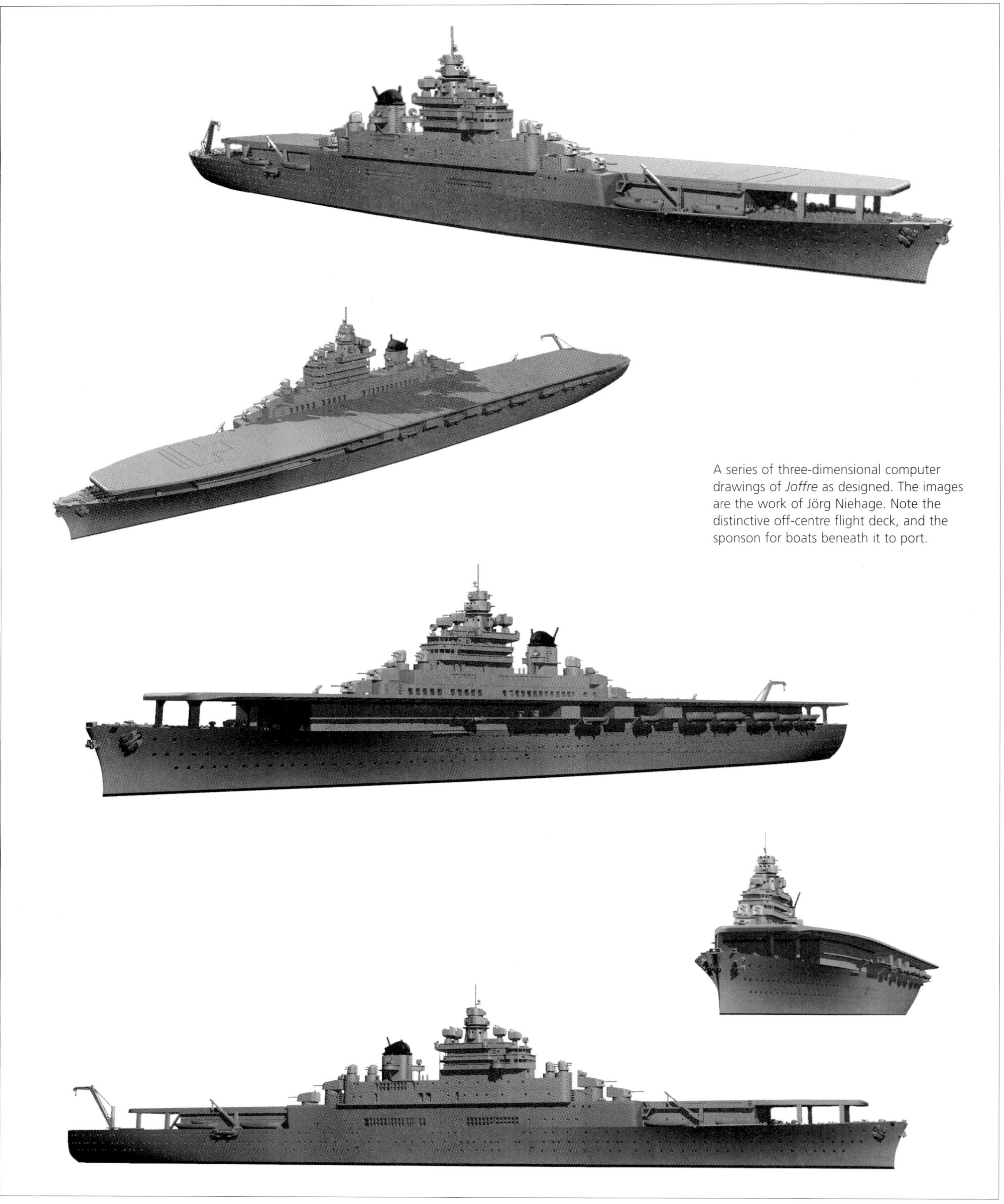

A series of three-dimensional computer drawings of *Joffre* as designed. The images are the work of Jörg Niehage. Note the distinctive off-centre flight deck, and the sponson for boats beneath it to port.

79 and 97), and the two aircrew ready rooms in the island at flight deck level.

The *Chef de l'arrimage*, translated here as 'Aircraft Stowage Officer', was responsible not only for aircraft stowage in the two hangars but also for all aspects of aircraft logistics, including arming and fuelling. Since aircraft were fuelled and armed on the upper hangar deck, not on the flight deck, this again was a logical arrangement. The Aircraft Stowage Officer had direct two-way communication with the forward and after aviation fuel pumping stations, the forward and after bomb magazines, and with the torpedo magazine and workshop. As he was stationed above decks, he delegated supervision of the hangars to three assistants. The control position for the first was on the port side of the upper hangar, adjacent to the forward lift. There was a second position just abaft of the upper hangar overlooking the 'warm-up area' and the after lift. The third position was at the forward end of the lower hangar, and was adjacent to the lift that served the two hangars (see Flight Deck & Hangars drawing).

## ARMAMENT

*Béarn*, in common with most of the early carriers, combined an anti-ship battery of 155mm casemate guns with a light HA armament of 75mm guns. By the 1930s, however, the dedicated anti-ship battery was being abandoned in the major navies in favour of a combination of heavy HA guns of 4.5in (RN) or 5in (USN/IJN) calibre with a dual-purpose capability[9] backed up by heavy multiple anti-aircraft cannon to provide a hail of fire at all angles of bearing and elevation, and light multiple machine guns for close-in engagement. This was the solution adopted for the *Joffre*, which was to have had an armament of eight 130mm (5.1in) dual-purpose (DP) guns in twin turrets, eight 37mm guns in automatic twin mountings, and twenty-eight 13.2mm Hotchkiss MG in quadruple mountings.

The 130mm dual-purpose mounting was a development of the twin mounting fitted in the fast battleships of the *Dunkerque* class, and had the same 20mm protective plating on the gunhouse. The lower mountings were virtually identical in configuration and layout to those of the battleships, but the superimposed mountings were extended to the rear to accommodate a trainable 5-metre rangefinder. The fixed rounds came up from the below-decks magazines via hoists that emerged onto a platform located at the level of the 3rd Deck between each pair of mountings; they were then transferred to the pusher hoists serving the guns (see drawing). Fire control arrangements were similar to those in *Dunkerque*. Two directors, the lower of which was equipped with a 6-metre rangefinder for anti-ship engagements, the upper with a 5-metre model for anti-aircraft fire, were superimposed on a short, stumpy tower atop the island superstructure, and were seated around the single mast. The transmitting station was located under armour, together with the lower steering position, immediately above the forward magazines (see Inboard Profile drawing).

9 Contemporary thinking was that the carrier would be accompanied by cruisers that could provide the necessary medium-calibre firepower and which were less vulnerable to crippling damage than the carrier herself.

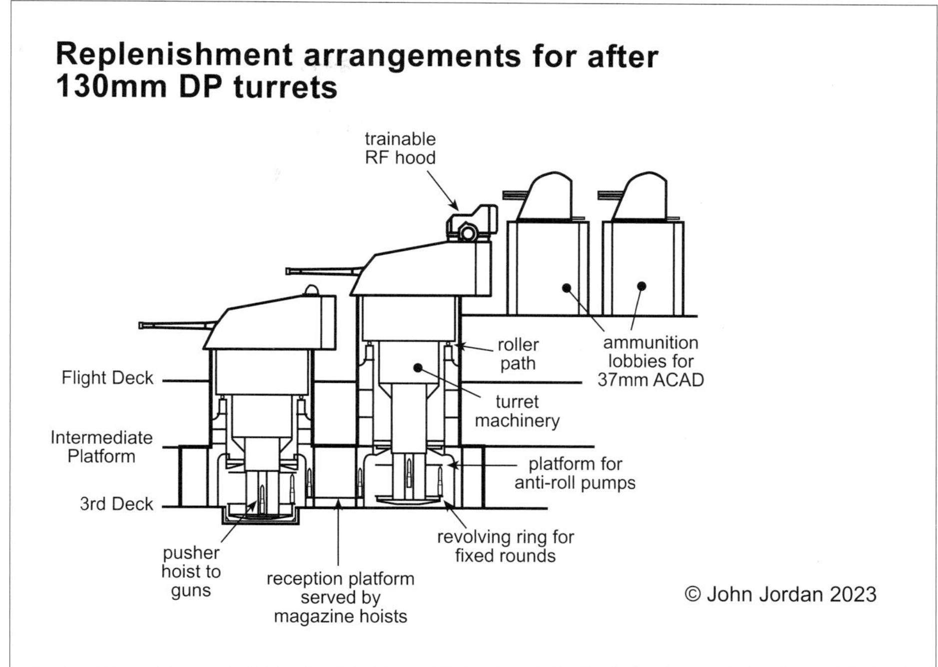


The 37mm mountings were to be of the advanced ACAD type, which had a theoretical rate of fire of 165rpg per gun per minute. They were mounted on cylindrical pedestals which formed their ammunition lobbies; continuous-feed belts constantly replenished by the gun crew supplied each gun with boxes of six cartridges, which were introduced automatically into the breech with loading at all angles of elevation. Early drawings of *Joffre* show superimposed 37mm mountings forward. However, once it was decided that the upper 130mm mountings would be fitted with tall, trainable rangefinder housings, the 37mm ACAD were mounted on the same (higher) level but *en echelon*, so that the port-side mountings had improved arcs when firing across the flight deck. Each of the 37mm ACAD mountings was controlled remotely from a director equipped with a 2-metre rangefinder via a remote power control (RPC) system driven by Sautter-Harlé electric servo-motors. The two forward directors were superimposed atop the island forward of the tower; the after directors were mounted side by side abaft the tower, overlooking the funnel.

The armament was completed by seven quadruple 13.2mm Hotchkiss Mle 1929 MG which, although comparatively lightweight weapons that would prove to be ineffectual except at the closest ranges, could deliver a high volume of fire. There were two mountings on the forecastle, two on the stern, and two atop the island abeam the forward ACAD directors. The seventh mounting was beneath the flight deck overhang to port, on a platform located forward of the ship's boats. Each of these mountings was provided with its own 1.5-metre rangefinder located close to the mounting.

## HULL, MACHINERY, PROTECTION

If the hull of *Béarn* was essentially that of a small battleship, that of *Joffre* was that of an enlarged cruiser of the period. She would have had the same two-shaft propulsion system and comparable protection to the contemporary light cruisers of the *De Grasse* class. As in the PA10/11 and PA13 studies, the unit machinery layout standard in contemporary

French cruisers was retained. The uptakes and ventilation trunking for the after boiler room, which was almost directly beneath the broad single funnel, emerged immediately forward of the short lower hangar aft, while those for the forward boiler room were led up to starboard of the hangar annexe, which was offset to port to facilitate this arrangement.

Power was increased over *De Grasse*, from 110,000cv to 120,000cv, with steam being generated by eight Indret boilers as opposed to four. The turbines for the port shaft were located in the Forward Engine Room, with the turbo-generators to starboard, while those for the starboard shaft were located in the After Engine Room, with the turbo-generators to port. The two-shaft arrangement had the advantage of simplifying the machinery layout and maximising the depth of the anti-torpedo system, but the power loading on each of the two shafts was exceptionally high for the period.[10] Maximum speed was to be 33.5 knots.

The protection system was likewise similar to that of contemporary cruisers, with an armoured citadel 120 metres in length to enclose the machinery spaces, the magazines, and the aviation fuel tanks, and a separate lightly armoured box over the steering gear (see drawing). The 105mm belt, which was approximately 3.7m deep, extended from the main deck to 1.45m beneath the waterline, and was enclosed at its ends by

10 Only twelve months previously, the designers of *De Grasse* estimated that 110,000shp was the maximum possible on only two shafts. The British went to three shafts for *Ark Royal* and the contemporary *Illustrious* class, which had slightly less powerful machinery. All of the earlier French interwar carrier projects were four-shaft designs.

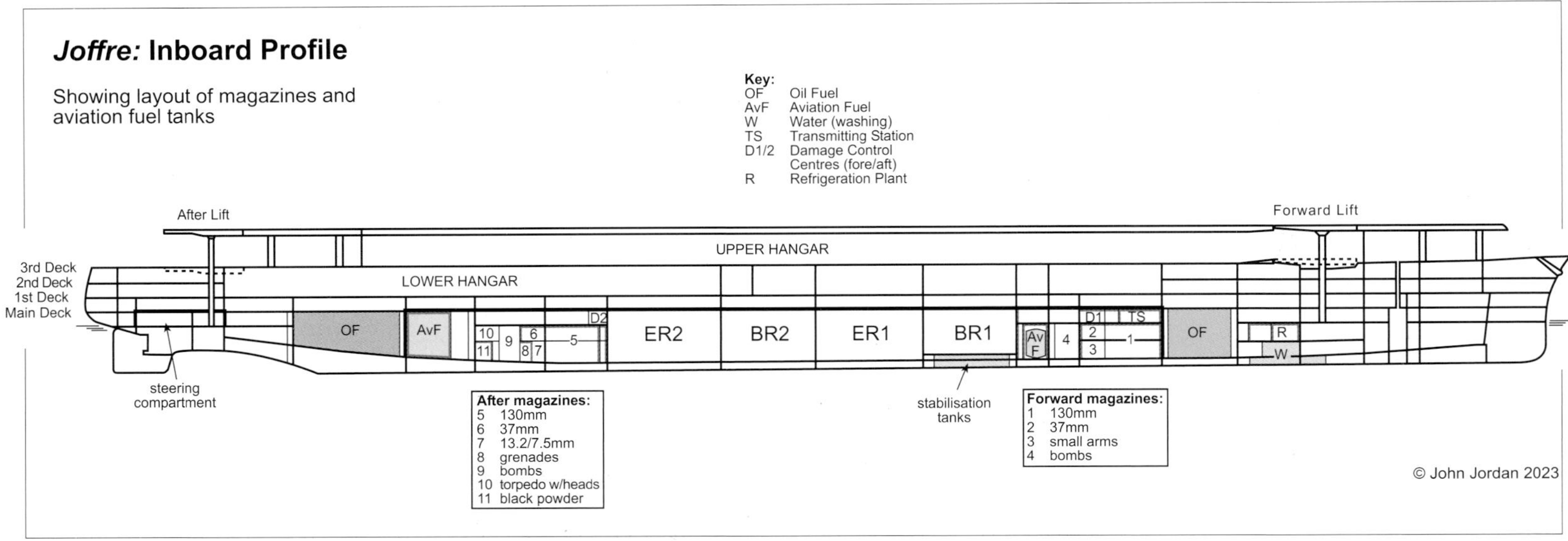


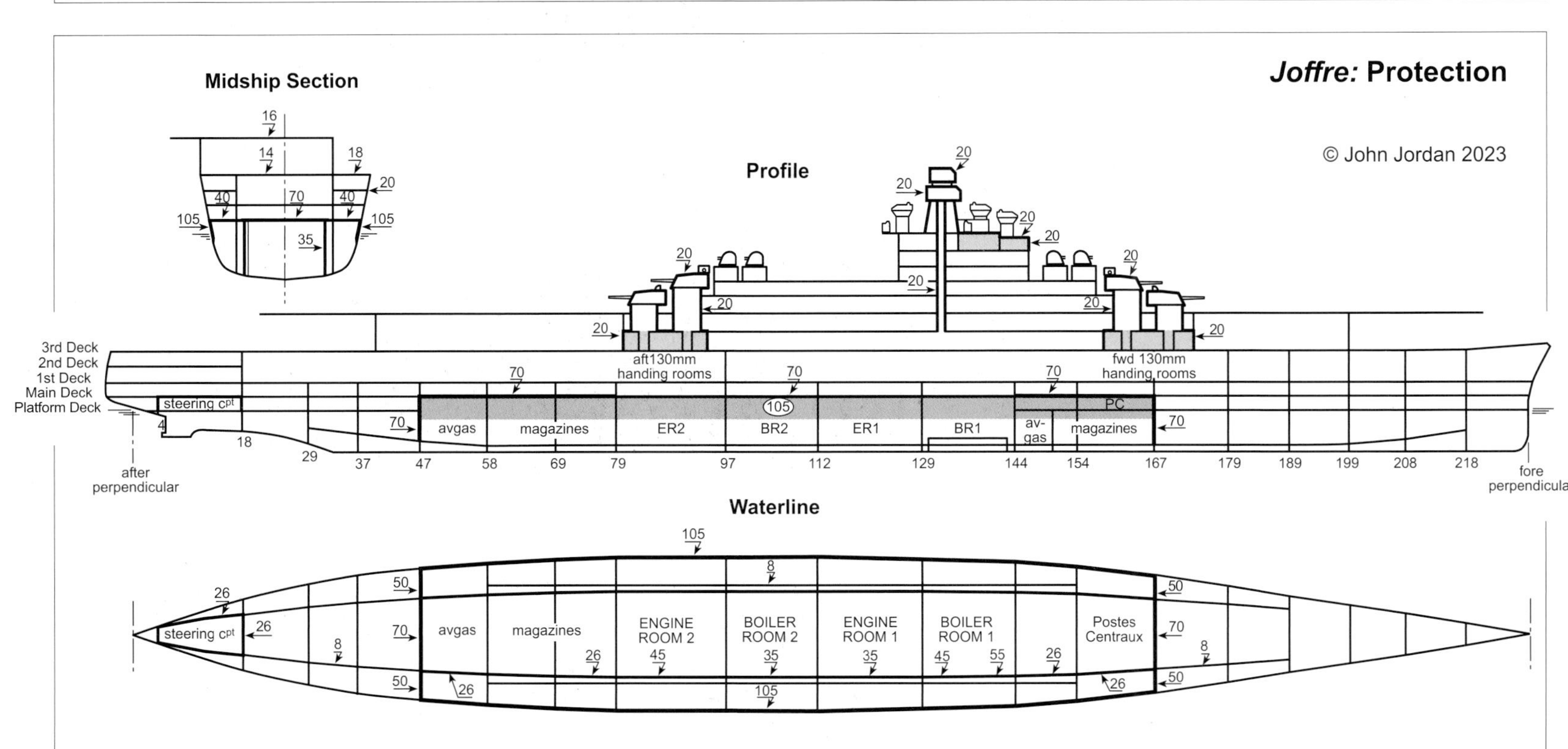

70mm transverse bulkheads. The armoured deck was a uniform 70mm over the magazines, avgas tanks and machinery spaces, reducing to 40mm outboard of the torpedo bulkhead; the latter varied in thickness between 35mm and 55mm abeam the machinery spaces, reducing to 26mm abeam the magazines fore and aft. Outboard of it was the customary 'sandwich' comprising alternate void compartments and heavy oil fuel tanks. Abeam the magazines the oil fuel was replaced by water – for washing or ballast – and abeam and beneath the forward engine room there was a tank stabilisation system similar to that devised for *Commandant Teste* to minimise roll in heavy weather. There was a holding bulkhead inboard of the torpedo bulkhead abeam the boiler and engine rooms. The maximum depth of the underwater protection system, from the outer face of the armoured belt to the torpedo bulkhead, was an impressive 6.6m.

The internal transverse bulkheads that separated the individual magazines and aviation fuel tanks fore and aft were sheathed in Alfol, an insulation material with a fire-resistant aluminium foil coating (see Inboard Profile drawing). The aviation fuel was stowed in three separate cylindrical tanks forward, each 3 metres in diameter and disposed athwartships between frame 145 and frame 149, but the more substantial aviation fuel stowage aft was a conventional full-width tank located between the torpedo bulkheads between frame 47 and frame 54, protected by Alfol and surrounded on all sides by void spaces or inert gas. The 130mm turrets, together with their hoists and upper handing rooms, were protected by 20mm plating, and there was similar plating for the command spaces in the upper part of the island, for the directors, and for the communications tube connecting the latter with the transmitting station.

## AIR GROUP

PA16 was designed at a time when aircraft technology was making a quantum leap forward. High-performance monoplanes were beginning to enter service with land-based air forces, compelling the navies operating carriers to raise their game and move to similar aircraft. In a further development, the US Navy had demonstrated the effectiveness of dive-bombing techniques against ships underway using purpose-designed biplanes such as the Curtiss SBC Helldiver (in service 1935), and despite the reservations expressed by naval staffs generally about the ability of aerial bombs to disable heavily armoured ships, the dive bomber was clearly a potentially useful addition to the carrier's air group. It initially seemed likely to the French that the carrier air group of the future would require many different types of aircraft, hence the emphasis on a large aircraft capacity in the designs that immediately preceded PA16. PA13, which featured two lower half-hangars with the funnel uptakes between them, was to have had a capacity of 70 aircraft (48 in the upper hangar, 22 in the lower); PA14, with only a single lower half-hangar, had a similar-sized air group and PA15, which had a full-length lower hangar, could stow 74 aircraft (44 + 30).

However, the primary missions of fighting for control of the air space over the battle fleet, reconnaissance and spotting for the battle fleet, and slowing the enemy battle line by torpedo attack remained to the fore. In the absence of a significant German or Italian naval air capability, there was no conception of independent carrier operations; the carrier would continue to operate close to and in support of the battleships. When she returned to operational service in 1935, *Béarn* was operating the following: the Wibault 74 high-wing monoplane fighter, which had entered service in 1932; the Levasseur PL.101 reconnaissance biplane, which was of similar vintage; and the large PL.7 biplane torpedo bomber, which had entered service in 1931. The fallow years of 1928–32, when the Navy had effectively lost control of naval aviation, had taken their toll, and in the haste to regain lost ground, a number of competing projects for new aircraft were

**Left:** Landing of a twin-engine Potez 56E on *Béarn* on 22 September 1936. *(Musée national de la Marine)*

initiated, most of which would deliver only prototypes before June 1940. Development would be protracted, and production correspondingly slow.

Despite these problems, some progress was made. A new high-wing monoplane fighter, the Dewoitine 373/376, was in the pipeline, but the first landings with this moderately capable aircraft would be made only in 1938. By this time, high-performance land-based fighters such as the German Messerschmitt Bf 109 and the Italian Fiat G.50 Centauro, both of which outclassed the D.376 by a considerable margin, were entering front-line service. The PL.101 was to be succeeded by a new three-seater biplane, the PL.108, in the spotter/reconnaissance role. Two prototypes, designated PL.107, were ordered in 1936 and underwent trials until 1939, but there were technical problems and the biplane configuration was increasingly questioned.

More interesting were the attempts to develop a satisfactory strike aircraft. As early as 1934, it was decided to investigate the possibility of using a twin-engine monoplane for the torpedo bomber role. Trials were conducted with a specially adapted transport aircraft, the Potez 56E, from 1936, the 2.6-tonne trials aircraft being fitted with an arrester hook and folding wings for the purpose (see Chapter 2). Developing an aircraft capable of lifting a 650kg torpedo had been problematic for the early carrier navies, and the additional lift and power generated by the twin-engine configuration was attractive – although there was a cost in terms of engine maintenance and fuel consumption.

At around the same time, the *Aéronavale* took its first steps towards developing a dive bomber, with a competition from March 1935 between the Gourdou-Leseurre GL.521 and the Nieuport Ni.140. The latter was a gull-wing monoplane similar both in conception and configuration to the German Ju-87 'Stuka'. Initial trials were followed by the construction of a prototype embarked aircraft, the LN.40, which first flew in June 1938. Six further 'pre-series' aircraft were ordered in 1937, and a further order for thirty-six production aircraft with tailhooks and folding wings (designated LN.401) for the *Aéronavale* followed. Production of the aircraft was slow – only twenty-four entered service before the Armistice. The engine proved to be underpowered, and problems were also experienced with series production of the planned gyroscopic bombsight, so that when the aircraft entered service they were limited to glide-bombing techniques with a diving angle of only 45–60 degrees, from 2000m to 300m.

It was against this fundamentally unsatisfactory background that discussions regarding the aircraft to be embarked on *Joffre* and her sister *Painlevé* took place in 1937–38. The first of the new ships would not be in service until late 1942 at the earliest, so it made sense to adopt a radical approach that took advantage of the latest developments in aircraft technology. Now that French capital ships and cruisers were generally equipped with catapult-launched seaplanes that could handle both reconnaissance and spotting, the key missions to be accomplished by carrier-based aircraft were: air superiority, area reconnaissance, and attack on enemy battleships and cruisers. *Joffre* was ultimately designed to accommodate an operational air group of forty aircraft, with the possibility of additional reserve aircraft being stowed in the lower hangar. At a time when the British Royal Navy was moving towards a moderately sized complement of multi-role aircraft of two basic types,[11] the French decided on a high-performance fighter capable of holding its own against land-based types, and a twin-engine multi-purpose attack aircraft capable of long-range reconnaissance, bombing and torpedo strike. Fifteen of the former and twenty-five of the latter would make up the ship's air group, a ratio that mirrored contemporary British practice.

The fighter was to be a navalised variant of the new Dewoitine D.520 currently under development for the *Armée de l'Air*. Design work for this aircraft, which was strikingly similar in configuration to the British Spitfire, had begun as a private venture in 1936, the first prototype flying only on 2 October 1938. An initial Air Force order for 200 production aircraft was followed by an order for 2,200 for the *Armée de l'Air* and 120 of a navalised variant with folding wings and an arrester hook (designated D.790) for the *Aéronavale* (see drawing for configuration and technical characteristics).

Specifications for the new attack aircraft were drawn up under the A47 Programme of 1937: speed was to be at least 300km/h, maximum weight 4–5 tonnes, and performance in each of the three roles was to be as follows:

- three-seat reconnaissance: two 75kg bombs, endurance 6hrs
- two-seat torpedo strike: one 650kg torpedo, endurance 3hrs
- three-seat bomber: four 150kg bombs, plus either two 225kg bombs or a single 450kg bomb; endurance 3hrs.

The aircraft would also be armed with three 7.5mm Darne MG.

Two prototypes were ordered in 1939: the CAO 600[12] and the Dewoitine D.750. Both were twin-engined aircraft with a twin tail boom, and had super-

**Table 3: PROTOTYPE ATTACK AIRCRAFT ORDERED 1939**

| | CAO 600 | D.750 |
|---|---|---|
| Dimensions: | | |
| wingspan | 16.5m | 15.9m |
| length | 12.4m | 10.4m |
| height | ??m | 2.9m |
| Engine: | | |
| type | Gnome Rhône 14M | Renault 12R |
| power | 2 x 670hp | 2 x 450hp |
| speed (max) | 380km/h at 1500m | 360km/h at 1500m |
| endurance | 900-1500km* | 900-1500km |
| Weight: | | |
| empty | ??kg | 2900kg |
| max load | 4660kg | 4500kg |
| Armament: | | |
| guns | two 7.5mm MG in wings | ditto |
| bombs | 4 x 150kg, 1 x 450kg | ditto |
| torpedo | 1 x 650kg | ditto |
| Crew: | | |
| torpedo attack | two | two |
| bomber/recce | three | three |

* The contract stipulated three hours as torpedo-bomber, 6 hours in recce mode.

**Source:** Dousset, *op cit.*

[11] The TSR Swordfish/FDB Skua pairing was to be followed by the similar Albacore/Fulmar combination.

## Dewoitine D.790

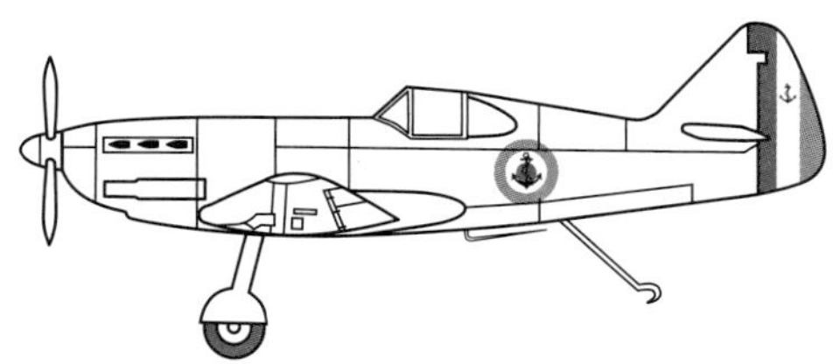

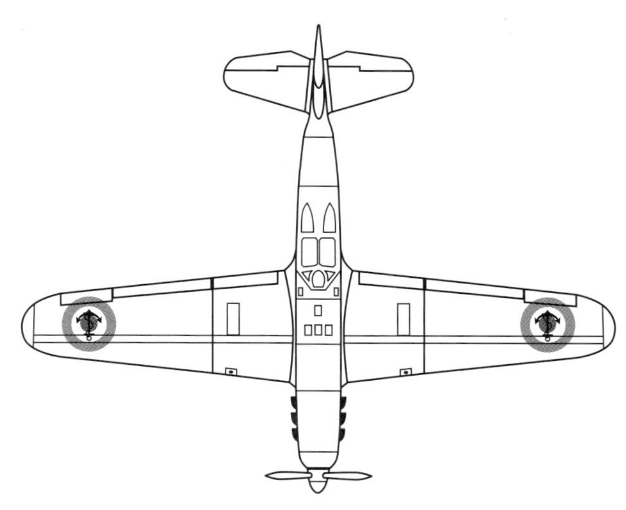

© John Jordan 2023

**Characteristics**

| | |
|---|---|
| Year: | adopted 1939; modified D.520 |
| Mission: | fighter |
| Construction: | metallic |
| Crew: | one |
| *Dimensions* | |
| Wingspan: | 10.3m (4.6m wings folded) |
| Length: | 8.8m |
| Height: | 2.6m |
| *Engine* | |
| Type: | Hispano-Suiza 12Y-45 V-type |
| Power: | 930hp |
| *Performance* | |
| Max. speed: | 550km/h @ 6000m |
| Ceiling: | 11,000m |
| Endurance: | 990km |
| *Weight* | |
| Empty: | 2150kg |
| Max. load: | 2800kg |
| *Armament* | |
| Guns: | one 20mm cannon in propeller boss<br>two 7.5mm MG in wings |

## Bréguet Br.810

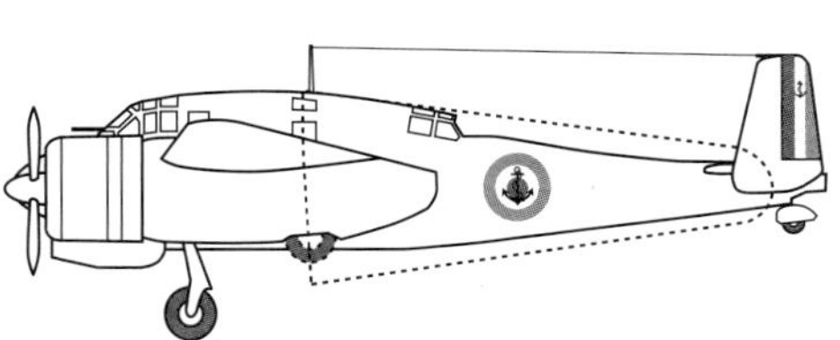

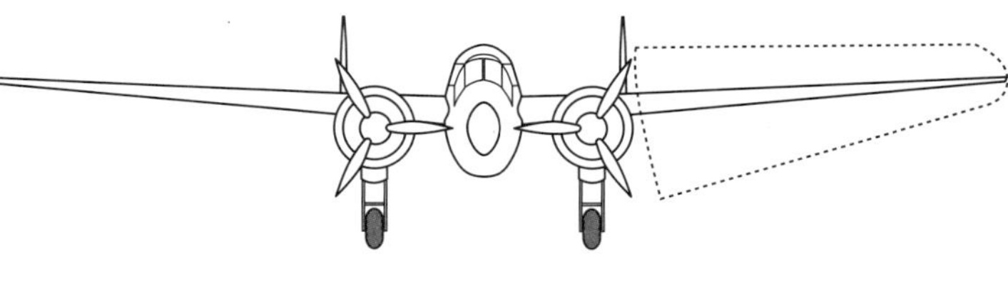

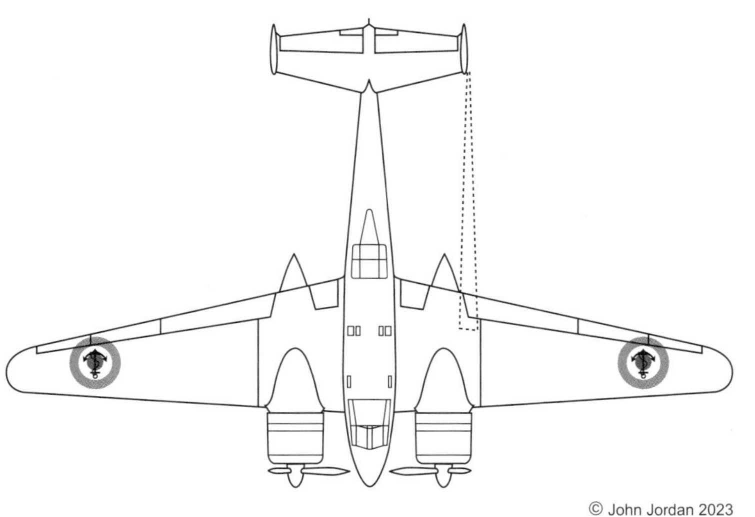

© John Jordan 2023

**Characteristics**

| | |
|---|---|
| Year: | adopted 1939; modified Br. 693 |
| Mission: | torpedo bomber |
| Construction: | metallic |
| Crew: | two/three |
| *Dimensions* | |
| Wingspan: | 15.36m (5m wings folded) |
| Length: | 10.3m |
| Height: | 3.2m |
| *Engine* | |
| Type: | Gnome-Rhône 14M-6 14-cyl. radial |
| Power: | 2 x 725hp |
| *Performance* | |
| Max. speed: | 490km/h @ 5000m |
| Ceiling: | 8500m |
| Endurance: | 1350km |
| *Weight* | |
| Empty: | 3700kg |
| Max. load: | 5470kg |
| *Armament* | |
| Guns: | one 20mm cannon<br>two nose, one fixed/one mobile rear 7.5mm MG |
| Bombs: | one M26DA torpedo or 400kg bombs |

imposed glazed positions forward for the pilot and for the bomber/navigator respectively. A wheeled variant of the single-engine Latécoère 299 torpedo floatplane, which had been adopted for the Aviation Transport *Commandant Teste* and had folding wings, was also seriously considered and a prototype ordered.

A new set of specifications issued in 1939 under the A80 programme eventually led to the adoption of a navalised variant of the *Armée de l'Air*'s Bréguet Br.693 bomber, the Br.810, which was similar in conception and general configuration to the British Bristol Beaufighter. The Br.810 would have had wings that rotated and folded back in the manner of some US Navy carrier aircraft (for configuration and technical characteristics, see the drawing).

## CONSTRUCTION AND FATE

The first of the two carriers authorised under the 1938 Estimates, *Joffre*, was duly laid down at Penhoët Saint-Nazaire on 26 November 1938. Work proceeded slowly, particularly after the mobilisation that accompanied the outbreak of war in September 1939, so that by the time of the Armistice in June 1940, the ship was only 20 per cent complete and probably the best part of a year from launch. Her sister *Painlevé*, due to be laid down on the same No 1 slipway following the launch of *Joffre*, was never begun. A third ship was to have been authorised in 1940 as a replacement for the elderly *Béarn* but the order never materialised. Construction of *Joffre* herself was effectively abandoned following the Armistice, and the hull was eventually dismantled on the slipway. The turbine machinery intended for the ship was installed in the Portzic underground power station built in 1947–51 to supply electricity to Brest Naval Dockyard.

Doubts regarding the ability of the French aviation industry to deliver modern aircraft suitable for carrier operation in sufficient numbers persisted, and in October 1938 – a month before *Joffre* was laid down – the American Vought company sent a SB2U-2 demonstrator to Paris with a view to selling the aircraft to the French. This led to an order for an export variant, designated V-156F, for the *Aéronavale*. A contract for twenty aircraft was placed on 19 February 1939, and a further batch of twenty was ordered three months

12 CAO = (Société des) Constructions Aéronautiques de l'Ouest.

**Below:** The carrier *Joffre* under construction on the Penhoët No 1 slipway. The photo was taken on 12 April 1939. In the background the 240-tonne 'Gusto' hammerhead crane towers over the Forme Caquot, where the battleship *Jean Bart* is under construction. *(CAA/SHD)*

later. The first aircraft arrived at Le Havre in July, and by the outbreak of war there were thirty-four V-156Fs in the inventory. The remaining aircraft were shipped to Canada to avoid being embargoed under the US Neutrality Act.

The V-156F would equip first AB1 Squadron, assigned to *Béarn* but subsequently redeployed ashore, then AB3. Landing trials with the latter squadron were conducted using *Béarn* in the Mediterranean during late April 1940 (see Chapter 2). The following month an order for a further fifty aircraft was placed with the American company. There were a number of important differences between the V-156F and the US Navy's SB2U-2 Vindicator. The throttle was reversed to deliver full power when the stick was pulled back, instrumentation was metric, French radio equipment was installed, and the French Darne 7.5mm MG replaced the US 0.30in MG. The French were not permitted to use the Vought bomb displacement gear; the French Alkan equipment was to be installed after delivery, but production and installation delays meant that combat missions over land during May 1940 were carried out using only the underwing bomb racks. The V-156F also had the wing-mounted fence-type dive brakes rejected by the US Navy. These aircraft could have operated from *Joffre*, but those delivered were employed for maritime patrol and, following the German invasion of Belgium and France, for ground attack missions.

With production of the *Armée de l'Air*'s D.520 fighter already experiencing serious delays due to technical problems, it was decided during the spring of 1940 to place an order in the USA for the Grumman G-36A, an export variant of the US Navy's F4F-3 Wildcat. The French order was for eighty-one aircraft to equip two carrier squadrons and a training squadron, plus a further ten aircraft for spares. The G-36A, which was powered by a Wright R-1820 Cyclone 9 radial engine and had non-folding wings, was to have been delivered unarmed and subsequently fitted with six 7.5mm Darne MG (two in the nose, two in each wing). In the event, these machines would be delivered to Britain, where they would be rearmed with four 12.7mm Browning MG and redesignated Martlet I.

## CONCLUSIONS

French experience with the PA16 programme shows just how difficult it was to kick-start the development of naval aviation after what was in effect a ten-year gap. In the early 1920s, the French had been just as enthusiastic about the aircraft carrier as Britain, the

Below: A close-up of the hull of *Joffre* under construction on the Penhoët slipway, taken on 4 January 1940. The hull is complete to the main deck, and the plating over the main machinery spaces is in place. *(CAA/SHD)*

**Right:** *Joffre* on 28 March 1940, two months before the invasion of France. The sides of the upper hangar are now in place. *(Lucien Morareau collection)*

USA and Japan. However, unlike the latter powers, France did not have large battlecruiser hulls suitable for carrier conversion, and *Béarn*, built on a battleship hull, proved too small and too slow. By the late 1930s, she was fit only for aircraft trials and training, whereas her contemporaries *Courageous* (RN), *Saratoga* (USN) and *Akagi* (IJN) remained very much first-line units. The absorption of the naval air arm into the *Armée de l'Air* in 1928 was undoubtedly a major setback. At a time when competitors were developing new aircraft and new operational concepts, French developments in carrier aviation were stuck in a time warp. When the Navy decided to build a new generation of carriers in 1937 it was faced by the need simultaneously to develop new ships and new aircraft, and to undertake a major expansion in the training of aircrew.

In addition to these very real practical difficulties, there were also philosophical difficulties to confront. The Washington Treaty of 1922 had left the *Marine Nationale* with a rump of elderly battleships, all of which by the 1930s were approaching the end of their active service lives. Their replacements, urgently required to match the new battleships of Germany and Italy, were costly in terms of both funding and infrastructure. Not only was there a distinct lack of influential aviators in the French naval officer corps, but many in the fleet were unconvinced of the value, and indeed of the survivability of aircraft carriers in the principal naval theatres in which the *Marine Nationale* would operate.

Most of the relevant indicators suggest a marked lack of conviction in the French carrier programme. *Joffre* was only 20 per cent complete after almost two years on the slipway, despite the urgency of first the political, then the military situation. Her sister *Painlevé* could not be laid down until she was launched; and in April 1940, the slipway on which the latter ship was to have been built was reallocated to the first of the new battleships of the *Alsace* class. Arguably the primary impetus for the construction of these ships came from the two German carriers laid down in late 1936. However, shortly after the outbreak of war, work on the second of these was suspended, and completion of *Graf Zeppelin* assumed a low priority. Moreover, the Royal Navy now had primary responsibility for the North Atlantic, and the British had numerous fleet carriers available for deployment with the Home Fleet, making the requirement for French carriers in this theatre superfluous.

The new carriers were competing with a new generation of battleships for a limited number of construction berths of the requisite dimensions and, in consequence, the PA16 programme effectively ground to a halt. Competition with the *Armée de l'Air* also made it highly unlikely that the aircraft intended for these ships would be delivered within an acceptable timescale, even if sufficient naval pilots and trained navigators could be provided for them. The aircraft ordered from the USA during 1940 could have deployed from *Joffre* had she been completed, but they could equally have been based ashore and deployed against Italian shipping.

Numerous tactical and operational lessons concerning the use of carriers were learned by the Allied powers during the first two years of the Second World War. Radar in particular had a major impact on carrier air operations, as the carrier could now defend herself against strikes from modern land-based aircraft by vectoring out combat air patrols to intercept attackers. The consequences of these developments were: the embarkation of high-performance aircraft able to compete with their land-based counterparts; more numerous air groups with a larger fighter component; virtually continuous, high-tempo air operations; and sufficient aviation fuel stowage to support larger air groups and continuous operations.

The air group intended for *Joffre* comprised modern, high-performance aircraft adapted from land-based types, the lifts allowed for more flexibility than their RN counterparts, and the capacious hangars could easily have accommodated more than the projected forty aircraft. However, it is not clear whether the navalised fighters and bombers of French manufacture would have been sufficiently robust for shipboard deployment; the D.520 fighter was remarkably similar in configuration to the British Spitfire, and the D.790 naval variant would undoubtedly have experienced the same problems as its RN counterpart, the Seafire. The configuration of the after part of the flight deck and after lift in the PA16 design was not conducive to landing over the stern, and the location of the arresting wires amidships would have precluded a deck park. Moreover, the limited aviation fuel stowage – approximately 270,000 litres – was insufficient for continuous operations even by the designed air group of forty aircraft, twenty-five of which were to be twin-engine models with relatively high fuel consumption. (In the revised PA16A design drawn up in January 1945 on the basis of war experience, avgas stowage was virtually doubled from 200 tonnes to 375 tonnes.) Despite a number of interesting and innovatory features, it is questionable how successful *Joffre* would have been as an operational carrier, and whether the design was sufficiently flexible to adapt to the high-tempo air operations that would become the norm during the Second World War.

## CHAPTER 6

# WAR AND POST-WAR

DURING THE OCCUPATION, THE NAVAL General Staff moved to Vichy, the new centre of government, but part of the *Services Techniques* remained in Paris. The Technical Bureau was attached to the *Service des constructions navales de la marine marchande* belonging to the Directorate of Naval Industries, which answered directly to the Minister for the Navy and the Colonies. Studies were undertaken with a view to ensuring that the Navy kept abreast of current technical developments abroad in preparation for a future change in the political situation, and also to ensure that the qualified personnel were not diverted to work on projects for the Germans (or even despatched to Germany).

Early wartime designs saw a continuation of the series of interwar studies, with particular attention being paid to underwater protection. PA17 (May 1942) was an enlargement of *Joffre*, with a trial displacement of 22,980 tonnes. Length between perpendiculars was 228 metres and beam 24.8 metres. Horsepower remained the same at 120,000cv, and the armament (4 x II 130mm DP, 4 x II 37mm and 7 x IV 13.2mm MG) was identical. The ship would have had the same arrangement of two superimposed hangars and three aircraft lifts, the third of which served the lower hangar.

The later PA18 (July 1943) had a broader hull based on that of the fast battleship *Dunkerque*, and had a trial displacement of 26,500 tonnes. Length was again 228 metres (pp), but beam increased to 28 metres and draught was 7.8 metres. The ship would have had a maximum speed of 30 knots with 90,000cv, and a range of 7200nm at 18 knots. There were superimposed hangars with three lifts, as in PA18, but the dual-purpose main armament of eight 130mm in twin turrets was complemented by a uniform light anti-aircraft battery comprising thirty-six of the new 25mm Hotchkiss MG.

A parallel study developed between May 1942 and March 1943, PA19 and PA19V, was for a hybrid carrier/cruiser with three triple 152mm turrets. PA19 would have had a trial displacement of 40,750 tonnes, and PA19V 45,000 tonnes. Dimensions were identical but in PA19V, which had improved protection, horsepower was reduced from 150,000cv to 120,000cv, and speed from 31.5 knots to 26 knots. The anti-aircraft armament comprised seven twin 100mm HA and forty-three 25mm MG for PA19 and eight twin 100mm and thirty 25mm for PA19V.

These studies for large fleet carriers were complemented by a smaller ship with a cruiser hull, which may have been inspired by the US Navy's CVL. With a length of 180 metres between perpendiculars, a beam of 22.5 metres and a draft of 5.8 metres, the ship would have had a trial displacement of only 11,000 tonnes. Two-shaft steam propulsion machinery rated at 56,000cv was to deliver a maximum speed of 29 knots. There was a single hangar and two aircraft lifts, and the ship was armed with six 100mm HA guns and twenty-two 25mm MG.

Projects 21 and 21V (dated February and April 1943) were based on the hull of the *Richelieu* class, and would have had a trial displacement of 42,270 tonnes and 45,513 tonnes respectively. These were hybrid battleship/carriers, armed with either a quadruple (PA21) or a triple (PA21V) 380mm turret, eight 100mm HA, eight twin 37mm and twenty single 25mm Hotchkiss MG, and had two superimposed hangars topped by a flight deck. Dimensions were 242m pp x 33m x 9.1m. PA21 had the standard

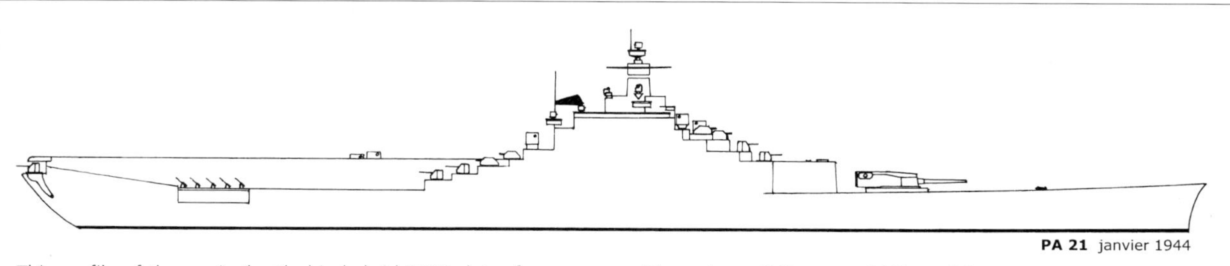


This profile of the carrier/battleship hybrid PA21 dates from January 1944. The hull is essentially that of the *Richelieu* class, with the forward 380mm turret retained. A double hangar topped by a flight deck has been constructed atop the original hull, and there is a long, stepped island to starboard to accommodate the uptakes from the boilers plus a powerful anti-aircraft armament. Characteristics were to have been as follows:

Displacement: 46,100 tonnes (trials)
Dimensions: 252m pp x 34.3m x 9.5m
Propulsion: 160,000cv = 31.5 knots
Endurance: 10,000nm at 18 knots
Armament: 1 x IV 380mm, 12 x II 100mm, 8 x II 37mm ACAD, 24 x I 25mm

Note that these studies would have provided a template for a future conversion of the battleship *Jean Bart*, only the forward turret of which had been completed prior to her escape to Casablanca. *(Drawn by Jean Moulin)*

*Richelieu* propulsion plant rated at 150,000cv for a maximum speed of 31 knots; in PA21V, this figure was reduced to 130,000cv. Endurance for both variants was 10,000nm at 18 knots.

The triple 380mm turret would have been the model planned for installation in the battleship *Alsace*. A further, slightly enlarged PA21 variant dated June 1943 and displacing 46,100 tonnes, would have had a quadruple turret forward. This would have provided a template for a conversion of *Jean Bart*, only the forward turret of which had been completed before her escape to Casablanca in June 1940.

An even larger design for a hybrid battleship/carrier, PA23, armed with eight 380mm guns in two quadruple turrets, was presented in January 1944. With a length between perpendiculars of 301 metres, a beam of 41 metres and a draught of 11.4 metres, the ship had a designed displacement of fully 78,500 tonnes. This 'paper' project was beyond the realms of fantasy: it could not have been built or accommodated in any of the current (or projected) docks, nor could it have been berthed in any of the current naval bases, either in metropolitan France or in the colonies, due to its exceptional draught.

On either side of this study were two more conventional carrier designs, PA22 and PA24. The former, dating from June 1943, had a hull 224 metres long and displaced 18,460 tonnes. A steam propulsion plant delivering 105,000cv could drive the ship at 32 knots. There was a single hangar with two aircraft lifts, and the armament comprised eight twin 100mm guns, twelve twin 37mm and twelve single 25mm Hotchkiss MG. PA24 was a larger, double-hangar design with a hull of identical length but with a beam of 29.6 metres compared with 24.3 metres. A figure of 120,000cv was necessary for the designed speed of 31 knots; endurance, an estimated 8000nm at 18 knots, was unchanged, as was armament, which was exclusively for use against hostile aircraft.

A series of designs designated PA25 featured alternative types of carrier. PA25 (no distinguishing letter) was a hybrid battleship/carrier with a quadruple 280mm (not a standard French gun calibre!) aft, and an anti-aircraft armament of twelve 115mm (4.5in) and thirty quad 25mm mountings. The design featured a 250mm belt and an upper armoured deck 130mm thick. Another variant of this study had eight twin 100mm mountings in place of the (non-standard) 115mm guns.

Other PA25 variants included: PA25A, a large fleet carrier designated 'war type' (*guerre*) of 28,000 tonnes; a light fleet carrier PA25C (June 1944), which had a 200-metre flight deck atop a single hangar and an armament of eight 100mm plus a mix of USN-type 40mm Bofors (8 x II) and 20mm Oerlikon guns (single), but a displacement of only 14,600 tonnes and a speed of only 22 knots (26,000cv); PA25D, which had a flight deck that ended 10 metres short of the bow and a uniform light AA armament comprising eight quad Bofors mountings; and PA25E, a 15,000-tonne auxiliary carrier designated '*paquebot*' (ocean liner), which could have attained 26.65 knots with 40,000cv or 29 knots with 70,000cv.

The PA26 series was for a large but conventional fleet carrier comparable to the US Navy's *Essex* class. PA26D would have had a designed trial displacement of 33,950 tonnes. Length between perpendiculars was 250 metres – the maximum that could be accommodated in the docks at Brest, beam 32.6 metres and draught 8.4 metres. The steam propulsion plant would

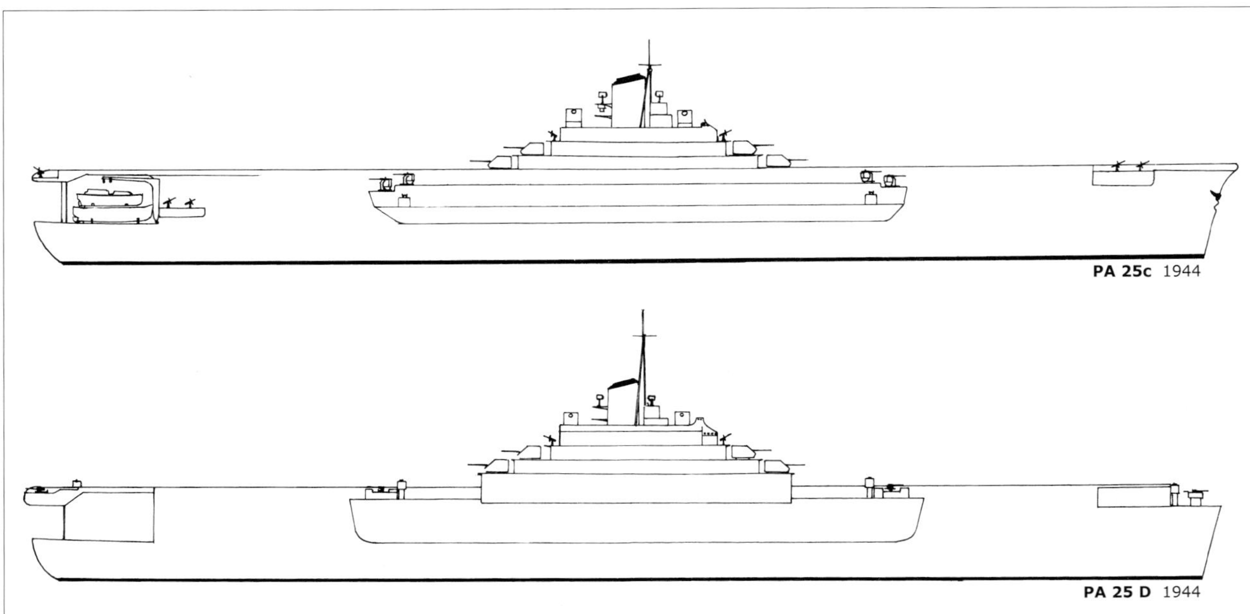


Project PA25C of June 1944 had a full-length flight deck and an enclosed bow, and may have been influenced by the British light carriers of the *Colossus* class. There was a single hangar with two lifts. Characteristics were as follows:

Displacement: 14,600 tonnes (trials)
Dimensions: 200m oa
Propulsion: 26,000cv = 22 knots
Endurance: 7400nm at 15.5 knots
Armament: 4 x II 100mm, 8 x II 40mm Bofors, 20 x I 20mm Oerlikon

PA25D had an open bow, reducing the length of the flight deck to 190 metres, and had a uniform light AA armament comprising eight quad Bofors.

*(Drawn by Jean Moulin)*

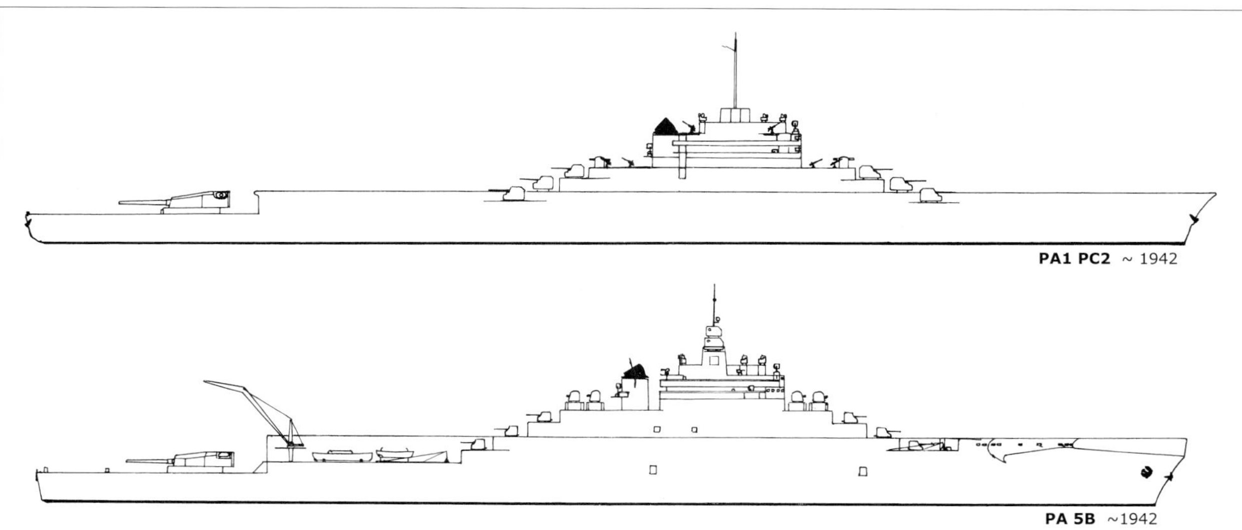


PA1 PC2 of 1943 was a hybrid battleship/carrier with a quad 330mm turret of the *Dunkerque* type mounted on the quarterdeck and offset one metre to starboard of the middle line. This series of studies featured a US Navy-style turbo-electric propulsion plant, which allowed considerable flexibility in the placing of the boilers and the machinery. Locating the big-gun turret aft nevertheless required permanent ballast forward. Characteristics were:

Displacement: 47,600 or 50,000 tons standard
Dimensions: 242m pp, 251.5m oa
Propulsion: 120,000cv on two shafts = 25? knots
Endurance: 7400nm at 15.5 knots
Armament: 1 x IV 330mm, 12 x II 115mm, 20 x IV 25mm Hotchkiss MG

In the PA5 series the calibre of the guns in the quadruple turret was increased to the 380mm of *Richelieu*. The characteristics of PA5B were:

Displacement: 42,065 tonnes (trials)
Dimensions: 238m pp x 31.7m
Propulsion: 110,000cv on two shafts = 25? knots
Armoured belt: 250mm
Armament: 1 x IV 380mm, 12 x II 115mm, 8 x 37mm ACAD

*(Drawn by Jean Moulin)*

have delivered 120,000cv for 31 knots, and there would have been two superimposed hangars and three lifts. The armament would have comprised eight twin 130mm DP mountings, six quad 40mm Bofors and twelve 20mm Oerlikon guns.

A further series of largely experimental designs, designated PA1–5 with multiple variants, was embarked upon between 1942 and 1944. These were large, hybrid battleship/carrier types that featured a triple or quadruple turret on the quarterdeck. The calibre of these guns was variously 280mm (11in), 305mm (12in), 330mm (as in *Dunkerque*) and 380mm (as in *Richelieu*). Most featured heavy protection. PA1 had a novel turbo-electric propulsion system, with two groups of electric motors driven by four turbo-alternators supplied with steam by four boilers; the two shafts and their propellers were located in a tunnel to provide a degree of protection against torpedoes. Several of these designs had a heavy armoured belt 250–327mm in thickness, and some had a 190mm armoured flight deck.

In the autumn of 1942, the Germans decided to complete the cruiser *De Grasse*, currently on the stocks in the Lanester ship hall at Lorient, as an auxiliary aircraft carrier. Construction of this vessel had been halted in June 1940 when she was 28 per cent complete. A study was duly undertaken, and *De Grasse* would have been completed as a carrier with a single hangar capable of accommodating thirty-three aircraft, a standard displacement of 11,400 tons, and a speed of 32 knots. Work began in late 1942 but was abandoned in early February 1943 due to a shortage of materials and labour. The ship was then struck by two Allied bombs. In May 1945, the *Commissariat de la Marine* found that the shipyard workers had concealed a large quantity of material within the lower hull as an act of sabotage. *De Grasse* would eventually be completed as an anti-aircraft cruiser.[1]

The *Forces navales françaises libres* (FNFL) in London had a severe shortage of personnel, which limited their

[1] See Jordan & Moulin, *French Cruisers 1922–1956*, Seaforth Publishing (Barnsley, 2013).

In August 1942, the Germans drew up plans for the completion of the cruiser *De Grasse* as an auxiliary aircraft carrier. She was to operate thirty-three aircraft and would have had a maximum speed of 32 knots. The weapons and sensors were to have been of German design and manufacture.

*(Drawn by Jean Moulin)*

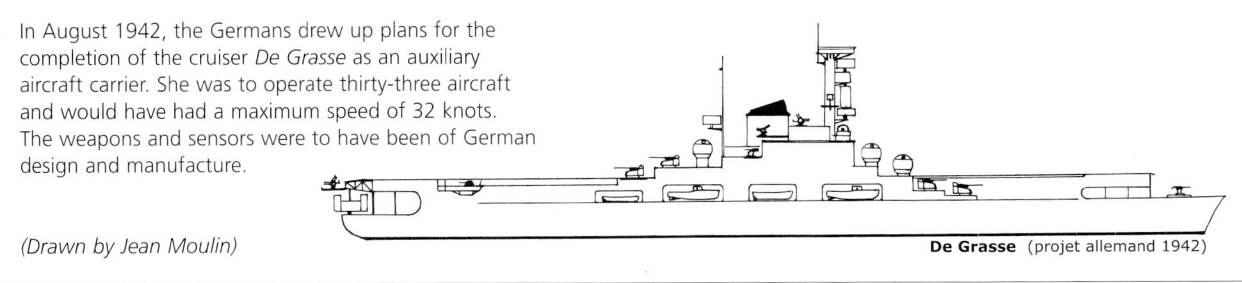

activities and their development. They would have liked to man a carrier with an air group but lacked the means to do so. There was a proposal to mount a catapult for a fighter following the British CAM model on the merchantmen *Cap des Palmes*, *Fort Richepanse* and *Indochinois*, but it came to nothing. Four pilots from the *Ile de France* fighter squadron were embarked on the carrier *Indomitable* in December 1942. The French also expressed an interest in acquiring one of the British escort carriers built in the USA.

The FNFL merged with the *Forces maritimes d'Afrique* (FMA) on 4 August 1943. Rear Admiral André Lemonnier, Chief of the Naval Staff, was committed to building a powerful new fleet. He requested the transfer of an escort carrier of the *Archer* class in July 1944, and proposals were advanced for the conversion of *Jean Bart*, *Commandant Teste* and one of the 10,000-ton cruisers – none of which were practical given the current political situation. Lemonnier also asked the Americans for the transfer of a fleet and an escort carrier. This would eventually lead to the transfer of the British CVE *Biter*, which became *Dixmude* (see Chapter 7).

## POSTWAR PROPOSALS

After the Liberation, studies resumed under more realistic conditions than during the Occupation. Not only did the studies resume, but the French returned to the numbering sequence established pre-war.

In May 1945, a study for an improved *Joffre*, designated PA16A, was drawn up and signed by Chief Engineer Paul Gisserot, who was responsible for the design of major ships. Displacement was 20,000 tonnes light, 22,132 tonnes trials and 24,800 tonnes full load. The 3rd Deck was raised by 0.6 metres and the flight deck by 0.8 metres. Clearance in the upper hangar remained the same at 5.8 metres, but was increased from 4.8m to 5.5m in the lower hangar in order to accommodate newer models of aircraft. An air group comprising eighteen VB.10 fighters and twelve SBCA.80 torpedo bombers was to be embarked; avgas stowage was 375 tonnes. Armament was to comprise eight 130mm DP guns in a modernised twin mounting, seven quad 40mm Bofors and sixteen 20mm Oerlikon AA guns. Horsepower remained at 120,000cv for a speed of 32.4 knots, and range was 8200nm at 18 knots with 3,960 tonnes of oil fuel. A PA16B variant would have had a slightly higher displacement (22,650 tonnes trial) and a speed of 32.5 knots.

In June 1945, the Minister of Marine and the *Conseil supérieur* requested three preliminary designs, all with a single hangar and a designed speed of 32 knots:

- a 'heavy' fleet carrier with an armoured flight deck, to be designated PA27
- a light fleet carrier with no protection, designated PA28
- a carrier with a waterline belt, designated PA29.

On 20 June, a study proposed a fleet of six aircraft carriers by 1950 to comprise the newly transferred escort carrier *Dixmude*, *Béarn*, plus conversions of the battleship *Jean Bart*, the aviation transport *Commandant Teste* and the cruisers *Duquesne* and *Tourville*. Given the wartime damage sustained by the naval dockyards and a difficult financial situation, it was recognised that such a programme was unachievable. It was, however, hoped to complete a carrier to the plans of *Joffre*, using steel and parts of the propulsion machinery that had been recovered. Only eight days later, on 28 June, the Minister cancelled *Joffre* and *Painlevé*, but approved a conversion of *Commandant Teste* and studies for a fleet carrier and an escort carrier.

In October, the *Service Technique* presented plans for PA27–29. PA27 had a standard displacement of 26,130 tons and a trial displacement of 29,450 tonnes. Variant A1 had a length of 234 metres between perpendiculars, and was powered by steam propulsion machinery delivering 144,000cv on four shafts. There was an armoured flight deck 90mm thick, and an armament of eight 130mm DP guns in twin turrets and ten quadruple 40mm Bofors. The air group comprised fifty-four aircraft. An A2 variant was 10 metres shorter and had sixteen 130mm guns, while an A4 variant was similar to A1 but had a HA armament of eight 100mm guns in twin mountings.

PA28 displaced 15,750 tons standard and had a number of features in common with the British light fleet carriers of the *Colossus* type. PA29 displaced 22,500 tons standard (25,400 tonnes trials) and had a length of 228 metres between perpendiculars. A four-shaft propulsion system similar to that of PA27 delivered 130,000cv, and there were eight 130mm DP guns and seven quad 40mm Bofors. The ship was designed for an air complement of fifty-seven. Of these three preliminary studies, only PA28 would be taken forward, becoming the *Clemenceau* of 1948 (see below).

Two further studies would be undertaken by the *Service Technique*. No details have been located for PA30, but PA31 (1947) was for a large fleet carrier displacing 38,000 tonnes.

On 2 October 1945, the *Conseil supérieur* considered that the purchase of an existing carrier from abroad or a new-build was essentially unaffordable, despite the Navy's desire to purchase two carriers and to lay down two new carriers from 1946. The PA29 design was abandoned in favour of the smaller PA28. Less than two weeks later, on 15 October, the *Conseil* acknowledged that it would be four years before the Navy

A post-war study for a conversion of the cruiser *Duquesne* and her sister *Tourville*. There was a full-length flight deck over a single hangar and an AA armament comprising quad 40mm Bofors guns and 20mm Oerlikons. Note the twin funnels that would have been required due to the unit arrangement of the steam propulsion machinery.

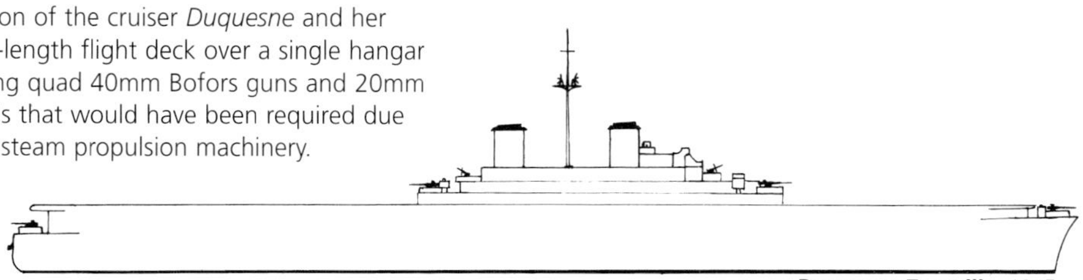

*(Drawn by Jean Moulin)*

**Duquesne Tourville** 1945

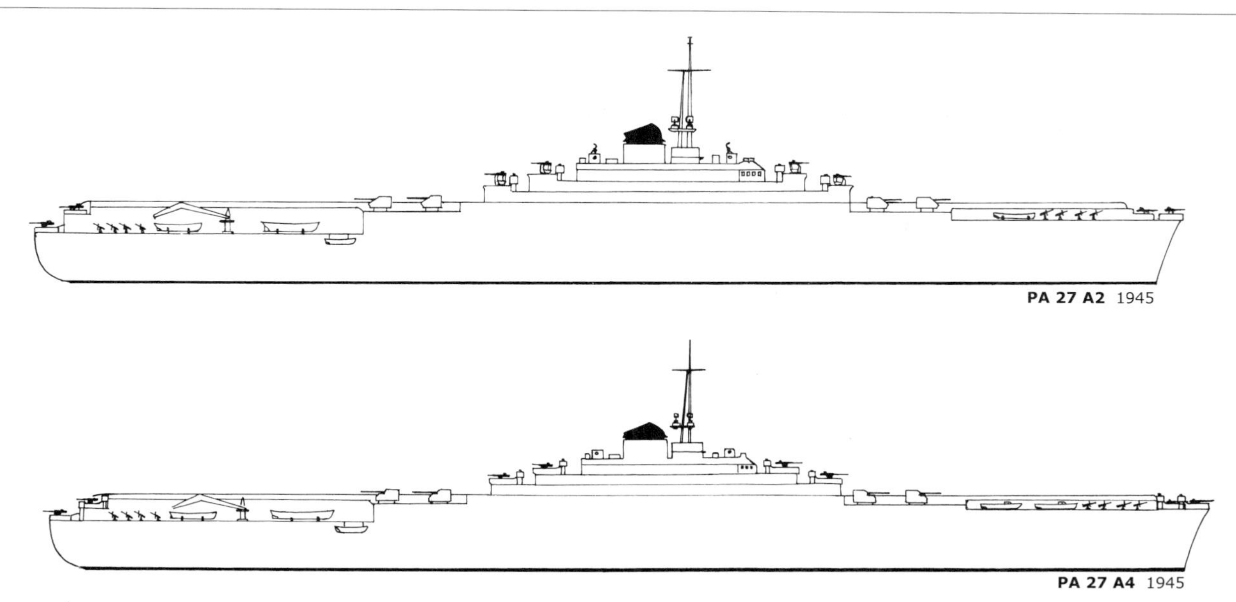


Variants A2 and A4 of the PA27 series, dated October 1945. The designed trials displacement for all variants was 29,450 tonnes (26,130 tons standard), but there were considerable differences in the respective armaments. A2 had no fewer than eight twin 130mm DP mountings and forty 40mm Bofors guns in a mix of twin, quad and single mountings; A4 had only four twin 100mm mountings but a larger air group of fifty-four aircraft. *(Drawn by Jean Moulin)*

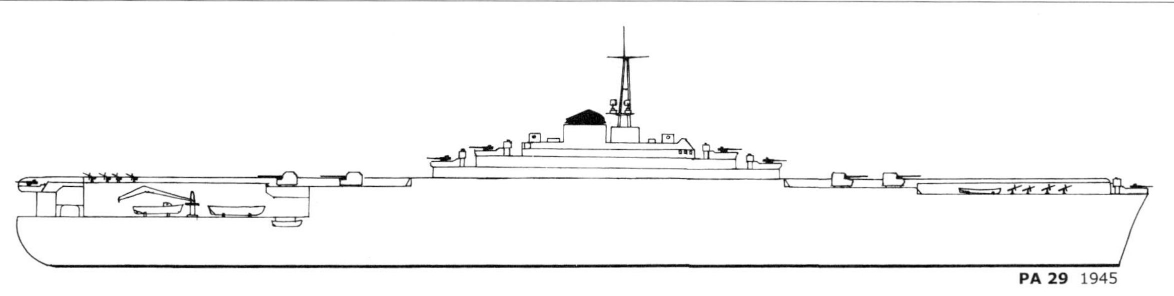


Drawn up at the same time as PA27 and PA28, PA29 displaced 22,500 tons (standard) and 25,400 tonnes (trials); length was 228 metres between perpendiculars, and the four-shaft propulsion plant could deliver 130,000cv for 32 knots. PA29 could operate fifty-seven aircraft, and was armed with eight twin 130mm DP guns and a mix of quad and single 40mm guns.

*(Drawn by Jean Moulin)*

would be able to complete a new carrier. It recommended a stop-gap conversion of *Commandant Teste*, the laying down of two light fleet carriers of the PA28 type, and preparation work on two protected 'combat' carriers to displace 27,000 tonnes.

A carrier of the PA28 type was to be ordered and, in early November 1945, Rear Admiral Nomy was despatched to London to secure the necessary material to recommission the aircraft transport *Biter* (*Archer* class) as a fully fledged carrier and to negotiate the transfer of a light fleet carrier of the *Colossus* class, which would materialise as the future *Arromanches*.

The need to reconstitute French naval and military infrastructure and to rebuild the merchant fleet meant that there was little money available for new naval construction, and what funds were available would be concentrated on the ships recovered in an incomplete state following the Liberation, notably *Jean Bart* and *De Grasse*. The rebuilding of the fleet would begin in earnest only with the 1949 programme.

Early plans for future force structures that dated from 11 January 1946 envisaged three 'high sea combat groups' (*groupes de combat de haute mer*) with five aircraft carriers. The plans were quickly modified and there were now to be two groups, initially centred on the battleships *Richelieu* and *Jean Bart*.

On 24 March 1948, the *Conseil supérieur* declared its support for a programme of four fleet carriers of 26,250 tonnes and three escort carriers of 8,000 tonnes, to be in service by 1960. A more modest proposal designated Plan 50, submitted by the Navy on 9 April 1948, envisaged the construction of a carrier of the PA28 type under the 1948 Estimates, and a second, with a slightly higher displacement of 20,000 tonnes, under the 1951 Estimates. The plan came to nothing due to budgetary restrictions, as did proposals for a 'naval law' (*statut naval*) put forward in August 1948 prescribing the construction of four carriers, and a similar proposal (for four/six carriers of 20,000 tonnes) in August 1949.

## PA28: THE FIRST *CLEMENCEAU*

The 1948 budget included a *tranche navale* that featured a single new vessel, PA28. The carrier was to be christened *Clemenceau*, the name given to a battleship laid down at Brest in 1939 and never completed.

## POST-WAR PROJECTS FOR CARRIER AIRCRAFT

Following the Liberation, a number of programmes were begun in an attempt to revive the French aero industry. Some of these were specifically aimed at the development of aircraft of modern design to operate from a new generation of aircraft carriers. The task proved to be more difficult than anticipated and none of these new designs would enter service, leaving French *Forces de l'aviation embarqué* dependent on the loan or purchase of British or American types.

The NC.1070 Noréclair, the prototype of a twin-engine embarked bomber, at Toussus in 1947. The first flight took place on 23 May. A version powered by two jet engines, the NC.1071, flew for the first time on 12 October 1948. *(ARDHAN)*

The SNCASO SO.8000 Narval was a single-engine, twin-boom naval fighter driven by two coaxial propellers. The first of two prototypes had its maiden flight on 1 April 1949. The Narval was abandoned in 1950. *(ARDHAN)*

The Arsenal VG 90 was France's first jet fighter. The first flight took place on 27 September 1949, but this first prototype crashed on 25 May 1950, and a second on 21 February 1952. The photo shows the first prototype at Brétigny in September 1949. *(ARDHAN)*

The prototype of the SNCAC NC.1080, a competitor for the role of embarked fighter jet, at Brétigny in 1950. It first flew on 29 July 1949, but crashed on 10 April the following year and was abandoned. *(ARDHAN)*

A third attempt at an embarked jet fighter was the Nord 2200, which first flew on 16 December 1949. The aircraft, seen here at Brétigny in May 1950, proved too heavy and the contract was terminated in 1951, although the prototype continued to fly until 1954. The failure of these projects led to the purchase of the British Sea Venom as the Aquilon. *(ARDHAN)*

The Bréguet Br.960 Vultur was a prototype anti-submarine aircraft with mixed propulsion, a combination of jet and turboprop. The first prototype flew on 4 August 1951. It was too heavy for the carriers currently in service, but a second prototype, developed as the Br.965, became a test-bed for the later Br.1050 Alizé, which would serve on board French carriers until the end of the century. The photo shows the second Br.960 prototype in 1953. *(ARDHAN)*

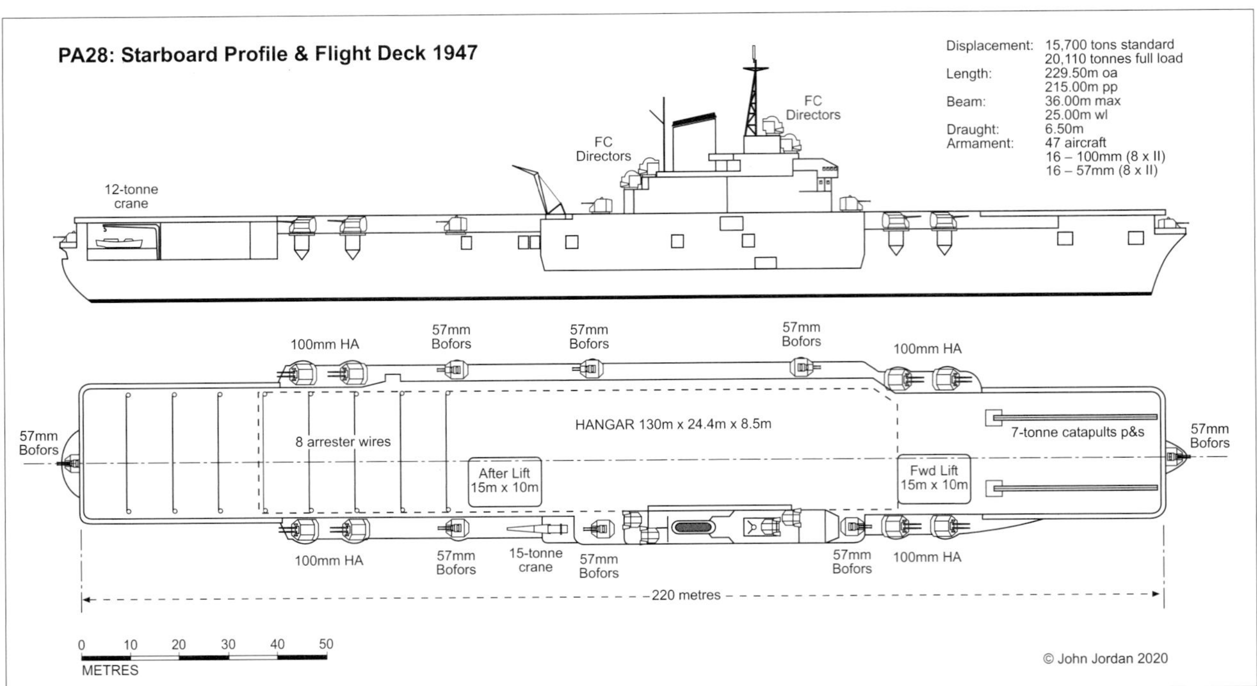


The hull of the new carrier would have been laid down in Dock No 8 at Laninon, with a completion date of 1954.

The programme was authorised under a law passed on 14 August 1947, and construction was assigned to Brest by a ministerial decision of 1 September 1947. The plans were still being refined and the first orders for steel and equipment made. However, a decree dated 9 October 1947 forbade any new expenditure, and on 7 March 1949, the Ministry of Defence advised that all work (except that on items already ordered) be halted; on 31 May, this was confirmed by the Government and the ship was effectively cancelled.

*Clemenceau* was the victim of the financial and industrial constraints of the immediate post-war period. However, there were other factors that influenced her cancellation, notably the continuing opposition to carriers from traditionalists in the Navy and the failed trials of the aircraft she was to embark. Sensing the way the wind was blowing, Lemonnier made a request in the autumn of 1948 for the Americans to transfer one of their own carriers. The request was renewed on March 1949, and the Americans agreed the loan of a light carrier (CVL) on 27 February 1950 (see Chapter 7).

The decision to cancel *Clemenceau* was eventually acknowledged to be the correct one. The carrier's designers lacked experience and were unfamiliar with the latest technical developments associated with embarked aircraft. Moreover, the three features that would characterise the new post-war generation of carriers – the angled deck, the steam catapult and the landing mirror sight – were as yet unknown. Admiral Nomy, who would become the driving force behind the post-war naval air arm and a new generation of aircraft carriers of French design, damningly characterised PA28 as 'a poor copy of *Arromanches*'.

## TECHNICAL CHARACTERISTICS

*Clemenceau* as designed had a displacement of 15,700 tons standard and 20,110 tonnes full load. Length was 215 metres between perpendiculars and 229.5 metres overall, beam 25 metres, and draught 6.5 metres. The hull was divided into thirty-two watertight compartments, but was otherwise unprotected.

The French constructors opted for a conventional steam propulsion plant. Initially it was proposed to fit machinery identical to that of *Joffre*, parts of which had been recovered, or half the machinery ordered for the battleship *Clemenceau* or, alternatively, machinery recovered from the cruiser *De Grasse*, which was lying incomplete at Lorient. In the end, a decision was made in favour of a completely new propulsion plant on two shafts comprising four Sural asymmetric boilers and two groups of Parsons turbines (HP, IP and LP) with single reduction gearing; the astern turbine was incorporated in the casing of the LP turbines. Total horsepower was 105,000cv. There were to be two auxiliary boilers and two turbo-generators.

The aviation installation comprised a 220-metre flight deck, four arrester systems with eight arrester wires and three barriers. The arrester systems could handle aircraft with a weight of 12 tonnes, and aircraft with a maximum take-off weight of 7 tonnes could be launched by the two bow catapults. The single hangar was 130m x 24.4m with a clearance of 8.5 metres. It could accommodate a total of forty-seven aircraft using the 'tricing' technique developed by the US Navy, twenty-two fighters being suspended from the roof beams. Two conventional aircraft lifts 15m x 10m with a capacity of 12 tonnes connected the hangar to the flight deck, and there were smaller bomb lifts fore and aft. There was an aircraft crane and a boat crane, with a capacity of 15 and 12 tonnes respectively, and tanks for 400 tonnes of avgas.

The armament comprised eight twin 100mm HA mountings controlled by four stabilised directors, and eight of the new twin 57mm mountings that would be a feature of the new escorts. The peacetime complement was to be 1,806 officers and men plus a possible admiral and his staff.

CHAPTER 7

# THE 'LOAN' CARRIERS

### *DIXMUDE* (EX-*BITER*)

On 4 August 1943, the day after the merging of the *Forces maritimes d'Afrique* with the FNFL, a joint naval committee in Algiers envisaged manning an auxiliary aircraft carrier of the *Archer* class and made a formal request to the British for such a transfer. On 18 December, a similar request was made to the Americans for the transfer of a fleet carrier. Neither request was particularly well received at the time, as both navies were fully extended by their own maritime commitments, and the Americans would continue to have reservations about an independent French naval force capable of reviving French colonial and imperial ambitions in the Far East. However, in May 1944 the Americans agreed to supply two squadrons of SBD Dauntless dive bombers, which were surplus to requirements with the delivery of the Curtiss SB2C Helldiver.

In September 1944 the French proposed the deployment of a Task Force centred on the battleship *Richelieu* to the Far East, and made a further request for a medium-sized carrier to accompany her. The US Navy stonewalled and suggested the French consult the British who, despite their doubts about French abilities to man and operate a carrier, offered to transfer either the CVE *Biter*, currently being employed as an aircraft transport, or *Nabob*, which had been torpedoed and not repaired. They also offered the old fleet carrier *Furious*, which decommissioned that same month. Following further French pressure, the transfer of *Biter* was finally agreed in December, but the ship (which was still technically US property) would not be allowed to deploy to the Far East.

The British imposed further conditions on the transfer: all work to fit the ship for service was to be undertaken by the French; the ship was to be towed to a French port; and she was to be used solely for French purposes, so that no requests for assistance would be made in the event of joint operations.

The US Munitions Assignment Board duly approved the transfer on 21 February 1945 and, following lengthy negotiations, the British agreed on 5 March to supply the materiel necessary to refurbish the ship

**Below:** *Dixmude* on 9 April 1945, the day she was formally handed over to the *Marine Nationale*. *(Jean Moulin collection)*

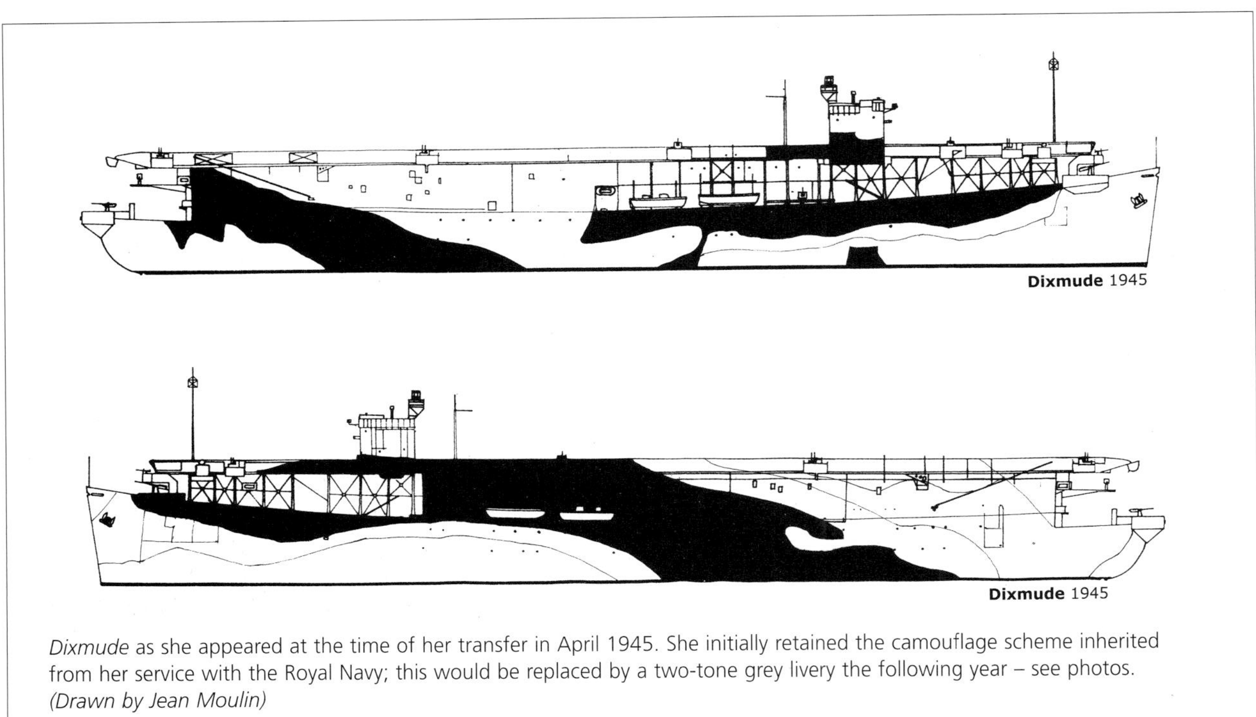


*Dixmude* as she appeared at the time of her transfer in April 1945. She initially retained the camouflage scheme inherited from her service with the Royal Navy; this would be replaced by a two-tone grey livery the following year – see photos. *(Drawn by Jean Moulin)*

and make her operational. On 7 April a French skeleton crew of twenty-five men arrived at Gareloch Head. The ship would be commanded by CF Yves Caron, and his chief engineer would be Julien Bertho. They found the ship moored at the end of a creek on the Clyde; she was in poor condition, with a pronounced list and secured with rusty chains.

### HMS *Biter*

*Biter* was laid down in December 1939 by the Sun Shipbuilding and Dry Dock Corporation, Chester (Pennsylvania), as the cargo ship *Rio Parana* (Type C3). Launched on 18 December 1940, she was towed to the Atlantic Basin Iron Works, Brooklyn, in September 1941 to be completed as auxiliary carrier BAVG-3.

Below: *Dixmude* in late 1945, with two Walrus amphibians of 4S on her flight deck. *(Musée national de la Marine)*

Transferred to the Royal Navy on 1 April 1942 under Lend-Lease, she was completed the following month and towed to the naval dockyard at New York, which fitted her electronics. She was officially handed over to the Royal Navy on 6 May, which christened her *Biter* with the pendant number D97.

*Biter* had an inauspicious start to life. Early trials and work-up were marred by a fire in the motor for the catapult and problems with her propulsion machinery. She embarked her first Fairey Swordfish aircraft – six Mk I belonging to 836 Squadron – on 2 June. She subsequently took part in Operation 'Torch' (November 1942), and undertook anti-submarine warfare (ASW) patrols in support of convoys in the North Atlantic.

In early August 1944 she returned to Greenock; her aircraft were disembarked and she was decommissioned. The Royal Navy had by now commissioned a large number of more modern and better-equipped escort carriers, and *Biter* was relegated to the role of aircraft transport and manned by the Merchant Navy. A serious fire broke out on board on 24 August and, with the British shipyards and dockyards at full capacity, it was decided to place her in reserve with a skeleton crew; she was moored in the Gareloch.

*Biter* had covered 59,900nm under the White Ensign, had escorted 21 convoys, and had performed 2,644 landings and 363 catapult launches (all of Wildcats). Although some aircraft had sustained damage, these had not resulted in any fatalities on board.

**Repair and Refurbishment**

On 9 April 1945, the same day that the French took over the ship, *Biter* was formally handed back to the US Navy; she would be stricken on 24 January 1951. The ship in her current state was habitable, but her machinery was in serious need of refurbishment. This was carried out at Gareloch by workers from Brest Naval Dockyard, with replacement parts supplied by Britain. Renamed *Dixmude*,[1] she was manned for trials on 26 July. Sea trials took place off Greenock, and the ship left for Brest on 21 August with 150 tonnes of materiel for the French Navy at Brest and for the Red Cross.

**Transport Missions**

Following the end of the Second World War, maritime transport was grouped into an inter-Allied pool under the overall control of the Americans, for whom Indochina was a low priority. French personnel therefore had to be transported there and others repatriated using regular warships. Following an inspection of *Dixmude* at Le Havre in early September, the Americans considered her unfit to embark their troops for a proposed transport mission to Southampton. She left Brest on the 16th with 450 tonnes of cargo for Casablanca, embarked 332 passengers and headed for Toulon via Oran.

A mission under Admiral Nomy was despatched to London, arriving on 30 October, to negotiate the acquisition of the necessary materiel to recommission *Dixmude* as an aircraft carrier. Radar and communications equipment to the value of £12,800 were agreed. In the interim the ship would continue to undertake the transport of materiel and personnel around the Western Mediterranean.

[1] The ship was named after the Belgian city of Diksmuide (French: Dixmude), and specifically in honour of the *Fusiliers Marins* at the battle of Diksmuide in October 1914.

**Above:** A Douglas SBD-5 Dauntless of 3F Squadron. These were the only combat aircraft to operate from *Dixmude*, and they saw extensive service in Indochina, operating both from the carrier and from land bases. *(ARDHAN collection)*

**The First Campaign in Indochina**

From 24 June to 12 October, work was undertaken at Toulon to enable *Dixmude* to serve as a training ship for aircraft landings, and she was finally fitted out as an aircraft carrier during a twenty-three-day refit that took place between December 1946 and January 1947. The Navy planned to deploy the ship to Indochina in place of *Arromanches*, which was not yet available.

The first deck landings took place using the SBD Dauntless dive bombers of 3F Squadron, and *Dixmude* left for Indochina on 28 January with the 9 SBDs of 3F, 17 Morane 500 liaison aircraft and 12 Spitfires broken down in cases intended for the *Armée de l'Air*, 360 tonnes of cargo and 36 passengers. The extent of the cargo precluded air operations, but the nine SBDs were catapulted off on 3 March when the ship arrived off Cape Saint-Jacques, and by the evening she was moored at Saigon. Deck landing practice for the pilots of 3F resumed after more than a month without training.

On 11 March, two SBDs were flown off for a photographic mission over Quang Ngai and Tam Ky. The first bombing missions in support of the ground forces were carried out in the same area on 15 March, during which one of the aircraft was damaged by the explosion of its own bomb. The carrier then headed for Tonkin. On 21 March, five SBDs were launched for a bombing raid on a munitions depot at Thai Nguyen. The launch of the fifth aircraft had to be aborted when the catapult sling ruptured and was unable to be repaired. The mission failed due to bad weather.

Without the catapult, the launch of a fully loaded aircraft required 22 knots of wind over deck, and *Dixmude* was capable of a maximum speed of 15 knots. The aircraft had to be lightened by removing the machine guns and leaving the external fuel tank empty, and missions were limited to two hours thirty minutes; the SBDs could be armed only with rockets, not bombs. However, further surveillance and attack

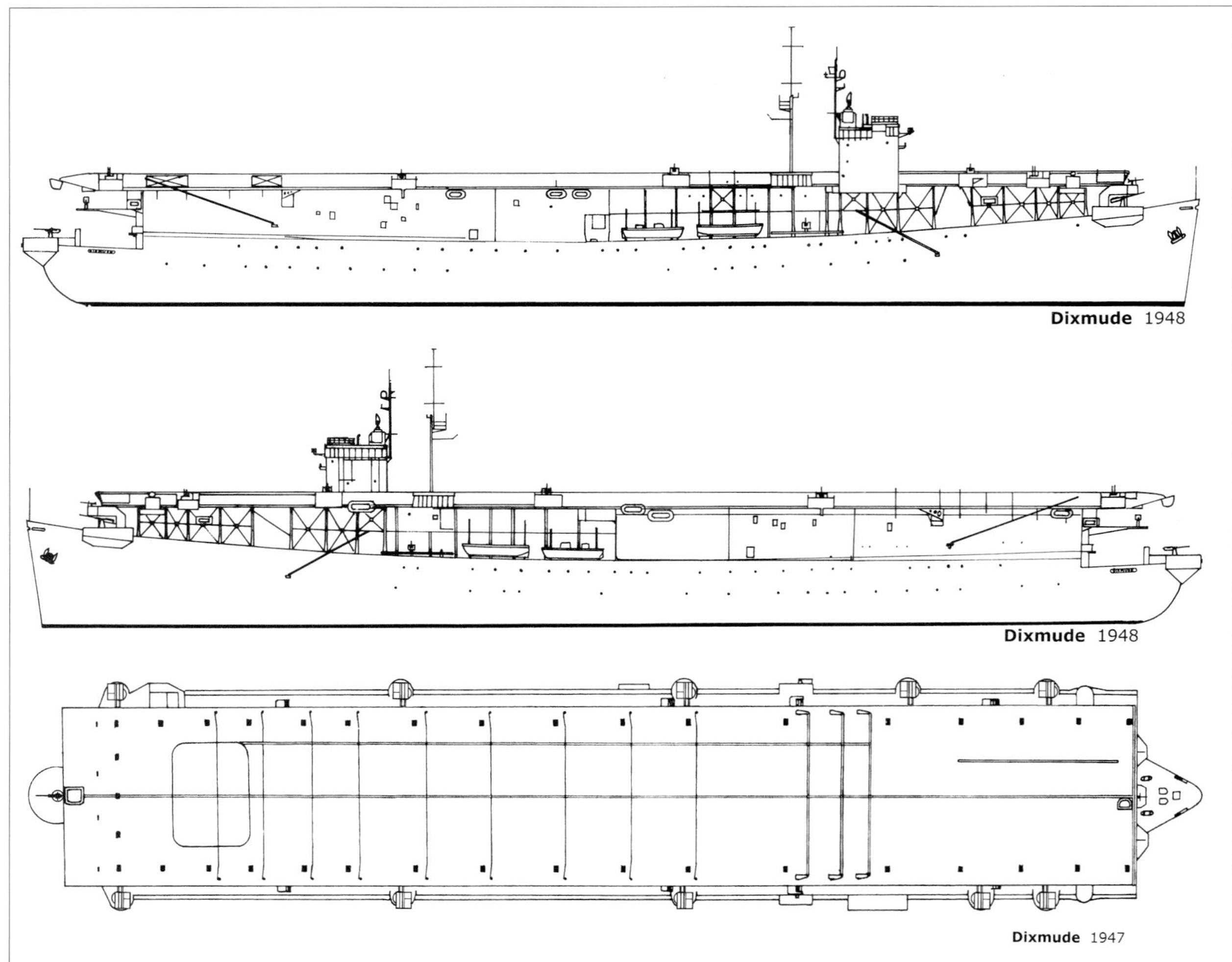


**Right:** *Dixmude* in French service in 1948. The only substantive changes made at this time were to the electronics – see separate drawing. *(Drawn by Jean Moulin)*

**Below:** An aerial view of *Dixmude* taken in the late 1940s. *(DR)*

missions were successfully undertaken during late March.

*Dixmude* returned to Tonkin, and two sections each of three SBDs bombed Tuyen Quang. It was the final mission of the campaign. A total of seventy-four deck landings had been achieved, but the only dive-bombing mission had been that of 15 March. She left Saigon on 14 April, returning to Toulon on 16 May. She then underwent a refit from 22 May to 18 August 1947.

On 15 September, she conducted trials with her newly repaired catapult. An SBD was launched and there were thirty-six deck landings, including two by Seafires.

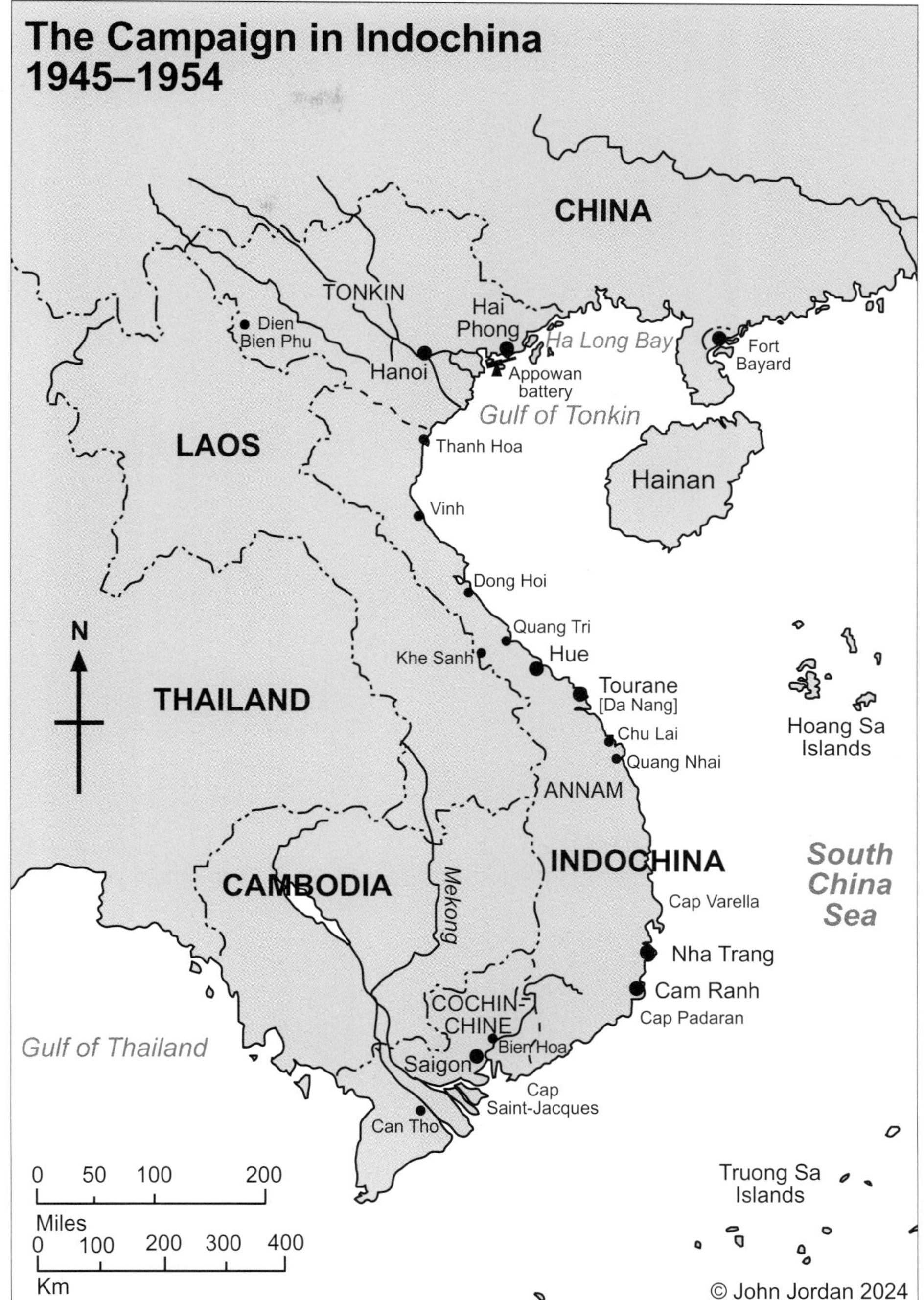


## Second Campaign in Indochina

*Dixmude* left again for Indochina on 16 September 1947, embarking the nine SBDs of 4F, together with twelve Spitfires and twelve AAC.1 Toucan transport aircraft – used as makeshift bombers in Indochina – for the *Armée de l'Air*. The SBDs were catapulted off near Cape Saint-Jacques on 20 October, and the ship moored at Saigon the following day. Three of the SBDs were despatched to Gia Lam, near Hanoi. They were followed by the remainder of the squadron on 1 November, where they conducted 67 missions (206 sorties) until mid-December for the loss of a single aircraft, returning occasionally to the ship for maintenance. On 29 October, a second SBD was lost during a dive-bombing demonstration near *Dixmude*, which remained moored at Saigon. She left the port on 1 November for Ha Long Bay via Cam Ranh Bay with twelve Morane 500 on board. The aircraft then took off for Cat Bi.

*Dixmude* left Tonkin on 16 November, and returned to Saigon on the 19th, departing two days later with nine Morane 500 and 160 passengers for Ha Long Bay. Catapult launches and practice deck landings followed during late November and early December; she re-embarked her air squadron on 15 December and returned to Saigon, arriving on the 24th. The SBDs were based at Tan Son Nhut.

*Dixmude* left Saigon on 2 February 1948, moored at Nha Trang, then Tourane, and returned to Cape Saint-Jacques after a single catapult launch and fourteen deck landings. Three replacement SBDs arrived in the cargo ship *Taurus* and were readied for operational deployment. The ship remained at Saigon until 4 March, when she left for Nha Trang, putting to sea on the 6th for six deck landings. Bad weather prevented planned air operations at Tonkin, and *Dixmude* returned to Saigon on 9 March. She departed for Toulon on 3 April, accompanied by the support ship *Commandant Robert Giraud* (formerly the German *Imelmann*), and returned to Toulon via Singapore, Colombo, Djibouti and Suez, entering the port on 1 May.

The two campaigns in the Far East had shown that *Dixmude* was too slow and too dependent on the strength of the wind to conduct air operations. She had proved capable of operating a maximum of six SBDs due to the constraints of the single aircraft lift and the fragility of the single catapult – it has to be acknowledged that the ship was designed for ASW operations in the North Atlantic, not for a colonial war in the Far East.

*Dixmude* left Toulon on 17 May to take part in exercises in the Atlantic, for which a *Force d'Intervention* was specially activated. With 4F Squadron embarked, she joined an aircraft carrier group centred on *Arromanches*. This would be the first occasion on which the French could muster a two-carrier force. Following manoeuvres off Morocco, *Dixmude* headed for Brest, taking part in a naval review in the outer harbour on 30 May. She left Brest on 21 June, conducted further exercises with the cruiser group and re-entered Toulon on the 28th. She was then docked for a major refit, which lasted from 1 August to 22 February 1949.

Following trials and work-up she left for Bizerte on 23 May and took part in Exercise 'Soliman' with 4F Squadron embarked; four of the SBDs were employed to observe the fire of the cruisers. This would be *Dixmude*'s last mission as a carrier; she left the Mediterranean Squadron on 1 June and prepared to undertake transport missions.

**Right:** *Dixmude* and the cruiser *Montcalm* at the Fleet Review at Brest on 30 May 1948. *(Musée national de la Marine)*

**Below:** *Dixmude* transporting twelve Morane 500 liaison aircraft from Saigon to Ha Long Bay from 1 to 5 November 1947 during her second campaign in Indochina. *(SHD-A)*

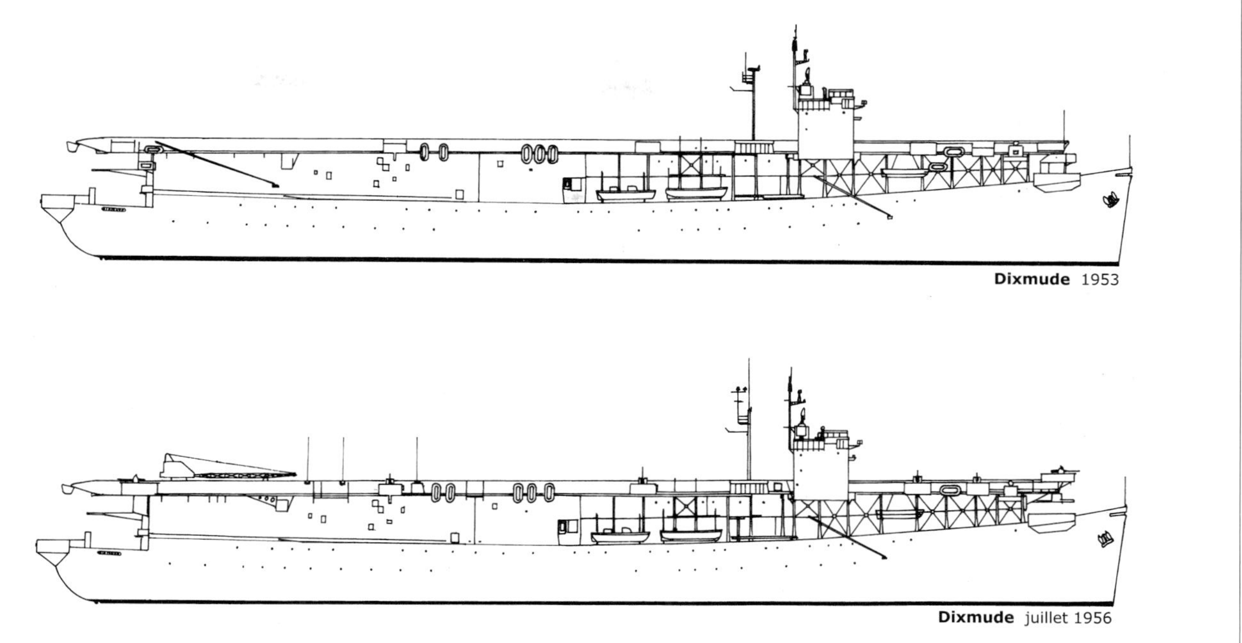


*Dixmude* as she appeared in the mid-1950s. Her original armament was landed in 1952, when the ship was redesignated *transport d'aviation*, but was replaced in 1955/56 by four single Bofors 40mm and ten 20mm Oerlikons on single Mk IV mountings. In the 1956 profile, note the crane aft, which was used to embark and disembark aircraft quayside in the transport role. *(Drawn by Jean Moulin)*

**Aviation Transport**

*Dixmude*'s first mission as an aviation transport was to the Far East, carrying 377 tonnes of cargo for the Navy and the Air Force, including 16 AAC.1 Toucan and 20 Bell P-63C Kingcobra aircraft to Saigon. She left Toulon on 16 June and arrived on 23 July. She returned to Toulon with 177 passengers and 572 tonnes of freight (including two AAC.1s) on 8 September.

On 28 November, off Hyères, two naval Seafire XVs

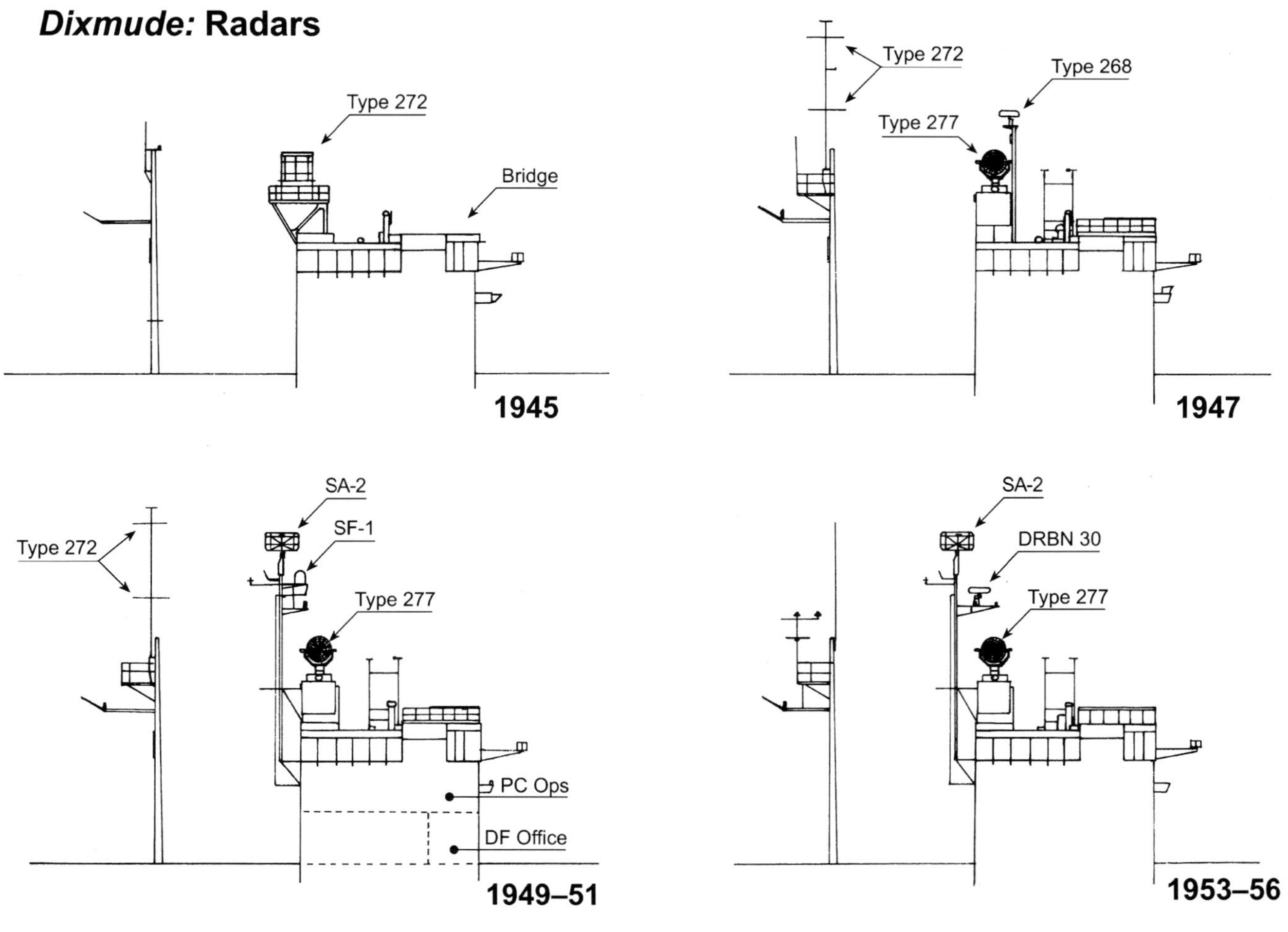

***Dixmude:* Radars**

Type 272
Bridge
1945
Type 272
Type 268
Type 277
1947
SA-2
SF-1
Type 272
Type 277
PC Ops
DF Office
1949–51
SA-2
DRBN 30
Type 277
1953–56

When transferred in April 1945, *Dixmude* had only the British Type 272 radar in its distinctive 'lantern', which had been designed to detect submarines on the surface; this was removed in 1946, when she was fitted with British-model air search (Type 79B) and surface surveillance (Type 268) radars. After 1949, these were replaced or complemented by US Navy 'small-ship' models, SA 2 and SF 1, the antennae for which were mounted on a new pole foremast at the after end of the island. *(Drawn by Jean Moulin)*

Above: *Dixmude* on 6 July 1951, the day before her arrival at Bizerte with seven TBM-3E, twenty-four F6F-5, ten F6F-5N and a decommissioned F6F-5. Note the 'L' markings on the flight deck. *(ARDHAN collection)*

Opposite, top: *Dixmude* in Ha Long Bay in early September 1954. She is serving as a helicopter carrier, with an HUP-2 (DX-1), a Morane 500 and two H-19 belonging to the *Armée de l'Air*. *(Berthault collection)*

Opposite, bottom: *Dixmude* decommissioned at Saint-Mandrier. She served as a base ship for the amphibious forces from 1960 to 1965. Note the crane on the starboard side of the flight deck aft, which was fitted in the mid-1950s to facilitate the embarkation and disembarkation of aircraft when quayside. *(DR)*

landed on *Dixmude* for the first time and took off again shortly after. These would be the last landings on the carrier.

After a short refit from 10 December 1949 to 17 January 1950, *Dixmude* served almost exclusively as an aircraft transport, ferrying aircraft delivered by the Americans under the Mutual Defense Assistance Pact (MDAP), signed by President Harry S Truman on 6 October 1949, to metropolitan France. This included a round-the-world tour in August, when *Dixmude* headed for San Francisco and Pearl Harbor via the Panama Canal, arriving at Saigon on 28 October. She returned to Toulon on 21 December at an average speed of 13.7 knots and underwent a refit lasting four months.

After a further transport mission to the USA in April, she left Toulon on 18 May 1950 with the personnel of 12F Squadron, who were due to operate from the loan carrier *La Fayette* (see below). In June she embarked thirty-five F6F Hellcat and seven TBM-3 Avenger plus spares at Norfolk, Va, and returned to Toulon via Casablanca, disembarking the aircraft at Bizerte. There was a further transport mission to the USA in August, followed by a short refit, and a third to Norfolk in late November. She returned to Toulon on 31 August.

*Dixmude* was formally redesignated *transport d'aviation* on 4 January 1952, with effect from 1 December 1951. She left for the USA on 7 January, taking the crews for destroyer escorts to be delivered under MDAP and returning with twenty-six SNJ trainers and twenty-one Helldivers; she arrived back in Toulon on 24 February. A second mission to the USA took place from 11 March to 5 May, with crews for two more destroyer escorts embarked in France and eighteen TBM-3 Avengers and nineteen Helldivers going in the opposite direction. From 15 May to 15 December, *Dixmude* underwent a major refit, during which all guns were disembarked.

Similar missions followed during her remaining years in service. Highlights were:

- 20 January–3 March 1953: To the USA to embark forty F4U-7 Corsair – the aircraft was specially modified for French service – plus a single F4U-4 (to be cannibalised for spares).
- 17 April–22 June 1953: To the USA to embark ten SNJ-4 trainers, fourteen F4U-7 Corsair plus a single F4U-4 (for spares) and six SB2C Helldiver.
- 3 August–1 October 1953: To the USA with 390 men to crew the loan carrier *Bois Belleau* (see below), and to embark 20 Beechcraft SNB-5 utility aircraft for Bizerte and 2 HUP-2 helicopters – used as plane guards – for Toulon.
- 12 March–26 May 1954: To the USA to embark eighteen TBM-3 Avenger, fifteen HUP-2 helicopters plus three Bell helicopters. Twelve of the Avengers were disembarked at Bizerte.
- 5 July–4 November 1954: Final campaign in Indochina. Combat aircraft transported to Saigon. After various transport missions along the coast she returned to Toulon with 12 Helldivers of 3F and 17

Hellcats of 11F (embarked by crane), 243 passengers, ammunition and materiel.

- 6 September–15 October 1955: Short refit at Toulon in which the catapults, arrester wires and barriers were removed. Four 40mm Bofors and ten 20mm Oerlikons were embarked.
- 21 January 1958: An explosion in the combustion chamber of one of the auxiliary boilers injured sixteen men.
- 13 June 1960: Placed in Special Reserve B and moored at Saint-Mandrier as the base ship for the *Fusiliers Marins* in place of *Jules Verne*. She would serve in this role until 30 January 1965. She was returned to the US Navy on 10 June 1966, which opted to use her as a target for the 6th Fleet; she was sunk off Toulon on 14 June. During her active service *Dixmude* had covered 513,235nm, of which 59,900nm were under the White Ensign, and had accumulated a total of 1,500 deck landings by French aircraft.

## Table 1: *DIXMUDE* (1946)

| | |
|---|---|
| **Displacement:** | 10,220 tons standard<br>15,700 tons full load<br>17,035 tonnes full load (1954) |
| **Dimensions:** | |
| length | 141.73m pp, 149.96m oa |
| beam | 27.17m wl |
| draught | 7.39m |
| **Aviation:** | |
| flight deck | 134.72m x 20m |
| catapult | one H2 (3170kg aircraft) |
| arrester wires | nine with seven braking systems |
| barriers | three |
| crane | 6350kg capacity, 13.71m reach |
| hangar | 60.67m (incl lift) x 18.62m max x 6.14m max |
| lift (L x W) | 12.8m x 10.36m (6580kg load) |
| air group | fifteen max (normally nine) |
| **Machinery:** | |
| engines | two Sun Droxford 2-stroke, 6-cylinder diesels |
| propellers | single 6.86m diameter |
| horsepower | 9,000bhp |
| speed | 15.2 knots |
| diesel fuel | 875 tonnes normal<br>2,700 tonnes full load |
| endurance | 14,500nm at 10 knots |
| generators | five diesel generators each 400kW |
| **Armament:** | |
| HA guns | three 102mm Mark V in single mountings |
| light AA | nineteen 20mm Oerlikon in twin/single mountings |
| **Electronics:** | Type 79B air search radar<br>Type 268 surface surveillance radar |
| **Complement:** | |
| private ship | 800 officers and men (includes air group) |

## *ARROMANCHES* (EX-*COLOSSUS*)

After persistent pressure from the French for the transfer of a 'true' aircraft carrier, the British finally agreed in February 1946 to a loan of HMS *Colossus* for a period of five years.

*Colossus* was the first of a class of ten light fleet carriers conceived as an emergency measure in 1941. The initial design was for an austere ship capable of operating the latest fighter aircraft, to be laid down in a variety of non-specialist shipyards. Built to mercantile standards, they were completely unprotected, mounted only light anti-aircraft guns, and had two-shaft steam propulsion machinery (half the installation of the cruisers of the *Fiji* class) capable of driving them at 25 knots. It was initially envisaged that they would serve only to the end of the war or for a maximum of three years. In the event they would prove remarkably successful and long-lived; the last vessel in service, the Brazilian *Minas Gerais*, decommissioned only in 2001. With a 690ft (210m) flight deck, two large rectangular centre-line aircraft lifts, and a capacious single hangar with a clearance of 17ft 6in (5.33m), they could operate a total of forty aircraft; the simplicity of the design made them remarkably adaptable, and they were able to accommodate the new high-performance aircraft developed post-war.

*Colossus* was laid down at Vickers' Walker Yard on the Tyne on 14 March 1942, launched on 30 September 1943, and completed on 16 December 1944. Following trials and work-up she was readied for deployment with the British Pacific Fleet. It was expected that the 11th Aircraft Carrier Squadron, comprising *Colossus* and sisters *Glory*, *Venerable* and *Vengeance*, would join 1 ACS (the armoured carriers) for Operation 'Olympic', the projected amphibious landings on the Japanese mainland in the autumn of 1945, but the Japanese surrendered shortly after their arrival in the Pacific. *Colossus* was operational with the BPF on 26 July 1945, with 1846 (24 F-4U Corsair) and 827 (Fairey Barracuda) Squadrons embarked. After covering British forces landed in Shanghai, she helped with the repatriation of British prisoners of war, returning to Portsmouth on 23 July 1946. She was promptly decommissioned, but retained a full outfit of stores on board in view of her imminent transfer to the French Navy.

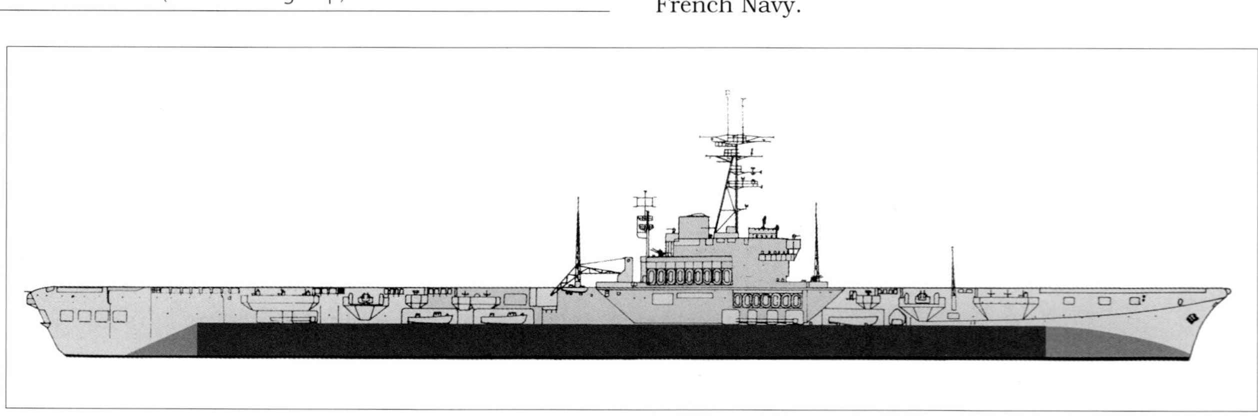

**Right:** HMS *Colossus* in 1945 in the RN livery in which she returned from the Pacific. She would be repainted light grey overall the following year. Although transferred to the *Marine Nationale* in August 1946, she would not be formally renamed *Arromanches* until March 1947. *(Drawn by Jean Moulin)*

**Above:** HMS *Colossus* in her late-war colour scheme, with Corsair Mk IV aircraft embarked. *(René Bail collection)*

**Left:** *Colossus* shortly before her handover at Portsmouth in August 1946. *(John Jordan collection)*

**Left:** *Colossus* at Portsmouth shortly after her handover; the gangway is guarded by a French sentry. Note the quad 2pdr (40mm) pom-pom forward of the island. *(Musée national de la Marine)*

### *Colossus* to *Arromanches*

The battleship *Richelieu* arrived in Portsmouth on 2 August 1946 with the crew destined for the carrier, and the formal transfer duly took place four days later, in the presence of the British Prime Minister and the French Minister of Defence. Captain (CV) Yves Caron took command of the ship, which had yet to be renamed. *Colossus* put to sea under the French flag for the first time on 20 August, and two days later a TBM Avenger piloted by a RN officer with Caron as his passenger landed on board, followed by a Seafire III piloted by Félix Ortolan, head of the French *Service Aviation.*

The ship left Portsmouth on 25 August escorted by the torpedo boat *Basque*, two minesweeping sloops and two corvettes. The group was met by *Richelieu*, accompanied by the destroyers *Marceau* (ex-German *Z 31*) and *Hoche* (ex-*Z 25*), before mooring in the outer harbour at Cherbourg, where various dignitaries came on board. She left on the 27th, landed a Seafire piloted by Ortolan, and headed for Toulon via Brest, Casablanca and Algiers, arriving on 19 September. The ship would be based at Toulon for her entire career. The previous day saw the formation of the *Groupe des porte-avions et de l'aviation embarqué*, to comprise the air groups of *Colossus*, *Dixmude*, 1F, 3F and 4F Squadrons, 54S and the base at Hyères, east of Toulon.

After a short docking from 16 to 30 October, the carrier sailed from Toulon on 6 November for work-up. The first deck landings since that of Ortolan took place from the 12th. There were fifty pilots of 1F, 3F and 4F who needed to qualify, including Admiral Edouard Jozan, formerly a pilot on board *Béarn*. Pilot training continued during the first quarter of 1947: there were 138 Seafire landings and 125 by SBDs.

On 4 March 1947, the ship was renamed *Arromanches* by ministerial decree and this was formalised during a ceremony on board on 15 March in the presence of the Mayor of Arromanches.[2]

### The *Force d'Intervention*

*Arromanches* left Toulon on 11 April 1947 with 1F and 4F Squadrons embarked; escorted by the ex-American destroyer escort *Marocain*, she took part in a tour by President Vincent Auriol of French West Africa (AOF). There were port visits to Casablanca, Agadir, Cap Blanc then, in company with *Richelieu*, to Dakar. On 22 April, a *Force d'Intervention* (FI) centred on the latter, under the command of Vice Admiral Robert Jaujard, was formed. A further visit to Casablanca from 10 to 20 May was marked by rocket-assisted (RATOG) take-offs using Seafires while *Arromanches* was at anchor in the port. The ship returned to Toulon on 21 June.

A cruise to the coasts of North Africa from 11 to 30 September was followed by docking and refit from 16 October 1947 to 16 March 1948. Deck landing training for the pilots resumed in April, which also saw the reconstitution of the *Force d'Intervention* under the command of Jaujard. The carrier group comprised *Arromanches* with 1F, 3F and a detachment from 54S and, from 21 May, *Dixmude* with 4F. Following exercises off Oran, *Arromanches* accompanied the cruiser group through the Strait of Gibraltar for Exercise 'Cachalot' off Casablanca. She then headed for Brest,

2 Arromanches was one of the key locations of the Normandy Landings of June 1944 that preceded the Liberation of France, and hosted one of two massive 'Mulberry' artificial harbours, the remains of which can still be seen today.

**Above:** An SBD-5 of 4F on *Arromanches*. *(DR)*

**Below:** A Seafire III emerges from the hangar onto the forward lift. *(ECPAD)*

**Above:** A Seafire III of 1F takes off from *Arromanches* in 1947. *(ARDHAN collection)*

**Right:** A Grumman F6F-5 Hellcat of 11F (formerly 1F) Squadron. *(ARDHAN collection)*

where she took part in a major naval review by the President of the Republic, anchoring on 5 June off Arromanches, the town from which she took her name. She returned to Toulon via Bizerte on 2 July 1948, then, in late September/early October, put to sea to work up 12F Squadron, newly formed with Seafire IIIs.

### A First Campaign in Indochina 1948–49

*Arromanches* was to be deployed to Indochina in place of *Dixmude*, which had limited capacity. However, the terms of the loan prohibited military operations without the authorisation of the British Government. The solution was to use her to transport aircraft for the *Armée de l'Air*; it was also agreed that she could undertake air operations to maintain order, as a 'policing' measure.

*Arromanches* duly embarked equipment, vehicles and 12 tonnes of notes for the Bank of Indochina, together with an air group comprising ten SBDs of 4F plus a section of two Seafires to be permanently attached to the ship. Seven twin-engine NC.701 Martinet light transport aircraft were embarked en route, at Bizerte, and the ship arrived at Saigon on 30 November, when Rear Admiral Pierre Barjot came on board. The SBDs were flown off to Tan Son Nhut, but were re-embarked on 11 November, when *Arromanches* headed for Ha Long Bay. She conducted air operations off Tonkin, returning to Saigon on 31 December. She left for metropolitan France on 4 January, arriving in Toulon on 1 February. Her aircraft had undertaken 152 sorties, but only a fifth of these had been from the carrier.

### The *Escadre* 1949–50

A new formation designated *L'Escadre* ('The Squadron') was created at Toulon on 1 April 1949. It comprised a carrier group with *Arromanches*, *Dixmude* and two escorts, a cruiser group and an anti-submarine group.

Following the loss of an SDB as a result of engine failure, all SDBs were grounded and were disembarked by crane. The Navy no longer had any aircraft compatible with carrier operations, but the British agreed to

**Table 2: *ARROMANCHES* (1946)**

| | |
|---|---|
| Displacement: | 14,000 tons standard<br>17,170 tonnes normal<br>18,330 tonnes deep load |
| Dimensions: | |
| length | 192.02m pp, 211.84m oa |
| beam | 24.38m wl |
| draught | 6.70m |
| Aviation: | |
| flight deck | 201.31m x 22.86m (abeam island) |
| catapult | one BH 3 (8165kg aircraft) |
| arrester wires | ten with five Mk 8 braking systems |
| barriers | two (6804kg) |
| hangar | 104.64m x 15.85m x 5.33m |
| lifts (L x W) | 13.72m x 10.36m (6804kg load) |
| crane | one flight deck (6350kg) |
| air group | forty-two max, normally thirty-four in French service (1953–54) |
| avgas | 377m$^3$ |
| Machinery: | |
| boilers | four Admiralty 3-drum, 27.5kg/cm$^2$ (370°C) |
| engines | two sets of Parsons geared turbines (HP + LP) |
| propellers | two 4.27m diameter |
| horsepower | 40,000shp |
| speed | 24 knots |
| oil fuel | 3,246 tonnes |
| endurance | 8,300nm at 20 knots |
| generators | two turbo-generators each 450kW<br>two diesel generators each 200kW |
| Armament: | |
| HA guns | twenty-four 2pdr Mark VIII in quad mountings |
| light AA | nineteen 40mm Bofors in single LS III/Boffin mountings |
| Electronics: | Type 79B air search radar<br>Type 277 surface surveillance radar<br>Type 281B air search (also used for ranging)<br>Type 293 FC radar |
| Complement: | |
| private ship | 1,300 officers and men (includes air group) |

**Left:** A Curtiss SB2C-5 Helldiver of 9F Squadron. *Arromanches* operated a combination of Hellcats and Helldivers throughout the campaigns in Indochina. *(ARDHAN collection)*

transfer fifteen Seafire XV fighters to enable the ship to take part in a major exercise, 'Verity', scheduled for July. They were distributed between two squadrons, 1F and 12F, which now made up the 1st Embarked Fighter Group (*1er GCE = Groupement de chasse embarquée*). Fourteen pilots qualified in deck landings on 28–29 June off Lorient. However, landing accidents involving Seafires on 4 July 1949 and 8 March 1950 resulted in the grounding of all Seafires. Fortunately the Navy was now in the process of receiving American carrier aircraft that were surplus to requirements. Squadrons 1F and 12F were duly re-equipped with F6F-5 Hellcats and Squadrons 3F and 4F with Curtiss SB2C-5 Helldivers, pilot qualification taking place between May and August.

*Arromanches* underwent a major refit from 24 November 1950 to 2 July 1951, when she began trials and work-up. The following month saw the purchase outright of the carrier on 4 August, for the sum of £1.5 million. The limitations on her employment no longer applied, and the French were free to send *Arromanches* to Indochina and to undertake the full range of air operations. After a final docking from 11 to 16 August, she embarked Squadrons 1F and 3F together with a Sikorsky S-51 rescue helicopter.

### Second Campaign in Indochina 1951–52

*Arromanches* departed Toulon on 28 August 1951 in company with the light cruiser *Le Malin*. Unfortunately her helicopter was damaged when landing at Djibouti and had to be left behind. The two ships arrived at Cape Saint-Jacques on 24 September, when eight Hellcats and three Helldivers were flown ashore to Tan Son Nhut to serve as an operational reserve and to free up the movement of the aircraft remaining on board. *Arromanches* was to operate off the coast of Indochina, providing support for the ground forces when weather permitted. Operations were to be co-ordinated with the Tactical Air Groups (GATAC) of the *Armée de l'Air*.

During operations off Tonkin from 14 to 21 October, a Helldiver was lost during a dive-bombing attack on the bridge at Thai Ke, probably downed by anti-aircraft fire. On 7 November, a second Hellcat was lost in similar circumstances when attacking the bridge at Chi-Tanh off Annam Province. When returning from the strike, bad weather compelled four Helldivers and a Hellcat to divert to Nha Trang. They were retrieved on the 12th with only 22 knots of wind over the deck.

The carrier returned to Tonkin on 14 November, remaining in the area until 9 January 1952. The *Armée de l'Air* was particularly impressed with the performance of the Helldiver, which could carry up to five 250lb (113kg) bombs. *Arromanches* was able to sustain twenty-four sorties per day, but she was now in serious need of maintenance. Marine growth (a major problem in the tropics) had reduced maximum speed to 22 knots, and there were shaft vibrations between 16 and 18 knots.

**Right:** *Arromanches* in Ha Long Bay during the early 1950s, with Hellcats and Helldivers embarked. Note the 'H' deck recognition letter. *(René Bail collection)*

Following a five-week docking period at Singapore from 16 January to 23 February, *Arromanches* returned to Cape Saint-Jacques, while twenty-one of her aircraft operated from Tan Son Nhut. She was off Tonkin from 6 March to 16 April, but on 14 April one of the Hellcats of 1F approached too fast, bounced over the barriers and landed on aircraft in the forward deck park. The accident resulted in four dead, two seriously injured and the loss of five Hellcats, which were ditched over the side.

After a joint exercise with the Royal Navy in late April, *Arromanches* left with *Le Malin* for Toulon on 18 May, arriving on 13 June. Her aircraft had flown for 3,454 hours and made 1,509 deck landings. She underwent a short refit, emerging on 13 August, and began work-up for a further deployment to Indochina, during which there were a number of minor accidents.

The drawing shows the impact of the accident of 14 April 1952. The accident resulted in four dead, two seriously injured and the loss of five Hellcats. *(Drawn by Jean Moulin)*

### Third Deployment to Indochina 1952–53

*Arromanches* left with the destroyer escort *Marocain* for Saigon on 29 August 1952, when the Minister of Defence and the Secretary of State for the Navy came on board and addressed the crew. The group arrived off Cape Saint-Jacques on 29 September.

On 15 October the catapult failed, leading to the loss of a Helldiver of 9F. Eight Hellcats of 12F were flown off to Cat Bi, and the remaining Helldivers had to take off using the full length of the deck until the catapult was repaired. A second Hellcat was lost during a patrol mission involving three Hellcats and four Helldivers on 19 December.

*Arromanches* visited Hong Kong from 7 to 13 January, then conducted further air support missions off Annam and Tonkin. By now she was in serious

**Left:** The forward deck park of *Arromanches* following the accident of 14 April 1952 – see text and drawing. *(René Bail collection)*

54S
DEFENSE
FUMER

A Hellcat of 54S has a problem disengaging its tailhook from the arrester wire in 1950–51. *(ARDHAN collection)*

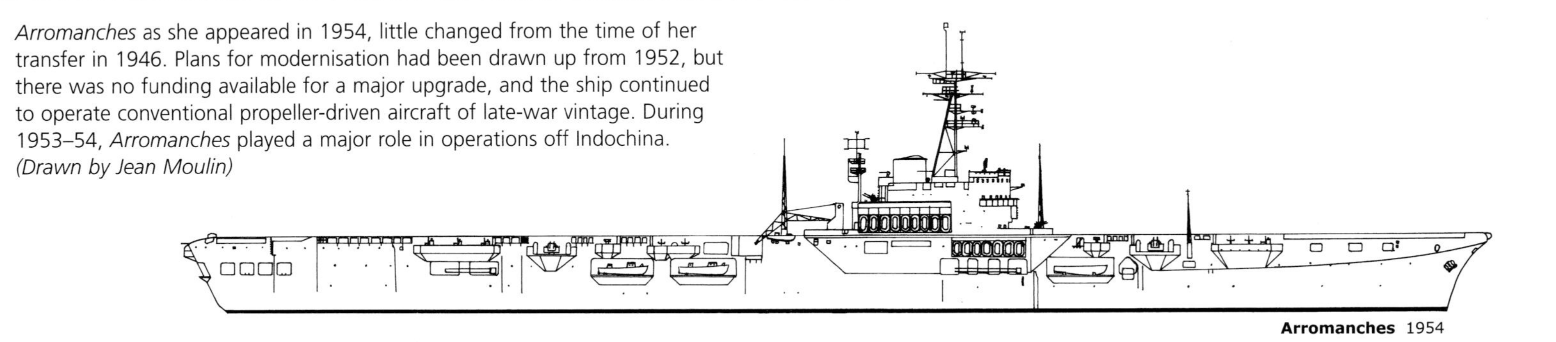


*Arromanches* as she appeared in 1954, little changed from the time of her transfer in 1946. Plans for modernisation had been drawn up from 1952, but there was no funding available for a major upgrade, and the ship continued to operate conventional propeller-driven aircraft of late-war vintage. During 1953–54, *Arromanches* played a major role in operations off Indochina. *(Drawn by Jean Moulin)*

need of a refit; she left Saigon at the end of February 1953 and entered Toulon on 18 March. Her air group remained at Cat Bi ready to embark on her replacement, *La Fayette*, which arrived in the Far East on 9 April. It had totalled 4,128 hours of flight and 1,433 deck landings.

**Fourth Campaign to Indochina 1953–54**

*Arromanches* emerged from the dockyard on 17 April 1953 and embarked sixteen Helldivers of 3F and eighteen Hellcats of 11F (formerly 1F), together with two S-51 plane guard helicopters of 58S. She left Toulon on 9 September and arrived at Cape Saint-Jacques on the 29th.

She departed on 4 October for Tonkin, operating off that province until 19 January 1954. Her escort, *Sénégalais*, joined in Ha Long Bay only on 10 October. Air support operations were directed principally by GATAC North, but *Arromanches* also conducted some operations in conjunction with GATAC Centre. Flying was often curtailed due to bad weather, and there were frequent landing accidents (four between 29 October and 25 November, of which three involved the same pilot!).

On 20 November, Operation 'Castor' began with a parachute drop into the bowl of Dien Bien Phu. Aircraft from *Arromanches* operated against enemy supply lines and, in the later stages of the battle, in support of the besieged troops. Two Hellcats were lost (to an air accident and enemy AA fire respectively) during November and December.

From 14 to 19 January 1954, six Hellcats and six Helldivers were based ashore while the catapult was being repaired. A further two Hellcats of 11F would be lost to enemy AA fire during February and March. The captain of the carrier decided to base the air group ashore, where the aircraft would be closer to their targets and would avoid the problem of deck landings during the poor weather prevailing. Squadron 11F was based at Cat Bi and 3F at Bach Mai. Losses continued to mount: two Helldivers of 3F, including the squadron commander, on 31 March and 9 April, and two Hellcats of 11F, downed by AA fire on 23 and 26 April. Other aircraft were hit but managed to return to base.

The air group of *Arromanches* was by now exhausted, and was relieved by the AU-1 Corsairs of 14F based at Bach Mai. The Hellcats of 11F returned to the carrier on 1 May, and the Helldivers of 3F would embark on *Bois Belleau*, which had recently arrived in Ha Long Bay, on the 3rd. Dien Bien Phu fell on 7 May. *Arromanches* was in Ha Long Bay from 9 to 24 May, when she re-embarked Squadron 3F. She then resumed air operations off North Vietnam until 23 June, during which another Hellcat was lost in action (17 June). Squadrons 3F and 11F were then transferred, together with support personnel and spares, to *Bois Belleau* while the two ships were moored in Ha Long Bay.

*Arromanches* departed on 16 July for Tourane. A ceasefire was signed on 20 July, and came into effect between 27 July and 11 August, depending on the zone. *Arromanches* was at Saigon from 14 to 20 August, disembarked 14 AU-1 to be handed back to the Americans in Manila, and returned to Toulon on 19 September 1954. Her aircraft had totalled 9,045 hours of flight and 2,275 deck landings.

Below: A Hellcat of 11F involved in an accident on board *Arromanches* in late September 1953. *(ARDHAN collection)*

**A Second Spell in the *Escadre* 1954–55**

*Arromanches* entered the dockyard for refit and repair on 20 September, emerging for trials on 19 January 1955. She would now be engaged in the training of pilots, participation in exercises with NATO ('Medflex 2', January) and with the *Escadre* ('Sans Atout 4', March). She took part in the spring cruise of April with Squadrons 4F and 6F embarked, visiting Lisbon, Brest, Plymouth, Cherbourg and Casablanca. Pilot qualifications and further 'Medflex' exercises followed during the summer and autumn.

A brief docking at Toulon over the Christmas period was followed by further pilot qualifications.

**Left:** The flight deck of *Arromanches* with the Helldivers of 3F and the Hellcats of 11F. *(René Bail collection)*

**Left:** *Arromanches* in Toulon roads, with a Hellcat at the forward end of the flight deck. *(Musée national de la Marine)*

Above: *Arromanches* in company with HMS *Birmingham* during a NATO exercise between July 1955 and April 1957. She remains relatively unmodified since her transfer from the Royal Navy. *(ARDHAN collection)*

*Arromanches* then took part in the spring cruise (13 April–14 May), which was followed by exercises with GASM. On 23 May, she embarked 9F Squadron and visited the ports of French West Africa; 9F was replaced by 14F during the visit to Casablanca. She was then docked from 6 to 13 August.

### Suez 1956

The nationalisation of the Suez Canal by Egyptian President Gamal Abdel Nasser on 26 July 1956 took the French Navy by surprise; it was traditionally a period of leave for the personnel, and this was also a moment of transition for the Navy, with the worn-out ships inherited from the Second World War in the process of being replaced by a new generation of vessels that were only just starting to enter service.

A *Force navale d'Intervention* (FNI) was constituted on 8 August. The French carriers in commission were as yet unable to operate jets, so fire support for the troops ashore would be provided by F4U Corsairs and anti-submarine protection by TBM Avengers. *Arromanches* sailed on 27 August, embarking Squadrons 9F at Ajaccio the following day and 14F at Bizerte on 1 August. Work-up and exercises off Les Salins, Bizerte and Algiers followed.

Finally she embarked fourteen F4U-7 Corsair of 14F and ten TBM-3W/S Avenger of 9F, together with two HUP-2 helicopters of 23S. *Arromanches* formed Task Unit 345.4.2 with *La Fayette*, the brand-new fleet escorts *Surcouf*, *Bouvet* and *Cassard* (T47 type), and the equally new fast escorts *Le Corse*, *Le Brestois*, *Le Boulonnais* and *Le Bordelais* (E50 type). The British committed the fleet carriers *Eagle*, *Albion* and *Bulwark* with Sea Hawk and Sea Venom jets, and Wyvern, Skyraider and Avenger propeller-driven aircraft, together with *Theseus* and *Ocean*, two sister ships of *Arromanches* recently converted to commando carriers with an air complement of Westland Whirlwind assault helicopters. The two groups met up on 30 November, but each group would be allocated its own operational zone.

The war began on 29 October with an Israeli attack on the Sinai Peninsula that halted 16km from the Suez Canal. Two days later the British bombed the Egyptian airfields. On the same day, *Arromanches* launched reconnaissance patrols that located two US Navy destroyers and Egyptian surface vessels. On 1 November, a TBM struck the Egyptian frigate *Tarik* with two rockets (out of eight launched) after it was fired upon. At 1000 on 2 November, catapult launches of Corsairs had to be halted due to lack of wind, and on 3 November, a TBM attack on a submarine was aborted when it was discovered that it was the American *Cutlass* (SS-478).

An attack on the Almaza air base (Cairo) was scheduled using eight Corsairs from *Arromanches* and ten from *La Fayette*, but the commander of 14F had to pull out due to a hydraulics problem and the strike was led by his second-in-command. The two groups attacked independently, losing one of the Corsairs. Of the six surviving aircraft, the last had to land on with its bomb still attached, the landing zone of the flight deck being cleared in advance. Four Corsairs were subsequently launched for an attack on a convoy of tanks and trucks. The two French carriers replenished on 4 November, resuming operations the following day.

On 5 November, the Corsairs provided fire support for British and French parachute landings on Port Fuad and El Gamil. Three of the aircraft from *La Fayette* landed on *Arromanches* following a crash on their own flight deck. However, wind over deck then declined to a point at which *Arromanches* could no longer land her aircraft, and it was *La Fayette* that recovered the last of them.

On 6 November, troops landed at Port Fuad and Port Said. A wind of 10 knots allowed *Arromanches* to operate as normal. Two sections each of two Corsairs were slated to observe the fire of the ships, but the naval bombardment was aborted at the last moment. The Corsairs were then redirected to attack ground targets with cannon fire. One patrol covered the pilot of a downed British Sea Hawk prior to his recovery by a Whirlwind.

The same evening, a ceasefire was announced. *Arromanches* remained in the zone, then was at Limassol (Cyprus) from 14 to 16 November, returning the following day after a boiler issue. Her two air squadrons were disembarked at Bizerte on 21–22 November, and she was repaired at Toulon. On 9 December she re-embarked the Corsairs of 14F and returned to Port Said to relieve *La Fayette*. She left Port Said for the last time on 21 December and covered the final re-embarkation of the troops. On the evening of the 24th, twelve Corsairs were catapulted off and landed at Karouba. *Arromanches* then headed for Toulon, returning on 27 December 1957 with the FNI.

Pilot qualifications in January 1958 were followed by participation in Exercise 'Medaswex 17' in mid-February and a trip to the USA to pick up 176 AT-6 Wolverine light attack aircraft and 17 helicopters. *Arromanches* returned to Toulon on 22 April to decommission prior to a major modernisation that had been planned since 1952.

**Above:** F4U-7 Corsairs of 15F on *Arromanches* during the mid-1950s. The F4U-7 variant of the Corsair was specially adapted for French service. *(ARDHAN collection)*

## Modernisation 1957–58

Work began on 6 May 1957; the ship was docked at Toulon between 31 July and 16 November, and fitting out continued until July of the following year.

The key elements of the modernisation were:

- an extension of the flight deck to port to create a landing deck angled at 4 degrees from the ship's axis and a deck parking area forward to starboard
- fitting of a mirror landing sight
- removal of all guns
- replacement of the older-model British electronics

**Left:** *Arromanches* in November 1956, when she took part in Operation 'Mousquetaire', the operation to retake the Suez Canal. Note the distinctive recognition markings on her F4U-7 Corsairs. *(René Bail collection)*

Profile and plan drawings of *Arromanches* following the major modernisation of 1958. The flight deck was extended to port to create a new angled deck 4 degrees from the ship's axis, but there was insufficient funding available for a modern steam catapult, so the only jet that could be operated was the Fouga Magister trainer. The Fouga jets and the Alizé turboprop ASW aircraft generally landed on the angled deck, but the original axial flight deck was retained for the older models of propeller-driven aircraft, hence the 4/6 division of the arrester cables between the two and the retention of the net barriers abeam the island. Radars and transmission systems of French design and manufacture were fitted in place of the original British models (see separate drawing), and the command and control facilities were completely revised and extended. The original armament was landed, as the ship would henceforth be employed principally for pilot training, with a subsidiary role as a helicopter carrier and assault ship. *(Drawn by Jean Moulin)*

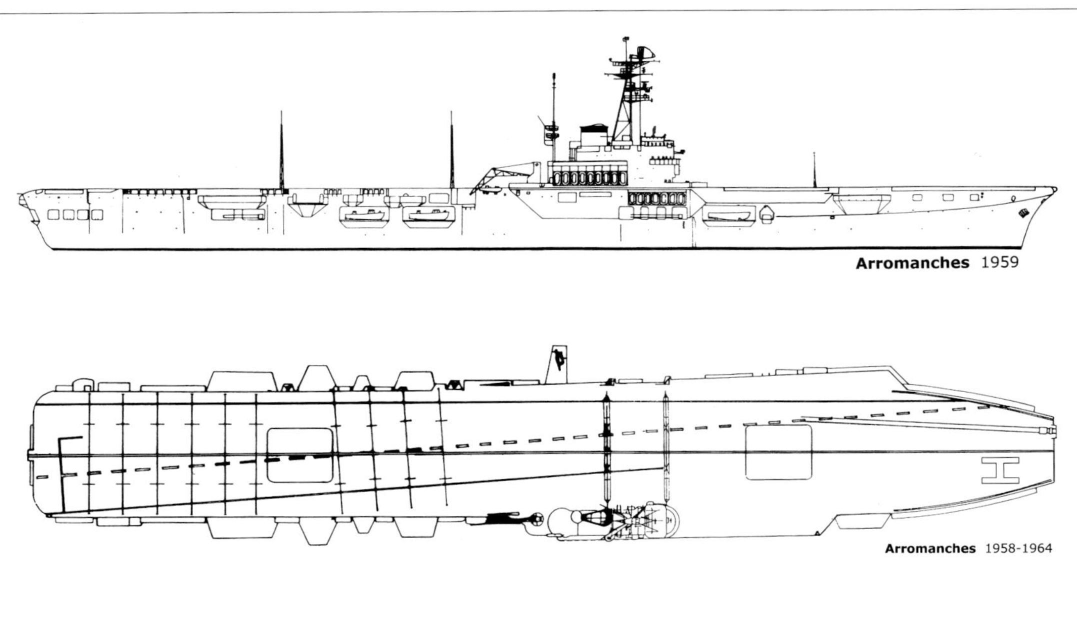


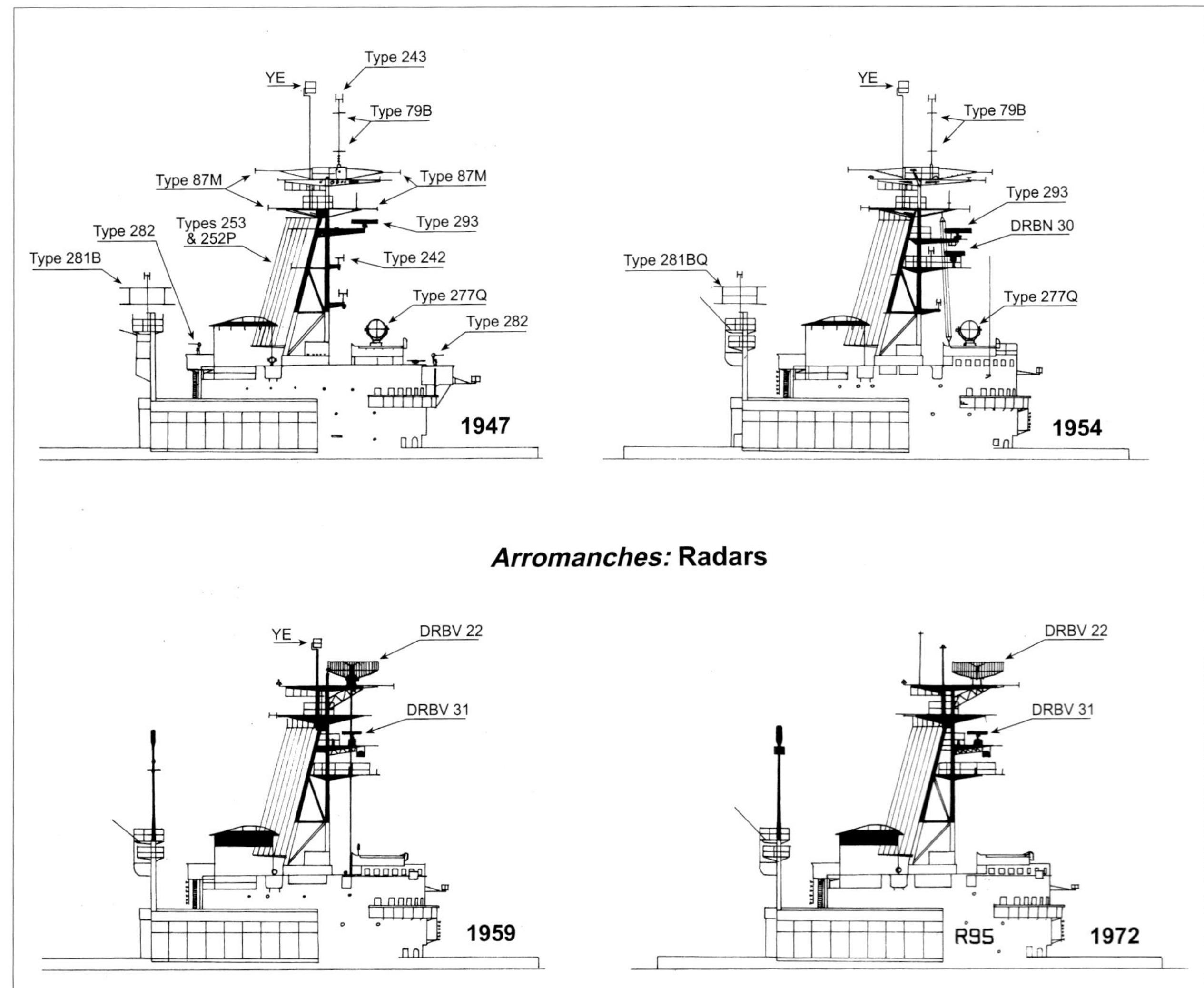


The radar fit of *Arromanches* when transferred from the Royal Navy would remain largely unchanged before her modernisation in 1957–58, when the British-type radars were replaced by models newly developed by French industry. The DRBV 22, the antenna of which resembled the contemporary US Navy SPS-6B, was a lightweight air surveillance radar with a range of 70nm against aircraft, and was fitted in the latest French escorts. *(Drawn by Jean Moulin)*

**Left:** Two Alizé ASW aircraft on the new angled deck of *Arromanches* during a press visit on 20 December 1958. The line marking the centre of the axial deck is yellow, the broken line of the angled deck white. Note the mirror landing sight on its platform to the left of the photo. *(Jean Moulin collection)*

by modern radars and communications equipment of French design and manufacture

- installation of a tank for jet fuel
- modernisation of the Combat Information Centre (*Centre d'Informations* or CI)
- concentration of all data into an Operations Centre (CO)
- reorganisation of damage control and installation of an NBC washdown system for the superstructures.

This was only a partial modernisation. A proposal for installation of a steam catapult to enable the ship to handle the Aquilon jet fighter aircraft was abandoned on the grounds of technical complexity and cost. The six after arrester wires were left in place to enable landings to take place on the axial deck, while the four forward cables were re-aligned with the angled deck. Two of the barriers for the axial flight deck were left in place, and a Mk 5A nylon barrier could be erected 15 metres forward of arrester wire 10. A deck officer was retained on the angled deck for safety reasons, although the pilot used the mirror landing sight to line up his aircraft. A light source was located on a platform 46 metres abaft the mirror sight, 48 metres forward of the point of impact, and the pilot was guided by the reflection of its beam in the mirror.

The tank for TR5 jet fuel (the French equivalent of JP-5) had a capacity of 97m$^3$. This would be almost doubled in a later refit in 1972 by converting a diesel tank.

The British Type 281B air search and Type 293 surface surveillance radars were replaced by the French DRBV 22 and DRBV 31 respectively, both mounted on the tripod foremast.

On 14 July 1958, the work on *Arromanches* was yet to be completed, but the ship was in a sufficiently fit state to take part in a naval review that took place in Toulon roads in the presence of General de Gaulle, President of the Council, who was embarked on the new fleet escort *Kersaint.*

*Arromanches* in the Indian Ocean in 1959. The aircraft parked on the after part of the flight deck are F4U-7 Corsairs. *(René Bail collection)*

The official date for completion of the refit was 30 July. *Arromanches* then began trials and work-up. She was the only carrier currently in service capable of operating classical piston-engine aircraft (Corsair/Avenger) from an axial deck and modern jet and turbo-prop aircraft (Fouga/Alizé) from an angled deck.

### From Algeria to Madagascar

Landing-on trials using the angled deck were conducted by TBM Avengers on 2–3 October. Pilot

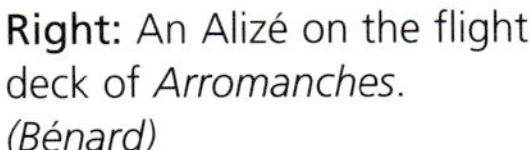

**Right:** An Alizé on the flight deck of *Arromanches*. *(Bénard)*

**Right:** Two Alizé ASW aircraft on *Arromanches*. An HSS helicopter can be seen landing at the after end of the flight deck. *(Bénard)*

qualifications followed, and 'touch-and-go' trials with Fouga jets and Alizé turbo-prop aircraft took place between the 19th and the 21st. The first landings and catapult launches using these two aircraft were carried out from 3 to 5 December.

On 4 January 1959, *Arromanches* launched strikes against rebel forces in Algeria – the only occasion on which she participated in the conflict. Routine activities, pilot training and exercises followed.

*Arromanches* left Toulon on 15 June with 15F and

**Left:** HSS helicopters lined up on the angled deck. *(Bénard))*

**Left:** Two Super Frelon heavy-lift helicopters on *Arromanches*. *(Bénard)*

Above: *Arromanches* with three Alizé ASW aircraft in the forward deck park. Note the antenna for the DBBV 22 air surveillance radar atop the foremast. *(Bénard)*

the fleet escort *La Bourdonnais* to support a tour by General de Gaulle, now President of the Republic, of the French Indian Ocean territories (Djibouti, Madagascar and La Réunion). She returned to Toulon on 5 August. In October, she conducted deck landings of Alizé and Fouga aircraft, trials of the Sikorsky HSS-1 helicopter in conjunction with GASM, and night landings by the Alizé. The ship was then docked in November and December.

The year 1960 was relatively uneventful except for a visit to the USA in December, when *Arromanches* embarked forty-two AD-4 Skyraiders for the *Armée de l'Air* at Norfolk, offloading them at Saint-Nazaire on 2 January 1961.

The first half of 1961 saw three visits to North Africa, with first 9F and then 12F embarked.

### Bizerte

The Tunisians threatened the naval base at Bizerte, then attempted to take it by force. An assault on 19–22 July was repelled by the garrison, which was reinforced by parachute troops. Corsairs of 17F Squadron, based at Karouba, provided fire support, but *Arromanches* only had a handful of aircraft from 14F on board, which were not engaged. She entered Bizerte on 22 July and remained on alert at Bône, returning to Toulon on 11 August.

*Arromanches* was placed in care and maintenance on 1 November, then entered the dockyard for a refit from 26 April to 27 June 1962. She was active from 26 January 1963. Pilot training followed, interrupted by a problem with a propeller coupling, and there were sorties to North Africa.

The last Corsair landings took place on 5 May 1963, which meant that the axial deck was no longer in use. Later that month, *Arromanches* took part in NATO Exercise 'Fair Game 2', followed by maintenance from May to September. She left for Norfolk on 3 October, where she embarked thirteen F-8 Crusaders intended for the new carrier *Clemenceau*; they would be disembarked at Saint-Nazaire on 4–5 November.

*Arromanches* visited Barcelona in late January 1965 and was then in maintenance until April. Exercise 'Fair Game 3' followed, and there were visits to Livorno and La Spezia in July. On 15 September, the Squadron became the Mediterranean Fleet.

### *Arromanches* as a Helicopter Carrier

In October 1965, the missions of *Arromanches* were redefined; she would now serve as:

- a helicopter assault ship
- an operational transport
- a training carrier for pilot landings
- an anti-submarine carrier capable of embarking a mixed air group comprising Alizé turbo-prop aircraft and HSS helicopters.

In early December she embarked on her first mission as an assault carrier, with HSS-1 assault helicopters of 33F and a battalion of US Marines embarked. In December 1966 she took part in a Franco-US exercise involving a landing on the coasts of Corsica. A major exercise off French West Africa the following year, 'Alligator 3', found *Arromanches* with fifteen HSS of 33F embarked. During the last two years, *Arromanches* had required regular maintenance periods; the ship was now more than 20 years old and in need of a major refit.

### The Major Refit of 1968–69

*Arromanches* was immobilised at Toulon from 1 January 1968 and in refit from 1 September 1968 to 2 September 1969. Judged to be still in good condition, she acted as a relief for *Clemenceau* and *Foch* for pilot training, and could be employed as a helicopter assault carrier and as a fast transport if required.

*Arromanches* participated in exercises with the Mediterranean Fleet throughout 1970, and embarked twelve HSS helicopters of 33F in early December for mission 'Petrel Alpha' in French West Africa; the helicopters were flown off before she entered Douala, and operated in Chad until March; the ship returned to Toulon on 30 December.

She left again on 29 April 1971 for the Antilles, with the Alizés of 9F, the HSS of 31F and a company of Marine commandos embarked. She was accompanied by the missile frigate *Duquesne*, the fleet escorts *Surcouf*, *Vauquelin* and *Du Chayla*, the fast escort *Le Normand* and the fleet tanker *La Saône*. There were numerous port visits in the region. During the return voyage a collision between a Soviet tanker and *Surcouf* resulted in the latter losing her bow, and the stern section was towed into Cartagena by *Tartu* on 7 June escorted by *Arromanches*, whose helicopters had taken part in the rescue of the crew. The carrier returned to Toulon two days later, on 9 June, leaving again on the 12th for exercises, still with 9F and 31F embarked.

On 19 June, *Arromanches* took part in a major naval review off Toulon by President Georges Pompidou, who was hosted on the carrier *Clemenceau*. Further exercises followed, off Corsica in August with 33F and commandos embarked, in the Western Mediterranean in October (9F and 31F) with port visits to Cartagena and Palma de Mallorca, and in November/December.

After a five-week maintenance period in January–February 1972, *Arromanches* was again involved in exercises and pilot training for Squadron 6F. The landing mirror sight then failed, rendering the ship incapable of operating as an aircraft carrier. A spring cruise to the Eastern Mediterranean followed. *Arromanches* was at Navy Week in Cherbourg, returning to Toulon via Lisbon on 28 June. The year concluded with a three-month maintenance period, with activity resuming on 22 January 1973, when the ship visited Venice with the HSS helicopters of 31F embarked. She then took part in the Fleet's winter cruise to West Africa with 33F, returning on 8 March.

A planned maintenance period was interrupted by a rescue mission following severe flooding in Tunisia. *Arromanches* left Toulon on 30 March with eleven HSS of 33F, the Jaubert commando unit and 38 tonnes of cargo. A total of 156 sorties were mounted by her helicopters and 230 people rescued. She left the area on 4 April, then embarked 31F for the spring cruise to the Eastern Mediterranean.

A six-month transport mission to Madagascar was abandoned, but the catapult was repaired and two Alizé embarked. Training for the pilots of 59S resumed in June. A maintenance period from 27 August to 1 October was followed by a sortie with the Fleet, with the helicopters of 31F and Fouga and Alizé aircraft of 59S embarked.

On 9 November, during an exercise off the Iles d'Or, Hyères, a Fouga jet of 59S caught the arrester cable but the cable parted on the starboard side and the aircraft veered to the right, crashed into an Alizé and fell into the sea. The pilot and one of the flight deck crew died, but the passenger in the plane was rescued.

**Above:** An aerial view of *Arromanches* with eight Alizés on the flight deck. During the late 1950s and early 1960s she was employed as an anti-submarine carrier, with a subsidiary role as an assault carrier. The angled deck has now been painted dark grey. Note the markings for the helicopter landing spots on the angled deck, and for the boundary of the forward deck park to starboard. *(Bénard)*

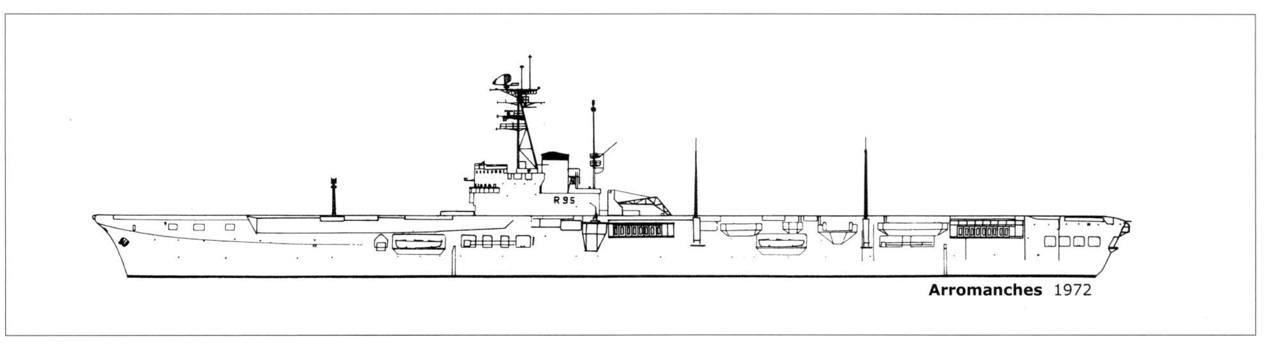


**Left:** *Arromanches* in 1972 in her final configuration, little changed since her modernisation in 1957–58. *(Drawn by Jean Moulin)*

**Above:** *Arromanches* at Toulon in 1972. *(Marc Piché)*

**Left:** *Arromanches* at Brégaillon, where she would be broken up. *(René Bail)*

This would be the last landing of an aircraft on board *Arromanches*, and the last catapult launch (with a second Fouga) took place that same evening.

*Arromanches* returned to Toulon on 16 November, and on the 28th the decision was taken to decommission the ship from 1 January 1974. The decision saved the cost of a planned refit in 1974 and freed up a complement of 572 officers and men. The ship was stricken on 5 September 1974 and became Q 525. The ship's bell was returned to the Royal Navy and is now on display in the Fleet Air Arm Museum at Yeovilton. The ship was purchased for scrap in early December 1977 and broken up at Brégaillon.

## THE AMERICAN CARRIERS

In 1945, the Americans were initially opposed to the return of the French to their former colony of Indochina. They tolerated a French purchase of decommissioned landing ships from the Philippines, but would have preferred the European presence in Southeast Asia to be permanently erased, to be replaced by an enlarged free-trade zone open to US manufacturers. However, Stalin's division of Europe into West and East by an 'iron curtain' prompted a move to rearm the countries of Western Europe, and this change in US strategy was accompanied by a softening of the position regarding the *Marine Nationale*.

Neither the Americans nor the British were keen on facilitating the reconstitution of a French ocean-going fleet, but the need for access to European ports for US troops in the event of a conflict on land led the Americans to boost the anti-submarine and minesweeping capabilities of the French Navy, and the NATO Alliance, formed by a treaty signed on 4 April 1949, prompted a cautious reversal of the American position. New surface units would be funded under the Mutual Defense Assistance Act, passed by Congress on 6 October 1949 and signed by President Harry S Truman, and the Americans finally agreed to loan a light carrier to France to compensate for the cancellation of PA28. The agreement was signed by both parties on 27 February 1950, but it was stipulated by the Americans that the ship could be used only for anti-submarine warfare; an initial project envisaged the transfer of three light fleet carriers to form two or three 'hunter-killer' groups in the North Atlantic. The transfer of a second carrier would be agreed on 15 June 1953, but by this time the American position had softened still further, and the carriers would be permitted (provisionally) to deploy outside the NATO area.

### *LA FAYETTE* (EX-*LANGLEY*)

The US light fleet carrier *Langley* (CVL-27) was the first to be handed over, on 16 October 1950. A sum of

**Below:** Task Force 58.3 makes a simultaneous turn to port from column formation, while entering Ulithi anchorage on 12 December 1944 after strikes against the Japanese in the Philippines. *Langley* (CVL-27) is in the foreground, with *Ticonderoga* (CV-14) beyond her. *(NHHC, 80-G-301354)*

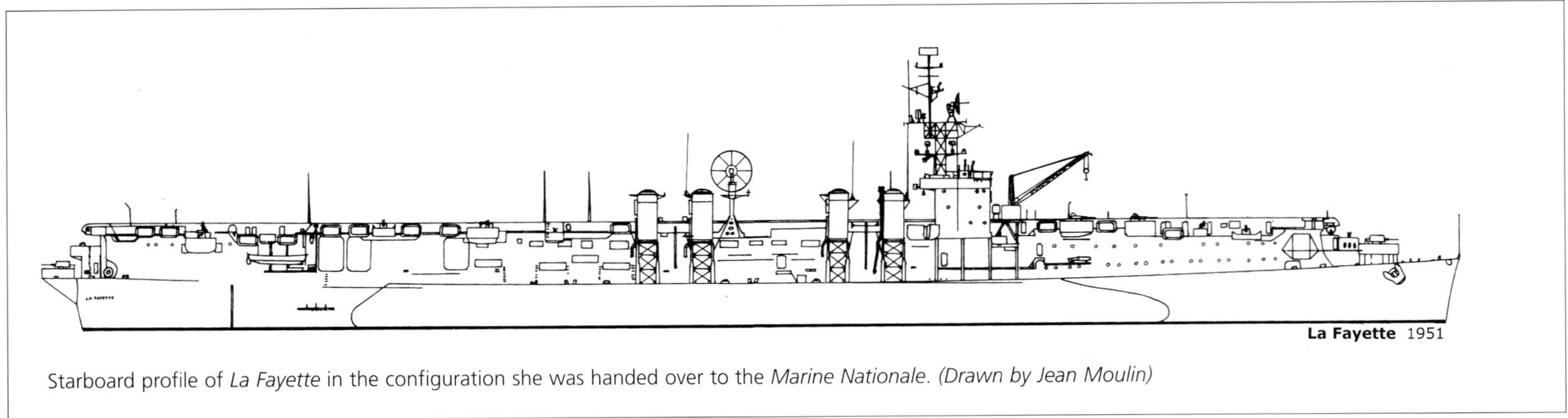


Starboard profile of *La Fayette* in the configuration she was handed over to the *Marine Nationale*. *(Drawn by Jean Moulin)*

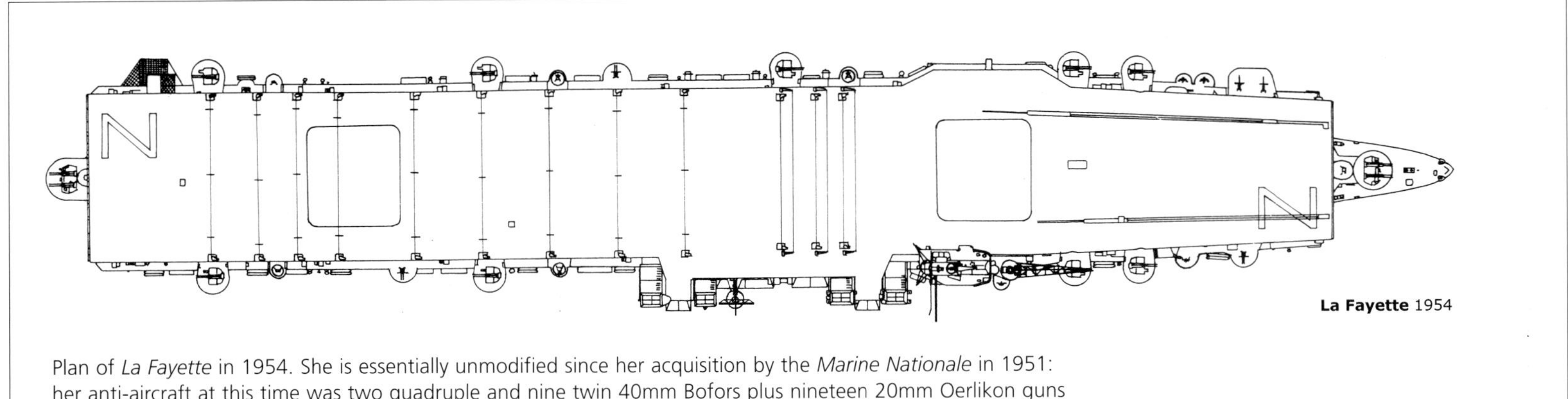


Plan of *La Fayette* in 1954. She is essentially unmodified since her acquisition by the *Marine Nationale* in 1951: her anti-aircraft at this time was two quadruple and nine twin 40mm Bofors plus nineteen 20mm Oerlikon guns in twin and single mountings. Note the nine arrester wires and the three barrier nets. *(Drawn by Jean Moulin)*

**Right:** Raising of the French *tricolore* as the ship is formally transferred to France in a ceremony at the Philadelphia Navy Yard, Pennsylvania, on 2 June 1951. Note the US Navy bandsmen in the centre. *(NHHC, 80-G-429464)*

US $700,000 was allocated to refurbish the ship under MDAP.

Built by the New York Shipbuilding Corporation, *Langley* was originally ordered as the light cruiser *Fargo* (CL-85), but by the time her keel was laid in April 1942, she had been redesigned as an aircraft carrier, using the original cruiser hull and machinery. Commissioned in August 1943, *Langley* served with the fast carrier task forces in the Pacific during 1944–45, taking part in most of the campaigns. She was decommissioned at Philadelphia Navy Yard on 11 February 1947 and 'mothballed'. Two of the class of nine would be refitted for ASW, and two would be transferred to the *Marine Nationale*; the remainder never recommissioned.

Work to prepare the ship for French service began at the Philadelphia Navy Yard on 9 January 1951, and the ship was docked from 3 to 21 March. It was planned to operate F6F-5 Hellcat fighters and TBM Avenger torpedo bombers from the ship, and these former US Navy aircraft were allocated to 12F and 4F Squadrons respectively. In April, *Langley* was renamed *La Fayette* after the French general who commanded the Continental Army during the siege of Yorktown in 1781, the final major battle of the American War of Independence, and the French *tricolore* was raised for the first time on 2 June 1951.

*La Fayette* first put to sea under French colours on 16–18 June. Flotillas 12F and 4F were at Norfolk on 12 July, and work on the ship was completed the following day. The cost of the refit was US $3.9 million – far greater than anticipated. The first deck landings took place off Norfolk on 19 July, but the second Hellcat approached too low and struck the after end of the flight deck, breaking up on impact; the pilot was rescued by an American HUP-1 helicopter. A period of intensive work-up that conformed to US procedures followed.

The carrier departed Norfolk on 1 September with the two air squadrons embarked. Further trials were undertaken during the crossing, including a speed trial that delivered 30.5 knots. *La Fayette* was met by the escort *Alsacien* (ex-German *T 23*) off Toulon. Thirty aircraft took off and landed at Hyères, and the ship entered the port on 14 September 1951.

During the last three months of the year there were visits to Algiers, Bougie and Ajaccio with 12F and 4F embarked, and on 14–15 December, the first landings with the Helldivers of 9F took place.

Left: The island of *La Fayette* on her arrival at Toulon in late September 1951. *(Musée national de la Marine)*

## Table 3: *LA FAYETTE* (1951)

| | |
|---|---|
| **Displacement:** | 11,000 tons standard<br>15,810 tonnes load |
| **Dimensions:** | |
| length | 190m oa |
| beam | 21.80m wl, 33.25m max |
| draught | 7.40m |
| **Aviation:** | |
| flight deck | 138.90m x 22.30m max |
| catapult | two H2-1 |
| arrester wires | nine with Mk IV Mod 6/7 brakes |
| barriers | three |
| hangar | 75.20m x 16.76m x 5.28m |
| lifts (L x W) | 12.43m x 13.05m (12,700kg max, 7600kg normal) |
| air group | twelve F4U Corsair, ten TBM Avenger (hangar) |
| crane | one flight deck (6350kg) |
| avgas | 462m$^3$ |
| **Machinery:** | |
| boilers | four Babccok & Wilcox boilers, 42kg/cm$^2$ (450°C) |
| engines | two sets of General Electric geared turbines (HP + LP) |
| propellers | four 3.60m diameter |
| horsepower | 100,000shp |
| speed | 31.5 knots |
| oil fuel | 2,700 tonnes |
| endurance | 10,000nm at 13/14 knots |
| generators | four turbo-generators each 600kW<br>two diesel generators each 250kW |
| **Protection:** | |
| belt | 127mm (5in) |
| main deck | 15–20mm (3/4in) |
| magazines | 50mm (2in) |
| **Armament:** | |
| light AA | twenty-six 40mm Bofors in two quad Mk 2 and nine twin Mk 1 mountings<br>ten 20mm Oerlikon in twin Mk 24 mountings |
| **Electronics:** | SK-2 air search radar<br>SC-2 air/surface surveillance radar<br>SG surface surveillance radar |
| **Complement:** | |
| private ship | 1,139 officers and men (peacetime)<br>1,178 officers and men (wartime) |

**Right:** A Grumman TBM-3S Avenger of 3F preparing for launch from the port-side catapult of *La Fayette*. *(ARDHAN collection)*

**NATO Hunter-Killer 1952**

*La Fayette* left Toulon on 15 January 1952 with 12F and 4F embarked to continue training for ASW using NATO procedures; there were several landing incidents, and a problem with a turbopump, damaged while mooring, restricted the ship to a maximum speed of 28 knots.

Visits to North Africa were followed by NATO Exercise 'Grand Slam', in which the carrier formed a hunter-killer group with four US Navy destroyers. *La Fayette* then visited Bizerte and Naples, returning to Toulon on 3 April for a brief maintenance period.

Squadron 12F embarked again on 26 April, followed by 9F on the 30th. On 1 May, the first night launch took place 50km off Toulon. Minor deck accidents continued. *La Fayette* then took part in the spring cruise of the Squadron between 7 May and 27 June with all three of her assigned squadrons (12F/4F/9F) embarked, escorted initially by the destroyer *Marceau* (ex-*Z 31*), then by *Kléber* (ex-*Z 6*). Exercises 'Sans Atout' and 'Tage' followed, with port visits to Oran, Lisbon, Brest, Le Havre and Mers el-Kébir. Squadrons 12F and 4F were disembarked and replaced by 6F with TBM Avengers between 11 and 24 June. After further port visits to West and North Africa, *La Fayette* returned to Toulon on 27 June. During the cruise there had been no fewer than 913 deck landings, with only 7 accidents.

Pilot qualifications and leave for the crew followed, and the ship was docked from 13 to 29 September. She emerged for trials on 10 October. On 14 October, there was a major incident when a Hellcat of 1F broke through the barrier and crashed onto the lift. Five aircraft were damaged, four of which had to be written off. Pilot training continued, with visits to Mers el-Kébir and Oran. There were a further two serious accidents involving the Hellcats of 1F during early November.

On 24 November, *La Fayette* left for the USA with a Beechcraft aircraft for the air attaché, but on 1/2 December she ran into a major storm off the Bermudas and suffered extensive damage; a roll of 44 degrees was experienced on the second day. The ship arrived at Norfolk on 4 December and entered

Portsmouth Navy Yard the following day, when a whaler, rafts and nets carried away by the storm were replaced. She embarked forty F4U-7 Corsairs, explosives and other materiel, disembarked the Corsairs at Bizerte and arrived back in Toulon on 24 December. She then underwent a short maintenance period in which the storm damage was repaired.

**First Campaign in Indochina 1953**

After further pilot training with Squadrons 1F and 3F during the early part of 1953, *La Fayette* left Toulon on 22 March with two Morane 500 aircraft on board, tasked with recovering the Hellcats and Helldivers of 12F and 9F left in Indochina by *Arromanches*. She arrived off Cape Saint-Jacques on 7 April, embarked two S-51 helicopters and headed for Tonkin, escorted by the patrol boats *Flamberge* and *Inconstant*. Six Hellcats of 12F took off from Cat Bi, but only two were able to land on board due to the fog. The remainder of the aircraft, eleven Hellcats of 12F and seven Helldivers of 9F, were finally able to embark on 12 April.

The poor weather precluded operations until 15 April, when four Helldivers attacked Quang Ngai in support of the garrison of Sam Neua, which was withdrawing towards the Plain of Jars. The last two Helldiver patrols had to return to Cat Bi due to the weather, but twelve sorties were made by Hellcats on the 17th. The air support missions continued until the 24th, often hindered by poor visibility. On the 26th, fifteen sorties were made with the aim of cutting enemy supply lines, and there were further ground support missions on 30 April and during early May.

*La Fayette* was in Ha Long Bay from 6 to 9 May, then left for Hon Me to take part in Operation 'Muguet'. There were eight sorties on the 9th, fourteen on the 10th and twenty-five on the 11th. She then embarked the aircraft, personnel and materiel left by *Arromanches* at Cat Bi and departed Tonkin for Saigon, arriving on the 18th. She returned to metropolitan France via Singapore, Djibouti, Suez and Port Said, re-entering Toulon on 10 June. Two sailings to Bizerte in late June/early July were followed by a

Below: *La Fayette* in Ha Long Bay in May 1953 with the F6F-5 Hellcats of 12F and the SB2C-5 Helldivers of 9F. *(ARDHAN collection)*

docking to inspect her port propeller shaft, which had been damaged by the mooring chain of a buoy during the passage through the Suez Canal, and was found to have a broken propeller blade and a deformed A-frame. On her three remaining shafts she was capable of only 27.5 knots.

She left for Bizerte on 27 July for pilot qualifications with the F4U-7 Corsairs of 14F. She was then docked and her propeller shaft removed for repairs on 1 August. The work was completed on 10 October, and *La Fayette* resumed her pilot qualification and training missions off Bizerte, with visits to Mers el-Kébir and Oran in the New Year. She then entered Toulon Dockyard for a major refit, which lasted from 16 February to 15 September 1954. The island was modified and a French DRBV 30 surface surveillance installed, while the original US SK-2 long-range air surveillance radar, the antenna of which was atop the lattice mast, was replaced by the more modern US Navy SPS-6. The repaired outer port shaft was replaced during this refit.

**The Evacuation of Indochina 1955**

*La Fayette* emerged from refit on 4 October 1954 to embark Squadron 12F; she was accompanied by the light cruiser *Le Terrible*. An H4B catapult was installed during 10 October–24 November. Two visits to Bizerte were followed by Exercise 'Ajax' off the coast of Provence from 15 to 17 December. Squadron 12F embarked with eight Hellcats, the Corsairs being currently grounded following an accident. There were two further exercises, including the NATO 'Medflex 2' in late January 1955, still with the eight Hellcats of 12F embarked. The Corsairs were cleared for flying in February, and twelve F4U-7 of 12F were embarked for Exercise 'Sans Atout' off Bizerte in early March. Further exercises off the ports of North Africa followed, and on 1 April the twenty Corsairs of 12F were assigned to the ship.

On 13 April, *La Fayette* left for Tonkin with 12F, four Helldivers and two HUP-2 helicopters embarked; she arrived at Cape Saint-Jacques on 2 May, and headed for Tourane on the 4th. From 8 to 18 May, the *Groupe des porte-avions d'Extrême-Orient* (GPAEO) comprised *La Fayette* with 12F, *Bois Belleau* with 14F, eight PB4Y-2 Privateer patrol bombers (28F), a squadron of Air Force B-26 bombers, and a section of Dakota Luciole aircraft at Tourane (all *Armée de l'Air*). On 8 May a Task Force 65 was created with the submarine tender *Jules Verne* as command ship. Task Group 65.1 comprised the two aircraft carriers, with the patrol ships *Trident* and *Flamberge*. The Haiphong bridgehead was evacuated in Operation 'Saumon', which was completed on 15 May. Squadron 12F was initially based at Tourane, then re-embarked, then flown off again to Tourane and embarked on *Bois Belleau*, to be replaced by 14F on board *La Fayette*. The latter then embarked 1,293 personnel, the 9

**Below:** An SB2C-5 Helldiver on *La Fayette* during her deployment to Indochina in 1953; the aircraft suffered damage when landing. *(René Bail collection)*

F4U-7 Corsairs of 14F, 2 HUP-2 helicopters, 3 Helldivers, 2 Morane 500, 8 Grumman Goose flying boats plus 3 F4U-7 from *Bois Belleau* and 2 LCVP landing craft. She left for Toulon on 11 June, flying off 14F at Bizerte en route and arriving back on 13 July.

*La Fayette* was at sea again on 19 September with 15F embarked. Pilot qualifications were followed by Exercise 'Medflex Champion', which ended on 30 September. In early October she was at Bizerte, embarking Vice Admiral Philippe Auboyneau for a visit to Malta. She returned to Toulon via Bizerte on 13 October, and underwent a short docking from 7 November to 5 December, by which time she had accumulated 10,805 deck landings under the French ensign.

In January 1956, *La Fayette* returned to Indochina, embarking sixteen Corsairs of 15F, two TBM-UT and two HUP-2 helicopters. She left for Saigon on the 20th, embarking a further four Corsairs en route at Bizerte and arriving on 11 February. Exercises with other French units and with the Royal Navy followed in late March (the British force included the carriers *Albion* and *Centaur*). During the latter exercise there were two landing accidents involving the ship's Corsairs. After visits to Manila and Hong Kong in April, *La Fayette* left again for metropolitan France on 3 May with her own air group, eight Grumman Goose, five Morane 500 and about a hundred personnel. Nine Corsairs were flown off as the ship neared Bizerte, where she disembarked the remaining aircraft and picked up two Corsairs, arriving back in Toulon on 3 June.

The carrier was immobilised from 15 June for repairs with the cabling to the boilers. She then left for Norfolk on 27 June, arriving on 9 July. She embarked 5 H-21 and 9 S-58 helicopters, and 94 T-6 trainers, together with 100 crated T-6. The trainers were disembarked at Pauillac (near Bordeaux), the helicopters flown off to Marignane and at Algiers. *La Fayette* returned to Toulon on 5 August.

### Operation '*Mousquetaire*' 1956

Routine activities in August/September were followed by assignment to a *Force d'Intervention* that was being assembled in preparation for an assault on the Suez Canal. *La Fayette* left Toulon on 22 October with twelve Corsairs of 15F and two HUP-2 rescue helicopters. A further ten Corsairs belonging to 12F and 14F were flown on when the ship was off Bizerte, where she refuelled on the 24th. She sailed on 27 October in company with *Arromanches* and the fleet escort *Cassard*. They were joined by the fleet escorts *Surcouf* and *Bouvet* and the fast escorts *Le Corse*, *Le Brestois*, *Le Boulonnais* and *Le Bordelais*. *La Fayette*'s air group comprised eighteen Corsairs of 15F and four Corsairs detached from 14F, plus the two HUP-2 helicopters.

Combat operations against Egypt began on the night of 31 October/1 November. The two French carriers were stationed to the north of Damietta. The

Below: *La Fayette* with the Corsairs of 14F embarked. *(René Bail collection)*

Corsairs were tasked with neutralising the Egyptian Navy. Eight Corsairs armed with 454kg (1000lb) bombs were readied, but the intervention of US Navy warships complicated proceedings. Eight Corsairs were launched against an Egyptian destroyer thought to be the *El Nasser* on 1 November, but the Corsairs found only a frigate identified as the *Tarik*; the bombs, released at 2400m, all missed. A second strike using aircraft armed with rockets failed to find its target. The following day saw a rocket attack on the French submarine *La Créole*, whose periscope wake was mistaken on the radar screen for a fast patrol boat; the submarine was forced into an emergency dive but was undamaged. During a second patrol a Corsair pilot was unable to fire one of its rockets, and the aircraft was lost while attempting to land due to pilot error; he was rescued by an HUP-2 helicopter. On the same day, twelve Corsairs armed with 454kg bombs attacked the air base at Dekheila, destroying two hangars and putting one of the landing strips out of action.

On 3 November, seven Corsairs of 15F attacked the air base at Almaza, shortly before an identical strike force from *Arromanches* arrived. *La Fayette*'s air group returned without loss, but one of the Corsairs from *Arromanches* failed to return. Four Corsairs then took off at midday with orders to strafe a military convoy on the road from Ismailia to Zagazig. When they returned, the two carriers withdrew to replenish.

On 5 November, the Corsairs were tasked with covering a dawn parachute drop. The carriers now operated independently, in part because of the relatively slow speed of *Arromanches*. Four Corsairs from *La Fayette* attacked the railway line between Port Said and Ismalia, destroying two locomotives, while at Port Said four Corsairs guided from a forward position (*poste de guidage avancé* or PGA) struck two buildings, an armoured vehicle and a trench that was only 100 metres away from the paratroops. The first of the Corsairs crashed on its return, putting the flight deck temporarily out of action; its three companions landed on *Arromanches*. A section of four Corsairs attacked guns, vehicles in hangars and a group of soldiers. *La Fayette* then recovered six Corsairs from *Arromanches* that could not land on the latter due to the lack of wind over deck. There were further strikes (totalling fourteen sorties) mounted from the carrier during the remainder of the day, using 226kg (500lb) bombs and machine-gun fire. During an attack on Port Fuad twelve trucks were destroyed. All aircraft were successfully recovered at dusk despite the lack of a night landing qualification of some pilots.

On 6 November, the Allied troops disembarked at Port Said and Port Fuad, supported by Corsairs from *La Fayette*. A 20mm cannon and a total of eight trucks were damaged or destroyed and a petrol dump went up in flames; no aircraft were lost. However, the night of 6/7 November saw the implementation of a ceasefire.

During the operation there had been ninety-four combat sorties from *La Fayette* with the loss of only a single aircraft. After replenishing at Limassol (Cyprus) the carrier was at Port Said on 15 and 26–28 November, and returned to Bizerte on 1 December after thirty-three days at sea. The Corsairs of 15F were disembarked at Bizerte and the ship returned to Toulon on 8 December. She was in refit from 20 December to 22 February 1957.

**Right:** *La Fayette* at anchor in 1955. Note the new, tall lattice mainmast for the US SPS-6B air surveillance radar. *(SHD-A)*

15
12

Above: *La Fayette* on 8 July 1958 with a deck-load of F4U-7 Corsairs. The photo may have been taken at Barcelona after the conclusion of Exercise 'Corrida'. *(Leo van Ginderen collection)*

Left: *La Fayette* in the anchorage at Fréjus following the catastrophic breach of the Malpasset Dam on the night of 2/3 December 1959, when she served as a base for rescue helicopters. *(SHD-M Toulon)*

**The Years 1957–58**

On 29 March 1957, *La Fayette* left for the USA for an aircraft transport mission. Delayed by four storms, she finally arrived at Norfolk on 10 April and embarked forty-five AU-1 Corsair,[3] ten Piasecki H-21 tandem rotor helicopters plus a single S-55 and an S-58. She left again on 10 April, disembarking the Corsairs at Bizerte on 2–3 May and returning to Toulon on the 4th. Deck landing training for 14F off Bizerte followed, with night landings for 6F at Arzew and Mers el-Kébir in June and July. Transport missions involving 1,506 parachute troops took place between Algiers and Marseille in July.

*La Fayette* sailed from Toulon on 6 September, and Squadron 4F was embarked on 7 September. She called in at Bizerte and Algiers, and took part in Exercise 'Seawatch' in the Atlantic; a port visit to Brest followed. The carrier then returned to the Mediterranean, disembarking Squadrons 4F, 6F and 9F at Bizerte before returning to Toulon on 10 October. She re-embarked 6F and took part in Exercise 'Medaswex 20' and visited Malta, returning to Toulon on 10 November having disembarked 6F at Bizerte.

*La Fayette* underwent a two-month refit at Toulon at the beginning of 1958, emerging for trials on 24 February. After pilot qualifications for 54S, 14F and 6F Squadrons, she took part in a number of small-scale national exercises, 6F being replaced by 15F on 12 March. Moorings at Arzew and Mers el-Kébir were followed by a port visit to Algiers from 19 to 27 March. On this last day, *La Fayette* launched four missions, each of two or three aircraft, against land targets at the request of GATAC 3. She then disembarked Squadron 9F at Ajaccio and returned to Toulon on 2 April. Squadron 15F was now officially assigned to her, and

[3] The AU-1 (originally F4U-6) was a development of the F4U-5 and was optimised for ground attack. It was used extensively by the US Marine Corps during the Korean War, but was officially retired from the USMC in 1957.

**Above:** An HUP-2 tandem-rotor plane guard helicopter takes off from the flight deck of *La Fayette*. Note the distinctive configuration of the DRBI 10 tracking radar fitted during the 1958–59 refit. *(René Bail)*

**Left:** *La Fayette* departing Mers el-Kébir in 1962. Note the HUP-2 helicopter used for plane guard duties at the forward end of the flight deck. *(René Bail)*

deck landings took place in mid-/late April. She left again on 16 May, and attempted to recover 9F off Cap d'Armes (Hyères), but a sudden squall prevented the last two of the seven aircraft from landing. Before the aircraft on deck could be secured, two TBMs slid across the deck and five were damaged.

*La Fayette* returned to Toulon on the 17th, and left the following day with 6F embarked for Exercise 'Medflex Fort'. She then headed for Malta and Bône, where she embarked 15F and half of 14F, departing on 27 May for the Gulf of Gabes in preparation for a possible intervention in Tunisia, accompanied by the fleet escorts *Dupetit-Thouars* and *Chevalier Paul*. She had on board ten F4U-7 Corsair of 15F and ten of 14F,

Above: Another view of *La Fayette* departing Mers el-Kébir in 1962. Note the HUP-2 helicopter used for plane guard duties at the forward end of the flight deck. *(René Bail)*

together with two TBM-UT Avenger of 9F. In response to a request from GATAC 1, she flew off eight Corsairs of 15F armed with rockets and machine guns for a ground support mission. Exercises 'Caïman 2' and 'Corrida' followed, with port visits to Tangier and Barcelona, and the carrier returned to Toulon on 10 July. On the 14th she took part in a major fleet review in Toulon roads, for which the President of the Council, General de Gaulle, was embarked on the fleet escort *Kersaint*.

### Refit and Modernisation 1958–59

From 4 August 1958 to 8 September 1959, *La Fayette* underwent a major refit during which the US SP fighter control radar was replaced by the French DRBI 10. Trials and work-up followed, with port visits to Ajaccio.

From 2 December, *La Fayette* served as a base for rescue helicopters at Saint-Raphaël following a breach in the Malpasset Dam that resulted in the deaths of 423 people. She returned to Toulon with a number of survivors on the 5th. A cruise with 14F embarked was interrupted by a second humanitarian mission in early March 1960, when *La Fayette* deployed to Agadir with a medical unit on board following an earthquake on the night of 29 February. She embarked 1,500 soldiers together with supplies and materiel at Casablanca and took control of air operations, losing one of her HUP-2 helicopters in the process. She then resumed her cruise; there were port visits to Port Etienne, Dakar and Abidjan, and the ship returned to Toulon via Mers el-Kébir on 5 April. Routine exercises, training and a short docking followed until the end of the year.

At around this time, it was a proposed to convert the ship into a helicopter carrier. However, it was decided that *La Fayette* would continue to operate Corsairs until 1963, when the new carrier *Foch* was due to enter service (see Chapter 7).

The carrier was at sea with the Squadron, with 14F embarked, in November/December, and again in January 1961. On the 24th, *La Fayette* departed Toulon for Bizerte with four HSS-1 helicopters of 31F and AU-1 (ground attack) Corsairs belonging to 12F. The helicopters were disembarked, but from 1 February, *La Fayette* then took part in Operation 'Harmattan', with ten AU-1 of 12F, two TBM-W and two TBM-UT of 3F, and two HUP-2 of 23S embarked. She visited Mers el-Kébir, Las Palmas, Port Etienne, Dakar, Libreville and Port Gentil, returning to Toulon via Dakar and Bizerte on 28 March. The port outer propeller suffered a bent blade during the cruise, and had to be changed.

The spring cruise with the Squadron to the Western Mediterranean took place between 23 May and 15 June, and there were visits to Valencia, Barcelona and Cannes. After a short docking and trials, *La Fayette* was then at the centre of Task Group 253.3 with the fast escorts *D'Estrées* and *Tartu*; the Task Group was deployed to Bizerte following the Tunisian attempt to impose a blockade on the naval base and enforce its evacuation in July. These deployments continued until late October, when the ship took part in the autumn cruise. They resumed in November/

## Table 4: NAVAL AIRCRAFT 1945–1960

| | Seafire Mk III | Seafire Mk XV | F6F-5 Hellcat | F4U-7 Corsair | AU-1 Corsair |
|---|---|---|---|---|---|
| Origin | UK | UK | USA | USA | USA |
| Type | fighter | fighter | fighter bomber | fighter bomber | fighter bomber |
| Crew | one | one | one | one | one |
| In service | 1946–49 | 1949–50 | 1950–59 | 1953–62 | 1954–62 |
| Number | 113 | 15 | 139 | 94 | 82 |
| Length | 9.21m | 9.70m | 10.23m | 10.51m | 10.39m |
| Span | 11.23m | 11.23m | 13.08m | 12.49m | 12.50m |
| Height | 3.50m | 3.50m | 3.99m | 4.50m | 4.50m |
| Weight (empty) | 2858kg | 3100kg | 5670kg | 4700kg | 4455kg |
| Weight (fl) | 2640kg | 4130kg | 2820kg | 8400kg | 8788kg |
| Power Unit | R-R Merlin<br>1608hp | R-R Griffon VI<br>1840hp | P&W R-2800<br>2000hp | P&W R-2800<br>2100hp | [as F4U-7]<br>2300hp |
| Max Speed | 590km/h | 550km/h | 630km/h | 715km/h | 638km/h |
| Ceiling | 10,500m | 10,800m | 11,400m | 12,600m | 9500m |
| Armament | two 20mm cannon<br>four 7.65mm MG<br>226kg bomb | [as Mk III] | six 12.7mm MG<br>900kg bomb | four 20mm cannon<br>1800kg bombs | [as F4U-7] |

| | SB2C Helldiver | TBM/TBF Avenger |
|---|---|---|
| Origin | USA | USA |
| Type | dive bomber | torpedo bomber |
| Crew | two | three |
| In service | 1950–58 | 1951–65 |
| Number | 110 | 173 |
| Length | 10.90m | 10.33m |
| Span | 15.15m | 16.51m [5.8m folded] |
| Height | 4.01m | 5.00m |
| Weight (empty) | 4870kg | 4920kg |
| Weight (fl) | 7471kg | 7600kg |
| Power Unit | Wright R 2600-20<br>1950hp | Wright R 2600-8<br>1900hp |
| Max Speed | 475km/h | 445km/h |
| Ceiling | 8900m | 6900m |
| Armament | 908kg bombs<br>two 20mm cannon<br>two 7.7mm MG | one torpedo or 908kg bombs<br>one 12.7mm MG<br>two 7.7mm MG |

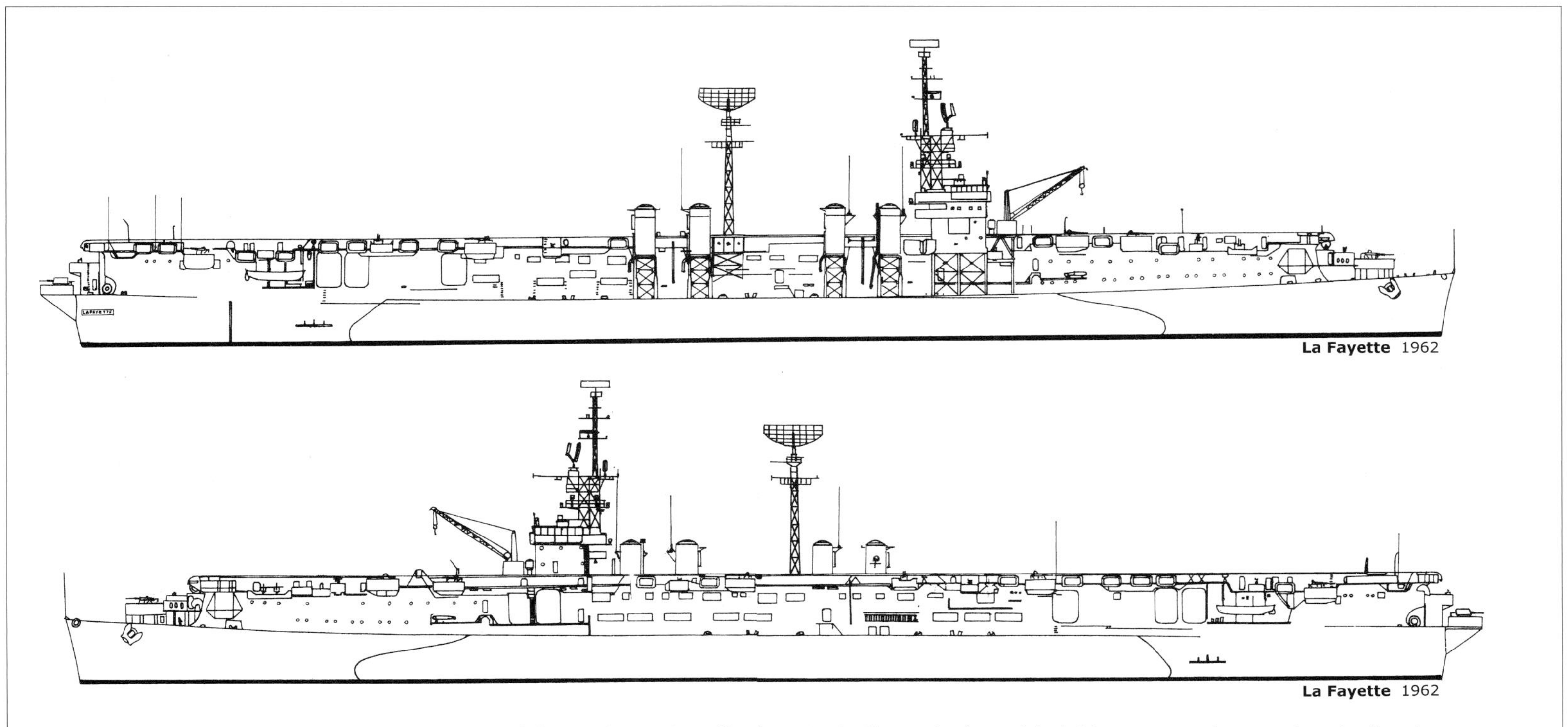


Starboard and port profiles of *La Fayette* in 1962, following her major refit of 1958–59. She retains her original AA armament, but now has the French DRBI 10 fighter control radar in place of the American SP, SPS-6 in place of the original SK-2, and DRBV 31 in place of SG-1b. *(Drawn by Jean Moulin)*

December, when training for the pilots of 31F, 15F and 17F took place.

Further training off Bizerte for 17F and TBM-3S bombers from 15 to 19 January 1962 was followed by Exercise 'Big Game' with the US 6th Fleet, with 14F embarked; the American carriers taking part were *Saratoga* (CVA-60) and *Intrepid* (CVA-11). The latter had, by coincidence, formed TG.84 with *Langley* (CVL-27), *Yorktown* (CV-10) and *Independence* (CVL-22) in March/April 1945.

*La Fayette* then joined the winter cruise in the Western Mediterranean from 6 March to 1 April with 31F and 14F embarked plus a section of TBMs employed as utility aircraft. Routine activity followed, and there was a series of rotations between North Africa and metropolitan France after the ceasefire in Algeria (19 March) with a view to repatriating French nationals and native Algerians ('Harkis') who had served as auxiliaries in the French forces. A total of 15,000 personnel, 450 vehicles and 178 helicopters were transported to metropolitan France.

*La Fayette* was decommissioned and put into care and maintenance with a reduced crew on 1 January 1963. The US radars and other materiel supplied with the ship were packed into cases and brought back on board, the French DRBV 31 radar was replaced by a DRBV 30, and the DRBI 10 tracking radar landed.

*La Fayette* left Toulon for the last time on 20 February 1963. She was at Ponta Delgada (Azores) from 25 to 26 February, and arrived at Philadelphia on 6 March. The ship was officially returned to the US Navy on 20 March and assigned to the Philadelphia group of the Atlantic Reserve Fleet. She was stricken in June 1963, sold to the Boston Metals Co, Baltimore, and broken up in 1964.

She had steamed 346,000nm under the French *tricolore* and performed 19,805 deck landings and 6,502 catapult launches.

Table 5: **NAVAL AIR SQUADRONS 1945–1960**

| Squadron | Aircraft | In service | Bases |
|---|---|---|---|
| 1F[1] | Seafire Mk III | Jan 46–Jun 49 | Hyères |
| | Seafire Mk XV | Jun 49–Apr 50 | Hyères |
| | F6F Hellcat | Apr 50–Jun 53 | Hyères |
| 3F | SBD Dauntless | Jan 46–Jul 49 | Hyères |
| | SB2C Helldiver | Apr 50–Dec 54 | Hyères |
| 4F | SBD Dauntless | Jan 46–Jul 49 | Hyères, Karouba[2] |
| | SB2C Helldiver | Apr 50–1951 | Hyères |
| | TBM Avenger | Apr 51–1960 | Hyères, Karouba |
| | Alizé | Feb 60– | Hyères |
| 6F | TBM Avenger | Mar 52–1959 | Hyères |
| | Alizé | 1959– | Hyères |
| 9F | SB2C Helldiver | Apr 51–1953 | Hyères, Karouba |
| | TBM Avenger | 1953–1960 | Hyères, Aspretto |
| | Alizé | Sep 60– | Hyères |
| 11F | F6F Hellcat | Jun 53–Jan 55 | Hyères |
| | Aquilon[3] | Apr 55–Apr 62 | Hyères |
| 12F | Seafire Mk III | Aug 48–Jun 49 | Hyères |
| | F6F Hellcat | Apr 50–Jun 53 | Hyères |
| | F4U-7 Corsair | Jun 53–Aug 63 | Hyères > Karouba |
| 14F | F4U-7 Corsair | Jan 53–Jan 59 | Karouba |
| | AU-1 Corsair | Jan 59–Oct 64 | Karouba > Cuers |
| 15F | F4U-7 Corsair | Oct 53–Feb 62 | Karouba > Hyères |
| 16F | Aquilon[3] | Jan 55–Apr 64 | Hyères |
| 17F | F4U-7 Corsair | Apr 58–Apr 62 | Hyères > Karouba |
| 31F | HSS (ASW) | Feb 60–Jun 79 | Algeria > Saint-Mandrier |
| 32F | HSS (ASW) | Feb 58–Jan 70 | Algeria > Saint-Mandrier |
| 33F | HSS (Assault) | Jul 59–Jun 79 | Algeria > Saint-Raphaël |

**Note:**

1 In a reorganisation of the French naval air squadrons that took place in 1953, F1 became 11F. From this point on, Squadrons F1–9 would comprise attack and anti-submarine aircraft, F11–19 embarked fighters, F21–29 land-based ASW aircraft, and F31–39 helicopters.

2 Hyères was the naval air base for Toulon, Karouba for Bizerte, and Lanvéoc for Brest; the Saint-Mandrier airbase was on the peninsula immediately south of Toulon.

3 In April 1955, 11F converted to the new Aquilon jet fighter, and in January of the same year a second squadron operating the Aquilon, 16F, was formed. The Aquilon was not able to operate from any of the 'loan' carriers. Of the three squadrons that converted to Alizé turbo-prop aircraft in 1959–60, only 9F operated from a loan carrier (*Arromanches* following her 1957–58 modernisation). For further details see Chapter 8.

## *BOIS BELLEAU* (EX-*BELLEAU WOOD*)

The French continued to press the Americans for the loan of a second carrier, and in 1953 they finally agreed to transfer one of *Langley*'s sisters, *Belleau Wood* (CVL-24), named after the battle of June 1918 near the Marne when the US 2nd and 3rd Divisions successfully fought alongside a French force of Senegalese *Tirailleurs*. The loan was subject to the same conditions as *Langley* in 1950 (modified 1952): primarily for employment as part of the NATO Alliance, with provisional use outside the NATO area. It was to remain in force until six months after the cessation of hostilities in Indochina or until 5 August 1958. The contract was signed on 2 September 1953; it would subsequently be modified on 3 February 1956 and on 22/26 August 1958. The ship underwent a major refit at Hunters Point until 5 September to prepare her for service.

*Belleau Wood* was formally transferred to France at San Francisco by Vice Admiral Francis S Low, and renamed *Bois Belleau*. The ship left Alameda on 30 September and arrived in San Diego on 2 October for work-up. The crew was complete on 15 October, and work-up continued with three TBM-3W and five TBM-3S Avengers of VS-23 and an HO3S-1 helicopter. There were 140 catapult launches, 18 unassisted take-offs, and 152 deck landings. The crew also practised replenishment at sea from the oiler *Navasota* (AO-106).

*Bois Belleau* sailed from San Diego on 14 November, transited the Panama Canal and arrived at Norfolk on the 24th. After a short docking, she left on the 10th and embarked sixteen TBM-3W Avenger torpedo bombers that were to arm Squadron 4F. The following day she headed for Toulon, arriving on 23 December having disembarked the Avengers at Bizerte, and was admitted into service the same day. She would then undergo some small modifications, including the fitting-out of a 'wine hold' (*cale à vin*) in the bows.

On 18 February 1954, *Bois Belleau* embarked fourteen F4U-7 Corsairs of 14F and six TBM Avengers of 6F. She then set course for Bizerte, taking part in Exercises 'Sans Atout 3' and 'Philbex' off North Africa with port visits to Bizerte, Algiers and Oran, and returned to Toulon on 7 March, having damaged a propeller on the 3rd. She was docked from 8 to 22 March.

**Above:** USS *Belleau Wood* (CVL-24) underway on 22 December 1943, shortly after her completion. *(NHHC, NH-97269)*

**Left:** *Bois Belleau* off San Diego on 5 October 1953, still with US Navy aircraft embarked. She had been handed over to the *Marine Nationale* in September. *(US Navy)*

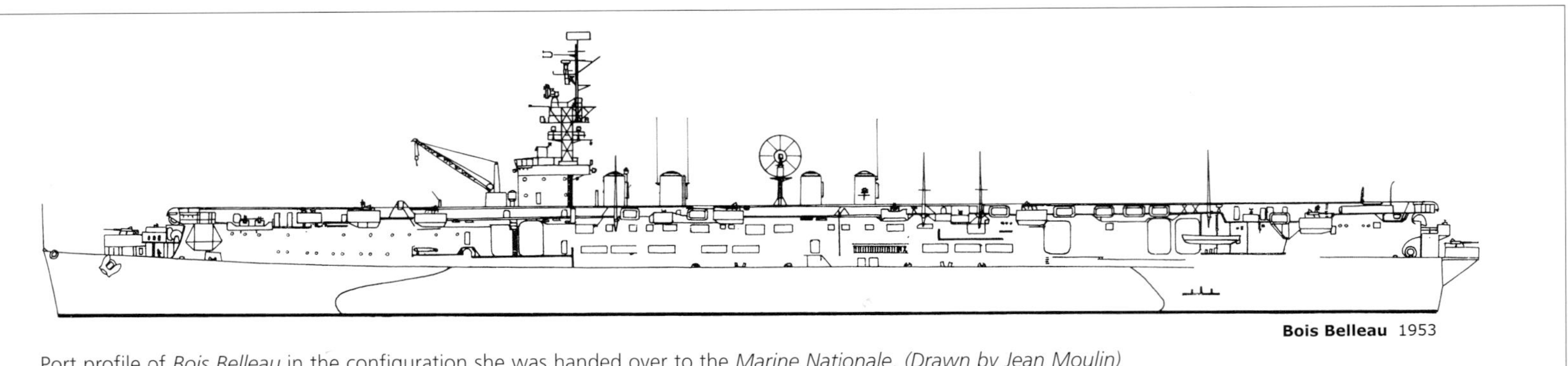


Port profile of *Bois Belleau* in the configuration she was handed over to the *Marine Nationale*. *(Drawn by Jean Moulin)*

**Right:** *Bois Belleau* with TBM Avengers on the quayside and an HUP-2 tandem-rotor helicopter on deck. The photo may have been taken at Bizerte in December 1953. *(René Bail collection)*

**Below:** *Bois Belleau* in Ha Long Bay during her twenty-month deployment to the Far East. *(DR)*

She left Toulon on 24 March and embarked thirty-two Dassault Ouragan fighter jets at Saint-Nazaire during 28–31 March. She returned on 4 April after suffering a burst boiler tube on the 3rd.

**Campaign in Indochina 1954–55**

*Bois Belleau* left for Indochina on 7 April 1954 with eleven Hellcats, nine Helldivers and two HUP-2 plane guard helicopters embarked, accompanied by the destroyer escort *Tunisien*. In addition to her air group she was to transport three Morane 500 liaison aircraft and the thirty-two Ouragans. On 9 April, the French secured an agreement with the Americans that spares for the ship would be provided free of charge if she deployed to Indochina. The Ouragans were disembarked at Bombay on the 19th, and the ship departed four days later and arrived at Cape Saint-Jacques on 30 April. She left the following day for Ha Long Bay, joining up with *Arromanches* on 3 May. She then transferred the Hellcats and four of the Helldivers to *Arromanches*.

The two carriers operated together until 11 May. *Belleau Wood* embarked Squadron 3F with nine Helldivers. On the 11th she departed Ha Long Bay with the escort *Sénégalais* to avoid a typhoon, moored at La Noisette on 11–12 May, and left on the 12th with five Helldivers and two HUP-2 helicopters embarked,

Above: The flight deck of *Bois Belleau* in April 1954, during her deployment to Indochina. *(ECPAD)*

accompanied by the escort *Tunisien*. She was at Hong Kong from 14 May until 7 July, when boiler No 3 was retubed.

On 9 July, *Bois Belleau* returned to Ha Long Bay to join *Arromanches*, embarking the latter's air group. She took over from her on 13 July; she now had twelve Hellcats, twelve Helldivers plus the two helicopters on board. The aircraft provided ground support from 25 to 30 July in the regions of Hue and Ding Hai. The last combat mission was flown by 11F on 29 July. The two squadrons were disembarked at Tourane on the 31st.

In August, the ship was at Cam Ranh Bay and Tourane, where she embarked 2,000 refugees on 20 August. She ferried them to Saigon, then returned to pick up another 1,000 refugees, returning to Saigon on 31 August. Further rescue missions followed, and on 20–21 September she re-embarked Squadrons 11F and 3F from Tourane and returned to Saigon, where the aircraft were transferred to *Dixmude* for repatriation to France; *Bois Belleau* retained only a 'service' section comprising four Helldivers and two HUP-2 helicopters. *Dixmude* had brought the sixteen F4U-7 Corsairs of 14F, and these were now assigned to *Bois Belleau*; they would be embarked on 21 October, when deck landings were practised off Tourane.

On 8 November, the Corsairs were grounded due to a problem with the propeller regulator. On the same day, the carrier was ordered to proceed to Tonkin, where she embarked 1,800 refugees who were landed at Saigon on the 12th. *Bois Belleau* left on

**Above:** A Chance Vought AU-1 Corsair of 12F in 1959. The AU-1 (originally F4U-6) was a development of the F4U-5 and was optimised for ground attack. It was used extensively by the US Marine Corps during the Korean War, but was officially retired from the USMC in 1957. *(ARDHAN collection)*

**Below:** *Bois Belleau* at Colombo, probably during November 1955, when she returned from her twenty-month deployment to the Far East. *(Marc Piché)*

22 November for Tourane, where she embarked the last five AU-1 Corsairs, which were returned to the Americans during a port visit to Manila on 10–12 December. She then headed for Hong Kong for a short refit, returning to Saigon on 30 December.

*Bois Belleau* left Saigon on 26 January 1955 for the coasts of Indochina. Corsair flights resumed at the end of February, and the carrier took part in Exercises 'Carême Cacao' and 'Carême Bravo' in early March, then headed for the Gulf of Tonkin. She would henceforth be based at Tourane, putting to sea for numerous training exercises with 14F. An agreement was reached with the Americans for the extension of her loan until 30 June 1958.

In April, *Bois Belleau* joined her sister *La Fayette* in Task Force 65, formed to cover the evacuation of Tonkin. Squadron 14F embarked on 7 May, but disembarked at Tourane on 28 May in order to return to France on board *La Fayette*. It was replaced by 12F, which was assigned to *Bois Belleau* on 1 June; 12F embarked with nineteen Corsairs on 5 June. The carrier returned to Saigon on 18 June, returning to Tourane on 13 July. She took part in Exercise 'Thermidor Bravo' from 20 August to 2 September, visited Manila from 5 to 9 September, and returned to Tourane on 11 September. On 22 September she re-embarked sixteen Corsairs of 12F and returned to Saigon.

*Bois Belleau* finally left for metropolitan France on 14 November. She disembarked 12F at Bizerte and entered Toulon on 16 December 1955, after a campaign that lasted twenty months.

### Major Refit 1956–57

On 1 February 1956, *Bois Belleau* began a major refit that lasted until 27 November. The work included the installation of an H4B catapult and an SPS-6 radar. During post-refit trials, on 19 December she attained 31.1 knots. She was back in service by February, departing on the 15th to take part in Exercise 'Medaswex', which ended with a port visit to Cannes. Night training for Squadron 4F took place at Bizerte during mid-March, and was followed by training for 6F. *Bois Belleau* then took part in Exercises 'Sans Atout' and 'Medflex Epic', returning to Toulon on 12 May.

On 18 May, the carrier, with 4F and an Alouette II helicopter embarked, departed Toulon for the USA, accompanied by the cruiser *De Grasse*, the fleet escorts *Dupetit-Thouars* and *Chevalier Paul*, and the

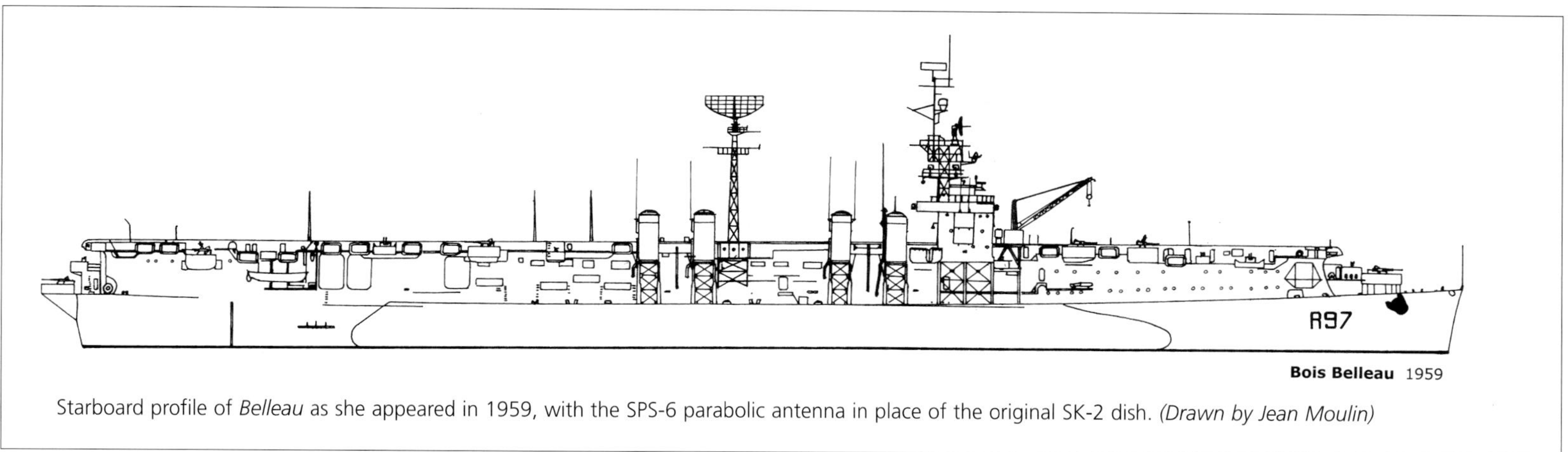


Starboard profile of *Belleau* as she appeared in 1959, with the SPS-6 parabolic antenna in place of the original SK-2 dish. *(Drawn by Jean Moulin)*

fast escorts *Le Gascon* and *Le Lorrain*. The formation was to take part in an international naval review on 12–13 June at Norfolk, in the presence of the US Secretary of Defense on the cruiser *Canberra* (CAG-2). *Bois Belleau* and *De Grasse* visited New York from 21 to 26 June. During the return transit, the carrier was being refuelled by the tanker *Elorn* off Morocco on 2 July, when a steering breakdown on the latter resulted in a minor collision between the two ships. A whaler was crushed, and two of the twin 40mm Bofors mountings and one of the Oerlikons suffered damage. *Bois Belleau* put in to Casablanca from 5 to 8 July and was back in Toulon on 12 July.

Pilot qualifications during late July were followed by

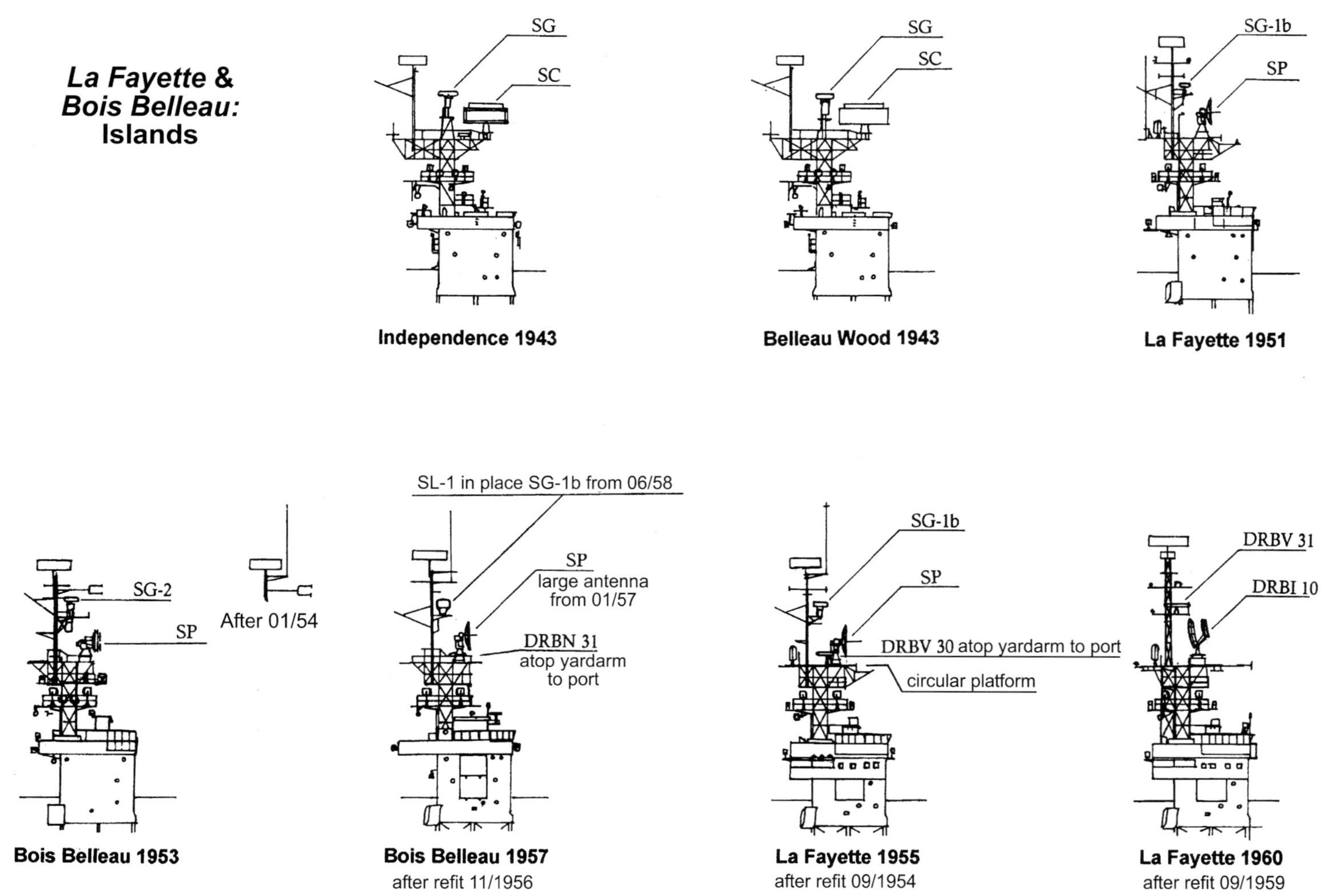

**La Fayette & Bois Belleau: Islands**

SG
SC
**Independence 1943**

SG
SC
**Belleau Wood 1943**

SG-1b
SP
**La Fayette 1951**

SG-2
SP
After 01/54
**Bois Belleau 1953**

SL-1 in place SG-1b from 06/58
SP large antenna from 01/57
DRBN 31 atop yardarm to port
**Bois Belleau 1957**
after refit 11/1956

SG-1b
SP
DRBV 30 atop yardarm to port
circular platform
**La Fayette 1955**
after refit 09/1954

DRBV 31
DRBI 10
**La Fayette 1960**
after refit 09/1959

The drawing shows the changes made to the island and the radar outfits during the 1950s. Both ships as completed had the antenna for the SG surface surveillance radar on the topmast platform and that of the SC air/surface surveillance radar atop the lower (lattice) section of the foremast. When handed over to the French, *Langley* and *Belleau Wood* retained later variants of the SG radar but had the SP fighter control radar in place of SC. The latter radar would later be replaced by the French DRBI 10 height-finder and tracking radar in *La Fayette*, which also had her SG surface surveillance radar replaced by DRBV 31. *(Drawn by Jean Moulin)*

### *La Fayette* & *Bois Belleau*: Mainmast Antennae

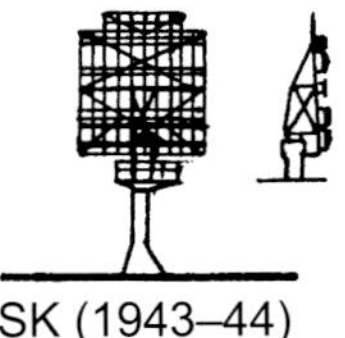

SK (1943–44)

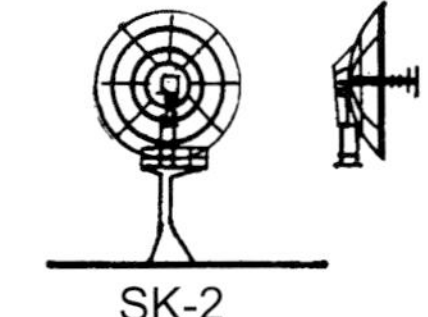

SK-2
*Langley* May 1951
*Bois Belleau* 1953

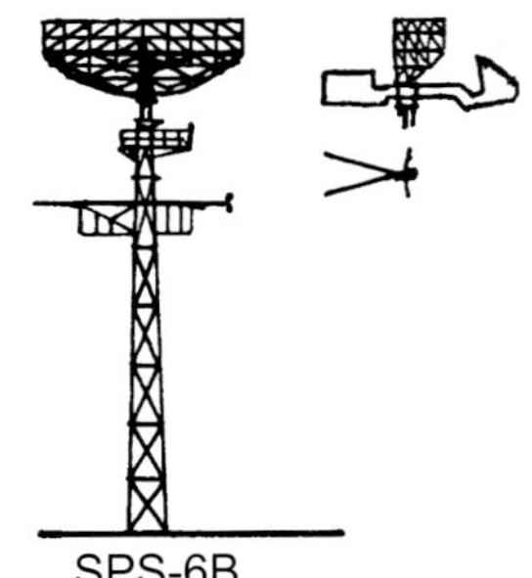
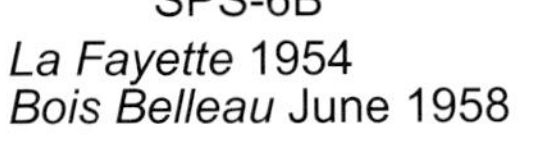

SPS-6B
*La Fayette* 1954
*Bois Belleau* June 1958

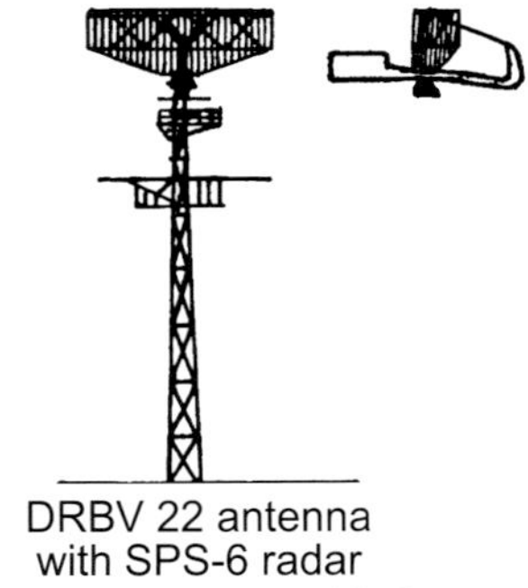

DRBV 22 antenna
with SPS-6 radar
*Bois Belleau* late 1956
to June 1958

The mainmast of these ships carried the long-range air surveillance radar. As completed, both ships were fitted with the large rectangular antenna for the SK radar, but by the time they were handed over to the French, SK-1 had been superseded by SK-2, which featured a 17ft (5.18m) dish antenna array intended to reduce side lobes. Both were capable of detecting an enemy bomber at 100nm. In 1954 SK was replaced in *La Fayette* by the standard post-war US SPS-6B radar, which used a new parabolic horn-fed antenna, atop a tall lattice mast and, from 1956 to 1958, *Bois Belleau* experimented with an SPS-6B installation allied to the French DRBV 22 antenna. *(Drawn by Jean Moulin)*

a short refit during 10–30 August, when the SG radar was replaced by an American SL surface search set. October and November saw routine sorties for training with 6F, and there was a trip to Corsica in December with 15F embarked.

**Algeria 1958**

In January 1958, Squadron 9F was embarked for a further visit to Ajaccio and Exercise 'Hélicasex'. On 24 January, a TBM-3W2 Avenger was lost on launch, resulting in the death of the pilot; the other two members of the crew were recovered by an HUP-2. A further visit to Ajaccio was followed by training for 15F. *Bois Belleau* was then docked for a propeller change.

On 11 February she was assigned 15F plus a detachment of 14F, and on the 15th she left for Mers el-Kébir, where she disembarked the eight HSS-1 helicopters of 32F. The conflict in Algeria had entered a critical phase and, on 25 May, *Bois Belleau* launched five Corsairs for a ground support mission at the

Right: *Bois Belleau* during her visit to the USA in mid-1957, when she took part in an international naval review. The ship in the background is the ocean escort *Norfolk* (DL1). *(Leo van Ginderen collection)*

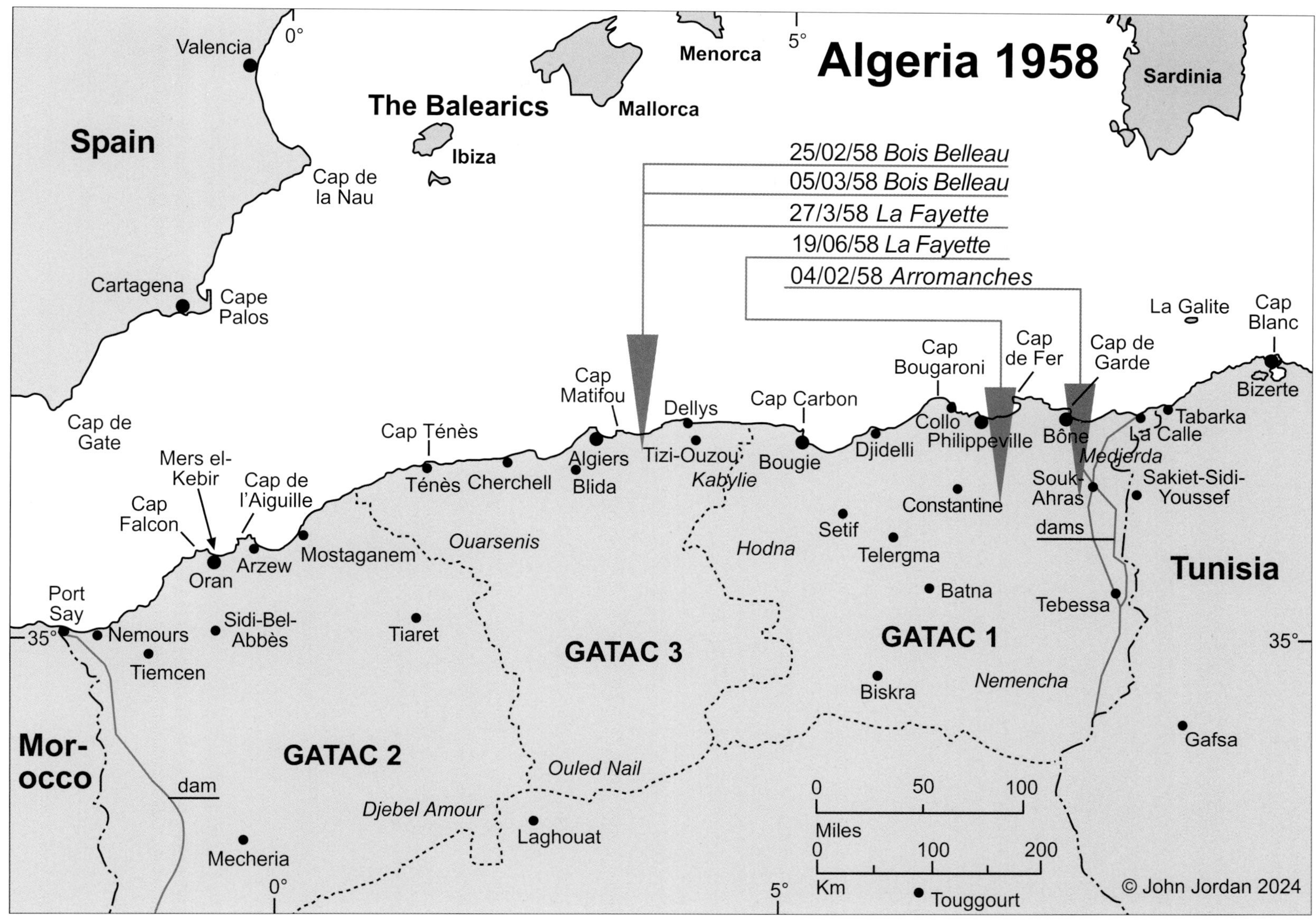


request of GATAC 3. A second ground support mission at the request of GATAC 3 was launched on 25 February when the ship was off Cape Matifou; there were twenty sorties to the Great Kabylie and Ouarsenis mountain regions. On 6 March she returned to Algiers, left on the 11th for Arzew and embarked 6F. *Bois Belleau* then took part in a series of exercises, returning to Toulon on the 22nd. Her air group was disembarked on 3 April.

Pilot qualifications were followed by manoeuvres off North Africa with 9F (from Ajaccio) and the officer cadets of the training ship *Jeanne d'Arc*, during which a second Avenger was lost due to a catapult failure. *Bois Belleau* returned to Toulon on 1 May, then embarked on training sorties for 15F, 6F and 9F. She took part in a naval review at Toulon on 14 July during a short refit, and was moored close to the battleship *Jean Bart*. Post-refit trials followed, and the loan of *Bois Belleau* was extended until 30 June 1960 due to building delays with the new carrier *Clemenceau*.

Training with 4F off Bizerte took place from 22 to 27 September, and routine activities to the coasts of North Africa and Provence continued until the end of October. A sailing from 12 to 17 November was cut short due to machinery problems, and in mid-December *Bois Belleau* damaged a propeller when coming alongside at Mers el-Kébir and needed to be docked at Toulon over the Christmas period until 12 January 1959.

## THE LAST YEARS: 1959–1960

Routine activities during the early part of 1959 were followed by the spring cruise with the Squadron from 11 April to 25 June, during which there were port visits to Naples, Milos, Piraeus, Phalerum, Istanbul and Bône. *Bois Belleau* was the only aircraft carrier present at an assembly of naval forces off Mers el-Kébir and Oran on 14 June. On the 19th, when moored off Algiers, she collided with the fleet escort *Châteaurenault* and suffered damage to the tubs for the 40mm Bofors.

On 1 September 1959, *Bois Belleau* was assigned to the 2nd Maritime Region based on Brest. She was then tasked with a number of transport missions to the USA for the *Armée de l'Air*. She left Toulon on 20 November, and embarked three AD-4 Skyraider and thirty-eight T-28 Trojan ground attack aircraft, returning to Brest on 20 December having disembarked the aircraft at Saint-Nazaire. She left for Norfolk again on 12 January 1960, and embarked sixteen AD-4 Skyraider and forty-seven T-28 Trojan from 20 to 30 November. She returned to Saint-Nazaire and entered the Joubert dock on 9 February. She left for Brest the following day and remained there until the 16th.

**Right:** *Bois Belleau* during the late 1950s, showing the extent of the roll of these ships in adverse sea conditions. The original SK-2 air surveillance radar was replaced by the US SPS-6 during a major refit that took place in 1956–57. *(René Bail collection)*

**Left and above:** Two views of *Bois Belleau* during the gathering of naval forces off Oran and Mers el-Kébir on 14 June 1959. *(René Bail)*

She would return to Norfolk for four more aircraft transport missions: 29 AD-4 and 27 T-28 in February/March; 29 AD-4 and 28 T-28 in April; 14 AD-4 and 38 T-28 in May; and 13 AD-4 and 38 T-28 in June. All the aircraft were disembarked at Saint-Nazaire.

On 23 August, *Bois Belleau* left Toulon for the last time with a reduced crew, arriving at Philadelphia on 1 September. She had steamed 183,216nm under the *tricolore*, and had performed 2,045 catapult launches and 6,420 deck landings. She was officially returned to the US Navy on 12 September but stricken on 1 October. She was sold for scrap to the Boston Metals Co of Baltimore, and broken up at Chester in 1961–62.

CHAPTER 8

# *CLEMENCEAU* AND *FOCH*

Below: The *Essex*-class carrier USS *Antietam* (CV-36) off Virginia Capes in January 1953 following the modifications to her flight deck, which now incorporated a fully fledged 8-degree angled deck. Note the six arrester wires aft, which had to be repositioned. *Antietam* would be the prototype for a series of later conversions. *(NHHC)*

ON 26 OCTOBER 1951, ADMIRAL HENRI NOMY, a former naval aviator, became Naval Chief of Staff. Nomy's accession saw a new plan published in July 1952 that aimed to take account of France's commitments to NATO and proposed the construction of three new carriers. On 28 July 1952, Navy Minister Jacques Gavini duly requested studies for an aircraft carrier of 12,500 tons to perform both the Atlantic ASW support and the overseas power projection missions. Studies began in late 1952, supervised by Paul Gisserot, head of the section *Grands bâtiments porte-avions* of the STCAN, who had been responsible for the PA28 design. However, 12,500 tons proved too small a displacement for operations in the Atlantic, particularly in the light of the increasing weight of modern jet and turboprop aircraft.

A Note from the General Staff dated 18 February 1953 (37156 S EMG/FC) requested a study for a more ambitious project designated PAX (= *Porte-avions 'X'*). There were to be two *avant-projets*: an unprotected variant (PAX) and an armoured variant designated PAX-P (P = *protégé*). The French were aware of the latest developments abroad, and in particular of the possibilities offered by a landing deck set at an angle to the ship's axis, which would permit powered landings by jet aircraft while obviating the need for crash

**Above:** The presentation of a model of the PAX on the occasion of the signing of the order to begin construction on 26 May 1954. In the centre are Admiral Nomy and the Navy Minister, Jacques Gavini. Note the resemblance of the island to that of the modified US Navy carriers of the *Oriskany* subgroup. *(Jean Moulin collection)*

barriers located alongside the island. The concept had been trialled in HMS *Triumph* during 1952, and had been enthusiastically taken up by the Americans, who rebuilt the flight deck of the *Essex*-class carrier *Antietam* and were conducting extensive trials from January 1953. Gisserot was keen to adopt an angled deck (initially termed 'skewed deck' in the RN and 'canted deck' in the USN) for the PAX design, but was conscious of the restrictions imposed by existing building and graving docks at Brest and Toulon, which could accommodate a ship with a maximum waterline beam of just over 30 metres.

On 25 March 1953, in response to the Note of 18 February, the *Service Technique* presented the two preliminary sketches. The baseline PAX had a displacement of 19,000 tons standard, a waterline length of 228 metres, and a flight deck 245 metres long incorporating a 7-degree, 164-metre angled deck. There were to be two 50-metre British steam catapults, aircraft lifts with dimensions 16.3m x 14m and 15.3m x 9m, and tanks for 750 tonnes of furnace fuel oil (FFO) and 550 tonnes of avgas. The ship was to be able to operate aircraft with an all-up weight of 15 tonnes. The steam turbine machinery would deliver 120,000shp on two shafts for a maximum speed of 32 knots, and protection was limited to tight subdivision. The island was modelled on that of the modernised units of the US Navy's *Essex* class, and the anti-aircraft armament was to comprise 24 x 57mm in four groupings, each of three twin mountings.

The armoured variant, PAX-P, had a displacement of 23,000 tons standard, and would have had a flight deck 50mm thick and an internal armoured citadel with 60mm sides and a 30mm crown. Propulsion machinery would have been identical, but the increase in weight would limit maximum speed to 31 knots. An even more heavily armoured variant, designated PAX-P2 (the earlier protected variant was redesignated PAX-P1) and presented for consideration on 20 June, would have combined a 30mm flight deck with an 80–100mm citadel; displacement increased by 720 tonnes, but 800 tonnes was saved by reducing the thickness of the flight deck armour. It was estimated that 32 knots would require four-shaft machinery, at a cost in both weight and volume plus a 10-metre increase in length. PAX-P2 was the variant preferred by the STCAN; Nomy likewise preferred the protected version but wanted 32 knots on two shafts. The version approved by the Minister on 8 August 1953 would be a modified PAX-P1.

There were numerous changes to the design specifications before the new ship, now designated PA 54,[1] was laid down. In July 1953 it was proposed to replace each of the twelve 57mm twin mountings by the new 100mm single mounting currently under development, which fired proximity-fuzed shells. On 19 October there was a request from Nomy to embark aircraft with a take-off weight of 20 tonnes and a landing weight of 15 tonnes. The air group was to comprise twenty-four British Sea Venom jet fighters (built under licence by SNCASE as the Aquilon), twenty-four attack and twelve anti-submarine aircraft (as yet undefined). New radars and electronic support measures (ESM) equipment of French design and manufacture would be fitted.

[1] The spacing in 'PA 54' and subsequent designations takes account of the change from the sequential numbering of projects to using the final two digits of the year.

There was now a focus on the layout of the flight deck. A study dating from late 1953 shows two catapults side by side and two aircraft lifts: one forward of the island, offset to starboard to clear the angled deck, the other as a side lift directly abaft the island. In January 1954, Gisserot visited the US-loaned carrier *La Fayette* and criticised the flight deck layout and the low capacity of the fuel tanks and magazines. Following his visit the angled deck of PA 54 was moved to port and the angle increased, the island was moved one metre to starboard – both measures were intended to increase the area available for deck parking – and the capacity of the avgas tanks was increased from 1000m$^3$ to 1200m$^3$.

The embarked aircraft were now posing problems. Studies of the Aquilon were completed; however, the dimensions and weight of future aircraft were unclear, so the aviation installations needed to be 'future-proofed'. The forward lift was lengthened by one metre (from 16.4m x 14m to 17.4m x 13m), and the capacity of the aviation fuel tanks further increased to 1350m$^3$, with the bulk allocated to JP-5 jet fuel. In late 1954, the relative positions of the catapults were reviewed in the light of current US Navy and RN thinking: one of the catapults was relocated to the angled deck to free up the forward part of the flight deck for parking to starboard.

On 14 June 1957, only six months prior to 'launch', the number of 100mm guns was reduced from twelve to eight. Finally, on 30 July 1957 Vice Admiral Philippe Auboyneau presented to the *Conseil supérieur de la Marine* (CSM) a proposal for atomic bombs to be delivered by aircraft from *Clemenceau* and her sister *Foch*. This would have an impact on the arrangements for air ordnance stowage and handling.

## CONSTRUCTION

PA 54 was authorised under the 1954 Estimates: she was to be laid down in October 1955 and ready for trials on 31 January 1959, and would be named *Clemenceau*. The turbines and gearing were ordered from the private shipbuilder Chantiers de l'Atlantique,

**Right:** A view of the assembly of the hull of *Clemenceau* (as yet unnamed and designated PA 54) in Laninon Dock No 9 at Brest in 1956. *(Jean Moulin collection)*

and the boilers from the state establishment at Indret; the propulsion and auxiliary machinery, together with the anchors and their handling gear, was to be installed by Ateliers et Chantiers de Bretagne. The order for the hull was duly placed with Brest Naval Dockyard on 28 May; work began in April 1955, and the keel was laid in Laninon No 9 Dock on 15 December 1955. At almost 258 metres, *Clemenceau* was the longest ship yet built at Brest.

Construction of the ship was a major enterprise: there were 200 draughtsmen and technicians charged with plans, and 2,500 men worked on the ship; 3,500 orders were sub-contracted to private industry. Each of the prefabricated elements weighed a maximum of 45 tonnes, and 500 tonnes were installed each month. The ends of the flight deck were fitted as two 50-tonne modules in November 1957, by which time the weight of the hull was 12,000 tonnes. The boilers were embarked from 12 August to 6 December 1957. Water was admitted to the dock on 20 December and the hull was formally floated out the following day (see photos); the 'launch' was attended by the Navy Minister and Admiral Nomy. The hull was then towed to the fitting-out quay at Laninon.

*Capitaine de vaisseau* (CV) Jean Lorrain was appointed in September 1958 to command the ship and supervise completion. The turbines and gearing were embarked between 12 June and 17 October. Fitting of the catapult on the angled deck began in September 1958, followed by the forward catapult in March 1959; the arrester gear was fitted from April 1959. The ship was manned for trials on 26 September of the same year.

## PA 55 *FOCH*

Funding for a sister *Foch* (PA 55) was authorised in August 1955. The hull was to be built by Chantiers de l'Atlantique of Saint-Nazaire and the armament installed by DCAN Brest. The contract envisaged official trials taking place in January 1960, six months

**Above:** The hull of *Clemenceau* is floated out of her building dock at Laninon, in a formal 'launch' ceremony on 21 December 1957, and towed to the fitting-out quay. *(Jean Moulin collection)*

Table 1: **BUILDING DATA**

| Name | Builder | Laid down | Floated out | Trials | Commissioned | In service |
|---|---|---|---|---|---|---|
| *Clemenceau* | Arsenal de Brest | 15 Dec 1955 | 21 Dec 1957 | 26 Sep 1959 | 18 Mar 1960 | 22 Nov 1961 |
| *Foch* | Chantiers de l'Atlantique/ Arsenal de Brest | 15 Feb 1957 | 23 July 1960 | 28 Apr 1962 | 1 Jan 1963 | 15 Jul 1963 |

The assembly of the hull of *Foch* in the construction area of the Jean Bart building facility at Saint-Nazaire. *(René Bail collection)*

The completed hull of *Foch* is floated across to the fitting-out dock of the Jean Bart facility on 13 July 1959. *(DCAN Brest)*

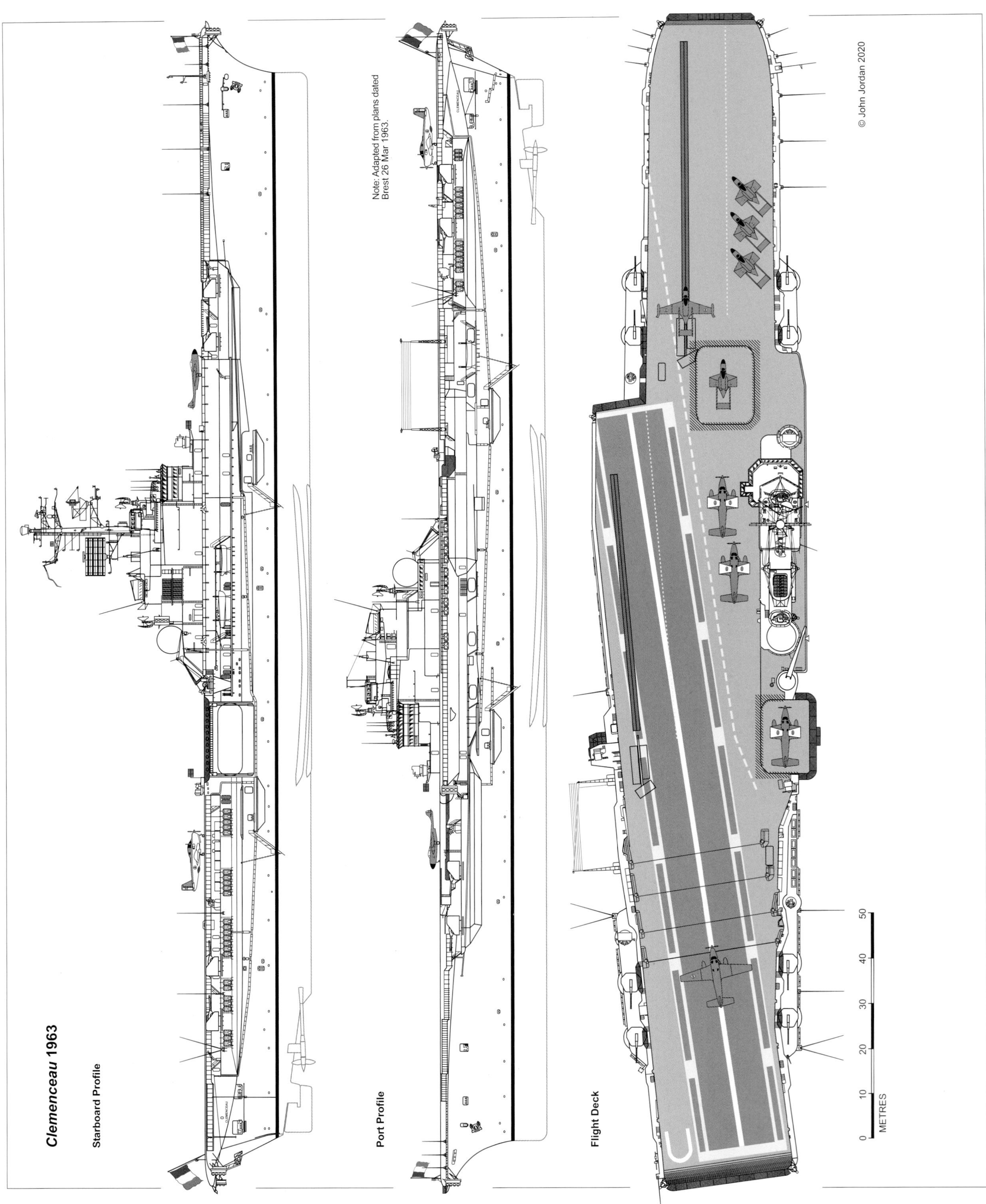

*Clemenceau* 1963
Starboard Profile
Port Profile
Flight Deck
Note: Adapted from plans dated Brest 26 Mar 1963.
© John Jordan 2020
0 10 20 30 40 50
METRES

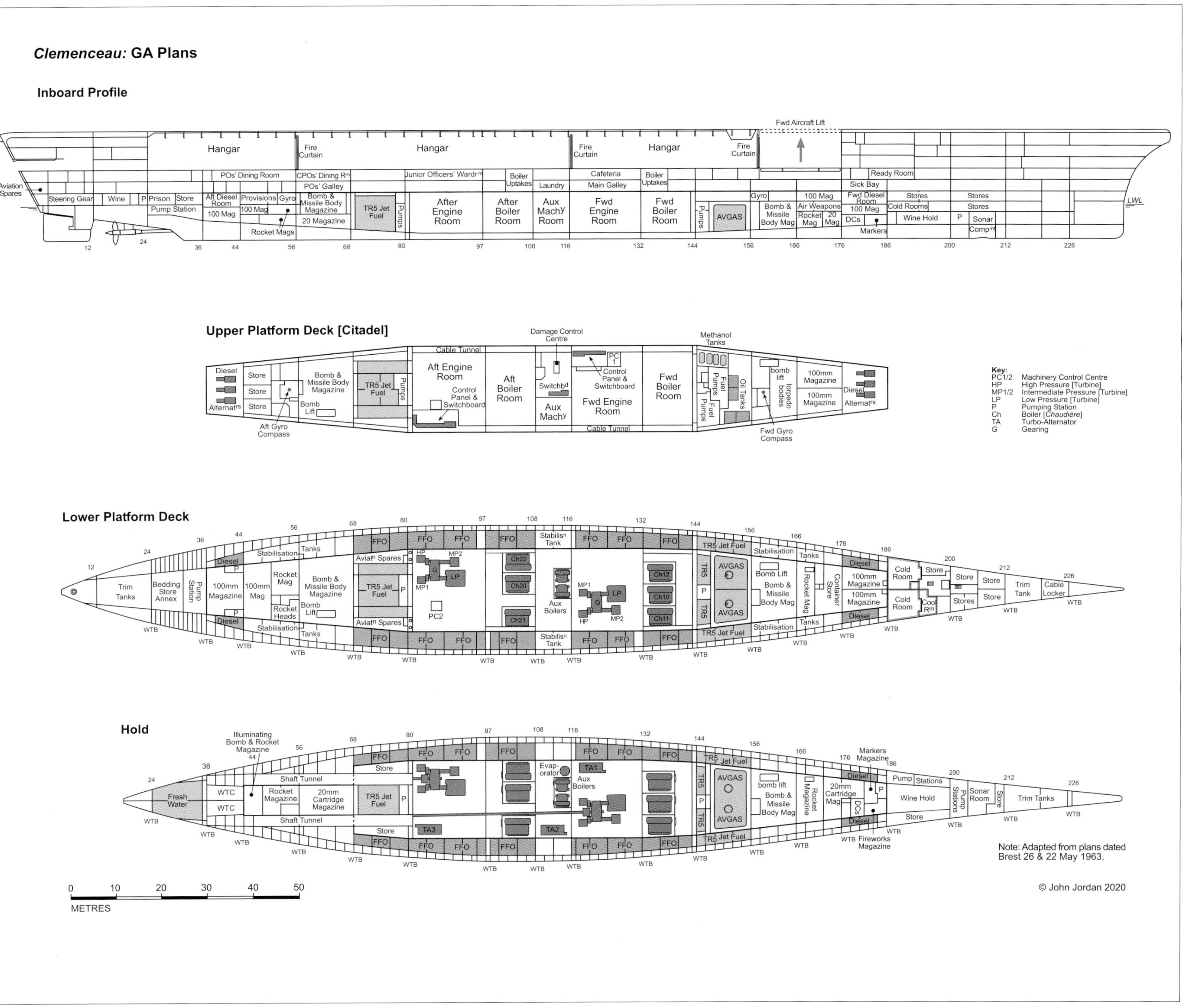
Clemenceau: GA Plans
Inboard Profile
Upper Platform Deck [Citadel]
Lower Platform Deck
Hold
Key:
PC1/2 Machinery Control Centre
HP High Pressure [Turbine]
MP1/2 Intermediate Pressure [Turbine]
LP Low Pressure [Turbine]
P Pumping Station
Ch Boiler [Chaudière]
TA Turbo-Alternator
G Gearing
Note: Adapted from plans dated Brest 26 & 22 May 1963.
© John Jordan 2020
METRES

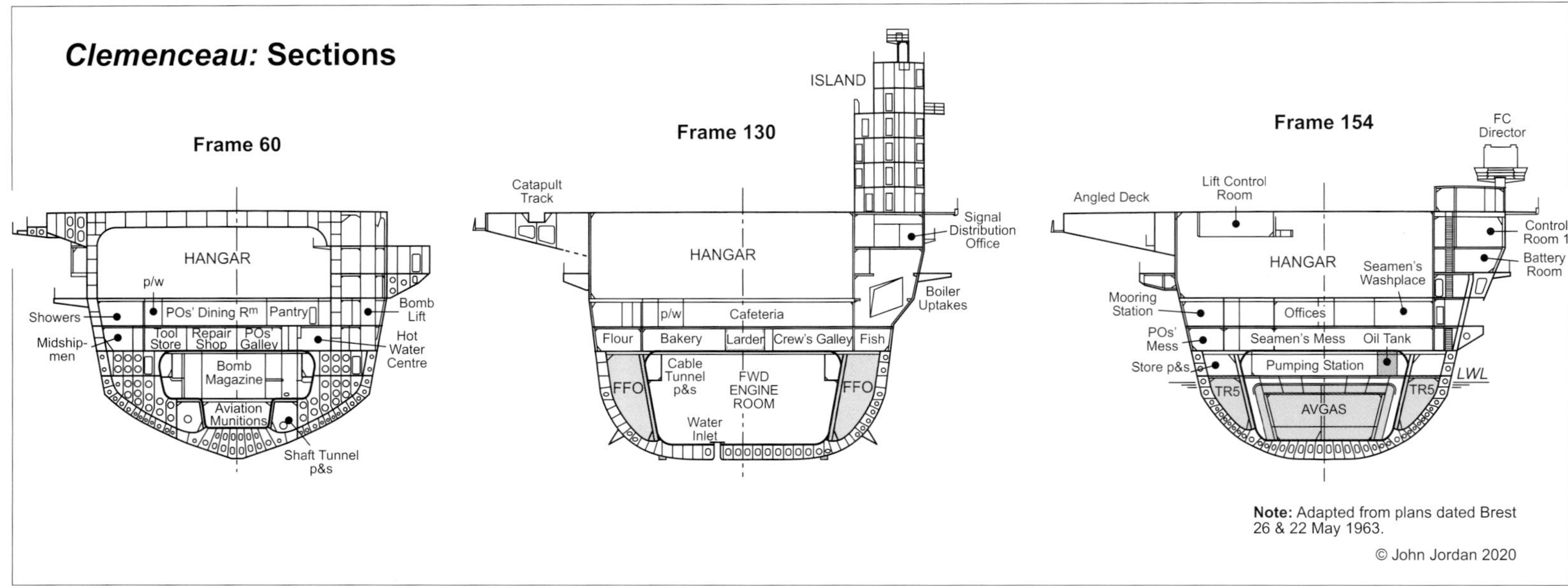


***Clemenceau*: Sections**

after *Clemenceau*. However, delays due to a shortage of labour and steel plating would lead to *Foch* entering service some twenty months after her sister.

Like *Clemenceau*, *Foch* was built in a dock, not on a slipway. The dock in question was that of the Forme Jean Bart (formerly Caquot), in which the battleship of the same name had been built. The completed hull was floated across from the 'dry' construction area to the 'wet' dock on 13 July 1959, and following stability trials was floated out of the facility and towed to Brest for fitting out. Budgetary problems then resulted in further delays, and trials began only in April 1962.

## A: TECHNICAL DESCRIPTION

### Hull and Navigation

Longitudinal construction was employed, the flight deck forming part of the hull girder as in British practice. The shell plating was 16mm, reinforced to 18–24mm at the bow. There were 1,200 Type 6Z galvanic anodes to prevent corrosion. The island was constructed of 10mm plates to port, 8mm to starboard.

Decks were as follows: Hold (No 3 Deck), Lower Platform (No 2), Upper Platform (No 1), Main Deck (No 0), First Deck (No 01), Hangar Deck (No 02), 1st Gallery (No 03), 2nd Gallery (No 04), and Flight Deck (No 05). The First Deck was the main circulation deck; beneath it the hull was divided into twenty watertight compartments (A forward to T aft) by nineteen transverse bulkheads. The island had six levels, numbered 06–011.

The ship was controlled from an enclosed bridge on Platform 3 of the island; the latter housed the engine room telegraphs, the steering column, a console for the DRBN 31 navigation radar display and an IPE 6 panoramic scope. The Admiral's bridge was on Platform 2 of the island; it had good views around the ship, but was fitted only with an IPE 6 panoramic scope.

During the early trials the metacentric height (GM) of 1.01m at light displacement was found to be insufficient, leading to excessive heel when turning or with a beam sea, and excessive roll and pitch when operating aircraft. The 3-degree heel experienced on trials was reduced to 2 degrees following the embarkation of lead ballast. At a displacement of 30,358 tonnes and with a GM of 2.03m, movement was much reduced. It was nevertheless decided to fit bulges (1966 in *Clemenceau*, on completion in *Foch*); these gave a GM in excess of 2 metres even at light displacement. The bulges increased waterline beam from 29.3 metres to 31.7 metres.

### Protection

The flight deck had 45mm armour plating between frames 24 and 159. The machinery spaces, magazines and tanks for the aviation fuel were contained within an internal armoured box formed with a 30mm roof at the level of the Main Deck and 50mm sides, joined top and bottom by curved corners with a 1.5-metre radius (see section drawings). The armoured box was closed at its ends (F186 and F36) by 40mm transverse bulkheads, and there was a third 40mm bulkhead at frame 68 where the shafts exited the hull. The steering gear compartment was protected by a separate 40mm box, and the compartments to the sides and at its after end were filled with 360 cubic metres of a waterproof compound. The gunhouses, aviation facilities and command spaces had light bullet-proof plating.

### Propulsion and Auxiliary Machinery

The high-pressure steam propulsion plant (45kg/cm$^2$, 450°C) was disposed in two boiler and two engine rooms in a 'unit' arrangement. The forward unit comprised three boilers (numbered 10–12) arranged side by side in a single compartment, followed by an engine room with the forward set of turbines driving the starboard shaft, and one of the three turbo-alternators (TA1 – see Hold drawing). The after unit was similar, with three boilers (20–22) in a single compartment followed by the turbines driving the port shaft, and the third of the turbo-alternators (TA3). The two propulsion units, each comprising a boiler room and an engine room, were separated by an auxiliary machinery room. Designated *tranche de mouillage* – it supplied power and 'hotel services' when the ship was at her moorings or alongside – it housed two Indret auxiliary boilers (rated at 27kg/cm$^2$, supplying 14t/h of steam) for use when the ship was in port and a third turbo-alternator (TA2); it was located amidships and had stabilisation tanks to the sides.

Each turbine grouping comprised high-pressure (HP), intermediate-pressure (MP1/MP2) and low-pressure (BP) turbines and drove the shaft via single reduction gearing, which reduced the turbine shaft rotation of 2000–3000rpm to 200rpm for the propeller shafts. There were two reversing turbines, HP and LP, the latter being incorporated into the main casing of the LP ahead turbine.

Each of the two engine rooms was divided vertically into two floors (see GA Plans): the upper for the control consoles and electrical switchboards; the lower for the turbines and the feed/lubrication pumps, and for the turbo-alternator. *Clemenceau* as completed had a machinery control centre (*PC machines*) in the forward engine room to port and a secondary control post in the after engine room; these control spaces were enlarged and differently arranged in her sister *Foch*.

Steam for the turbines was supplied by six Indret asymmetrical SURAL small-tube boilers with natural circulation and direct firing. The boilers had a single large water collector at the base and a steam collector offset at the top, and were equipped with economisers, superheaters and air reheaters. Each boiler was in its own airtight box, and the six exhaust uptakes were combined in a single funnel.

High temperatures in the machinery spaces were found to be a major problem during trials. In February 1961, *Clemenceau* ran a two-hour trial with an external temperature of 28.6–30°C; the temperature recorded at the control panel in the forward boiler room was 34–38°C, that in the after engine room 40–52°C!

The shafts were of nickel-chrome steel. The four-bladed propellers fitted in *Clemenceau* were 5.52m in diameter and weighed 21,700 tonnes; *Foch* had a slightly different model. Pitting of 25–30mm was registered after 8,000 hours of operation, and some modifications were required during the late 1960s.

The maximum speed attained by *Clemenceau* on trials was 33.39 knots with forced draught on 11 December 1959; the maximum speed for *Foch* was recorded (following correction) as 33.27 knots on 24 August 1962. An increase in displacement of 1,000 tonnes was found to cost 0.5 knots, and there was a loss of a further 0.5 knots with a dirty hull. Peak vibration was around 28 knots (176rpm).

**Electrical Supply**

The electrical supply for general service was 440V. There were three Rateau-Jeumont turbo-alternators, each rated at 2000kW, located in the forward engine room, the *tranche de mouillage* and the after engine room respectively. Each generator was powered using the steam from the main turbines and had its own switchboard (*Tableau Principal* – designated TP2/3/4 from aft); the turbo-alternators could be coupled together.

For back-up and when alongside there were six SACM-Jeumont diesel alternators, each rated at 480kW: three located side by side in the after diesel room, which was on the Upper Platform Deck at the after end of the armoured citadel, and three in the forward room, which was on the same level at the forward end (see GA Plans). The switchboards were designated TP1 (aft) and TP5 (forward), and as with the turbo-alternators, the two groups could be coupled together. Normal electricity consumption at sea was 2400kW in peacetime.

**Fresh Water Supply**

When completed, *Clemenceau* was equipped with three evaporators, each with a capacity of 160 tonnes per day, distributed between the three machinery spaces. Consumption was found to be greater than anticipated: 3 tonnes per hour for the boilers, 200/300kg per catapult launch, plus 185 tonnes of fresh water per day for the crew. In practice, only 300–350 tonnes of water per day were produced to top up the initial 540 tonnes carried in the tanks. In theory, endurance was unlimited with three evaporators on line provided there was no air activity, but with air operations it was only twenty days. Additional evaporators were embarked in 1978–81, and a more modern osmosis unit was installed in *Clemenceau* in 1992.

**Table 2: CHARACTERISTICS: *CLEMENCEAU* (AS COMPLETED)**

| | |
|---|---|
| Displacement: | 22,000 tons standard<br>27,520 tonnes normal<br>32,570 tonnes deep load |
| Dimensions: | |
| length | 238m pp; 257.5m oa |
| width at flight deck | 46.3m |
| beam | 29.3m wl |
| mean draught | 8.34m deep load (9.25m incl propellers) |
| Aviation: | |
| flight deck | 257.5m x 28/46m |
| height above w/l | 15.89m |
| angled deck | 168m x 20m at 8°40′ |
| hangar | 180m x 26m x 7.15m |
| lifts (LxW) | fwd: 17.4m x 13m (15 tonnes)<br>aft: 16.4m x 11m (15 tonnes) |
| catapults | two BS 5 steam (20-tonne aircraft) |
| arrester cables | four (18-tonne aircraft at 112kts) |
| cranes | one fixed (15 tonnes), one mobile (10–15 tonnes) |
| Machinery: | |
| boilers | six Indret asymmetrical SURAL boilers<br>45kg/cm², 450°C |
| engines | two-shaft Parsons geared turbines (HP, 2 x IP, LP) |
| horsepower | 126,000cv |
| propellers | two 4-bladed, 5.524 diameter |
| speed | 32 knots max (33.4kts on trials) |
| endurance | 7500nm at 18 knots |
| electricity | three Rateau-Jeumont turbo-gens each 2000kW<br>six SACM Jeumont diesel gens each 480kW |
| Protection: | |
| flight Deck | 45mm (F24–F159) |
| citadel | 50mm sides, 30mm roof |
| transverse b/heads | 40mm |
| Armament: | |
| main guns | eight 100/55 ACAS Mle 1953 (8 x I) |
| aircraft | forty (normally 34–36 + 2 helicopters) |
| Electronics: | |
| air search | DRBV 20C (B-band) |
| height-finder | two DRBI 10 (E/F-band) |
| target designation | DRBV 23 (D-band) |
| surface search | DRBV 50 (G-band) |
| fire control | four DRBC 31C (I/J-band) |
| navigation | DRBN 31 |
| CCA | NRBA 50 |
| sonar | SQS-503 |
| Complement: | |
| private ship | 2,239 officers and men |

Right: The stern of *Foch* is seen here in dock during her modernisation in 1987. The large single rudder and the two four-bladed propellers are prominent. *(DR)*

Below: *Clemenceau* passes through the harbour mouth at Brest on 23 November 1958. There was a near-collision at the harbour entrance with a sand hopper barge (see page 225), which can be seen here off the port bow. The carrier then headed out to sea for machinery trials. The armament and most of the electronics outfit have yet to be fitted, and there are as yet no markings on the flight deck. *(ECPAD)*

## ARMAMENT

### Guns

Eight of the new 100mm/55 ACAS (*Automatique Contre-Avions Simple*) Mle 1953 guns were fitted on completion. The gun was housed in a pseudo-turret with a fixed ammunition hoist supplied from a working chamber directly beneath the mounting. A rotating twelve-round drum (*barillet*) in the working chamber revolved around a fixed vertical hoist (three rounds), and the feed in the gunhouse comprised two quarter-cheese trays with eighteen rounds; the first thirty rounds could be fired without human intervention. Once the ready-use (RU) supply was exhausted, the drum needed to be replenished by two/three loading numbers.

The theoretical maximum rate of fire was 60rpm, but once the RU supply was exhausted this was reduced to 35rpm. The gun could be elevated to +80° and depressed to -15° and could be locked between +5° and +20° when not in use; there was water cooling for the barrel between the ejection of the cartridge and the loading of the next round.

The gun mounting could be controlled remotely using Ward Leonard RPC, or locally by the turret commander (*chef de tourelle*) using an electrical director; it was equipped with binocular sights with a wide field of vision. The mounting was manned by the turret commander, a 'supervisor' (*surveillant*), who checked that the breech opened for the first round, a gunlayer and an *aide-surveillant*, charged with supplying gun range and deflection data in local control. The working chamber was manned by the chamber commander (*chef de relais*) and two loading numbers. The gun could open fire without any of the gun crew present.

### Ammunition

The fixed OEA Mle 1954 round was fitted with a mechanical (DM/DE) or proximity fuze. The Mle 1956 detonator activated on impact or after a predetermined interval. The OEA Mle 1954 would be superseded by the F1 with prefragmentation, then the F4 with 1,530 1-gramme balls, both intended for use against thin-skinned missiles.

The ammunition for the 100mm guns was stowed in six magazines within the armoured citadel; electric hoists raised ammunition at a rate of twenty boxed cartridges per minute to handing rooms on the 1st Gallery Deck beneath the mountings. Capacity was 9,400 OEA combat rounds plus 300 OEALp semi-ballasted exercise rounds. The fixed ammunition was stowed in individual cylindrical cases of light alloy.

Each of the eight working chambers had an RU supply of 190 rounds; fuzing was carried out in an adjacent space. The magazines were equipped with a spray system, and there was forced ventilation for the magazines and the handing rooms.

### Fire Control

There was a director for each of the four groups of guns. All were fitted with radar and – unusually for the period – two were equipped with an optical stereoscopic rangefinder. The DRBC 31C radar was optimised for the automatic tracking of aerial targets, but could also be used to direct anti-surface fire (*but flottant* or BF). The 100mm guns could also be employed against an invisible target on land (*tir contre la terre* or CT) provided the ship was stationary or moored 17,000m away; this was done in local control using the auxiliary sights.

The two directors fitted with optical rangefinders, which had a base length of 4.2 metres, were designated TT (*tourelle de télépointage optique et radar*). Each weighed 8 tonnes, was 4.5m wide, and was stabilised on four rotational axes. The director was able to train through 350 degrees, could elevate from -8° to +90°, and was stabilised for 10 degrees of pitch and 22 degrees of roll. It was normally manned by a gunlayer, a rangetaker and a control officer, but was able to operate with one man or unmanned.

The two light directors, which were designated TR (or TRA = *télépointeur radar artillerie*) were uniquely for radar-controlled fire against aircraft. The platform was again stabilised in four axes. The director carried only the antenna for the DRBC 31 radar and a black-and-white TV camera that facilitated remote optical pointing from the *Poste Central*.

Fire control groupings were as follows:

- Group 1 (starboard forward): director TT1 plus mountings 1 & 3.
- Group 2 (port forward): director TR2 plus mountings 2 & 4.
- Group 3 (starboard aft): director TR3 plus mountings 5 & 7.
- Group 4 (port aft): director TT4 plus mountings 6 & 8.

Group 2, which was forward of the angled deck, was located 1.5m lower than the others. Each of the four directors was able to control (i) its own group, (ii) the group on the same side of the ship, or (iii) both groups. Director TT1, which was on a raised deckhouse at the forward end of the island, was also able to control Group 2. Each group had two calculating positions with three cabinets. Performance was limited to aircraft with a speed of 25m/s out to a range of 8,000 metres. The groups were under the overall command of the *Chef de défense* (Platform 6 of the island) or the target designation officer (*Officier de désignation d'objectif*, or ODO).

### Crotale and Sadral

In early 1958, when the ships were under construction, there was a proposal to fit the Tartar medium-range area defence system in place of half the 100mm battery. Two cylindrical magazines, each holding forty missiles and topped by a single-arm launcher, were to be fitted on enlarged sponsons forward to starboard and aft to port; an alternative arrangement would have seen the two installations replacing both the after groups of guns.

The proposal came to nothing, but when *Clemenceau* and *Foch* were approaching their major half-life refit in the mid-1980s it was decided to fit two Crotale close-range air defence missile systems in the original arrangement proposed for Tartar: one installation replacing the forward guns to starboard, the other the after guns to port. The total weight of the two installations was 90 and 120 tonnes respectively.

Crotale was initially developed for the French Air Force as a short-range missile system to defend air bases, and was designed and built by Matra and Thomson/CSF. The development contract for the

Below, left: A close-up of the island of *Clemenceau* in 1960, with two Aquilon jet fighters parked beneath. Note the large carrier-controlled approach (CCA) radar housed within a dome at the after end. *(DR)*

Below, right: The foremast of *Clemenceau* in 1960, now with her full complement of radar antennae, including the large mattress antenna for the DRBV 20C long-range air search radar (left), the DRBV 23 target designation radar (right), the DRBV 50 surface surveillance radar (above), and one of the two DRBI 10 heightfinders atop the bridge. *(SHD-M Toulon)*

navalised variant was placed on 1 February 1974 and, following testing on the missile trials ship *Ile d'Oléron*, the first production launcher was installed on board the frigate *Georges Leygues* in 1978.

In early versions of Crotale the fire control radar found it difficult to detect low-flying anti-ship missiles because of surface clutter, particularly in rough seas. The EDIR (*écartométrie différentielle infrarouge*) variant, developed specifically for naval use, used an infrared camera to detect the flare from the missile rocket motor and was capable of intercepting sea-skimming missiles manoeuvring at 5g down to 3 metres above the surface; range was 13,000m, and the missile reached a maximum speed of Mach 2.3. It was associated with the DRBV 15 target indication radar and a dedicated control console in the Operations Room (see below). *Clemenceau* would be the first French surface unit to receive the EDIR variant, during her refit in 1985–86. She would be followed by her sister *Foch* in 1987–88.

Each of the eight-cell missile launchers was located, together with its Thomson K-band tracking radar, atop a housing for the electronics. In addition to the eight on-mount missiles there was a magazine for eighteen reloads close to the mounting. Two missiles could be replaced simultaneously; the time needed for a full reload was thirty minutes.

In 1996–97, *Foch* received two six-round Sadral launchers for the Matra Mistral short-range 'fire-and-forget' missile to supplement Crotale in the anti-sea-skimming missile role. The missile was effective at very low altitudes (less then 3 metres) out to 6,000 metres. *Clemenceau* never received this system.

## ELECTRONICS

### Radars

*Clemenceau* was fitted on completion with a complete suite of the latest models of radar of French design and manufacture.

The DRBV 20C (with NRBI 20 IFF) was a long-range air search radar with a large rectangular mattress antenna, and was also fitted in the contemporary anti-aircraft cruiser *Colbert*. In theory it could detect a jet fighter out to 150nm, but this varied with the altitude and radar cross-section of the aircraft.

DRBV 23 (likewise with NRBI 20 IFF) was not available until mid-1961; the smaller and less capable DRBV 22C, which was widely fitted in ships of destroyer/frigate size, replaced it as a temporary measure. DRBV 23 was a long-range target designation radar capable of detecting a fighter out to 110nm; it used a parabolic antenna and was normally synchronised with DRBV 20C.

The aerial detection and tracking suite was completed by two DRBI 10 heightfinding radars, the antennae being fitted at either end of the island; they could be synchronised at an angle of 180 degrees, and detection range was 80nm on an aircraft flying at 21,000 metres.

A DRBV 50 radar for surface surveillance was fitted above DRBV 23 on a platform angled to starboard, which gave it a blind arc between 200 and 230

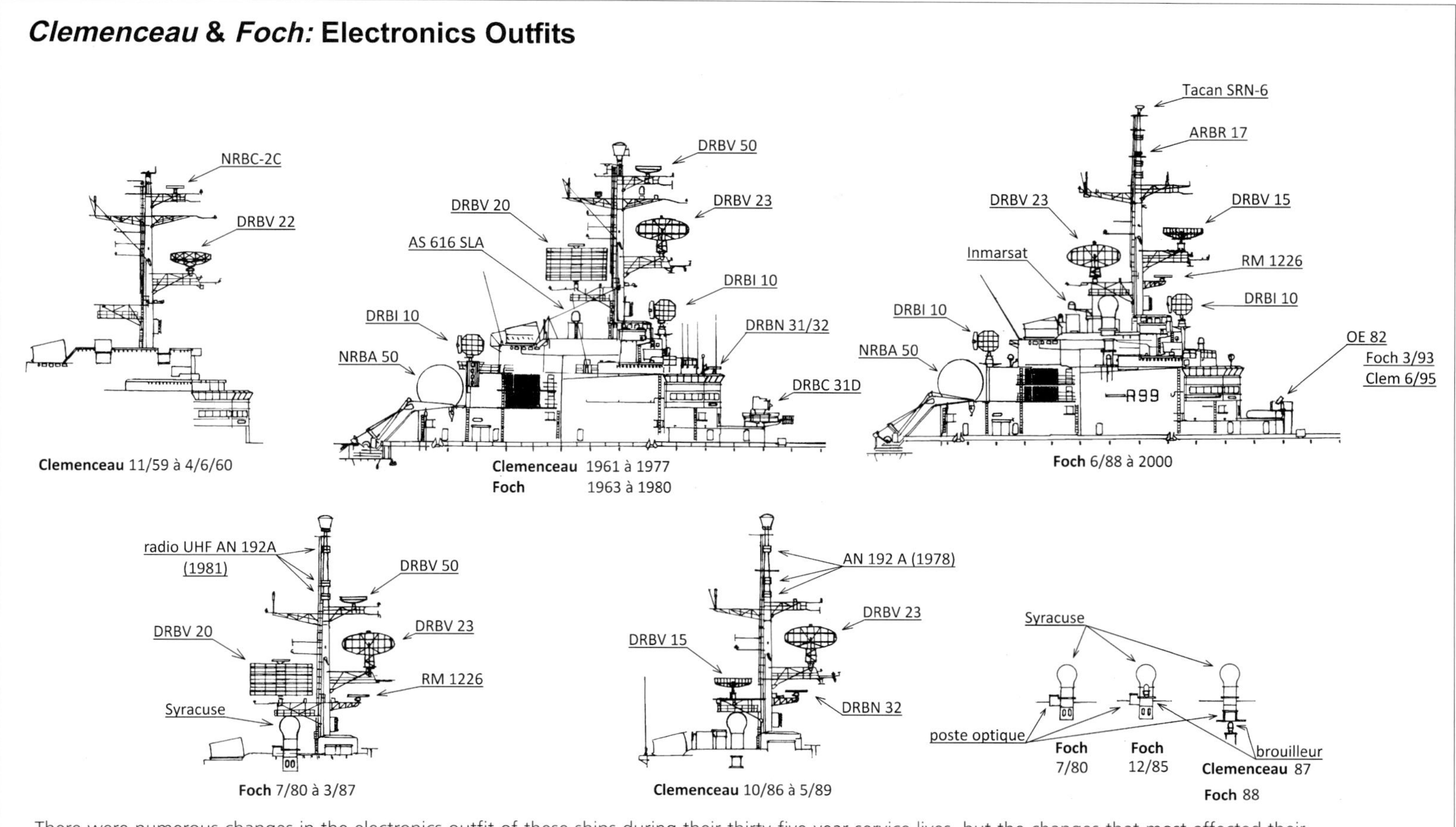


There were numerous changes in the electronics outfit of these ships during their thirty-five-year service lives, but the changes that most affected their appearance relate to the major life-extension refit of the mid-/late 1980s, when the antennae for the original DRBV 20 long-range air search and the DRBV 50 surface surveillance radars were replaced by the parabolic, horn-fed antenna of the DRBV 15 target indication radar associated with Crotale, and paired radomes for the Syracuse satellite communications system were fitted. *(Drawn by Jean Moulin)*

degrees; it could detect a large surface unit at 30nm and a destroyer at 20nm. It was complemented by the smaller DRBN 31 for navigation, which was capable of detecting a destroyer at 12nm; the antenna was fitted atop the navigation bridge and had a blind arc between 130 and 230 degrees. DRBN 31 would be replaced by the more capable DRBN 32 in 1969–70 (1971 in *Foch*).

The carrier-controlled approach (CCA) radar was the NRBA 50, the aerial for which was housed within a large radome at the after end of the island (there was a 100-degree 'dead zone' forward). It could detect an Alizé ASW aircraft at 25nm and the smaller Etendard strike fighter at 15nm. A TACAN beacon, carried at the masthead, enabled a high-flying aircraft to home in on the carrier from a maximum range of 200nm. The original NRBP 20A model was replaced by the more advanced SRN-6 in August 1961.

There were numerous issues with these emitters due to their close proximity, and some could not be used simultaneously at full power. The DRBV 20 and DRBV 50 radars would be landed and replaced by the DRBV 15 target indication radar for the Crotale short-range air defence and anti-missile system (see above) during the ships' half-life refits in 1985–88.

### Sonar

The sonar, which was housed in a retractable dome, was SQS-503, a 10kHz medium-frequency model widely fitted in the US Navy. It was usable in good weather up to 28 knots, although performance deteriorated above 22 knots. Speed had to be reduced to 20 knots in order for the dome to be raised or lowered; at higher speeds it had to be lowered and locked. SQS-23 would be replaced by the US SQS-505 panoramic sonar around 1971. The sonar was landed during the mid-life refits of 1985–88.

### ECM/ESM

Electronic support measures (ESM) to detect, monitor and analyse hostile emissions comprised the French ARBC 10C (detection + analysis) and the US Navy's AN/SLR-2 (analysis); ARBC 10 would be superseded by ARBR 16 (*Clemenceau*), then by the particularly effective ARBR 17 (both ships) during the late 1980s. There was provision for the fitting of electronic countermeasures (ECM), and ARBB 31 jammers were installed during the early 1970s. However, chaff dispensers, which were key to decoying anti-ship missiles, would not be embarked until the late 1980s, when two ten-tube Sagaie decoy launchers developed and manufactured by the French Compagnie de Signaux et d'Entreprises Electriques were installed. One launcher was installed forward of the island, the other abaft the port-side Crotale installation.

### Tactical Data and Command Systems

The French Navy was not as advanced as the British Royal Navy or the US Navy of the 1960s with regard to data processing and co-ordination. When *Clemenceau*

**Above:** A later view, taken on 19 July 2000, of the island of *Foch*. The antenna for the DRBV 23 radar has been relocated to the platform abaft the mast, and replaced by DRBV 15. *(Jean Moulin)*

and *Foch* were first completed there was only a *Central Information* (CI) housing the consoles for the DRBV 20, 23, 50 and DRBI 10 radars, located on the 2nd Gallery Deck to starboard, beneath the forward end of the island.

A *Poste Central Opérations* (PC Ops), located on Platform 2 of the island directly behind the admiral's bridge, was tasked with co-ordinating surface and air operations. The latter space proved too small, particularly when an admiral and his staff were embarked. The *Chef de défense*, stationed in a glazed 'gazebo' on Platform 6, provided situational input via 'indicators' (*indicateurs*).

A proposed installation of the French-developed SENIT data system was delayed by funding issues. A SENIT 2 system from the fleet escort *Jauréguiberry* (T53 type) was finally installed in *Clemenceau* in 1977–78, and *Foch* received the SENIT 2 from her sister *Tartu* in 1980–81. The original CI was enlarged and redesignated the Operations Centre (*Central Opérations*, or CO). SENIT would subsequently be upgraded with NATO Links 11 and 14 and a doubling of computer capacity.

### Satellite Communications

The cabling and infrastructure for the French Syracuse (*Système de radiocommunication utilisant un satellite*) satellite communication system was installed in *Foch* during the early 1980s, and the installation completed in 1985; *Clemenceau* had Syracuse installed during her major half-life refit in 1985–86. The position of the distinctive white-painted paired radomes can be seen in the drawings. The radomes were some 30 metres above the waterline and added 15 tonnes of topweight. *Foch* had her system upgraded to Syracuse II during her last modernisation in 1996–97.

In 1987–88, both ships were fitted with terminals for Inmarsat (INternational MARitime SATellite). This civil system used eight geostationary satellites to give global coverage for telephones, telex and fax.

Finally, the US Navy's Fltsatcom (FLeeT SATellite COMmunication) UHF communication system, designed to support Link 11 data transfer between ships, was installed during the early 1990s. This was connected to the French Sachem system in 1997.

## COMPLEMENT

The theoretical complement when *Clemenceau* entered service was 179 officers, 560 petty officers and 1,500 men (total 2,239). All personnel had bunks, and there was cafeteria messing. There were separate galleys for the admiral, officers, petty officers and seamen. The change in balance between specialist petty officers and ordinary seamen during the ships' service lives led to constant modifications to the accommodation.

There was a large, well-equipped sick bay with twenty-four beds on the First Deck forward of the first aircraft lift. This would later be refitted as a seventeen-bed hospital.

## AVIATION FACILITIES

### Flight Deck

The flight deck was 257.5 metres long and between 28 and 46 metres wide. At deep load it was 15.89 metres above the waterline. To starboard of the island was a narrow passageway for deck tractors and other handling gear. The angled deck measured 168m x 20m and was inclined at 8°40' to the ship's axis; its length was calculated to allow aircraft to clear the deck at the stern by at least 3 metres when landing on to allow for pilot error and pitching of the deck.

The strength of the flight deck was calculated to bear the weight of a 20-tonne stationary/catapulting aircraft and a 15-tonne aircraft on landing (once fuel had been expended and ordnance disposed of). There were 800 attachment points on the flight deck, and when the angled deck was in use there was sufficient space for twenty-three parked aircraft: fifteen forward, four abreast the island, two on the forward lift and one on the after lift. From 1970 there was an additional spot for aircraft to be rapidly fuelled and catapulted.

The flight and hangar decks were initially given a coat of Tankastral paint, and from 1964, Ferrox non-

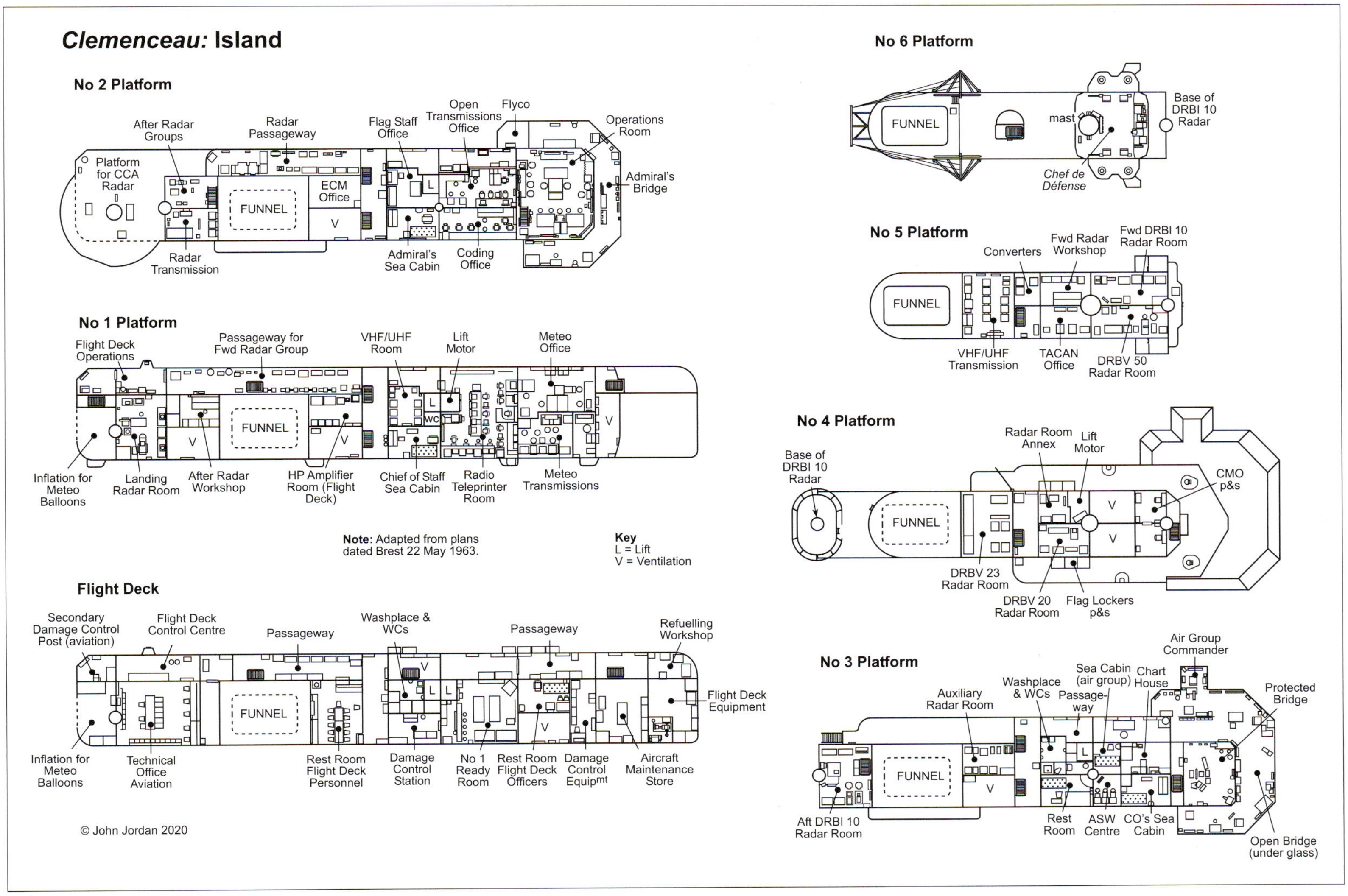

## *Clemenceau:* Island

### No 2 Platform

After Radar Groups
Radar Passageway
Flag Staff Office
Open Transmissions Office
Flyco
Operations Room
Platform for CCA Radar
FUNNEL
ECM Office
V
L
Admiral's Bridge
Radar Transmission
Admiral's Sea Cabin
Coding Office

### No 1 Platform

Flight Deck Operations
Passageway for Fwd Radar Group
VHF/UHF Room
Lift Motor
Meteo Office
FUNNEL
V
L
WC
Inflation for Meteo Balloons
Landing Radar Room
After Radar Workshop
HP Amplifier Room (Flight Deck)
Chief of Staff Sea Cabin
Radio Teleprinter Room
Meteo Transmissions

**Note:** Adapted from plans dated Brest 22 May 1963.

**Key**
L = Lift
V = Ventilation

### Flight Deck

Secondary Damage Control Post (aviation)
Flight Deck Control Centre
Passageway
Washplace & WCs
Passageway
Refuelling Workshop
Flight Deck Equipment
FUNNEL
V
L
Inflation for Meteo Balloons
Technical Office Aviation
Rest Room Flight Deck Personnel
Damage Control Station
No 1 Ready Room
Rest Room Flight Deck Officers
Damage Control Equip$^{mt}$
Aircraft Maintenance Store



### No 6 Platform

FUNNEL
mast
Base of DRBI 10 Radar
*Chef de Défense*

### No 5 Platform

Converters
Fwd Radar Workshop
Fwd DRBI 10 Radar Room
FUNNEL
VHF/UHF Transmission
TACAN Office
DRBV 50 Radar Room

### No 4 Platform

Base of DRBI 10 Radar
Radar Room Annex
Lift Motor
CMO p&s
FUNNEL
V
DRBV 23 Radar Room
DRBV 20 Radar Room
Flag Lockers p&s

### No 3 Platform

Air Group Commander
Auxiliary Radar Room
Washplace & WCs
Sea Cabin (air group)
Chart House
Passage-way
Protected Bridge
FUNNEL
V
L
Aft DRBI 10 Radar Room
Rest Room
ASW Centre
CO's Sea Cabin
Open Bridge (under glass)

**Left:** The hangar of *Foch*, looking aft, on 19 July 2000. Note the open bay for the side lift on the left, and the sliding fire doors that divided the hangar in the event of a fire. *(Jean Moulin)*

slip, anti-oxidising paint was applied to the flight deck. The *Poste de contrôle pont d'envol* (PCPE) organised the stowage of aircraft on deck and in the hangar using models; it controlled movement in collaboration with the *Bureau technique aviation* (BTA). Both were at flight deck level at the rear of the island: the PCPE to port and the BTA to starboard. Directly above the PCPE was the *Passerelle pont d'envol* (lit 'flight deck bridge'), which had large glazed bays that gave it good views over the flight deck.

**Hangar**

The hangar was offset to port, as in PA28 and the prewar *Joffre*. It was divided into three zones (*sous-hangars*) numbered 1 (F158–116), 2 (F116–56) and 3 (F56–24) by four sets of metal fire doors with electrical controls (F176, 158, 116, 56), and there were fire curtains at frames 24 and 12 to isolate the engine maintenance spaces (see below). The layout of the hangar was a compromise between British and US practice: the starboard side of hangar was completely enclosed, with operational spaces outboard and access by air lock; the port side was partially open, with bays closed by sliding doors. The flight deck was supported from the main deck on transverse beams 1.5m high, reducing the usable height of the hangar from 8.5m to 6.9m.

The zone forward of the first lift was originally an extension of the hangar measuring 16m x 15m x 5.1m. Between March and November 1961 it was converted into a workshop for airborne missiles; *Foch* was completed with this arrangement. At the after end of the hangar, between frames 24 and 12, there was a space for dismantling and reassembly of Atar and J-57 aero-engines to starboard with associated workshops to port.

The total length of the hangar following modification was 164 metres, of which 134m was usable (taking account of the forward lift). Maximum width was 26 metres (of which an average 21m was usable). There was a control platform for the hangar at frame 122 to starboard, and damage control cabins in the centre of each of the three fire zones to port.

The spray system comprised nine networks on the hangar roof, ten water screens along the doors, four transverse water screens, plus diffusers in the lift well and water spray ramps for the control cabins and air locks. Ten foam stations on the First Deck (five per side) fed nine main and four secondary canons, and the fire suppression outfit was completed by mobile $CO_2$ and water dispensers.

Heavy items could be moved by block and tackle, with five engagement points each capable of lifting 10 tonnes and one of 3 tonnes, plus two 0.5-tonne davits in the port-side bays.

Below: An Etendard IVM strike fighter on the side lift to starboard in 1970. Note the SAGEM optical landing aid directly abaft it; this would later be removed. *(ECPAD)*

**Lifts**

The two aircraft lifts were built by Applevage. Each was powered by two 150hp electric motors from Sautter-Harlé; a single emergency motor delivered 30hp. The lifts could raise 15 tonnes from the hangar to the flight deck. Four speeds were available: two 'normal' (one or two main motors), two 'slow' (single main motor/emergency motor); it took nine seconds to travel the 8.5m with two motors, one minute with the emergency motor.

The forward lift was 17.4m long and 13m wide, and was offset 3 metres to starboard. The after, US-style side lift measured 16.4m x 11m. The access bay for this lift was 5.5m high, and was closed by double-leaved sliding doors operating at 30m/s.

**Catapults**

The two British BS 5 catapults were built by Brown Bros, with the bow catapult offset to port and the second at the forward end of the angled deck and inclined at 5°21' to the axis of the ship. This arrangement was adopted to maximise parking forward.

The BS 5 could launch a 20-tonne aircraft at 90 knots with 2.8g acceleration. In theory the interval between launches was thirty-five seconds; in practice it was forty-five seconds. There were two driving cylinders side by side beneath the flight deck; twin rams ran inside the cylinders under steam pressure; the rams were linked by a cradle, and a bridle was attached to the aircraft. The steam accumulators were located on the 1st Gallery Deck, the operating spaces, elevation motors for the blast deflectors, catapult workshop and stores on the 2nd Gallery Deck. The catapult had to undergo onboard maintenance after 400 launches, and a major maintenance period of six weeks in a dockyard was required after 1,600–2,000 launches.

Hinged blast deflectors abaft the catapults protected the crew and the aircraft on deck; the original MacTaggart model was replaced during the Crusader refit of 1967–68. The new Bréguet model had identical dimensions but had water cooling. The blast deflectors were hydraulically operated from a retractable 'howdah', and took fifteen seconds to elevate or lower. When in the raised position they had a vertical angle of 60 degrees and an angle of deflection 120 degrees to port.

Initially the catapult bridles were simply ditched on launch, but the bridles for the Crusader were five to ten times more expensive, and two bridle catchers (Mk 2 Mod 2 forward, Mod 0 angled deck) were fitted from January 1966 to January 1967 (*Foch* August 1965–January 1966). In 1964 *Clemenceau* carried 720 (disposable) bridles for the Etendard and 420 for the Alizé. Following two incidents, catchers were no longer used for the Etendard, but they continued in use for the Crusader.

**Arrester Wires**

*Clemenceau* was equipped with four arrester wires that ran perpendicular to the axis of the angled deck at frames 40, 48, 56 and 63. The cables were 114mm thick and 29 metres across at rest, extending to 65–70m when engaged by an aircraft on landing. They could cope with an 18-tonne aircraft with a maximum landing speed of 112 knots. Each cable was linked to a British MacTaggart Mk 13 hydraulic brake, comprising a cylinder filled with a glycerine-based fluid that was displaced by a piston via a small opening. A cabin located on the starboard gallery monitored the arrester wires.

In the event of a failure of the tailhook to engage the arrester wires, a barrier could be installed between collapsible posts at frames 72–77. The force was absorbed by a system of nylon bags. The barrier was used only once, for an Aquilon on 20 February 1961.

**Mirror Landing Aids**

Aircraft adopted a speed of approach of 130 knots for a maximum 112 knots when engaging the arrester wires; the angle of approach was 3°30' and the vertical speed of impact 3 metres per second. *Clemenceau* was initially fitted with a British Mk IA mirror landing sight manufactured by John Curran with SAGEM stabilisation; it was located on a platform between frames 84 and 88, with the light source at F37. There was also an emergency SAGEM model, which was purely optical and used Fresnel lenses, to starboard at frame 78, immediately abaft the side lift (see Profile and Plan). In 1967, *Clemenceau* had the mirror sight replaced by a second optical landing aid – *Foch* had two optical models on completion; the starboard installation was landed in 1970.

**Cranes**

A fixed crane capable of lifting a 15-tonne aircraft was located at the after end of the island forward of the side lift: it had a 300-degree radius to enable it to serve the flight deck, side lift and quay. Built by Caillard, it had a height of 22–26 metres in the raised position, a reach of 12.2–8.7 metres, and could lift or lower at 0.3 metres per second.

There was also a 27-tonne mobile crane mounted on a Berliet 90hp diesel tractor that could lift 10 tonnes at 6 metres, and 15 tonnes at 3.5 metres. Some of the deck tractors initially embarked proved too lightweight for the task; they were replaced in 1967 by ten diesel tractors with a pull rating of 2.3 tonnes.

**Aviation Fuel**

When *Clemenceau* entered service the transition was being made from conventional propeller-driven aircraft to jets; the former used *essence aviation* (avgas), the latter TR5 jet fuel (the French equivalent of JP-5), which was less volatile and had a higher flash point. *Clemenceau* initially embarked 400m$^3$ of the former and 1180m$^3$ of TR5. *Foch*, which was completed less than two years later, embarked 1800m$^3$ of TR5 and only a small quantity of avgas (9m$^3$) for helicopters.

The avgas tanks were of the 'saddle tank' design, and were always filled with liquid to prevent the accumulation of combustible vapours; petrol that was consumed was replaced by seawater, which because of its higher density sat on the bottom of the tank.

*Clemenceau* as completed had two groups of tanks forward (see GA Plans), each comprising an external reservoir, an internal reservoir and a pumping reservoir located one inside the other and surrounded with nitrogen. Distribution was via two collectors: the port-side collector supplied the hangar, that on the starboard side the hangar and flight deck. There were three distribution stations (40m$^3$/h at 7kg/cm$^2$) for the flight deck and two for the hangar.

## Appearance Changes: *Clemenceau*

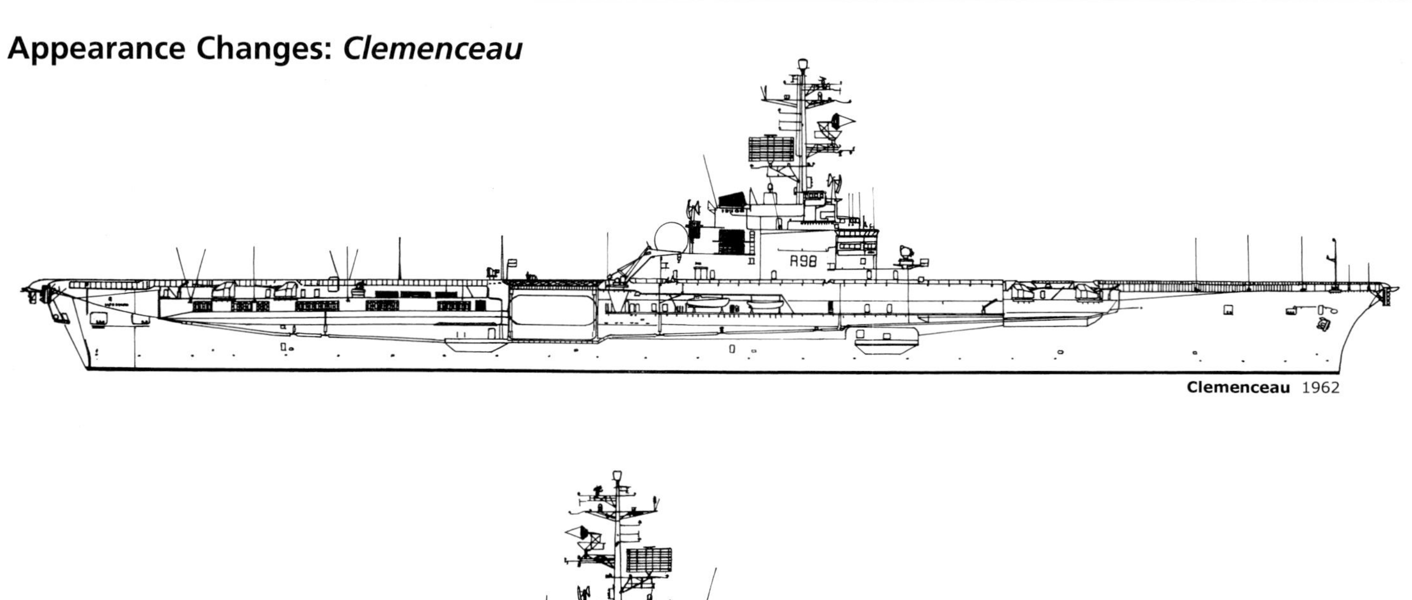


**Clemenceau** 1962

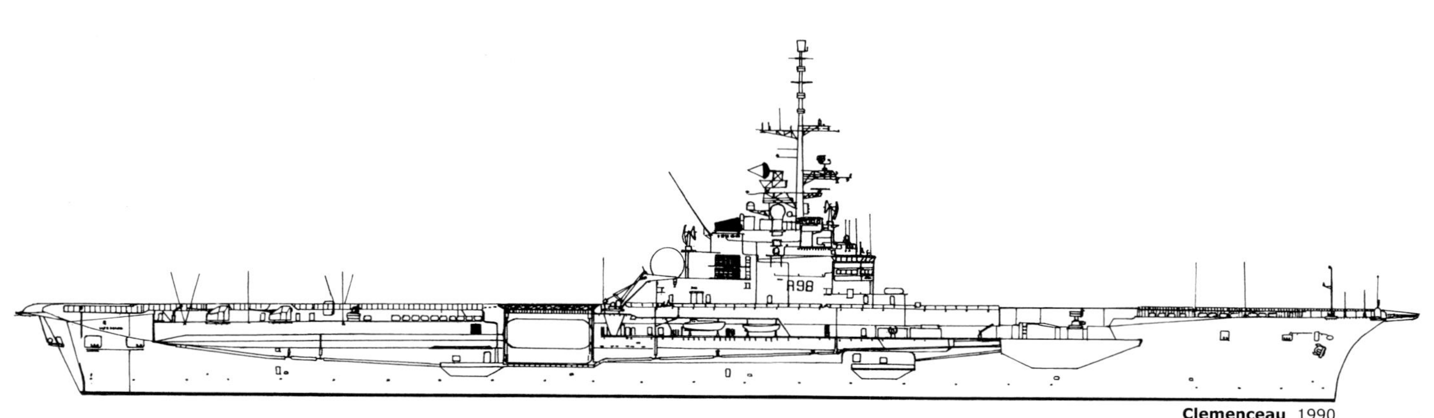


**Clemenceau** 1990

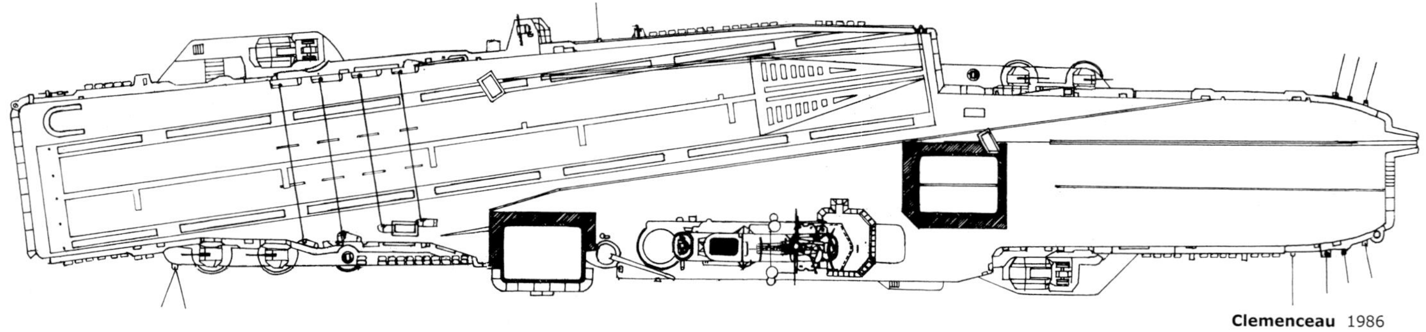

**Clemenceau** 1986

*(Drawn by Jean Moulin)*

## Appearance Changes: *Foch*

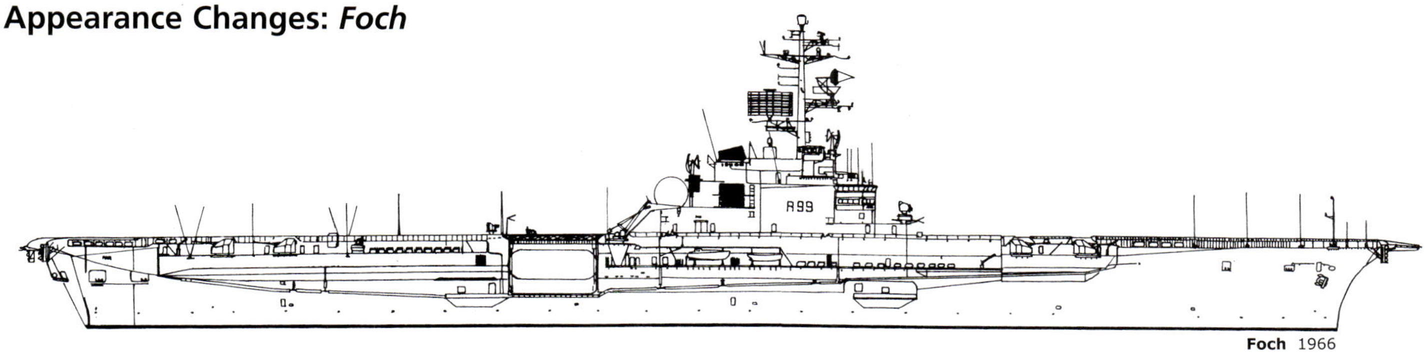

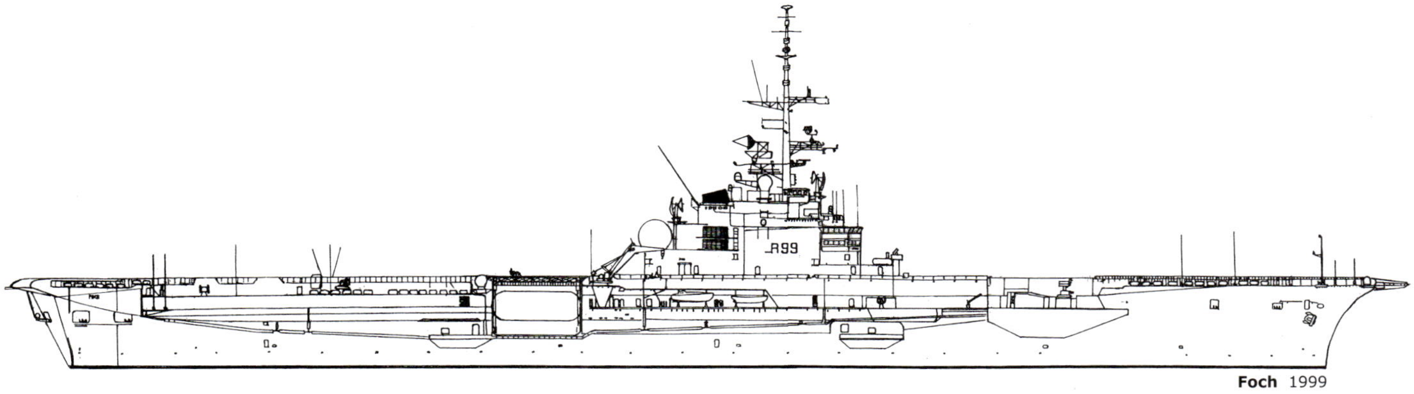

**Foch** 1966

**Foch** 1999

*(Drawn by Jean Moulin)*

The TR5 jet fuel was stowed in two groups of tanks with a total volume of 1180m$^3$ (1360m$^3$ at deep load). Each group comprised two stowage tanks, two feed tanks plus two decontamination tanks. There were two electrically driven pumps per group rated at 90m$^3$/h at 7.5kg/cm$^2$ for distribution, two 40m$^3$/h pumps for transfer and two water separators. Distribution was via collectors to port and starboard linked by transverse lines. *Clemenceau* had ten 40m$^3$/h distribution stations to starboard and four to port.

The avgas capacity of *Foch* had to be increased from 9m$^3$ to 109m$^3$ in 1965–66 prior to the embarkation of Sikorsky HSS helicopters. However, following the retirement of the helicopters in June 1979 there was no further need for avgas, and the TR5 jet fuel capacity was increased to approximately 2000m$^3$ in both carriers.

**Air Ordnance**

A total of 1,300 tonnes of air ordnance could be embarked: on completion *Clemenceau* had no fewer

**Left:** An Aquilon jet fighter of 16F in the early navy blue livery of the *Aéronavale* in 1959. *(ARDHAN collection)*

## Table 3: MAJOR REFITS AND MODIFICATIONS

All the major refits involved refurbishment of the catapults and the propulsion machinery. The modifications are listed below:

***Clemenceau***

15 Jan–4 Mar 1960: installation of DRBI 10 and DRBV 20 radars, together with a signals bridge.
1 May–7 Jul 1960: fitting of eight 100mm guns; embarkation of 1,295 tonnes of ballast.
15 Jun–15 Nov 1961: installation of workshop for air-launched missiles, together with SQS-53 sonar; replacement of DRBV 22 radar by DRBV 23.
10 Aug 1963–17 Mar 1964: major refit.
1 Jan 1966–10 Jan 1967: major refit: removal of ballast and fitting of bulges; installation of bridle catchers for catapults and new jet blast deflectors.
23 May 1969–15 Mar 1970: IPER; refurbishment of boilers; replacement of DRBC 31D by DRBC 32A on two main FC directors.
13 Jul 1977–22 Nov 1978: refit and modernisation: mast raised; magazine for AN 52 tactical nuclear bomb; installation of SENIT 2 (from *Jauréguiberry*) and inertial navigation centre for Super Etendard strike fighter; two new auxiliary boilers and modifications to accommodation to match new ranking system.
17 Dec 1979–3 May 1980: IPER: adaptations for AM 39 Exocet ASM; Telemir installation for SUE.
3 Sep 1985–28 Oct 1986: IPER and modernisation: replacement of four 100mm guns and main FC directors (TT) by Crotale (starboard fwd, port aft) and DRBV 20 by DRBV 15; installation of new EW outfit with Sagaie decoy launchers and ARBR 16 ESM; installation of SPIN; replacement of DRBC 31D by DRBC 32A on two light FC directors (TR); fitted for Syracuse satcom; reinforcement of lifts and removal of sonar.
16 May 1989–17 Nov 1989: IPER; positions of DRBV 15 and DRBV 23 radars reversed.
21 Jun–23 Aug 1993: adaptations for ASMP missile; fitting of AIDCOMER command system.
24 Sep 1994–28 Jun 1995: IPER: installation of FltSatCom.

***Foch***

22 Feb 1965–12 Feb 1966: modifications for F-8E Crusader, including bridle catchers.
4 Apr 1967–17 May 1968: major refit.
19 Apr 1971–15 May 1972: major refit: replacement of DRBC 31D by DRBC 32C on two main FC directors.
Sep 1975–3 May 1976: IPER: modifications to catapults; refurbishment of accommodation.
19 Feb–24 Aug 1979: IPER.
15 Jul 1980–15 Aug 1981: major refit and modernisation: mast raised; magazine for AN 52 tactical nuclear bomb; installation of SENIT 2 (from *Tartu*) and two inertial navigation centres for SUE; two new auxiliary boilers; reinforcement of catapults and arrester cables.
24 Aug 1983–30 Mar 1984: IPER: Syracuse satcom installed.
1 Mar 1987–1 Jun 1988: IPER & modernisation: replacement of four 100mm guns & main FC directors (TT) by Crotale (starboard fwd, port aft) and DRBV 20 by DRBV 15; installation of new EW outfit with Sagaie decoy launchers and ARBR 16 ESM; SNTI; replacement of DRBC 31D by DRBC 32A on two light FC directors (TR); reblading of turbines and removal of sonar.
4 Feb–19 Jul 1991: IPER: installation of SPIN.
29 Mar 1992–15 Mar 1993: IPER: replacement of LP turbines; modifications for Rafale trials; installation of FltSatCom and AIDCOMER.
5 Feb 1996–31 Jul 1997: IPER: replacement of remaining four 100mm by SADRAL; installation of Syracuse II; removal of asbestos; replacement of steam collectors.

than twenty magazines in two groups fore and aft of the machinery spaces, served by twelve lifts. Each of the two groupings had upper and lower bomb lifts, with transfer at the level of the First Deck, and separate lifts for rockets and cartridge ammunition.

On *Clemenceau* the upper bomb lifts emerged to port of the forward aircraft lift and directly abaft the after lift (see flight deck plan). The lifts were manufactured by Sautter-Harlé; they measured 3.8m x 1.1m and could raise ordnance 2.5m at 0.6m/sec. The length of the lifts was limited by the 4-metre distance between the frames, but this had to be increased to 5.5m between 1978 and 1981 to enable them to handle the new generation of air-launched missiles.

Nuclear weapons were embarked from 1978. The AN 52 900kg gravitational bomb needed special handling arrangements and limited the number of conventional bombs carried. It would later be replaced by the ASMP air-to-ground missile.

When the Super Etendard was embarked in the late 1970s, stowage for the associated AM 39 Exocet missile was considered insufficient, and it was decided that additional missiles would be stowed externally in airtight canisters on the gun sponsons.

## AIR GROUP

*Clemenceau* and *Foch* were originally designed to operate sixty aircraft, but aircraft became larger and heavier during build, and the air group when they commissioned comprised thirty-four to thirty-six fixed-wing aircraft plus two helicopters for plane guard duties. Capacity was also reduced by the reassignment of the forward part of the hangar to stow large items. This led to some discussion about reducing the number of different types of aircraft to be embarked.

The capability of the new carriers would be limited by the capability of their embarked aircraft, which was in turn limited by the comparatively low displacement and light construction of the ships, and also by the limited funding available for specially adapted carrier aircraft. Only the US Navy can be said to have anticipated the increase in size and weight of modern jet aircraft during the post-war period, building 'super-carriers' that could comfortably operate jets (and large turboprop aircraft such as the E-2 Hawkeye) with all-up weights in excess of 25 tonnes and high landing speeds. The *Aéronautique navale*, on the other hand, had to purchase (or build under licence) foreign aircraft with moderate weights and dimensions, or

## Table 4: EMBARKED AIRCRAFT

### Aquilon

French variant of British Sea Venom built under licence by SNCASE. Five prototypes (01–05) followed by 96 production models:

- 25 Mk 20 2-seat trainer (1–25) – not fitted for carrier landing
- 25 Aquilon 202 with R/F (26–50)
- 40 Aquilon 203 all-weather fighter with APQ-65 + FC computer (51–90)
- 6 Aquilon 204 2-seat trainer night fighter (91–96)

Characteristics:

| | |
|---|---|
| Type | single-seat fighter |
| Weight | 6820kg fully loaded |
| Dimensions | 11.14m(L) x 13.07m(S) x 2.31/3.00m(H) |
| Performance | powered by Ghost 103 turbojet; 960km/h at 15,000m; 420nm radius |
| Armament | 4 x 20mm Hispano HS 404 cannon, later 8 x 5in rockets, then Nord 513 AAMs *or* AS 20 ASM + 2 x Matra R.511 AAM |

| | |
|---|---|
| Flotille 11F | 1955–62 |
| Flotille 16F | 1955–64 |

### Bréguet Br.1050 Alizé

Evolved from the post-war Br 965, a specialised ASW aircraft that worked in pairs: one for detection, the other for attack. The Alizé was designed for both roles. The prototype flew 5 Oct 1956. Followed by 87 production aircraft of which 75 for the *Aéronavale* + 12 for Indian Navy. First flight Mar 1959. Thirty aircraft modified to ALM standard with upgraded electronics 1978–83. Fifteen aircraft further modified to ALH standard for airborne early warning (AEW) 1995–96.

Characteristics:

| | |
|---|---|
| Type | 3/4-seater ASW aircraft (pilot, navigator, radar op + spare seat); later used for AEW |
| Weight | 8200kg fully loaded |
| Dimensions | 13.86m(L) x 15.60m(S) x 5.00m(H) |
| Performance | turboprop, powered by RR Dart 21; 435km/h upwards at ground level; cruise speed 250–380km/h; 4h 45 in flight for total range 685nm |
| Electronics | DRAA 2A radar + various receivers/interrogators/detectors; 14 sonobuoys |
| Armament | 5 x DC (3 in weapons bay, 2 underwing); also bombs and rockets; Mk 43>44>46 A/S torpedo *or* 2 x AS 12 ASM |

| | |
|---|---|
| Flotille 6F | 1959–2000 |
| Flotille 4F | 1960–97 |
| Flotille 9F | 1960–72 |

### Dassault Etendard IVM

Designed to meet requirement for light strike fighter to replace US Corsair F4U-7. Pre-series of 5 (02–06) ordered 31 May 1957. Followed by 69 production aircraft delivered Dec 1961–May 1965.

Characteristics:

| | |
|---|---|
| Type | single-seat strike fighter |
| Weight | 10,800kg max catapult launch |
| Dimensions | 14.35m(L) x 9.60m(S) x 3.85m(H) |
| Performance | powered by SNECMA Atar 8C turbojet without afterburner; 1100km/h (Mach 1.3); range 980nm |
| Electronics | DRAA 2A radar + various receivers/interrogators/detectors |
| Armament | 2 x DEFA 30mm cannon, 2 x Sidewinder AIM-9B (later Matra R.550 Magic); 1300kg bombs on hardpoints, 2 x Matra rocket pods, 2 x Nord AS 20 ASM (later AS 30) |

| | |
|---|---|
| Flotille 15F | Jan 1962–Jan 1979 |
| Flotille 11F | Apr 1963–Sep 1978 |
| Flotille 17F | Jun 1964–Jun 1980 |

Not equipped for all-weather combat and limited capability at night; could be refuelled in air; single engine had no back-up. Replaced from 1978 by Super Etendard.

### Dassault Etendard IVP

Reconnaissance variant of above: cannon replaced by CER 10 chassis with three cameras; could also embark container with 3 more cameras externally. Total of 21 delivered Oct 1962–May 1965.

Flotille 16F May 1964–Jul 2000

To compensate for attrition of IVP, four IVM converted 1977–79. Last five aircraft retired Jul 2000; replaced by modified Super Etendard.

### Vought F-8E Crusader

Replacement for Aquilon. Trials with two US aircraft from *Clemenceau* Mar 1962; contract signed 31 Jul 1963 for 40 x 8E variant + 6 x 2-seat trainers built to French requirements: F-8E (FN). Two-seat version abandoned by US Navy so order modified to 42 single-seat. Order arrived from USA in two batches: 13 on *Arromanches* Oct 1964, 28 on *Foch* Feb 1965. Final machine – first completed and used for trials USA – arrived on USS *Forrestal* Sep 1965.

Characteristics:

| | |
|---|---|
| Type | all-weather interceptor |
| Weight | 13,000kg max catapult launch |
| Dimensions | 16.61m(L) x 10.72m(S) x 4.80m(H) |
| Performance | powered by Pratt & Whitney J57-P-20A with afterburner; 2220km/h (Mach 1.8); range 1500nm (2.5hrs) |
| Electronics | AWG-4 FC comprising Magnavox AN/APQ-104 + AN/AAS 15 infrared detector + gyroscopic sight and computers |
| Armament | 4 x 20mm Colt-Browning cannon, 2 x Sidewinder 1A (>1986) *or* Matra R.530 (1965–91) radar/infrared *or* R.550 Magic (1979>) infrared AAMs |

| | |
|---|---|
| Flotille 12F | Oct 1964–1999 |
| Flotille 14F | Mar 1965–Apr 1979 |

Variable-incidence wing to permit supersonic speed in flight with lowered speed on landing. Speed on take-off reduced by 9% in FN model (180km/h) by varying incidence of wing (5°>7°) and providing Boundary Layer Control (BLC) – air blown onto upper surfaces. Refuelled in air. Seventeen Crusaders underwent life extension refurbishment 1991–96 (F-8P; 'P' = *Prolongé*); some updates to avionics.

### Dassault Super Etendard (SUE)

After investigating the possibility of purchasing the US Navy Skyhawk or A-7 Corsair and a navalised version of the Sepecat Jaguar (Jaguar M), the Navy opted for a modification of the Dassault Etendard with a new engine and upgraded avionics. First flight of a modified IVM took place on 28 October 1974, first flight of a series model 24 November 1977. Planned total of 100 aircraft was reduced to 71, together with 14 for Argentina. Production ended in 1982.

Characteristics:

| | |
|---|---|
| Type | single-seat strike aircraft |
| Weight | 12,000kg max catapult launch |
| Dimensions | 14.31m(L) x 9.60m(S) x 3.85m(H) |
| Performance | powered by SNECMA Atar 8K-50 turbojet; 1200km/h (Mach 1.3); range 850nm (2h 15min) |
| Electronics | Thomson-CSF Agave radar with UAT-90 computer + various receivers/interrogators/detectors |
| Armament | 2 x DEFA cannon, 2100kg ordnance, 4 x LR 130 *or* 1 x AM 39 ASM |

| | |
|---|---|
| Flotille 11F | Sep 1978–2012 |
| Flotille 14F | Jun 1979–1991 |
| Flotille 17F | Sep 1980–2016 |

Twenty-four aircraft fitted to launch AN 52 nuclear bomb, operational Jan 1981–late 1991 (later ASMP missile). Fifty-four modernised to SEM standard 1991–98: new Anémone radar + ATLIS laser. Half of these modernised to S3 standard with AS 30 laser from 1998. Further S4 upgrade Dec 2000 onwards. Eight CRM 280 pods ordered to permit SEM S4 to conduct recce missions as replacement for Etendard IVP.

alternatively adapt small combat aircraft in service with the French Air Force.

The first jet strike fighter embarked was the Aquilon, a French adaptation of the British Sea Venom (see Table 4 for data). The Aquilon entered service with the *Aéronautique navale* at about the same time that the Sea Venom was being superseded in the Royal Navy by the larger, heavier and more capable Sea Vixen. It was complemented by the Bréguet Alizé, a large turboprop anti-submarine aircraft similar in conception to the Royal Navy's Fairey Gannet, equipped with radar, ESM detectors, sonobuoys, depth charges and A/S torpedoes. The Alizé was a successful machine, and remained in service (following a number of upgrades to its weaponry and avionics) until the year 2000.

The requirement for a light tactical strike fighter proved more difficult to meet. A Dassault model intermediate in size between the Mystère and Mirage land-based aircraft was developed as the Etendard IVM, and was delivered between December 1961 and May 1965. An Etendard IVP variant had its cannon replaced by a CER 10 chassis with three cameras, and was employed for photo reconnaissance. This lightweight, single-engine aircraft was not equipped for all-weather combat and had a limited night capability. Deployment was delayed following a series of four accidents, three of which were fatal, during 1963–64. It was planned to replace the Etendard with a navalised variant of the Jaguar, but this was abandoned after two years of trials. It would eventually be superseded by the Super Etendard, which was essentially an upgraded Etendard with a more powerful engine and superior avionics.

The Aquilon was already obsolescent after only two years in service, and various foreign aircraft were considered as replacements. The US McDonnell Douglas F-4 Phantom was too large and heavy to operate from *Clemenceau* and *Foch*, and following trials with two F-8 Crusader interceptors on *Clemenceau*, a contract was signed with Vought on 31 July 1963 for forty F-8E aircraft built to French requirements plus six two-seat trainers. When development of the latter was abandoned the order was increased to forty-two single-seat aircraft, to be designated F-8E (FN). The French variant incorporated a variable-incidence wing to permit supersonic speed in flight with a lowered speed on landing. Speed on take-off was reduced to 180km/h by varying the incidence of the wing and by providing Boundary Layer Control (BLC) – air blown onto the upper surfaces. The

**Above:** A Bréguet Alizé turboprop ASW aircraft of 59S about to be catapulted. *(René Bail)*

**Right:** A Bréguet Alizé anti-submarine aircraft of 4F at Landivisiau on 19 June 1988. *(Jean Moulin)*

Crusader was longer and heavier than the Etendard IV, and its operation required the fitting of bridle catchers and modification of the blast deflection plates, which were undertaken during 1965–67.

The Crusader was successful in service, but finding a replacement was to prove problematic. The French considered buying the F/A-18 Hornet from 1978, but this proposal was abandoned in 1989 in favour of the French-built Dassault Rafale, which was then delayed. Seventeen Crusaders therefore underwent a limited life extension refurbishment during 1991–96 and were redesignated F-8P (P = *Prolongé*).

## B: SERVICE HISTORY

### *CLEMENCEAU*: TRIALS AND WORK-UP

As the first of class and the first of a new type of warship, *Clemenceau* underwent extensive trials of her machinery and other systems from September 1959. Her first commanding officer was Captain (CV) Lorain, who headed a crew initially of 500 officers and men.

The after catapult was tested with dummy aircraft between 4 and 15 November. The ship was due to sail for the first time during the second half of November, but Lorain was keen to leave the dockyard at the first opportunity, and decided not to wait until the guns and certain radars were fitted in order to gain time. On 16 November *Clemenceau* cast off from the fitting-out quay and moored to a buoy in the inner roads. Her machinery was fired up for her static trials the following day.

The first deck landings took place on 23 November: two Alouette helicopters that landed on at 0900 were followed by a third at 1100 with the President of the Trials Commission, Admiral Robert Barthélémy, on board. *Clemenceau* duly cast off at 1400 with both engines slow ahead. There was a near-collision at the harbour entrance with a sand hopper barge, which passed under her bow. The carrier then headed out to sea.

This first sortie lasted four days. Speed was increased around 1900 and the ship remained at half power for the next twenty-four hours, before power was increased first to 80,000cv, then 100,000cv, then 115,000cv. *Clemenceau* sustained a power ratng of 114,310cv for ten hours – the contract stipulated only 110,000cv. She moored overnight at Groix (25/26) and Morgat (26/27), returning to Brest at 1425 on the

**Below:** An F-8E Crusader interceptor on *Clemenceau* during the late 1960s. *(ARDHAN collection)*

27th. A large part of the machinery trials had taken place at night to avoid fishing boats in the area between Penmarc'h and Lorient. She was then docked until 5 December.

Preliminary trials were completed on 11 December, when 126,000cv were recorded. The official trials then followed, with a seven-hour full-power trial followed by two hours with forced draught. The trial took place on the Penmarc'h–Guilvinec course, and a maximum speed of 33.40 knots was attained. However, on the morning of the 18th, when running at a speed of 28 knots off Groix in heavy seas, the forward part of the ship plunged into the waves and green seas swept the forward end of the flight deck, causing damage to watertight hatches and minor flooding. The ship also showed a tendency to excessive heel when turning. This led to further basin tests of a model from 30 December to 2 January 1960. The issues were resolved by reinforcement of the bow plating and the embarkation of fixed ballast during a two-month spell in the dockyard from May to July (see below).

Machinery trials continued on 5–10 January, but the ship was then immobilised at Brest for a visual inspection of her machinery and for the completion of her aviation installations. The DRBV 20 long-range air search radar and the two antennae for the DRBI 10 height-finding and tracking radar were embarked between 1 February and 7 March. *Clemenceau* then commissioned (*armement définitif*) on 18 March, putting to sea the same day and again on the 22nd with the fleet escort *Surcouf*.

The first deck landing took place on 25 March, when Alizé No 3, piloted by LV Michel Mosneron-Dupin, made three 'touch-and-go' landings, followed one hour later by Alizé No 2. Both aircraft were in the hangar when the (seawater) spray system was inadvertently activated, and the aircraft had to be washed down with fresh water and their systems checked.

*Clemenceau* returned to Brest the following day, and left port again on the 29th, accompanied by *Surcouf*, for aircraft trials which took place over the next five days off south Finisterre, within range of the naval air base at Lann-Bihoué. There were forty-nine catapult launches and fifty deck landings by Alizé ASW aircraft, and the first landing of an Aquilon jet fighter, by the commander of 11F, LV Gaultier de la Ferrière, took place on 30 March. Further trials followed during 4–9 April, when two Fouga Zéphir jet trainers made their first landings.

A cut-out in the turboprop fuelling system resulted in the loss of Alizé No 2 on 6 April as the aircraft left the catapult. It touched down on the water 150 metres from the carrier, and the two crewmen were rescued by the HUP-2 helicopter. The aircraft ended up on the bottom at a depth of 100 metres. While attempting to locate it 10nm south of Groix in fog,

Above: *Clemenceau* during one of her many inclining trials. Initial stability problems in the light condition were resolved first by the embarkation of permanent lead ballast in the double bottom, and subsequently by the fitting of bulges. *(René Bail collection)*

Opposite, top: *Clemenceau* during her aircraft trials. She has now received flight deck markings, with the angled deck prominent. She would retain these markings, albeit with some later additions, throughout her service life. *(DR)*

Opposite, bottom: The first landing of an Alizé on board *Clemenceau* in March 1960. *(DR)*

*Surcouf* was in collision with the cargo ship *Léognan* and had to put into Lorient. The foggy weather caused a temporary suspension of the trials, and *Clemenceau* returned to Brest from 9 to 11 April, putting to sea again on 12–15 and 19–22 April. On 21 April she returned to Brest roads to embark the Armed Forces Minister, Pierre Messmer, who spent the following twenty-four hours on board. The carrier returned to Brest at 0835 on the 23rd, having conducted 77 catapult launches for the Alizé, 162 for the Aquilon and 64 for the Zéphyr.

Final fitting-out work and modifications resulting from trials followed from 1 May to 7 July. The eight 100mm gun mountings were finally installed, and 1,295 tonnes of lead ballast was set in concrete in the double bottom; there was also some lightening of the upperworks, particularly the framework of the hangar roof. A SAGEM optical landing aid was put in place abaft the island. A failure of the catapult on the angled deck on 9 July meant that it would not be operational until October. A heeling trial took place with the ship moored at a buoy on 19 July, and the ship was then docked again until 1 August.

*Clemenceau* left Brest for further trials off Groix on 3 August and proceeded to conduct training for the pilots and personnel of 4F (Alizé) and 16F (Aquilon). The first night-time catapult launches and deck landings took place on 9 August, including the first night-time landing by an Aquilon of 16F, piloted by Mosneron-Dupin.

The carrier was back at Brest from 21 August to 5 September, then left to embark ten Alizé of 4F and seven Aquilon of 16F, returning on the 7th. While moored in the inner harbour at Brest she landed an Alouette II, three HUP-2 and three H-19D helicopters. President Charles de Gaulle dined on board, then disembarked by motor boat. Further trials off Lorient followed, which focused on the calibration of the radars. The first deck landing by one of the new Etendard IVM strike fighters took place on 18 September, when prototype 02 was piloted by LV Jean-Pierre Murgue. The ship finally returned to Brest on 24 September, having completed 141 catapult launches of the Alizé, 117 with the Aquilon and 21 with the Etendard, all using the forward catapult. The catapult on the angled deck was now repaired and tested on 13–14 October.

*Clemenceau* left Brest again on 22 October for an operational evaluation off North Africa. The Alizés of 4F were embarked then, off Bizerte, thirteen Aquilon of 11F. The ship moored at Bizerte on the evening of the 26th. A failed arrested landing led to the loss of an Aquilon over the bow, although the pilot was rescued. The ship arrived in Toulon on 29 October, and personnel from ORTF (the French national broadcasting service) embarked to make a TV programme about the ship. She left on 2 November, mooring off Les Salins overnight. A rehearsal took place on the 5th and filming was on the 6th, involving eight Aquilon, four Alizé and the fleet escort *Maillé Brézé*. The ship then returned to Toulon, and trials with the Etendard IVM resumed in November, ending with a catapult launch of aircraft 02 off Marseille. Further trials took place in December, during which an HUP-2 helicopter was damaged on take-off, and the ship returned on 16 December for Christmas in Toulon.

After routine activity in early 1961, *Clemenceau*

## Table 5: NAVAL AIR SQUADRONS 1961–2000

| Squadron | Aircraft | In service | Bases |
|---|---|---|---|
| 4F | Alizé | Feb 60–Jun 97 | Hyères[1] > Lann-Bihoué[1] |
| 6F | Alizé | Oct 59–Sep 2000 | Hyères > Nîmes-Garons |
| 9F | Alizé | Sep 60–Jul 72 | Hyères > Lann-Bihoué |
| 11F | Aquilon | Apr 55–Apr 62 | Karouba |
| | Etendard IVM | Apr 63–1978 | Hyères > Landivisiau[1] |
| | Super Etendard | Sep 78–2012 | Landivisiau |
| 12F | Crusader | Oct 64–Dec 99 | Lann-Bihoué > Landivisiau |
| 14F | Crusader | Mar 65–1979 | Lann-Bihoué > Landivisiau |
| | Super Etendard | Jun 79–Jul 91 | Landivisiau |
| 15F | Etendard IVM | Jun 62–Jan 69 | Hyères > Landivisiau |
| 16F | Aquilon | Jan 55–Apr 64 | Hyères |
| | Etendard IVP | May 64–Jul 2000 | Hyères > Landivisiau |
| 17F | Etendard IVM | Jun 64–1980 | Hyères |
| | Super Etendard | Sep 80–2016 | Hyères > Landivisiau |
| 31F | HSS (ASW) | Feb 60–1979 | Algeria > Saint-Mandrier |
| | Lynx | Dec 78–Jun 10 | |
| 32F | HSS (ASW) | Feb 58–Jan 70 | Algeria > Saint-Mandrier > Lanvéoc |
| | Super Frelon[2] | Jan 70–Jan 10 | Lanvéoc |
| 33F | HSS (Assault) | Jun 57–Jun 79 | Algeria > Saint-Raphaël > Saint-Mandrier |
| | Super Frelon[3] | Jun 79–Oct 99 | Lanvéoc |

**Note:**

1 Hyères was the naval air base for Toulon, Lann-Bihoué for Lorient, and Landivisiau and Lanvéoc for Brest.

2 The Super Frelon helicopters of 32F were initially for ASW then, from 1981, for assault.

3 The Super Frelon helicopters of 33F were initially for assault then, from the 1990s, for SAR.

departed on 31 January for a cruise to the Western Mediterranean and French West Africa. She had on board Admiral Jean Philippon, senior officer for the carriers and embarked aviation (ALPA), and Squadrons 4F and 16F (twelve Aquilon), and was accompanied by the carrier *La Fayette*, the cruiser *Colbert* and twelve escorts. After port visits to Mers el-Kébir and Las Palmas, she arrived at Dakar on 14 February, then took part in Exercise 'Harmattan D'. When 90nm off Monrovia on 20 February an Aquilon had a wing aileron damaged by the catapult bridle on launch and had to be halted by the net barrier on landing – the only time the barrier was deployed during the service life of *Clemenceau* and *Foch*.

After the exercise concluded, *Clemenceau* returned to Brest, where she underwent contractual checks. An SQS-503 sonar was fitted, and the DRBV 22 air surveillance radar embarked as a temporary measure was replaced by the more advanced DRBV 23. The forward part of the hangar was converted into a workshop for air-launched missiles, and the planned NBC washdown system for the superstructures was installed. The official completion date for the ship (*clôture d'armement*) was 15 September.

*Clemenceau* put to sea on 18 September, escorted by the fleet escort *Du Chayla*, for final trials of her aviation equipment, sonar and guns, with overnight moorings at Groix. Trials, which included a stability trial and qualifications for the pilots of 11F and 16F, continued throughout the autumn, and the ship returned to Brest on 18 November. *Clemenceau* officially entered service on 22 November, then left for Toulon on the 24th. She arrived on the 29th, having hoisted the flag of Rear Admiral Francis Lainé the previous day. Routine activity along the coast of Provence followed in December.

**Right:** An Aquilon jet fighter is about to engage one of the four arrester wires on *Clemenceau* in 1962. *(ECPAD)*

**Left:** Landing of the Aquilon of LV Borney on *Clemenceau* on 20 February 1961, the only landing that required the barrier net. *(Borney)*

**Left:** *Clemenceau* visiting Hamburg in 1962. In the background is the AA cruiser *Colbert. (Leo van Ginderen collection)*

## MEDITERRANEAN SQUADRON 1962–65

From 10 January 1962, *Clemenceau* made three two/four-day sorties from Toulon with Squadrons 9F (Alizé), 16F (Aquilon) and 31F (HSS helicopters) embarked, then took part in NATO Exercise 'Big Game' from 29 January to 3 February. Routine visits to the coasts of Provence followed and, on 7 March, test firings of the new Matra R.511 air-to-air missile took place using the Aquilon fighters of 16F.

On 15 March, *Clemenceau* left Toulon for landing trials with the American F8U-2N Crusader. The following day two Crusaders from VF-32 of USS *Saratoga* (CVA-60) completed ten landings and catapult launches, the ship mooring at Les Salins overnight; she returned to base on the 17th. On the 19th she left for NATO Exercise 'Dawn Patrol II'. She called in at Gibraltar on the outward and inward passage, and British Gannet and Sea Vixen aircraft were landed and catapulted from her flight deck. She returned to Toulon on 4 April.

On 4 May she left with the Squadron for the spring cruise, with Alizés and twelve Aquilon of 16F embarked. After moorings at Brest and Groix there were port visits to Le Havre, Rotterdam and Hamburg; the latter visit marked an important stage in Franco-German reconciliation. The carrier returned to Toulon via Brest on 13 June, putting to sea again on 18–20 June for Aquilon firing trials with the new AS.20 air-to-surface missile (similar in conception to the US AGM-12 Bullpup). She then underwent a brief docking in July.

On 1 August she headed for Mers el-Kébir to embark the helicopters of 33F, which she brought back to Toulon. She left again on 6 August with 4F, 9F and 31F embarked to take part in Exercise 'Rip Tide', which took her as far as Lisbon, returning on the 21st. During a sortie on 26 September, an Alizé was lost overboard when landing off Hyères; two of the four-man crew were rescued by the helicopter, but two were lost with the aircraft. On 1 October, two F4U-7 landed on the carrier for the first time.

Further aircraft and missile evaluation trials took place during October involving not only the Alizé turboprop aircraft of 4F and the Aquilon jet fighters of 16F, but also four Etendard IVM of 15F. It was determined that the operational capacity of *Clemenceau* was between thirty-six and forty aircraft, with eighteen of these normally parked on deck. On 20 November she was docked, spending the next two months in dockyard hands.

*Clemenceau* emerged from her maintenance period on 26 January 1963. After a brief sortie at the end of the month she departed Toulon on 11 February for a cruise in the tropics, with Squadrons 4F, 16F and 33F embarked. She visited Las Palmas, Dakar, Pointe Noire, Libreville, Port Etienne and Casablanca, and returned to her home base on 23 March.

Squadron 32F (HSS helicopters) was embarked during a short cruise from 27 April to 10 May, and on the latter date a US Navy Skyraider landed on board. *Clemenceau* then took part in Exercise 'Fair Game' with her regular air group. The Mediterranean Squadron's spring cruise followed, from 28 May to 5 June, punctuated by a port visit to Naples. There was routine activity in June, including a Families Day and firing trials with the Matra R.511 AAM. This would be the last time the Aquilon would be embarked. *Clemenceau* then entered the dockyard for a major refit, which lasted from August 1963 to March 1964.

Sonar trials with the Alizé were undertaken in May/June, and pilot qualifications for the newly formed 17F, which would operate the Etendard IVM strike fighter. *Clemenceau* was then the subject of a film (*Le Ciel sur la Tête*) during July. She left Toulon on 29 July and embarked a single squadron of Alizés and two of Etendards. A joint scene with her sister *Foch* involving NBC washdown led to a decision to separate training and filming in favour of the latter. *Clemenceau* then took part in a naval review on 15 August, during which President de Gaulle embarked in the new missile patrol boat *La Combattante*. The film crew finally disembarked on 19 August following a further brief sortie.

*Clemenceau* took part in Exercise 'Lavezzi 2' in October, and there was a port visit to La Spezia and moorings at Porto Vecchio and Ajaccio. She then took part in Exercise 'Libeccio', returning to Toulon on the 20th. There were air defence exercises supervised by the Fleet Training Centre (CEF) in November and December, with overnight moorings at Les Salins in order to economise on fuel. A mixed air group was found to pose problems, particularly with the folding of the helicopter rotors, which required speeds of less than 15 knots over the deck, and this formula would be abandoned, at least in the short term.

After a brief docking in January 1965, *Clemenceau* put to sea on 22 February for a cruise christened 'Lobis' with 31F, 33F and 4F and a commando battalion embarked. A helicopter assault was practised at Fuerteventura in the Canaries on 9–10 March. The ship then moored at Lanzarote, Las Palmas and Casablanca, returning to Toulon on 26 March.

On 28 April, *Clemenceau* left Toulon for the first deck landings of the French Crusader fighter, which involved three French and two American pilots. CC Dominique Lefebvre, flight commander of 12F, made the first landing. The ship returned to port on 6 May. She then made six sorties in May/June for work-up with Etendard and Alizé aircraft and, on occasion, the HSS helicopters of 31F. The first landing of the IVP reconnaissance variant of the Etendard, an aircraft piloted by CC Bernard Klotz (flight commander 16F), took place on 4 May.

From 17 to 26 May, *Clemenceau* took part in Exercise 'Fair Game', and from 10 to 12 June in Exercise 'Alligator' with *Arromanches* and *Jeanne d'Arc*. The exercises were followed by a visit to Palma de Mallorca on 18–21 June.

On 15 September 1965 there was a major reorganisation of the Atlantic and Mediterranean Squadrons. The *Groupe des porte-avions et aviation embarquée*, under ALPA, was attached to the Mediterranean Squadron. From 4 to 16 October *Clemenceau* took part in training Exercise 'Lavezzi 3' with the Squadron, which was followed by pilot qualifications for 12F (F-8E Crusader) and a port visit to Ajaccio in November. The ship departed Toulon for a major refit at Brest on 30 November, calling in at Lisbon on 3–6 December and arriving on the 11th.

## REFIT BREST 1966–67

The refit at Brest involved the following work:

- the installation of bridle catchers at the forward ends of the flight deck and angled deck

- the fitting of new jet blast deflectors
- fitting-out of an operational ready room for the pilots
- removal of 1,300 tonnes of ballast from the double bottom and the fitting of bulges similar to those in *Foch*.

*Clemenceau* did a heeling trial on 7 January 1967 and a static machinery trial on the 10th. She went to sea for the first time post-refit on the 19th, and conducted training with 4F (Alizé), 12F (Crusader) and 15F (Etendard IVM) until 3 March, then with 4F and 17F (Etendard IVM) from 6 to 17 March. On 2 March, an Etendard IVM of 11F was lost following a catapult launch; the pilot was rescued by the Alouette III plane guard helicopter. The ship finally left Brest on 10 April with 12F embarked, arriving at Toulon on the 16th. During an ALPA training session from 17 to 29 April she embarked a full complement of aircraft belonging to 9F, 12F, 15F and 16F (Etendard IVP). Although declared available following her major refit, *Clemenceau* remained quay-side for a CEFDAM air defence operation on 13 May, which continued at sea from 10 June with Squadrons 9F (Alizé), 12F, 15F and 16F embarked. She left Toulon for Brest with 12F on 12 June, arriving on the 17th after manoeuvres.

From 21 to 28 August, *Clemenceau* took part in Exercise 'Alligator III' off Côte d'Ivoire with 4F, 11F, 12F, 16F and 17F embarked. She was at Dakar on 6 September, covered an amphibious landing exercise at Monogaga from 10 to 15 September, and returned to Brest via Lisbon on 13 October. She left for Toulon without her air group, arriving 5 November, then

Above: *Clemenceau* being fitted with bulges to improve stability; the photo was taken at Toulon on 27 March 1966. *(SHD-M Toulon)*

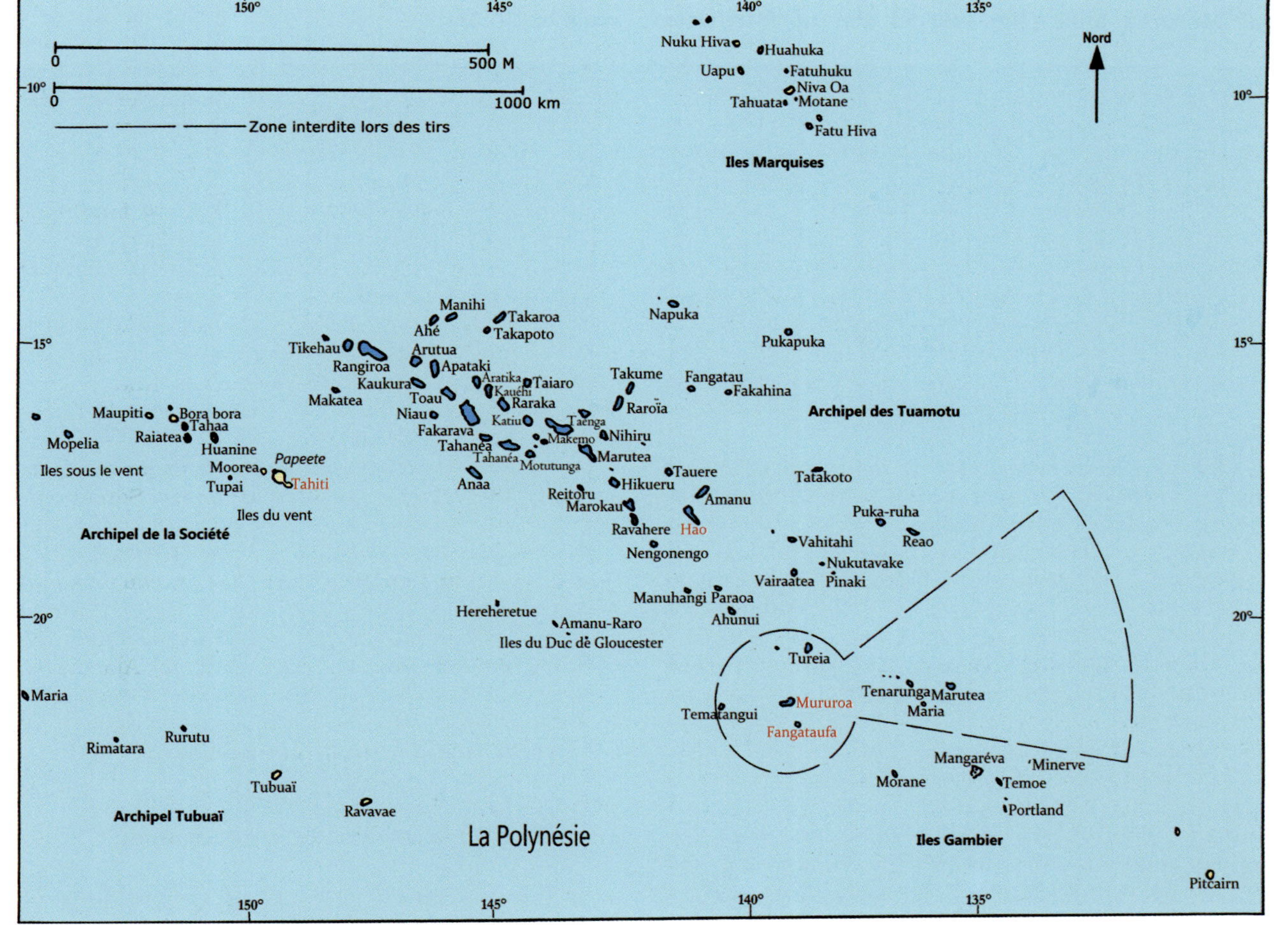


The area enclosed by the broken line marks the exclusion zone during the nuclear tests. *(Drawn by Jean Moulin)*

undertook qualifications and training for the pilots of 9F, 14F, 15F, 17F and 59S.

## THE FIRST CAMPAIGN IN POLYNESIA

Following a short refit over Christmas, *Clemenceau* left Toulon on 29 January 1968 to help in the search for the submarine *Minerve*, with which contact had been lost on 27 January; she had Squadrons 31F and 33F embarked.

The ship had been designated flagship of 'Force Alfa', tasked with policing the French nuclear tests in Polynesia, and she now embarked the air group for the coming campaign: Squadrons 9F, 17F, 31F and 22S. The first of four large Super Frelon helicopters landed on 7 February. *Clemenceau* departed for the Far East on 12 March. Force Alfa was to comprise the fleet escorts *Forbin*, *La Bourdonnais* and *Jauréguiberry* and the fleet tanker *La Seine*, which accompanied the carrier to Polynesia. They would be joined by the support ships *Le Rhin* and *Aber Wrac'h*, which proceeded independently.

On 20 April, when the force was crossing the Indian Ocean, an Etendard IVP reconnaissance aircraft was lost 130nm from the carrier as a result of engine failure; the pilot was rescued by helicopter after forty minutes in the water. *Clemenceau* finally arrived at Nouméa on 6 May, remaining there until the 11th. On 16 May she disembarked the Super Frelon helicopters of 27S at Hao, and headed for Tahiti, mooring at Vairao to the south from 18 May. Some of the Alizé and Etendard aircraft were flown off to the Tahiti-Faa air base, and the helicopters of 22S were likewise disembarked, leaving only a detachment for plane guard duties.

Force Alfa left Tahiti on 10 June and was stationed off Mururoa atoll. The first of the nuclear tests ('Capella') took place on 7 July, the second ('Castor') on the 15th and the third ('Pollux') on 3 August. The 24th marked the first 'H'-bomber drop, at Fangataufa, using a balloon, and the last test of the campaign ('Procyon') took place at Mururoa on 8 September. Between the tests *Clemenceau* returned to her moorings at Vairao.

She left, accompanied by *La Seine*, on 16 October. Force Alfa was accompanied by the tanker *Isère* until the 23rd. It passed Cape Horn on the 30th, then engaged in pre-planned manoeuvres, first with the Argentine Navy then with the Brazilians. *Clemenceau* then headed for Gabon, which was being threatened by Nigeria. Following an aerial demonstration of force, she rejoined her three escorts south of Abidjan, exercised with the officer training ship *Jeanne d'Arc* on 4 December, and visited Dakar on 5–6 December. Force Alfa returned to Toulon on 12 December and the air squadrons were disembarked. *Clemenceau* left Toulon on 19 December for a short refit at Brest, which lasted until 4 February 1969.

## ATLANTIC 1969–72

Following her refit *Clemenceau* was attached to the *Groupe des porte-avions*, which was then incorporated into the Atlantic Squadron. She departed Brest on 7 February with 4F, 6F (both Alizé), 32F, 33F and 23S (helicopters) embarked for the Squadron's winter cruise. She called in at Madeira, then Las Palmas, and took part in Exercise 'Atlantide' from 25 to 28 February. She was at Toulon on 3 March for pilot qualifications with 59S, 4F and 6F, returning to Brest with a reduced crew and without her air group on 27 March for a major refit that would begin on 23 May. In the interim she experienced a fire in the after boiler room on 24 April.

**Right:** Catapult launch of an Etendard IVP. On 5 October, one of *Clemenceau*'s aircraft achieved a record flight time of three hours six minutes. *(Marine Nationale)*

Left: A prototype Jaguar M strike aircraft lands on *Clemenceau*. The first trials took place during July 1970. *(Marine Nationale)*

The refit involved the replacement of both propellers, major work in the boiler rooms, maintenance checks on the catapults, and the replacement of the original DRBC 31D GFCS radars by two DRBC 32A. She also received a Sippican bathythermograph, and the platform for the landing officer was relocated farther aft.

Her complement was at full (peacetime) strength on 1 February 1970, and *Clemenceau* engaged in the customary trials and work-up, which included night qualifications for Etendard and Crusader pilots. On 1 April an Etendard IVP was lost during a catapult launch when the ejector seat activated prematurely; the pilot was rescued by helicopter. During May the ship took part in Exercises 'Goéland' and 'Datex'.

*Clemenceau* left Brest with the Squadron on 1 June for the spring cruise to the North and Norwegian Seas, with visits to Rotterdam and Oslo. She returned to Brest 20 June for a 'Families Day', then underwent a short docking. From 8 to 13 July she conducted trials with the prototype Jaguar M (M = Marine), which was being considered for the tactical support role, off Lorient. A total of twelve landings and catapult launches involving three different pilots were made.

*Clemenceau* sailed again on 28 September and operated off Brittany and the Bay of Biscay. On 5 October an Etendard IVP achieved a record flight time of three hours six minutes. However, there were two accidents involving Crusaders during this period. On 7 October a Crusader of 14F had a complete loss of power during a night qualification and the pilot had to be rescued by the fleet escort *Du Chayla*. Then, during the evening of 22 October, a Crusader of 12F struck the after edge of the flight deck on landing. The pilot ejected and was rescued by the fleet escort *Kersaint*, but when the carrier returned to Brest the following day the rear end of the aircraft was still in place, welded to the after edge.

During a training exercise from 1 to 6 November the Crusaders of 12F and 14F were tasked with intercepting a Mirage IV supersonic strategic bomber. The year ended with further exercises with the aircraft of 6F, 9F, 11F and 12F.

*Clemenceau* was active again from 31 January 1971, when she left Brest for exercises off Toulon. She took part in joint manoeuvres by the Mediterranean and Atlantic Squadrons in the Bay of Biscay from 24 February and provided assistance to two British tankers in difficulties in early March. She returned to Brest on 13 March, then put to sea for Exercises 'Finisterex' and 'Toucan 5'. A short refit followed from 29 March to 12 May. On 18 May, four Etendard IVM conducted a firing exercise off Lorient against a towed target; one of the aircraft experienced an engine failure and the pilot had to eject. A second Etendard IV was lost off Hyères during pilot qualifications on 2 June, when the aircraft struck the surface when turning sharply after a 'wave-off' and the pilot, who was making his first landing, was lost.

The carrier was back in Toulon two days later, and put to sea on 11 June with twenty-four Etendard, six Crusader and six Alizé embarked for Exercise 'Méditex 71'. On 19 June, President Georges Pompidou embarked on *Clemenceau* for a naval review off Toulon. The ship then left for Brest, arriving on the 26th. She departed again for Toulon on 15 October for further trials with the Jaguar M in the Gulf of Lion, when the two pilots performed catapult launches and landings; the carrier returned to Brest on 5 November.

On 22 November, *Clemenceau* left for the autumn cruise off West Africa. When in the Bay of Douarnenez she embarked Squadrons 4F, 12F, 14F, 16F, 17F and 23S. Two Crusaders were catapulted off on the 23rd and landed at Dakar having been refuelled in flight.

They were joined the following day by some twenty Etendard. These aircraft were re-embarked on the 26th, shortly before the ship's arrival at Dakar. *Clemenceau* returned to Brest on 17 December after a short stay in Las Palmas. The large radome protecting the approach radar had been damaged by a refuelling rig on the tanker *La Saône* on the 11th.

In January and February 1972, Crusader and Alizé aircraft were catapulted off while the ship was moored at Brest. On 9 February, an Alizé that was being catapulted from the angled deck struck a second Alizé on the forward catapult while it was deploying its wings; the latter aircraft, which suffered a jammed aileron, had to make a forced landing at Lann-Bihoué.

On 17 February, *Clemenceau* left with the Squadron for a winter cruise to West Africa. She then transited the Strait of Gibraltar to take part in Exercise 'Petit Liré' with ships of the Mediterranean Squadron. After the completion of the exercise, she embarked 1,300 men of the 11th Parachute Division, Marine commandos, and the helicopters of 32F and 33F at Toulon, and took part in Exercise 'Frégate' off the northern coast of Corsica, in which troops were landed in the Désert des Agriates. She returned to Toulon on 10 March, and proceeded on to Brest, arriving on the 16th.

On 16 May, *Clemenceau* put to sea with the Atlantic Squadron for its spring cruise, with eight Crusader F-8E of 14F, twelve Etendard IVM of 17F, six Etendard IVM of 11F, four Etendard IVP of 16F, and ten Alizé of 4F embarked (a total of forty aircraft). There were port visits to Hamburg, Kristiansand and Bergen. The Squadron went as far as 73°00' N, with simulated attacks on Bear Island by the Etendard strike fighters, and Soviet patrol aircraft intercepted by the ship's Crusaders. *Clemenceau* then headed for the Orkneys. She was joined by her sister *Foch* on 10 June, and the two ships exchanged air groups. From this point on, the two carriers would alternate in the roles of PA 1 and PA 2. PA 1 would be fully operational as an aircraft carrier while PA 2, when not in refit or repair, would operate with a reduced crew as a helicopter carrier, with the possibility of embarking Alizé ASW aircraft and able to be employed for pilot qualifications and deck landing training. *Clemenceau* now had an air group comprising four Super Frelon helicopters, four Alizé of 4F and a single Etendard IVP. She was at Scapa Flow from 11 to 14 June, then at Cherbourg with *Arromanches* for Navy Week. She returned to Brest for a short refit on 23 June. Operating as a helicopter carrier with four Super Frelon of 32F embarked, she participated in a group sortie from 17 to 23 October, and joined up with *Foch* for Exercise 'Sterne' from 6 to 9 December, returning to Brest on the 13th.

## DEPLOYMENT TO THE INDIAN OCEAN 1974–75

*Clemenceau* operated as a helicopter and training carrier throughout 1973; she would not resume PA 1 status until 1 June 1974. On 28 September she was incorporated into a Task Group 624.2 with the newly completed ASW frigate *Tourville*, the fleet escort *Bouvet*, and the support ships *La Saône* and *Aber Wrac'h* for a mission christened 'Saphir'. Her air group comprised four Alizé of 4F, eight Crusader of 14F, fourteen Etendard IVM of 17F, three Etendard IVP of 16F, two Super Frelon of 32F and eight HSS of 33F, with two Alouette III of 22S as plane guard. The Jaubert Commando unit was also embarked.

She left Brest on 8 October and headed for the Indian Ocean. When the group was approaching La Réunion, it was joined on 1 November by the 'Mousson'

**Above:** *Clemenceau* at Cape Town in 1975. *(Marc Piché)*

group comprising the missile frigate *Duquesne* and the fleet escort *Jauréguiberry*, which had been in the Indian Ocean since May. *Clemenceau* moored at La Réunion, then proceeded to Djibouti, arriving on the 15th. There were exercises in late November, followed by port visits to Bombay and Karachi in December.

In February 1975, accompanied by *Bouvet*, she gave assistance to Ile Maurice following a typhoon. She then returned to the Atlantic Ocean via the Cape, visiting

Cape Town and Dakar before re-entering Brest on 25 March; 17F had been catapulted when off Oléron, destined for Hyères, before her arrival. A three-month maintenance period (IPER = *Immobilisation périodique pour entretien et réparations*) followed.

Early July saw the first sea trials of the Super Etendard, with prototype aircraft 01 and 03 totalling fifty catapult launches and landings, and on the 5th an Alizé landed off Brest with Prime Minister Jacques Chirac on board.

**Below:** Another view of *Clemenceau* at Cape Town in 1975. *(Marc Piché)*

On 4 October 1975, *Clemenceau* left Brest for Toulon, arriving on the 10th. It had been decided to transfer the aircraft carriers, together with their escorts, to the Mediterranean. Between 1975 and 1977, *Clemenceau* and *Foch*, together the cruiser *Colbert* and the missile frigates *Suffren* and *Duquesne* (all three armed with the Masurca area defence missile), would move to their new home base.

## SECOND INDIAN OCEAN DEPLOYMENT AND REFIT 1976–78

On 3 February 1976, *Clemenceau* participated in the winter cruise of the Squadron, visiting Istanbul from 13 to 18 February and returning on the 27th. Further trials with the Super Etendard then took place, followed by Exercise 'Dawn Patrol' from 3 to 13 May and the Squadron's spring cruise to the Eastern Mediterranean from 19 May to 5 June, with a port visit to Alexandria. *Clemenceau* then replaced *Foch* and embarked President Valéry Giscard d'Estaing for a naval review that took place between Nice and Toulon. The unavailability of *Foch* disrupted the planned maintenance programme, which had to be broken down into two periods (July/September and October/December) to enable the ship to take part in NATO Exercise 'Display Determination' in early October.

After further trials of the Super Etendard during January–March 1977, *Clemenceau* departed Toulon for a second deployment to the Indian Ocean ('Saphir II'), to cover the transition to independence of Djibouti. She embarked six Alizé of 4F, ten Crusader of 12F, sixteen Etendard IVM of 17F, four Etendard IVP of 16F and two Super Frelon of 32F, with two Alouette III of 23S as plane guard. She arrived at Djibouti on 16 April. On 7 May, two of her Crusaders intercepted two Mig 21 fighters from South Yemen. However, on 18 May, a Super Frelon was lost on take-off at Ali-Sabieh; the crew and the commandos on board survived. And on 11 June, an Etendard IVP went down with its pilot in the Gulf of Tadjoura.

On 12 June, *Foch* joined *Clemenceau* in the Red Sea, and materiel and personnel were transferred across by helicopter. *Clemenceau* then returned to Toulon via the Suez Canal, arriving on the 21st. Following trials with the Alidade system and the Super Etendard in early July the carrier began a major refit, from which she would emerge only in late 1978. There was a major overhaul of the machinery and the catapults, and the crew accommodation and cafeteria were brought up to date. Trials of the ship took place in late November, and aviation trials with 23S, 6F, 14F, 16F and 17F during December and January 1978.

## MEDITERRANEAN 1979–83

On 22 January 1979, *Clemenceau* was again designated PA 1. On 11 March, an Etendard IVM of 17F and its pilot were lost following a malfunction of the catapult on the angled deck, and there were five casualties among the deck crew. The catapults were out of service for a while, and only Alizé turboprop aircraft could take off (using the axial deck) before the ship returned to Toulon on 20 March.

During Exercise 'Dawn Patrol' from 9 to 24 May, A-7 Corsair light attack aircraft from USS *America* (CV-66) made 'touch-and-go' landings on the carrier, but the ship had to return to Toulon on the 24th due to turbine problems that took three months to repair. Routine activity followed before the ship re-assumed the role of PA 2 on 17 December. *Clemenceau* then underwent a planned five-month refit (IPER), the focus of which was to enable her to operate the new Super

Etendard strike aircraft, for which the Telemir navigation system was fitted.

After post-refit trials during May 1980, *Clemenceau* made two sorties in June, then took on the role of PA 1, taking part in Exercise 'Display Determination' from 30 September, followed by port visits to Suda Bay and Piraeus, and returned to Toulon on 23 October. From 24 November she undertook qualifications for the pilots of the Super Etendard, which was due to replace the Etendard IVM in 17F. Further day/night pilot qualifications followed in February 1981.

On 9 March, *Clemenceau* departed Toulon for Exercise 'Aries 81' with the combined Mediterranean and Atlantic squadrons, then took part in Exercise 'Dual Dagger' in May, while pilot qualifications continued in April and June.

On 3 September, the Defence Minister, Charles Hernu, landed on board in an Alizé off Toulon and *Clemenceau* took part in the NATO Exercise 'Ocean Safari', which concluded with a visit to Hamburg. The ship returned to Toulon via Brest on 4 October. On 26 October a Crusader of 12F was lost, together with the pilot, following a catapult launch off Saint-Tropez. On the same day, ten Air Force Puma and seventeen Gazelle helicopters were embarked for Exercise 'Farfadet', which involved a landing in Corsica. The ship returned to base on 31 October. Routine activity followed, and on 2 December, *Clemenceau* resumed the role of PA 2, conducting trials with Super Etendard strike aircraft armed with the new Exocet AM 39 anti-ship missile in December.

*Clemenceau* continued to serve as PA 2 until 19 November 1982, when she again became the Navy's first-line carrier. Two days later she left Toulon with thirty-five aircraft embarked. She passed through the Strait of Gibraltar and joined her sister *Foch* for Operation 'Thiof', with the participation of the nuclear-powered attack submarine (SNA) *Rubis*. After a visit to Casablanca she returned to Toulon on 6 December.

The year 1983 began with pilot qualifications, but a sortie with the Squadron on 7 February had to be abandoned when the steam supply to both catapults failed and the ship was forced to return to Toulon; the air group had to be disembarked by crane. Relegated to PA 2 status, *Clemenceau* conducted trials with her catapults in March, then took part in Exercise 'Farfadet 83' with fifteen fixed-wing aircraft and twenty helicopters from 17 to 22 April. Landings took place at Le Racou, just to the north of the Spanish border. Routine activity followed, with port visits to Genoa and Naples. Late July saw the first female personnel embarked.

## 'OLIFANT' 1983–84

On 30 September, *Clemenceau* left without her air group and headed for Beirut to replace *Foch* in the role of PA 1. Helicopters and landing craft from the TCD *Ouragan* transferred 592 personnel and 120 tonnes of materiel between Cyprus and Lebanon, and Rear Admiral Bernard Klotz, commanding TF 452, embarked with his staff. On 6 October, the air group was landed off Larnaca: six Crusader of 12F, fifteen Super Etendard of 11F, 14F and 17F, three Etendard

**Right:** An aerial view of the flight deck of *Clemenceau* in 1987 following her half-life modernisation. The white arrow markings at the forward end of the angled deck are prominent. Alizé ASW aircraft and Crusader fighters are parked forward. Note the Crotale installation to port. *(Marine Nationale)*

IVP of 16F, five Alizé of 6F and six Super Frelon of 32F and 33F. The carrier's mission, designated 'Olifant XVIII', was to provide cover for the Multi-national Security Force at Beirut; she would put into Larnaca for replenishment. Only Alizé aircraft were launched in order to reduce the load on the catapults. On the morning of the 8th, five Super Etendard landed, and after refuelling were catapulted off and headed for Iraq, where they were to be loaned.

Bombing atrocities in Beirut resulted in the deaths of 241 US troops and 58 French among the Multi-national Force. *Clemenceau*'s helicopters brought many of the wounded on board and secured communications with the ground forces. Her fighters provided aerial cover during visits to Lebanon by first the Minister of Defence, Charles Hernu, then the President. *Clemenceau* maintained permanent cover with a radar-equipped Alizé in the air and a Crusader ready for catapult launch.

On 17 November, a strike on a Hezbollah training centre (Operation 'Brochet') was mounted by eight Super Etendard armed with bombs in three waves, escorted by two Crusaders. The Americans supplied cover using Prowler EW aircraft. However, the base had already been evacuated due to a tip-off. On the 30th, 'Olifant XVIII' became 'Olifant XIX' and Vice Admiral Louzeau replaced Vice Admiral Klotz in command of TF 452. The carrier remained on station until the end of the year.

On 4 January 1984, Admiral Louzeau transferred his flag to the missile frigate *Suffren*, and *Clemenceau* left for Toulon with 180 men of the Parachute Regiment on board, arriving on 8 January. She left again on 25 January with six Crusader of 12F, ten Super Etendard of 11F and 14F, three Etendard IVP of 16F, five Alizé of 4F, four Super Frelon of 33F plus seven smaller helicopters, arriving off the coast of Lebanon on the 29th. On 9 February, Admiral Leenhardt, Chief of the Naval General Staff, came on board, followed by the Minister for Foreign Affairs, Claude Cheysson, on 3 March. On 15 February an Alizé was damaged by a surface-to-air missile but

**Left:** The island of *Clemenceau* in 1987, with Crusader fighters below. The large antenna for the DRBV 20 air search radar on the after mast platform has been replaced by the smaller antenna for DRBV 15. *(Marine Nationale)*

**Right:** An overhead view of *Clemenceau* in 1989 with Super Etendard strike fighters embarked. *(Marine Nationale)*

Above: *Clemenceau* landing a Gazelle helicopter belonging to ALAT during the late 1980s. The forward installation for Crotale is prominent on the right of the photo. *(Marine Nationale)*

managed to land on with minor damage. On 14 March, 'Olifant XIX' became 'Olifant XX' and Admiral Klotz returned to the ship.

The foreign detachments finally left Lebanon, the French being the last to leave (Operation 'Carrelet' 30–31 March). *Clemenceau*'s helicopters evacuated 1,342 personnel and 16 wounded. Following a visit to Alexandria from 14 to 21 April, the carrier left for Toulon, arriving on 4 May after a deployment that lasted 101 days. She was in maintenance for almost three months, recommissioning as PA 1 on 31 July. However, a turbine problem meant that planned sorties for pilot qualifications had to be cancelled, and she was replaced as PA 1 by *Foch* after an exchange of personnel while both ships were alongside at the Milhaud piers. *Clemenceau* was then towed into the dockyard for repairs that lasted from 17 September 1984 to 10 January 1985.

The year 1985 began with routine activities, port visits and pilot qualifications. The carrier took part in NATO Exercise 'Distant Hammer' from 4 to 16 May. On 9 May, a Crusader of 12F struck the after edge of the flight deck; the pilot managed to eject but the plane struck another Crusader, writing off both aircraft. On 28 May, between visits to Port Said and Naples, an Alizé of 6F went down aft of the carrier, resulting in the death of the pilot. Exercise 'Farfadet' in early June was followed by a training sortie. *Clemenceau* was then relegated to PA 2 status (1 August), and prepared for a major refit that aimed to extend the life of the ship by ten years to 1995, the date the new nuclear-powered carrier was due to enter service.

## MODERNISATION 1985–86 AND 'PROMÉTHÉE' 1987–88

During her refit at Toulon, *Clemenceau* underwent a complete refurbishment of her machinery and her accommodation. Four of the 100mm DP guns were replaced by two Crotale short-range air defence systems, and there was a complete upgrade of the ship's electronics, the most significant being the replacement of the DRBV 20 air search radar by the DRBV 15 target indication radar (see technical section above and the accompanying drawings).

Post-refit trials began on 31 October 1986 and were completed on 23 January 1987; the ship was declared operational on 6 February, assuming the role of PA 1 on the same day. Pilot qualifications followed. On 30 April the demonstrator of the new Dassault Rafale naval jet fighter practised approaches without, however, touching down – the undercarriage was not designed for carrier operation. In May the ship took part in Exercise 'Dragon Hammer', followed by a cruise during which there were port visits to Barcelona, Brest and Casablanca. On 12 June a Crusader suffered damage in a deck landing and had to be written off. The carrier returned to Toulon on 25 June.

A crisis with Iran provoked by an attack on the

**Left:** Task Force 632.2 steaming in formation during 1987, with *Clemenceau* at its centre. *(René Bail collection)*

container ship *Ville d'Anvers* led to the formation of Task Force 632.2, comprising *Clemenceau*, the missile frigates *Duquesne* and *Suffren* and the fleet tanker *Meuse*, commanded by Rear Admiral Hervé Le Pichon. The air group comprised eight Crusader of 12F, fourteen Super Etendard of 11F and 17F, two Etendard IVP of 16F, six Alizé of 4F, two Super Frelon of 32F, two Lynx of 31F and two Alouette III of 23S. The group passed through the Suez Canal on 5 August and arrived in the Gulf of Aden on the 10th. Operation 'Prométhée' began on the 13th, with strikes planned against Iranian bases and installations. The carrier was positioned off Oman ready to provide cover for French mercantile traffic. It was planned that the ship would spend thirty days at sea followed by twenty days at Djibouti, when part of the air group would operate from the Ambouli air base. Four patrols were carried out during the final months of the year, punctuated by visits from Minister of Defence André Giraud and President François Mitterand, and a port visit to Bombay. On 1 December an Iranian P-3F Orion was intercepted by a Crusader.

On 3 January 1988, Admiral Pichon was replaced by Rear Admiral François Deramond, and on 20 January two Soviet Il-38 'May' maritime patrol aircraft were intercepted. A fifth patrol took place between 14 February and 15 March, and there was a joint training exercise with the US carrier *Enterprise* (CVN-65). *Clemenceau* then returned to Djibouti until 7 April. The next patrol period was marked by mine damage to the US frigate *Samuel B Roberts* (FFG-58) on 13 April and by attacks by US naval aircraft against Iranian oil platforms and warships on 18 April. There were further interceptions of Iranian Orion and Soviet Il-38 patrol aircraft.

Following a rest period at Djibouti from 6 to 25 May, *Clemenceau* carried out a 'presence' mission in the Indian Ocean, with port calls at La Réunion and Port Louis (Mauritius). On 17 July a Super Etendard struck the after edge of the flight deck. The front end remained on the ship, but the after section fell into the ship's wake and sank; the pilot was air-lifted to Djibouti but later died.

*Clemenceau* returned to Djibouti on 15 August, and left for metropolitan France with the fleet escort *Du Chayla* and the tanker *Var*, returning to Toulon on 16 September with the Prime Minister, Michel Rocard, on board. Her aircraft had spent 12,300 hours in the air and made 5,633 deck landings during the mission.

## REORGANISATION OF THE NAVAL AIR SQUADRONS AND A MAJOR FIRE 1989–91

During this period a clear division developed between a northern and a southern naval aviation group. The northern group comprised the squadrons at Lann-Bihoué (4F) and Landivisiau (11F, 12F, 14F, 16F) and the southern group those based Hyères (17F) and Nîmes-Garons (6F). The Crusaders and Etendard IVP, all currently in the north, could be assigned to either grouping.

*Clemenceau* put to sea for Mission 'Icare' with the northern air group embarked on 26 November, visiting Palermo before returning to Toulon on 10 December. There was further routine activity in early 1989 that included a visit to Valencia. On 4 February, during Exercise 'Phinia', a Crusader was lost during the interception of a US aircraft in the Mediterranean, and a second Crusader was damaged in a collision with an Atlantic maritime patrol aircraft on the 8th; it managed to land on the carrier but had to be rebuilt. *Clemenceau* re-assumed PA 2 status on 7 April, and underwent a refit (IPER) from 16 May to 17 November. She recommissioned on 14 December but continued as PA 2, conducting training and pilot qualifications during the early part of 1990. On 28 March, the ship anchored in the roads at Les Vignettes and hosted the Soviet Minister of Defence, General Yazov. Exercises with Puma and Gazelle helicopters belonging to ALAT (*Aviation légère de l'Armée de Terre*) followed, and trials with modernised Super Etendard (SEM) took place from 18 to 29 June.

On 9 August, during a period of leave and renewal of the crew, *Clemenceau* was placed on stand-by following the invasion of Kuwait. On 12 August, she embarked 4 Puma and 30 Gazelle helicopters, together with 70 vehicles and 600 personnel belonging to the 5th Regiment of Combat Helicopters (5e RHC). She was to form Task Group 623.2 with the cruiser *Colbert* and the tanker *Var* under the flag of Rear Admiral Wild for Mission 'Salamandre'. The group left Toulon on the 13th, and *Clemenceau* embarked four Alizé of 4F, a further eight Puma (5e RHC) and two Dauphin helicopters of 23S. The ships passed through the Suez Canal on the night of 17/18 August and arrived at Djibouti on the 22nd. The group manoeuvred in the Gulf of Oman with the forces of the UAE. *Clemenceau* then landed the troops and their helicopters in Saudi Arabia and returned to Toulon, being promoted to PA 1 on 1 November. Further trials with the SEM followed.

After routine activity in the early part of 1991, *Clemenceau* departed Toulon on 22 May, and visited Lisbon in early June before taking part in NATO Exercise 'Ocean Safari'. She returned to Toulon on 18 June, then conducted trials with a Grumman E-2C Hawkeye, no deck landings being involved.

When quayside at Toulon on 21 July with a reduced crew, a fire broke out in the mezzanine above hangar No 3 just after 1500. It spread despite the efforts of forty naval personnel equipped with fire extinguishing apparatus and other firefighters helicoptered in from Marseille. It took four hours to extinguish the blaze; five men were injured and there was significant material damage, including to the arrester system. An investigation concluded that the fire was the result of sabotage by a younger member of the crew who did not wish to go to sea. As a result of the fire, *Clemenceau* was relegated to PA 2 status on 12 August and spent the remainder of the year as a helicopter carrier until her next refit (IPER), which took place from 2 January to 5 June 1992.

## THE *FORCE D'ACTION NAVALE* 1992 AND 'BALBUZARD' 1993–94

On 1 June 1992, the Atlantic and Mediterranean Squadrons were abolished and the *Force d'Action Navale* (FAN) established, with the naval aviation command (ALAE) subordinated to it. *Clemenceau* was recommissioned initially as PA 2 then, on 3 September, as PA 1. The remainder the year was occupied with work-up and various exercises.

The year 1993 began with pilot qualifications, but on 28 January the ship departed Toulon with the Minister of Defence, Pierre Joxe, the Chief of Staff,

Admiral Lanxade, and the Chief of the NGS, Admiral Coatanéa, on board and headed for the Adriatic for Operation 'Balbuzard'. *Clemenceau* was to head Task Force 470 commanded by Rear Admiral Jean Wild, and embarked four Crusader of 12F, eighteen Super Etendard of 11F and 17F, three Etendard IVP of 16F, six Alizé of 6F, four Super Frelon of 32/33F, and two Dauphin and an Alouette III of 23S. She arrived on station on 31 January, and returned on 15 March after a four-day visit to Trieste. She left again with half a commando unit on board.

On 31 March, the UN Security Council established a 'no-fly zone' over Bosnia. The ship was again at Trieste from 19 to 24 April and the 'southern' group of naval aviation was replaced by aircraft of the northern group (11F and 4F). *Clemenceau* conducted her first aerial reconnaissance mission over Bosnia with an Etendard IVP on 17 May. She returned to Toulon on 21 June, being relieved by her sister *Foch*. Relegated to PA 2 status, she was in maintenance until the end of August.

Restored to PA 1 status, *Clemenceau* departed Toulon on 2 September with fifteen Super Etendard of 11F, four Etendard IVP of 16F, six Alizé of 4F, two Super Frelon of 33F, and two Dauphin and an Alouette III of 23S, together with two Pumas from ALAT. Various dignitaries, including the Prime Minister and the Minister of Defence, came on board by helicopter the following day. The ship was again on station on 7 September, and there were overflights of Bosnia by her Super Etendard aircraft, ready to provide support if required. *Clemenceau* moored off Corfu from 20 to 26 September, but a turbine problem forced a return to Toulon on 15 October for repairs.

During power trials in mid-March 1994, *Clemenceau* attained a speed of 32 knots – a remarkable figure for a thirty-year-old ship. She left Toulon on 24 March for her fourth 'Balbuzard' mission with Rear Admiral Alain Witrand and half a commando unit on board. A Super Etendard of 11F was lost to engine failure on 27 March; the pilot, who had ejected, was rescued by helicopter. On 15 April, two Etendard IVP were launched for a reconnaissance mission over Sarajevo, Rogatica and Gorazde. One of the two aircraft was struck by an SA-14 'Gremlin' surface-to-air missile that tore away part of its control surfaces; escorted by his wingman, the pilot managed to land on at a speed of 300km/h with the ship steaming 32 knots. On 21 April, strikes against the Serbs were planned following their invasion of the 'safe zones', but in the

**Above:** A fine overhead view of *Clemenceau* in company with the fleet escort *Du Chayla* and the tanker *Var*. The photo was probably taken in September 1998 during her return from Djibouti to metropolitan France. Crusader, Super Etendard, Etendard IVP and Alizé aircraft are parked on deck. *(Marine Nationale)*

**Left:** A Super Etendard of 11F with a Phimat pod on the flight deck of Clemenceau during Operation 'Prométhée' in the Indian Ocean in 1987. *(Feuilloy, ARDHAN collection)*

**Left:** *Clemenceau* entering Portsmouth Harbour on 16 June 1997 during her final round of port visits. *(Leo van Ginderen collection)*

**Below:** *Clemenceau* at Toulon awaiting disposal in 2005. *(Raymond Reboul)*

end only further reconnaissance missions were launched, and the ship returned to Toulon on 3 May.

On 1 June, command of the FAN was formally handed over, Vice Admiral Lefebvre being replaced by Rear Admiral Patrick Lecointre. Exercises 'Iles d'Or' and 'Dam/Tam' followed.

On 4 July, *Clemenceau* departed Toulon for a fifth 'Balbuzard' mission. Her air group comprised four Crusader of 12F, fourteen Super Etendard of 11F, four Etendard IVP of 16F, five Alizé of 4F, two Super Frelon of 33F, and two Dauphin and an Alouette III of 23S. The deployment included a passage to Corfu, and the ship returned on 29 July. She took part in a naval review off the coast of Provence on 13–14 August, resumed PA 2 status, and prepared for a major refit (IPER) that lasted from 2 October 1994 to 28 June 1995.

## THE LAST YEARS 1995–97

Trials and pilot training took place during June/July 1995, but in November *Clemenceau* was immobilised for boiler repairs. On 14 December, an Alizé suffered engine failure during flight and went down south of Toulon; the crew was rescued.

On 17 December, *Clemenceau* left Toulon with TF 470 (Rear Admiral Jacques Célerier) for Mission 'Salamandre', with the southern air group embarked, and on 20 December the first missions over Bosnia were launched (Operation 'Decisive Edge'). Admiral Charles Lefebvre, Chief of the Naval General Staff, came on board on 24 December. On 19 January 1996, operations resumed, with the ship providing a combat air patrol for 'Decisive Endeavour'. The Prime Minister, Alain Juppé, and the Defence Minister came on board on 25 January. A second 'Salamandre' mission was undertaken during March. From 16 to 27 March, *Clemenceau* was the only carrier on station in the Adriatic and her aircraft conducted a number of support missions. She returned to Toulon on 29 March. Routine pilot training and exercises followed.

On 17 July 1996, the Defence Minister, Charles Millon, announced that *Clemenceau* would decommission during 1997. She continued to be active in the interim. An Alizé ALH, a variant of the aircraft specially equipped for airborne early warning, made its first landing on 23 October, and on 25 November the carrier left for a third 'Salamandre' mission, returning to Toulon on 9 December.

During the first part of 1997, *Clemenceau* resumed training and pilot qualifications and took part in Exercise 'Iles d'Or'. On 23 May, an Etendard IVPM was lost to engine failure when being catapulted southeast of Toulon; the pilot was recovered. There were visits to Portsmouth (UK) on 16–20 June, Brest on 21–27 June and La Coruña on 30 June–3 July, and a farewell sea day for former commanding officers on 17 July. The decommissioning ceremony took place on 1 October. The ship had covered 1,063,708nm during her service career and totalled 77,683 deck landings.

*Clemenceau* was cannibalised for parts for her sister *Foch* and was stricken on 16 December 2002, becoming Q 790. After several false starts and controversies too complex to be detailed here, *Clemenceau* finally left Brest on 3 February 2009 towed by the tug *Anglian Earl*, and arrived at Hartlepool on the 8th to be broken up by Able UK. The work was completed in 2010.

## *FOCH*: TRIALS AND WORK-UP

The completion of *Foch* was delayed for two years due to a lack of funding. The forward catapult was embarked in July 1960, the catapult on the angled deck between August and December 1961. The forward machinery group was installed during January–February 1961 and the after group during July–August of the same year. The final cost was 518 million francs.

The boilers were lit for the first time on 19 February 1962, and *Foch* was manned for trials on 28 April under the command of CV Jean Bied-Charreton. Following a static trial on 16 July, the ship was docked for installation of the sonar dome. *Foch* sailed under her own power for the first time on 24 July. The reduction gearing was tested during a sortie to Groix that was, however, hampered by poor visibility. Trials of her machinery continued, culminating in a two-hour trial during which she attained 126,710cv.

Trials in open waters began on 16 August, when a seven-hour trial at a displacement of 31,936 tonnes delivered a speed of 32.39 knots with 126,863cv. This speed would be exceeded during a full-power trial on 24/25 August, when the ship achieved 32.91 knots with 139,976cv.

The first deck landing, with an Alizé of 3F piloted by EV Michel Rochard, took place on 6 September, and was followed on 7 September by the first landing of an Etendard IVM of 15F. Trials continued off Groix and Morgat with Alizé and Etendard fixed-wing aircraft and HUP-2 helicopters. Replenishment trials with the fleet tanker *La Seine* took place on 16–17 October, and the ship was then docked at Brest until the end of the year for the customary inspections of her machinery. *Foch* was commissioned (*armement définitif*) on 1 January 1963.

Trials and work-up continued until June, when the ship left for her long-distance cruise. With the Alizés of 9F embarked, she crossed the Atlantic, mooring off the Ile d'Orléans in the St Lawrence River before visiting Quebec (17–22 June) and Boston (26 June–2 July). She then headed back towards the

**Left:** An F-8E Crusader of 12F in flight. *(16F Flotilla, ARDHAN collection)*

**Left:** *Foch* disembarks F-8E Crusader fighter aircraft in the Joubert Dock at Saint-Nazaire on 16 February 1965. *(DR)*

Mediterranean via Funchal, replenished at Mers el-Kébir and arrived at Toulon on 15 July, the day she officially entered service.

*Foch* put to sea from 11 to 18 September for pilot qualifications with 11F (Etendard IVM). On the 17th, a catapult problem resulted in the loss of one of the aircraft and the pilot; in consequence all Etendards were grounded pending an investigation.

On 16 October, *Foch* departed Toulon with part of the Squadron (the AA cruiser *De Grasse* and seven escorts) for a cruise christened 'Mousson' ('Monsoon') in the Indian Ocean, embarking sixteen Alizé of 9F, four HSS of 33F and two Alouette III of 23S, together with six Air Force Skyraiders destined for Djibouti. After visits to Djibouti, Nosy-Be and Diego Suarez (Madagascar), Pointe des Galets (La Réunion), Aden and Massawa, she returned to Toulon via the Suez Canal on 20 December.

The year 1964 began with routine activities and port visits which included Ajaccio and Palma de Mallorca. *Foch* remained quayside during the naval review on 15 August to mark the landings in Provence. The first landing of an Etendard IVP took place on 15 September, but on 13 October an aircraft of the same squadron fell into the sea after being catapulted; the pilot was rescued by an Alouette III.

On 24 January 1964, *Foch* left Brest for Norfolk, Va, where she embarked the last twenty-eight of the forty-two F-8E Crusaders ordered. She returned to Brest, and was moored there on 14–15 February with ten Crusaders on deck for a visit by President Charles de Gaulle, who also visited the Ecole Navale. The carrier then proceeded to the Joubert Dock at Saint-Nazaire, where she disembarked the Crusaders on 16–17 February, returning to Brest on the following day for a twelve-month refit during which the aviation facilities were adapted for operations with the US-built fighters; these modifications included the fitting of bridle catchers at the forward end of the catapults.

Trials and work-up took place from 17 January 1966. *Foch* was placed under the control of the senior office for aircraft carriers (ALPA), and arrived in Toulon on 12 February. She landed her first Crusaders, now assigned to 14F, between 29 January and 17 February.

## 'FORCE ALFA' 1966

The first nuclear tests at the Pacific Test Centre (CEP) were due to take place in 1966, and were to be supported by a naval 'Force Alfa' centred on a carrier. *Foch* commanded a group that comprised the fleet escorts *Forbin*, *La Bourdonnais* and *Jauréguiberry* and the fleet tanker *La Seine*, together with the support ships *Rhin* and *Aber Wrac'h*, which would make their way to Polynesia independently via the Panama Canal. *Foch* had the following air group embarked: twelve Alizé of 9F, eight Etendard IVM of 15F, four Etendard IVP of 15F, ten HSS helicopters of 31F, plus six Alouette II and six Alouette III of 23S.

Force Alfa left Toulon on 23 March, and arrived at Tahiti on 22 May having called in at Dakar, Diego Suarez and Nouméa. During an aerial demonstration for the local authorities an Etendard IVP was lost in a collision with a IVM, which managed to land at Faa'a air base.

The carrier was then positioned off Mururoa for three nuclear tests that took place on 2 July

Above: *Foch* at anchor at Vairao, Tahiti, on 12 October 1966, overflown by two Etendard IVM of 15F. *(Marine Nationale)*

('Aldebaran'), 19 July ('Tamouré') and 24 July ('Ganymède'), following which she returned to the anchorage at Vairao.

A second series of tests took place in September: 'Bételgeuse' (11 September), in the presence of President de Gaulle, who had embarked on the cruiser *De Grasse*, 'Rigel' (24 September), and 'Sirius' (4 October). *Foch* returned to the Vairao anchorage on 7 October, and on the 29th her aircraft sank the elderly colonial sloop *Francis Garnier* (formerly the Italian *Eritrea*).

*Foch* finally left Vairao on 2 November. Force Alfa was accompanied by the fleet tanker *Isère* until 7 November, then by *La Saône* after passing Cape Horn. She returned to Toulon via Las Palmas on 7 December.

*Foch* departed Toulon for Brest, her new base port, on 9 December, arriving on the 13th. She was then docked for radiological testing, which found nothing of consequence. From 15 January, the carrier was again under ALPA. Training with the Etendard IVM strike fighters of 14F followed, during which one of the aircraft was lost after being catapulted; the pilot managed to eject. The carrier then underwent a major twelve-month refit, which lasted from 4 April 1967 to 17 May 1968.

## ATLANTIC 1968–71

Post-refit machinery trials began on 17 May 1968, and aviation trials with Squadrons 4F, 6F (Alizé) and 15F (Etendard IVM) took place from 10 to 21 June. They were followed by anti-submarine trials on 3 July, then further aviation trials and pilot qualifications.

On 24 September, *Foch* left Brest for Toulon, and from 9 October conducted exercises off the coasts of Provence and Corsica with aircraft of 4F, 14F (Crusader) and 15F Squadrons together with three HSS helicopters of 33F. Filming for a TV series took place during late September and early October, followed by Exercise 'Eden Apple' from 4 to 8 November and an exercise involving both the Atlantic and the Mediterranean Squadrons, for which Admiral André Patou, Naval Chief of Staff, was on board. The carrier then passed through the Strait of Gibraltar and headed for a short refit at Brest, entering the port on 23 December.

*Foch* left Brest on 8 February 1969 for joint exercises with the squadrons based at Brest and Toulon, with 6F (Alizé), 11F (Etendard IVM), 12F (Crusader) and 16F (Etendard IVP) embarked. However, weather hindered operations, and she returned on 1 March following visits to Las Palmas and Lisbon. During a demonstration with Etendard and Crusader aircraft in the presence of the Prime Minister, Couve de Murville, the local Maritime Prefect, the senior officer of the Atlantic Squadron and ALPA, there was an incident involving a minor grounding that resulted in the flooding of the sonar compartment. Although the aerial demonstration proceeded successfully it was subsequently found that the double bottom had been staved in over a length of 100 metres and a propeller blade bent. The damage was not serious, and it was decided that definitive repairs would be postponed until the next refit of the ship.

*Foch* then conducted day- and night-time training and qualifications for the pilots of 11F, 12F and 9F, and the same squadrons, together with a detachment of Etendard IVP of 16F, were embarked for exercises with the Squadron in May and in the North Sea in June, when the ship visited Hamburg. She damaged a propeller when leaving the port and this was replaced when she returned to Brest. Further exercises and aviation training followed.

Routine activity in September and October culminated in Exercise 'Gemex 69' from 24 to 31 October with Squadrons 11F, 12F, 14F and 32F embarked. On 27 October, an Etendard IVM of 11F was lost following a catapult launch at night, but the pilot was recovered by the fleet escort *Dupetit-Thouars*. After further brief sorties, *Foch* left Brest on 1 December for Toulon, and took part in Exercise 'Fair game VII' from 8 to 19 December. On 13 December, an engine failure led the pilot of an Etendard IV to eject, suffering severe injuries in the process. The ship returned to Brest on 23 December.

On 11 January 1970, a fire broke out in one of the auxiliary boilers but was quickly extinguished. On 12 February, during a sortie with 4F, 14F, 16F and 17F embarked, *Foch* suffered damage in heavy seas. During the same period she provided assistance to two merchant ships in difficulty. In May there was a visit to Rotterdam with six Super Frelon helicopters of 32F embarked.

The year 1971 began with routine activities. On 16 March, *Foch* left for the West African port of Douala to embark the twelve HSS helicopters of 33F that had been engaged in Chad since February 1970. The helicopters were disembarked at Toulon on 12 April, and the ship then left for a major refit at Brest, during which 400m$^2$ of the double bottom plating was replaced.

## ATLANTIC 1972–76

Post-refit trials began on 15 May 1972. On 8 June, *Foch* left Brest with four Super Frelon of 32F embarked, visited Portsmouth, then joined *Clemenceau* north of the Orkneys on the 11th. The air group of the latter was transferred to *Foch*, which became PA 1, and the two carriers moored at Scapa Flow until the 14th. *Foch* then returned to Brest. On 21 September, two Douglas A-4M Skyhawk strike aircraft from the trials unit of the US Marines landed on board.

She joined up with *Clemenceau* again on 20 November, but the rupture of an arrester wire during the landing of an Etendard IVM resulted in the death of a petty officer. The two carriers took part in Exercise 'Sterne' from 6 to 9 December, and *Foch* returned to Brest on the 19th following a port visit to Lisbon.

**Above:** A Douglas A-4M Skyhawk belonging to the Patuxent River Training Centre on board *Foch*, 21 September 1972. *(ARDHAN collection)*

In February 1973, *Foch* took part in the winter cruise of the Atlantic Squadron, returning on 9 March after visiting Málaga. During a spring cruise by the Squadron in May she visited the Azores, Fort-de-France, Jacksonville and New York, where she was joined by the cruiser *Colbert* following her major modernisation. A navigation incident when departing New York resulted in damage to the forward starboard sponson and its two 100mm guns. The ship returned to Brest via the Azores on 18 June. On 14 November, a McDonnell Douglas AV-8A Harrier belonging to the US Marines landed on board for trials. *Foch* then took part in Exercise 'Capricorne', visiting Genoa and Toulon before returning to her home port on 13 December.

During the winter cruise of February/March 1974, the Atlantic and Mediterranean Squadrons joined units of the Spanish Navy for Exercises 'Escuadras 4' and 'Inés II' off the Canaries. The carrier returned to Brest on 2 March following port visits to Las Palmas and Lisbon, and embarked Super Frelon helicopters in her role as PA 2. She underwent a short refit and maintenance period (IPER) from March to May. Exercise 'Sterne' followed in mid-June with the Pumas of ALAT embarked.

At the end of November, *Foch* embarked the HSS helicopters of 33F, four Super Frelon (32F), Pumas belonging to ALAT and commando and gendarmerie units, and left with the cruiser *Colbert* for the Antilles, where she was to provide security for a meeting between French President Giscard d'Estaing and US President Gerald Ford that took place in Martinique during 14–16 December. She returned to Brest on the 23rd.

The early months of 1975 saw *Foch* still operating as PA 2; only the forward catapult was in service, the one on the angled deck having suffered a failure. Routine activity followed, with a visit to Rotterdam in March. During a refit period (IPER) from September to the following April, the catapult was repaired and the accommodation refurbished.

The first post-refit deck landings took place on 13 May 1976 with Squadrons 4F (Alizé), 14F (Crusader), 16F (Etendard IVP) and 59S. On 9 June, *Foch* departed Brest for her new base port of Toulon, arriving on 23 June having participated in Exercise 'Archipel' and visited Lisbon. She was due to take part in a major review of the fleet by President Giscard d'Estaing to be held on 11 June between Nice and Toulon, but a machinery problem led to her being replaced by *Clemenceau* and the ship remained pier-side at Milhaud. During a sortie in late November an Alizé of 59S landed, struck a Crusader and fell into the sea; the two crew members were lost.

## TOULON 1977–80

After training and work-up in May 1977, *Foch* left Toulon for Mission 'Saphir II' in the Indian Ocean, with thirty-six aircraft of 11F (Etendard IVM), 14F (Crusader), 6F (Alizé) and 16F (Etendard IVP) embarked, together with two Super Frelon of 32F and two Alouette III of 23S. She arrived at Djibouti on the 12th and, having disembarked personnel and materiel, became PA 1 and relieved her sister *Clemenceau*, which returned to Toulon. Djibouti celebrated its independence on 27 June.

On 15 July, a problem with the starboard propeller shaft off Djibouti forced a return to port, but *Foch* then continued operations in the Indian Ocean, visiting Ile Maurice from 1 to 7 August and Colombo from 11 to 17 October. She finally left Djibouti on 3 December and returned to Toulon via the Suez Canal on 10 December.

In January and April 1978, *Foch* conducted trials off the *Centre d'essais des Landes* (CEL) with the new variant of the Dassault Etendard, the Super Etendard, and its Alidade carrier reference navigation system. In late April, Super Frelon helicopters delivered a first consignment of the Matra R.550 Magic AAM – the lightweight French counterpart to the US Sidewinder – to the ship while she was off the CEL.

**Below:** Preparing to launch an Alizé of 6F on board *Foch* in 1985. *(Marine Nationale)*

**Above:** Two Royal Navy Sea Harrier V/STOL aircraft on board *Foch* in 1980. *(ARDHAN collection)*

A visit to Lisbon from 2 to 6 May was followed by participation in NATO Exercise 'Dawn Patrol' during 15–31 May. *Foch* was then in maintenance from 3 July to 5 September. On 13 September, during a demonstration for reservists off Porquerolles, an Etendard IVM and its pilot were lost when the aircraft struck the surface. On 4 October, she embarked eight HSS helicopters of 33F and a commando group for Exercise 'Trinôme' off Corsica, returning to Toulon on the 10th after a port visit to Ajaccio. The month of December saw further evaluation trials of the Super Etendard, which was now assigned to 11F.

In January 1979, *Foch* undertook a sortie for ALAT, being designated PA 2 on the 22nd, and was then in refit (IPER) from 19 February to 24 August. Trials with the Lynx helicopters of 31F took place in January and July. Routine activity followed until late November, when the ship reverted to PA 1 status. She left Toulon on the 29th for Exercise 'Njambour II', which took place off West Africa from 3 to 22 December, with Etendard aircraft and helicopters embarked. A landing incident involving an Etendard IVM on 11 December rendered the flight deck non-operational, and two other Etendards were forced to land in Gambia. The return from Dakar to Toulon was marked by an encounter with exceptionally heavy seas off Cape Nao that caused significant damage to the bow area, including the starboard gallery. The ship finally entered Toulon on 22 December.

Between 14 and 18 January 1980, the first night landings by Super Etendard strike fighters took place. *Foch* then embarked Squadrons 4F (Alizé), 12F (Crusader), 16F (Etendard IVP) and 17F (Etendard IVM) for a short cruise from 18 to 29 January christened 'Salammbô', visiting Palma de Mallorca from 22 to 26 February. March saw further night operations with the Super Etendard. The carrier participated in NATO Exercise 'Dawn Patrol' from 5 to 23 May. On 14 May the pilot of a Crusader ejected due to a lack of thrust on launch; the pilot was rescued but the plane continued to fly for forty-five minutes!

On 3 June, *Foch* became PA 2, and on the 12th put to sea with reservists on board. During the afternoon a Super Frelon of 33F was approaching to embark some of the reservists when a rotor failure caused the helicopter to fall into the sea with the loss of three of the four-man crew. The last flight of an Etendard IVM took place on 13 June, the aircraft being piloted by an American on an exchange. During the same month it was decided that the medium-range nuclear air-to-ground (ASMP) missile would be embarked in *Foch*.

The carrier began a twelve-month refit (IPER) on 15 July. The work undertaken included the revision of the magazine arrangements to accommodate the AN 52 nuclear weapon and the AM 39 Exocet anti-ship missile, the adaptations necessary to enable *Foch* to operate the Super Etendard, and the installation of a SENIT 2 data management system removed from the decommissioned fleet escort *Tartu* (see Technical section).

## TOULON AND 'OLIFANT' 1981–87

*Foch* began her post-refit trials on 17 August 1981. Aviation trials took place between 25 August and 30 October. On 16 October she was designated PA 2, and during November there were joint trials with *Clemenceau* and the Super Etendard armed with the AM 39 Exocet. She was declared operational on 4 December and became PA 1 the following day. In December she took part in a short cruise christened 'Mécène', during which she visited Naples.

On 22 February 1982, *Foch* left Toulon for a cruise christened 'Decabel' with 6F (Alizé), 11F (Super Etendard = SUE), 12F (Crusader), 14F (SUE) and 16F (Etendard IVP) embarked. She returned to port after a visit to Palma de Mallorca. During April and May she took part in a number of exercises, including NATO Exercise 'Distant Drum' (4–14 May). On 26 May an Alizé of 6F suffered engine failure during a catapult launch and fell into the sea; the crew was rescued by helicopter. There was a second incident the following day, when a Super Etendard of 17F struck the sea when returning from a mission off Ajaccio and the pilot was lost. The carrier then returned to Toulon for a refit from 3 June to 4 July.

On 14 July, *Foch* participated in a naval review by President François Mitterand in the ASW corvette (later 'frigate') *Georges Leygues* which took place in the Vignettes roads. He then landed on board *Foch* in the corvette's Lynx helicopter.

A short maintenance period (IE) due to be completed on 20 September was interrupted by the need to evacuate the Multi-national Force from the Lebanon, for which *Foch* was to provide cover. She left for Operation 'Olifant IV' on 7 September with Squadrons 6F, 16F, 17F (SUE), 32F, 33F and 23S embarked. The Super Frelon helicopters brought over the men who had already embarked on the French dock landing ship (TCD) *Orage*. *Foch* landed 595 men of the Parachute Regiment at Corsica on the 17th and returned to Toulon the following day.

With the situation in Lebanon deteriorating, France put together a detachment of 1,100 troops of whom 300 were embarked in *Foch* for 'Olifant VI'. She left on 23 September, landed the troops on the 28th and returned to Toulon on 8 October. *Clemenceau* took on her role as PA 1 on 18 November. Two days later, *Foch* left with her sister and the nuclear attack submarine (SNA) *Rubis* for Mission 'Thiof' off the coast of West Africa. She had ten Super Etendard of 17F, four Etendard IVP of 16F and three Super Frelon of 33F embarked, together with ten Puma and four Gazelle helicopters of the 5th Combat Helicopter Regiment and troops. A landing was conducted off Dakar, and the ship was subjected to a simulated attack by eight Jaguar strike aircraft. The ten Pumas were re-embarked, then flown off to Lanzarote on 8 December. *Foch* returned to Toulon on 16 December after a four-day visit to Las Palmas, and began a maintenance period (IE) the following day.

The maintenance period was cut short and *Foch* became PA 1 on 15 February 1983, the air group of *Clemenceau* being transferred by crane while alongside. Work-up followed, and a night landing incident involving a Super Etendard on 16 February caused a small flight deck fire. *Foch* then took part in a number of routine activities and exercises before being diverted to Beirut for 'Olifant XIII' during mid-May. NATO Exercises 'Distant Drum' (19–27 May) and 'Ocean Safari' (6–16 June) followed, with ten Super Etendard, six Crusader, four Alizé and two Alouette III embarked. On 7 June, a British Sea Harrier landed on *Foch*, and a US Vought A-7E Corsair made 'touch-and-go' landings the following day. On 13 June, a catapult failure resulted in the loss of a Crusader of 12F; the pilot was recovered. The catapult was now out of service, and the ship returned to Toulon ten days earlier than anticipated, on 28 June. Before her return she achieved a record of 111 launches in a single day from her one serviceable catapult.

A maintenance period (IE) scheduled from 11 July to 6 September was cut short to enable *Foch* to head Task Force 452 under Rear Admiral Klotz. For the mission, designated 'Olifant XVII', she embarked six Crusader, fifteen Super Etendard, three Etendard IVP, five Alizé of 6F, six Super Frelon of 32F and 33F, and three Alouette III. *Foch* arrived off Beirut on 6 September, and reconnaissance flights with her Etendard IVP aircraft began the following day. On the 9th the French embassy in Beirut was bombed (five dead, fourteen injured), and the Super Frelon helicopters brought the wounded on board. The reconnaissance missions located the batteries that were shelling the French positions, and after a brief stay at Larnaka a reprisal raid was mounted on the 22nd. Eight Super Etendard (four wih rockets, four with bombs), guided by two Etendard IVP, attacked a battery of 130mm guns some 20km from Beirut. One of the two Etendards was struck by splinters from a surface-to-air missile of Soviet origin, but managed to land on safely and was repaired in four days. A second missile narrowly missed an Etendard IVP the following day but the aircraft was undamaged. Hostilities ended on the 26th after a ceasefire.

*Foch*, relieved by *Clemenceau*, was relegated to PA 2 status on 6 October. The customary transfers of personnel and materiel took place at sea and at Larnaca. *Foch* returned to Toulon via Naples and Hyères, where she undertook pilot qualifications, arriving at her home port on 16 October. Eight days later she began a major refit (IPER) during which the infrastructure for the Syracuse satcom system was installed. The refit was scheduled to last until June 1984, but was interrupted by the need to relieve *Clemenceau* in May.

*Foch* embarked on her post-refit trials on 20 March, followed by work-up. She was declared operational on 1 May. She took part in Exercise 'Circé' in June, becoming PA 2 on 31 July. On 15 August she hosted the Prime Minister, Laurent Fabius, and ceremonies took place to celebrate the anniversary of the landings in Provence in 1944. She resumed her IPER on 20 August but this was again suspended on 17 September due to *Clemenceau*'s unavailability with machinery problems. *Foch* took on the role of PA 1 on 20 September, but only a single catapult was operational. She departed Toulon on the 22nd for Operation 'Mirmillon', a presence mission off Libya, which was in conflict with France over Chad. Night strike missions were planned and three rehearsals carried out. On 15 October, a Crusader of 12F intercepted two Libyan Mirage jets. Following five-day visits to Trieste and Naples, *Foch* returned to Toulon on 13 November. An intermediate maintenance period (PEI) followed, the ship remaining at three days' notice.

*Foch* resumed her PA 2 status on 15 January, and underwent a refit (IPER) from 21 January to 3 May. Aviation trials followed, notably with the catapult on the angled deck that had been repaired. In early June she took part in Exercise 'Farfadet' with the Pumas and Gazelles of the 1st Combat Helicopter Regiment, together with two Super Frelon and two Alouette III helicopters belonging to her own air group.

A planned short maintenance period (PEI) that began on 17 June had to be extended due to problems with the port IP turbine, but as *Foch* was due to resume PA 1 status she was kept at seventy-two-hour readiness. She left Toulon on 12 September with twelve Super Etendard, three Etendard IVP, ten Alizé, two Super Frelon, two Lynx and two Alouette III for a sortie marked by a visit from the US Secretary of State for the Navy, John Lehman, at the invitation of Rear Admiral Guirec Doniol (ALPA) on the 16th. Pilot qualifications and routine activities followed.

A group sortie took place from 14 to 18 October; *Foch* had four Crusader, sixteen Super Etendard, three Etendard IVP, eight Alizé, two Lynx and two Alouette III embarked. Exercise 'Iles d'Or' followed in November, and pilot qualifications in early December. On the 3rd an Etendard IVM of 59S was lost following a catapult launch, but the pilot was rescued. *Foch* began a short maintenance period (PEI) on 16 December.

*Foch* was again available from 31 January 1986. She then took part in a cruise christened 'Centurion' from 10 February to 15 March, with sixteen Super Etendard, four Crusader, three Etendard IVP, eight Alizé, two Lynx and two Alouette III embarked. There were visits to Las Palmas and Santa Cruz in the Canaries. On 26 May, *Foch* hosted the Minister of Defence, and on the 30th one of her Super Etendard strike aircraft sank the hull of the former fleet escort *Jauréguiberry* with an AM 39 Exocet missile.

Following Exercise 'Trident' from 2 to 15 June, she put in to Taranto, where divers found a problem with the port propeller shaft, which required a docking at Toulon on 26–28 May. She then took part in a group sortie ('Poseidon') and Exercise 'Ephaistos'. A planned maintenance period (PEI) that began on 15 July was cut short on 23 August to enable the carrier to cover the evacuation of the Multi-national Force from southern Lebanon (Exercise 'Zinnia'). She embarked ten Super Etendard, two Etendard IVP, four Alizé, four Super Frelon, four Lynx, nine Puma, six Gazelle and half the Jaubert commando unit for the operation.

During a subsequent sortie on 11 September a Super Etendard of 17F was lost at sea when one of her rockets malfunctioned; the pilot ejected and was recovered. *Foch* took part in NATO Exercise 'Display Determination' later in the month then, from 29 September to 19 October, in a cruise by the Squadron to the Eastern Mediterranean with twelve Super Etendard, three Crusader, four Alizé, two Super

**Left:** The carrier *Foch* at Barcelona on 21 May 1989. *(Marc Piché)*

**Above:** A Sud Aviation SA.321G Super Frelon heavy-lift helicopter. *(René Bail)*

Frelon, two Lynx, two Alouette III, nine Puma, six Gazelle, plus two Etendard IVP that were not permitted to fly. A visit to Port Said during 6–11 October was followed by Exercise 'Osiris'. The end of the year was taken up with pilot qualifications.

On 1 March 1987, *Foch* began a major modernisation, during which two groups of 100mm guns were replaced by Crotale installations and the DRBV 20 long-range air surveillance radar was replaced by the DRBV 15 (see Technical section). The magazine stowage was revised to accommodate the ASMP missile.

## TOULON 1988–92

*Foch* went to sea for the first time after her refit on 1 June 1988. The first Crotale firing took place on 28 June. In July she operated with the northern air group, and on 21 July, during a 'Families Day', the prototype Rafale fighter made several approaches without touching down. On 16 September, *Foch* put to sea to welcome *Clemenceau*, which was returning after a fourteen-month period of activity. Work-up with the southern air group followed in late September and early October. *Foch* then underwent a course at the Fleet Training Centre (CEF), with ten Super Etendard of 14F, six Alizé of 6F, two Lynx of 31F and two Alouette III of 23S embarked.

Training and work-up continued into 1989. *Foch* was equipped as a helicopter carrier for Exercise 'Phinia', then underwent a maintenance period (PEI) until 7 April, when she was designated PA 1. Routine exercises and sorties to the Western and Eastern Mediterranean followed, with visits to Naples, Alexandria and Barcelona.

The Navy was anxious to acquire the F-18 Hornet to bridge the gap between the ageing Crusader and the Dassault Rafale, which was in the early stages of development and would not be available for some years. Trials with the F-18 were planned to take place on *Foch* from 28 August. However, French politicians were unhappy with the idea of purchasing an American aircraft, and the Government imposed the Rafale on the

**Right and opposite:** Two photos of *Clemenceau* and *Foch* operating together in 1992. *(PM Pascal Fournier, Marine Nationale)*

Navy in December 1989. No trials with the Hornet took place, and it was decided that the life of the Crusader would be prolonged; this modernisation focused on safety rather than an upgrade of the avionics.

An emergency mission to the Eastern Mediterranean ('Capselle') took place on 19 August; *Foch* returned to Toulon via Taranto on 25 September. There was further routine activity in October and November. During a sortie in late October two Alizé were engaged in a rocket attack on the hull of the former *Petrel* and mistook their target, resulting in one dead and one injured. The year ended with a maintenance period (PEI) from 13 November to 22 December.

Work-up with the northern air group took place in January 1990, followed by a short cruise christened 'Médoc', a visit to Valencia and a further maintenance period from 26 February to 13 April.

For 'Héraklès' on 17 April, *Foch* embarked fifteen Super Etendard of 11F, eight Crusader of 12F, six Alizé of 4F, a detachment of Etendard IVP of 16F, two Super Frelon of 32F and two Alouette III of 23S. The sortie began with Exercise 'Farfadet' on 23 April, followed by a visit to Ponta Delgada (Azores) on 30 April. On 4 May a Crusader of 12F was lost in mid-Atlantic due to a fuel transfer problem, but the pilot managed to eject and was rescued by helicopter twenty minutes later. *Foch* then visited Puerto Rico, Fort-de-France, Cayenne and Dakar before returning to Brest, where she hosted Minister of Defence Jean-Pierre Chevènement (13–14 June). She participated in Exercise 'Suroît' from the 15th to the 21st, returned to Brest from the 22nd to the 26th, visited Casablanca from 30 June to 4 July, and returned to Toulon on 7 July, where she began a two-month maintenance period (PEI).

*Foch* went to sea again in September to prepare for a possible deployment to the Gulf. An Etendard IVP was lost on 10 October when the control surfaces jammed; the pilot ejected and was recovered by a Super Frelon but suffered injuries. And on the night of 20/21 November, two Alizé collided when forming up; one managed to land at Nice, but the other fell to the sea and sank; the crew was recovered by the frigate *Commandant de Pimodan*. *Foch* became PA 2 on 30 November and in January of the following year prepared for a refit (IPER) that lasted from 4 February to 19 July 1991.

Following post-refit trials *Foch* became PA 1 on 19 August, and engaged in work-up during September. On 4 October an Alizé of 4F touched down forward of the arrester wires and took off again, but struck the water twenty seconds later and sank; the crew was

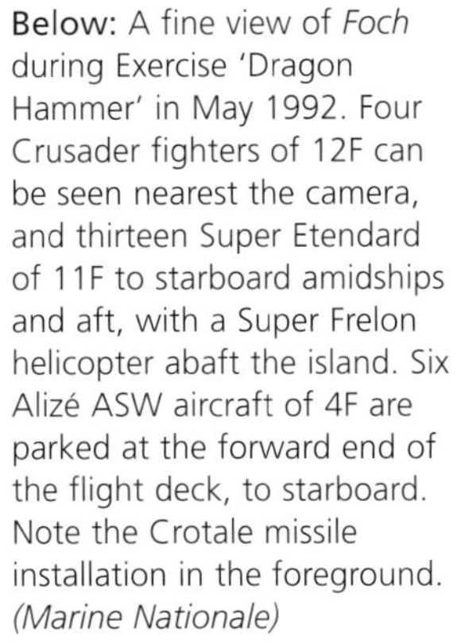

Below: A fine view of *Foch* during Exercise 'Dragon Hammer' in May 1992. Four Crusader fighters of 12F can be seen nearest the camera, and thirteen Super Etendard of 11F to starboard amidships and aft, with a Super Frelon helicopter abaft the island. Six Alizé ASW aircraft of 4F are parked at the forward end of the flight deck, to starboard. Note the Crotale missile installation in the foreground. *(Marine Nationale)*

rescued by a Super Frelon. Routine activities were followed by Exercise 'Iles d'Or' from 5 to 16 November, and there were visits to Barcelona (22–26 November) and Naples (6–10 December).

*Foch* put to sea for work-up with the southern air group during the first months 1992, embarking twenty-nine aircraft from 20 to 24 January. During training Exercise 'Terpsichore' on 23 March–14 April, a Crusader of 12F was diverted to Kalamata air base in Greece due to bad weather but crashed near Militsa Mountain with the loss of the pilot. After visits to Antalya (Turkey) and Athens, *Foch* took part in NATO Exercise 'Dragon Hammer' from 5 to 21 May.

On 1 June 1992, the Mediterranean and Atlantic Squadrons were replaced by the *Force d'action navale* (FAN) at Toulon and the *Groupe d'action sous-marine* (GASM) at Brest. During the same month, *Foch* participated in Exercises 'Damtam' and 'Farfadet'. She then prepared for a refit (IPER) that began on 29 September: her Parsons LP reaction turbines were replaced by new impulse turbines, and modifications were made to enable the ship to operate the Rafale fighter.

## TOULON AND 'BALBUZARD' 1993–96

*Foch* went to sea again on 15 March 1993. During machinery trials on 23–24 March she attained a top speed of 32.2 knots – an impressive performance for a thirty-year-old ship. From 13 April to 7 May she conducted trials with the first Rafale Marine fighter (M01), and a demonstration was attended by the Minister of Defence, François Léotard, on the 29th, three days after the carrier's redesignation as PA 2. In all, there were thirty-one catapult launches and deck landings.

On 25 June, *Foch* left Toulon to relieve *Clemenceau* in Mission 'Balbuzard' in the Adriatic, becoming PA 1 two days later. She had on board 11F (SUE), 4F (Alizé), and detachments of 16F (Etendard IVP), 32F and 23S together with a Puma detachment from ALAT. Her aircraft conducted reconnaissance and ESM missions over Bosnia. There were breaks in Corfu and Ancona (July), and Trieste (August). Two Sea Harriers landed on board on 8 August. *Foch* returned to Toulon on 29 August, resuming PA 2 status on 1 September. She then underwent a brief maintenance period (PEI).

In October she put to sea for pilot qualifications and took part in Excercise 'Ardente 93'. She again became PA 1 on 18 November, and after a visit to Valencia and participation in Exercise 'Tarot 93' (8–10 December) she took part in training with the ASMP missile. She left on the 11th for another 'Balbuzard' mission. She was at Trieste from 20 to 23 December, and returned

**Below and overleaf:** Three images showing the trials of the Dassault Rafale on *Foch*; the photos were taken on 19 July 1993. *(CEV)*

R99

**Opposite:** The last catapult launches of the F-8E Crusader from *Foch* in October 1989. *(Alexandre Paringaux)*

to Toulon on 30 December for a maintenance period (PEI), which lasted until 24 January 1994.

A series of trials with the M01/02 prototypes of the Rafale fighter took place in late January and early February, but these were cut short to enable the carrier to return to the Adriatic from 6 February to 20 March, after which *Foch* became PA 2. Pilot qualifications followed, and trials with the Rafale were then resumed; between 11 April and 3 May there were fifty-six catapult launches and arrested landings. After a maintenance period (PEI) from 9 May to 29 July, *Foch* took part in a naval review that took place between Villefranche and Toulon in the presence of President François Mitterand, who landed on the carrier in a helicopter. She became PA 1 on 18 August. Further work-up with the ASMP missile and trials with the Rafale took place during September and October, with twenty-five catapult launches and arrested landings.

On 14 November, Squadron 17F embarked with the upgraded SEM (Super Etendard *modernisé*) strike fighter – the first operational deployment of the aircraft. A new 'Balbuzard' mission in the Adriatic from 6 to 23 December saw the first SEM mission over Bosnia on the 11th. On the 17th, an Etendard IVP was damaged by a missile, but managed to land at Gioia del Colle (Italy).

The PEI ended on 3 February 1995, and three days later, *Foch* left for the Adriatic. She was at Trieste from 17 to 20 February and Alexandria from 2 to 7 March, returning to Toulon on 10 March. A second 'Balbuzard' mission took place from 25 April to 24 May, with a brief stay in Suda Bay from 8 to 12 May. The carrier departed Toulon again on the 28th with 37 helicopters belonging to ALAT and 250 men of the Special Operations group for Operation 'Hermine', which involved the extraction of French personnel from the UN Protection Force (FORPRONU). In the end it was the TCD *Ouragan* that embarked these troops at Split. *Foch* was at Trieste from 21 to 28 June and 9–13 July. On 14 July, the Minister of Defence, Charles Millon, came on board, and the ship returned to Toulon on 20 July for a maintenance period, which lasted until 8 September.

A fourth series of trials with the Rafale took place from 11 to 18 September, when aircraft M02 made twenty deck landings. On 11 December, *Foch* became PA 2 and prepared for a major refit (IPER), which began on 5 February 1996. Originally planned to last six months, the refit was extended in order to replace the steam collectors and remove asbestos. The four remaining 100mm turrets were replaced by the short-range Sadral anti-missile system.

## TOULON 1997–2000

The refit was completed on 31 July 1997. Following trials and work-up, *Foch* became PA 1 on 24 September, visiting La Spezia in October. From 24 to 26 November she conducted trials with SEMs modified to Standards III and IV. On 5 December, when *Foch* was returning from Exercise 'Hera' in the Western Mediterranean, an Etendard IVP was lost due to a catapult failure; the pilot ejected and was rescued.

The fifth series of trials with the Rafale M took place between 19 January and 6 February 1998, with thirty-eight deck landings, and two pilots were qualified to fly the Crusader. *Foch* then put to sea for Exercise 'Safran 1', was at Brest from 3 to 6 March, and took part in NATO Exercise 'Strong Resolve' from 6 to 23 March. Exercise 'Safran 2' followed from 27 March to 3 April.

With the commissioning of the nuclear-powered carrier *Charles de Gaulle*, it became difficult to maintain two aircraft carriers in active service. Some thought was given to putting *Foch* into reserve, to be

**Right:** The angled deck of *Foch*, seen here at Toulon on 19 July 2000. *(Jean Moulin)*

reactivated during the first planned immobilisation of the new carrier around 2004–05. It was eventually decided that she should be placed in Reserve A on 31 December 1999.

Routine training activity continued until 15 June, when the carrier underwent a three-month maintenance period (PEI) that ended on 4 September. On 21 September she left Toulon with fourteen SEM of 17F and 11F, four Etendard IVP of 16F, six Crusader of 12F, six Alizé of 6F, two Super Frelon of 33F and a detachment of 23S for Exercise 'Pean'. She visited Beirut from 1 to 5 October and was put on alert for a possible participation in the First Gulf War (Operation 'Salamandre'). She arrived at Antalya on the 12th, but left the same day for the Ionian Sea. 'Pean' was followed by Mission 'Trident', which began on 15 October. The Minister of Defence, Alain Richard, came on board on 23 October, and *Foch* returned to Toulon on 12 November after a six-day visit to Trieste.

After a brief maintenance period (PEI), *Foch* left Toulon for the Adriatic on 26 January 1999 at the head of Task Force 470 (Rear Admiral Coldefy). Her air group comprised fourteen SEM of 11F, a detachment of Etendard IVP of 16F, six Crusader of 12F, six Alizé of 6F, three Super Frelon of 33F and two Dauphin and a single Alouette III of 23S. On 28 February, five Crusaders escorted President Jacques Chirac when he flew over the ship. On 1 March, the Crusader was finally withdrawn from service due to its outdated electronic warfare outfit, and the group was reinforced by eight SEM of 17F. *Foch* was at Trieste from 2 to 8 March. Operations against the Serbs began on the evening of 24 March. On the 27th, the Super Frelon helicopters were put on alert after the loss of a US F-117 Nighthawk stealth attack aircraft; the pilot was eventually recovered by the Americans. The SEM were engaged in operations against the Federal Republic of Yugoslavia from 5 April. They provided close air support (CAS), intervention against targets when requested, and battle air interdiction (BAI) against targets identified before launch. The Etendard IVP conducted reconnaissance, and the Alizé maritime surveillance. *Foch* returned to Trieste for a rest period from 22 to 26 April, then resumed her patrols, returning to Toulon on 3 June; she began a maintenance period (IE) four days later. During the 119 days of the operation she had flown 476 combat missions.

**Below:** The former French carrier *Foch* as the Brazilian *São Paulo*. She was purchased by the Brazilian Navy to replace the elderly *Minas Gerais* in September 2000, and operated a mixed group of Douglas AF-1 (A-4UK) Skyhawk fighter bombers and helicopters. After abortive attempts to dispose of the ship, she was scuttled in the South Atlantic in 2023.

The Yugoslav conflict ended on 10 June. *Foch* then took part in Exercise 'Pean' from 4 to 29 October. Three Crusaders of 12F embarked for the last time for the final week of the exercise. The last catapult launch of the fighter, by the commanding officer of 12F (CF Antoine Guillot), and the last arrested landing (LV Bertrand Denis) took place on the 28th.

Due to delays with *Charles de Gaulle*, the service life of *Foch* would be extended by another few months. Following a brief maintenance period, she again went to sea for trials on 10 January 2000, and on the 15th for a final round-the-world trip christened 'Myrrhe', embarking twelve SEM, three Etendard IVP, six Alizé, plus helicopters. She passed through the Suez Canal on the 22nd, was at Jeddah on 24–26 January, then took part in Exercise 'Golfe 2000' from 31 January to 10 February. After visits to Abu Dhabi (9–13 February), Messaid (Qatar, 14–17), Bombay (24–28), La Réunion (9–13 March), Capetown (22–27 March), Rio de Janeiro (6–12 April) and Dakar (20–23 April) she returned to Toulon on 30 April.

A sea day for her former commanding officers took place on 8 June and, on 13 June, *Foch* took part in Exercise 'Eolo 2000', making a final visit to Valencia from 15 to 18 June. The last night landing, by an SEM of 17F, took place on 24 June. On 27 June, the air group was catapulted off, and *Foch* returned to Toulon on 28 June to pay off. She had covered 1,105,376nm since her entry into service, with 85,147 catapult launches and 74,999 deck landings. In theory she remained in commission as a helicopter carrier pending the availability of *Charles de Gaulle*, but was now due to be transferred to Brazil, and the first elements of the new crew arrived during July.

*Foch* was officially sold on 26 September for US $12 million and stricken on 1 October. She passed *Charles de Gaulle*, which was steaming in the opposite direction, during a brief sortie at the end of October. She finally left Toulon on 2 November for Brest, where she was to undergo a refit and modernisation prior to her transfer. The Crotale and Sadral missile systems and the Syracuse satcom were landed and, on 15 November, the ship was officially handed over and renamed *São Paulo*.

Post-refit trials began on 25 January 2001, and *São Paulo* departed on 1 February, arriving in Rio on 17 February after a brief stop at Dakar. She would be operational from 3 September, embarking a mixed air group of Douglas AF-1 (A-4UK) Skyhawk fighter bombers and helicopters. Service with the Brazilian Navy was marked by a number of serious boiler room fires, and she was decommissioned on 22 November 2018.

CHAPTER 9

# FROM PA 58 TO *CHARLES DE GAULLE*

A DIRECTIVE SIGNED BY ADMIRAL NOMY on 14 March 1955 envisaged the construction of a third carrier identical to *Clemenceau* and *Foch*, with the aim of having three such ships in service by 1963. However, the project fell foul of the customary budgetary problems, and future French carrier construction was then complicated by the perceived need to embark nuclear-capable bombers.

It was now envisaged that the 1958 budget would feature a larger, 35,000-ton aircraft carrier and a 5,000-ton missile-armed escort.[1] Staff requirements for a carrier capable of nuclear strike were drawn up on 5 March 1957, and studies were ready by 15 October that year. The sixty-strong air group was to comprise three nuclear bombers plus three refuelling aircraft, eight all-weather interceptors, twenty-four light strike fighters, twelve ASW aircraft plus six ASW helicopters, six AEW aircraft and two plane guard helicopters. The nuclear strike, aerial refuelling and all-weather interceptor missions were to be performed by a new aircraft designated CB 62; take-off weight was limited by the capacity of the catapults, hence the requirement for in-flight refuelling of the bombers. The strike fighter was to be either an 'M' (= *Marine*) variant of the Bréguet 1100 currently under development or the Dassault Etendard IV, and the Bréguet 1050 was to have ASW and AEW variants.[2]

PA 58, as the project was subsequently known, was for a ship with a length between perpendiculars of 262 metres and a beam of 34 metres (the maximum

[1] This would eventually become the 'missile frigate' *Suffren*.

[2] The British would adopt similar arrangements during the 1960s using the Fairey Gannet.

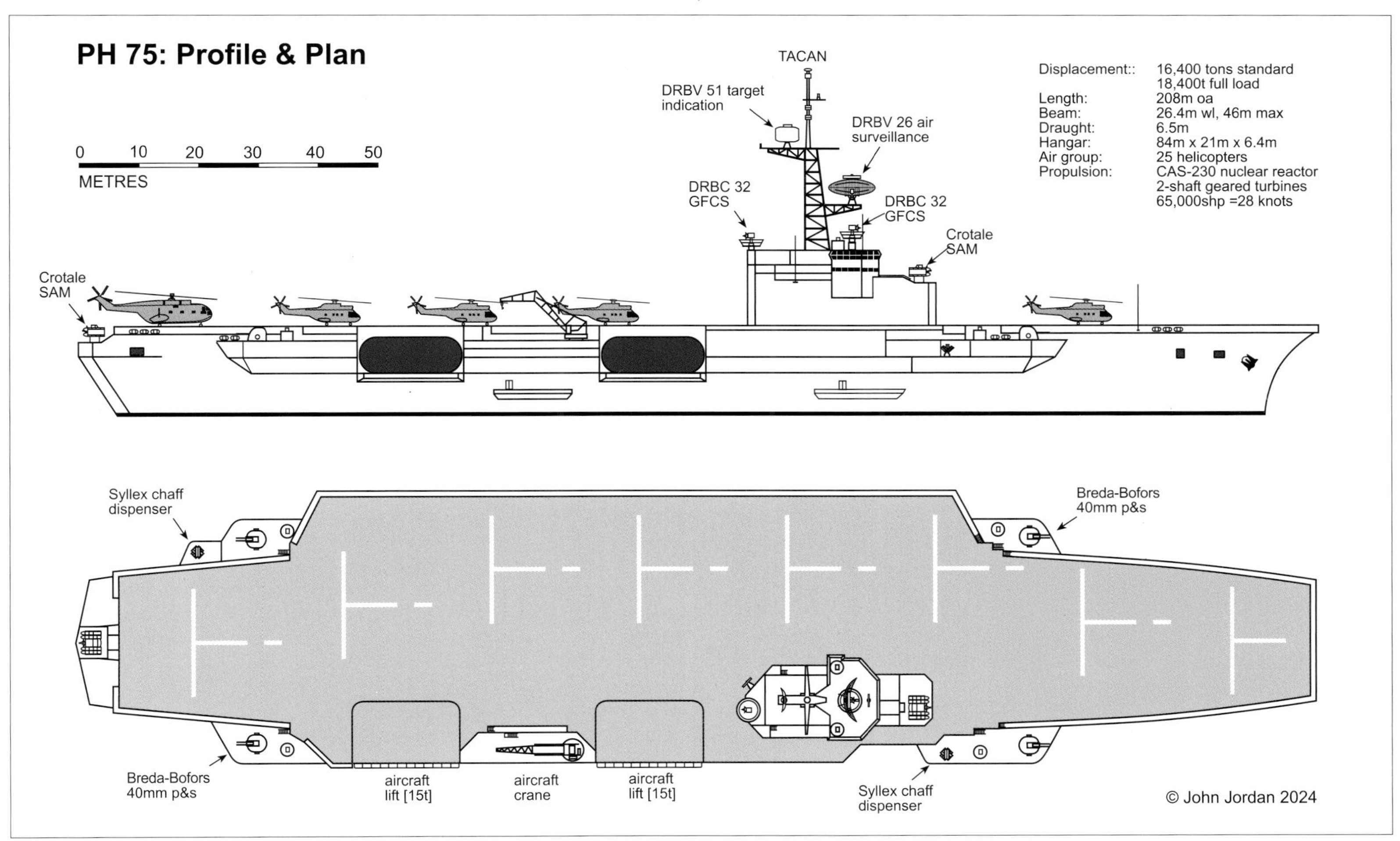

**Right:** A model of the PH 75 helicopter carrier.

that could be accommodated in the current building docks), a standard displacement of 35,000 tons, a normal displacement of 42,000 tonnes and a deep load displacement of 45,550 tonnes. The flight deck was 280 metres long and had a maximum width of 58 metres; it incorporated an 8°30' angled deck 192 metres long. The two catapults, each 75 metres long, were disposed as in *Clemenceau*, with one to port forward and a second on the angled deck. There were two side lifts 17m x 14m disposed fore and aft of the island. The four-shaft propulsion system comprised eight boilers and four sets of geared turbines, and was designed to deliver 200,000shp; maximum speed was 32.5–33 knots (35 knots were hoped for on trials). Armament was to comprise eight 100mm DP guns and two twin launchers for the new Masurca surface-to-air missile system – a similar arrangement to the contemporary USS *Kitty Hawk* (CVA-63). The name *Verdun* was mooted.

The Navy, committed to a third carrier to ensure permanent availability of at least one ship, was prepared to sacrifice the two 5,000-ton escorts proposed for 1958 and beyond, but the Minister of Defence refused to allow the carrier to be inscribed in the budget. The third carrier was finally abandoned in 1961, by which time it had been decided that France would develop an independent submarine-based nuclear deterrent, initially designated the *Force de Frappe* (later *Force de Dissuasion*). The financial outlay involved would constrict the funding available for the surface fleet for the following decades.

## PH 75

During the early 1970s, the *Marine Nationale* hoped to replace *Arromanches*. Following a number of abortive studies for a conventionally powered ship similar in conception to the American *Iwo Jima* (LPH-2) but incorporating a docking well, a project was evolved for a ship initially designated PH 75 (PH = *porte-hélicoptères*), designed to operate as either an assault carrier, embarking Super Frelon and Puma assault helicopters (see accompanying drawing), or as an ASW carrier, embarking the Super Frelon and Lynx. With a conventional 'through deck' and an island to starboard, the ship was to have nuclear propulsion to provide unlimited range, and displacement was to be 16,400 tons standard.

In the intervention role the ship would carry a special landing force of units from the *Forces terrestres d'intervention* (FTI) and their supporting air units (CAFI), plus a Helicopter Movement Command Centre. One thousand troops could be accommodated in designated quarters, with a further 500 in supplementary spaces in the hangar if required. PH 75 was to be fitted as a command ship, with an action information centre, an ASW centre and an amphibious operations centre. She would also be equipped for disaster relief, and had extensive hospital facilities.

PH 75 was to have been laid down at Brest in 1976 with completion scheduled for 1981, but the start of construction was delayed until 1981 due to funding issues. By this stage it was envisaged that PH 75 would operate British Harrier V/STOL aircraft, and she was redesignated PA 75. However, it was subsequently decided that PH 75 was too small, and that the performance of V/STOL aircraft was markedly inferior to conventional carrier aircraft. The concept of the carrier with nuclear propulsion, however, formed the basis of the *Charles de Gaulle* design.

## *CHARLES DE GAULLE*

The replacement of *Clemenceau* and *Foch* was already being considered during the 1970s, but decisions on the future carrier force would be constantly postponed.

In 1979, Chief Constructor (*Ingénieur général de l'armement*) Joseph Tretout reviewed the PH 75

project. Studies for a new aircraft carrier were already underway when Tretout was joined by Admiral François Deramond. The cost of the new vessel had already been determined, and dimensions were limited by the existing docks, with 32 metres being accepted as the maximum beam.

The programme was initiated in 1982 by the Chief of the Naval Staff. The studies concluded with the adoption of a conventional aircraft carrier of 32,000 tonnes equipped with catapults and arrester wires but with nuclear propulsion. In the absence of a clear decision regarding future aircraft, the aviation installations were based on the American F-18 Hornet, the purchase of which was currently favoured by the Navy. The programme was transmitted to the DCN in May 1985, and a meeting of the Council of Ministers approved the inclusion of the carrier in the 1986 budget proposal. The accompanying table gives a timeline for authorisation and construction of the ship.

## FLIGHT DECK AND AVIATION

The overall dimensions of the hull were similar to those of *Clemenceau* after she was bulged in 1966. However, the dimensions of the flight deck were maximised in order to allow more parking space. Length increased only slightly, to 261.5 metres, but the width of the flight deck was increased from 46 metres to 64 metres, the overhang being supported on deep sponsons. The island was shorter due to the elimination of boiler uptakes with the adoption of nuclear propulsion. The angled deck was similar in conception to that in *Clemenceau*, being offset at 8°30' to the ship's axis. However, the increased overall width of the flight deck meant that there was more 'parking space' to port and starboard, particularly at the after end of the ship. As completed the angled deck measured 199 metres by 20 metres, but following trials it was found necessary to increase the length by 4 metres at the forward end in order to ensure safe

Below: Assembly of the hull of *Charles de Gaulle*, 22 January 1990. *(DCAN Brest)*

handling for the E-2C Hawkeye, which had gained weight since the carrier's conception. The fight deck was initially covered with the French GPA 84 non-slip paint used on *Clemenceau* and *Foch*, but this was superseded in 2001 by a GPA 96 paint trialled on *Foch* in 2000, which aimed to reduce wear and tear for the arrester wires.

The two American C13-3 75-metre catapults were disposed as in *Clemenceau*, with the forward catapult parallel to the ship's axis to port and the after catapult on the angled deck. However, the greater length of the C13 meant that the forward catapult impinged on the angled deck, thereby precluding simultaneous catapult launches and arrested landings. This was accepted as the price of being able to launch heavier aircraft (up to 25 tonnes); relocating the catapult to starboard to clear the angled deck would have prevented aircraft being parked forward.

For landing aircraft, *Charles de Gaulle* was equipped with three US Mk 7 Mod 3 arrester wires spaced 13 metres apart, with a run-out of 96 metres reduced to 75 metres. A safety barrier was available for emergencies such as the loss of the tailhook. An OP3A landing mirror sight was fitted on a sponson to port; a portable emergency manual back-up device could be installed. A new departure was a laser landing guide desig-

## Table 1: TIMELINE

19 Sep 1985: PAN 1 included in 1986 budget; to be named *Richelieu*.
4 Feb 1986: construction approved by Minister of Defence.
18 May 1987: construction announced by Prime Minister Jacques Chirac during visit to Ile Longue (SSBN base); to be renamed *Charles de Gaulle*.
24 Nov 1987: first steel cut in presence of the Maritime Prefect, VAE Dominique Lefebvre, and Ing Gén Tretout.
14 Apr 1989: first two blocks (140t/60t) assembled in Laninon dock No 9.
22 Jan 1990: central part assembly completed.
23 Feb 1990: forward blocks in place, but construction then delayed by budgetary cuts 1990/1991/1993/1995.
19 Aug 1991: bow in place.
11 Sep 1991: 1st turbo-alternator installed and deck closed.
9 Mar 1992: last block of stern in place.
19 Dec 1992: hull floated out and supports moved 3 metres to west.
8 Jan 1993: hull back in dock for fitting of flight deck overhang sponsons.
19 Aug 1993: bow section of flight deck fitted.
20 Oct 1993: first set of turbines embarked.
24 Mar 1994: first aircraft lift installed.
6 Apr 1994: mast stepped.
7 May 1994: official ceremony for floating out in presence of President François Mitterand, Prime Minister Edouard Balladour, Minister of Defence François Léotard and 4,000 invited guests; ship covered with 30,300m$^2$ of blue, white and red fabric; removed by two DCN technicians and forty Marine commandos; however, weather delayed floating out until 13 May, when towed to fitting-out quay.
22–25 Jun 1994: two nuclear reactors installed.
17 Sep 1994: first crew formed.
7 May 1996: small fire beneath island; quickly extinguished.
14 Jun 1996: first landing by Lynx of 34F, followed by Super Puma with President Jacques Chirac on board; installation of catapults began same day.
24 Oct 1996: crane installed.
1 Feb 1997: manned for trials; CV Richard Wilmot-Roussel + 650 crew.
28 Feb 1997: DRBV 15C installed.
4 Apr 1997: ship turned at fitting-out quay for catapult trials beginning 18 June, initially with dummy aircraft.
12 Jun 1997: DRBJ 11B installed.
22 Oct 1997: docked for fitting of propellers 22 Dec onwards.
23 Feb 1998: floated out.
25 May 1998: after reactor activated, followed by forward reactor 10 June. SUE embarked by crane for catapult trials.
20 Dec 1998: left fitting-out quay for static machinery trials and helicopter trials, Bay of Roscanvel (Dauphin/Lynx/Alouette III/Super Frelon).
23 Dec 1998: returned to quay, then towed to Bay of Roscanvel for inclining.
26 Jan 1999: first sea trials; returned to Brest on 28th due to overheating of feed pump.
18 Mar 1999: left Brest for further trials; 20 knots with 50 per cent power attained on 20th, but vibration issue with steering gear and rudders at higher speeds; returned 30 Mar.
18 Apr 1999: on third sortie covered 3600nm and attained 28 knots at full power, but vibration problem persisted; returned 29 Apr.
14 Jun 1999: fourth sortie to prepare for aviation trials; returned 18 Jun.
5 Jul 1999: aviation trials; first landings by SUE and Rafale M02 6 Jul; first catapult launch with Rafale 7 Jul; thirty-three catapult launches and landings by Rafale, thirty by SUE plus one by SEM; returned 20 July.
2 Aug 1999: trials with E-2C Hawkeye; first landing on 3 Aug; returned 13 August.
23 Aug 1999: trials with SEM of 11F; hosted President Jacques Chirac, who witnessed catapult launch and landing of E-2C Hawkeye 28 Aug.
14 Sep 1999: first RAS trials with fleet tanker *Marne*: 28m$^3$ diesel, 20m$^3$ aviation fuel + 1.7t stores transferred.
1 Oct 1999: RANAE (*remise à niveau après essais*) until 15 May 2000; ship docked in Laninon No 8 17 Oct–12 Feb.
15 May 2000 onwards: further aviation and RAS trials + trials of Sadral; first night landing 30 June.
27 Sep 2000: official completion date (*clôture d'armement*).
30 Sep 2000: left Brest for Toulon.

nated DALAS (*dispositif d'aide à l'apportage au laser*).

The hangar was 138 metres long and 29 metres wide, and had a clearance of 6.1 metres to allow for the 5.6-metre height of the E-2C Hawkeye. It could be divided into two sections by a fire door. Theoretical capacity was twenty-three aircraft and two helicopters – just under two thirds of the standard air group. The hangar was served by two identical side lifts, both located abaft the island; dimensions were 21m x 12m and load capacity 36 tonnes, allowing them to lift two SEM or two Rafale multirole fighters simultaneously. There were also two smaller lifts that could raise bombs and missiles to the flight deck. No fewer than twenty aviation workshops were provided at hangar level, and there was a test bench for aero-engines at the after end, with an exhaust outlet set in the stern. The aircraft crane abaft the island could lift 37 tonnes, and was complemented by a mobile flight deck crane.

**Left:** The hull of *Charles de Gaulle* in Laninon No 9 dock on 7 April 1992. *(Jean Moulin)*

**Above:** *Charles de Gaulle* during the final stages of fitting out at Brest. Both aircraft lifts are in the lowered position. *(Marine Nationale)*

**Opposite:** *Charles de Gaulle* on her sea trials in 1999. *(Marine Nationale)*

Aviation fuel capacity when the ship was completed was 4000m$^3$, and the air ordnance magazines could hold 600 tonnes of munitions.

## MACHINERY

The main machinery spaces of *Charles de Gaulle* occupy five central compartments on four levels. Steam is supplied by two K 15 nuclear reactors, each of which is located in its own protected compartment. Rated at 150MW, the reactor is the same model employed in the SSBNs of the *Le Triomphant* type but was specially adapted to allow for the frequent changes of speed to be expected in a surface ship. Radiological protection was initially to CIPR 26 standard, but was adapted to the much stricter CIPR 60 standard adopted in France in May 2000 during the post-trials refit (RANAE), at a cost of 137 tonnes. The nuclear cores have a life of around eight years.

The steam produced is used to power two groups of geared turbines, each comprising a single HP and a single LP turbine driving one of the two shafts via double-reduction gearing. It also powers two turbo-alternators, two condensers each capable of producing 130 tonnes of fresh water per day, and the two reservoirs for the catapults. Total horsepower is 83,000cv for a maximum speed of 27 knots; the cruise speed is set at 25 knots.[3] This is significantly less than in *Clemenceau* and *Foch* (126,000cv/32 knots), and necessitated the adoption of the longer, more powerful catapult to compensate for the reduction in wind speed over deck.

3 Damage to a propeller early in the career of *Charles de Gaulle* necessitated the temporary fitting of propellers from *Clemenceau*, which reduced maximum speed to 25 knots.

**Right:** An overhead of *Charles de Gaulle* on 18 March 2010. On the flight deck: four Rafale interceptors, six Super Etendard strike fighters, an E-2C Hawkeye with wings folded, and a plane guard helicopter. *(ARDHAN collection)*

The machinery compartments are arranged as follows: Engine Room No 1 (turbines driving starboard shaft); Reactor Room No 1; Nuclear Control Room; Reactor Room No 2; Engine Room No 2 (turbines driving port shaft). The total volume of these five compartments is 15,000m$^3$ and the total weight of machinery 5,000 tonnes.

The two four-bladed propellers each have a diameter of 5.9 metres and weigh 19 tonnes. The twin rudders were initially offset from the line of the shafts so that the propellers could be removed without the rudders having to be dismantled. However, this arrangement was found to result in severe vibrations during trials and, in the refit (RANAE) that followed, the rudders were moved 0.83 metres to realign them with the shafts. Each of the rudder assemblies weighs 30 tonnes.

Electrical power when the ship is underway is supplied by four turbo-alternators, each rated at 4000kW. These are supplemented by four diesel alternators each of 1100kW. Back-up for these systems is provided by two emergency gas turbines each rated at 250kW, which ensure electrical supply for the vital organs of the ship, for the nuclear reactors and for the navigation systems. The diesel alternators are primarily for use when alongside, and these and the gas turbines can be started instantaneously. There are two electrical mains, arranged symmetrically port and

**Right:** Inside the hangar of *Charles de Gaulle* on 22 March 2010. A Super Etendard strike fighter is under tow in the foreground, with an E-2C Hawkeye beyond. *(ARDHAN collection)*

**Left:** The stern of *Charles de Gaulle*, with the exhaust duct for aero-engine testing prominent to starboard. The photo was taken when the ship left for the Eastern Mediterranean on 18 November 2015. *(ARDHAN collection)*

starboard, each with a main station, an auxiliary station and an emergency station; current is 440V at 60Hz, reduced to 220V for the crew spaces.

Arrangements for stabilisation of the platform are particularly complete. The SATRAP (*système automatique de tranquilisaion et de pilotage*) system comprises two pairs of fins that combine with the twin rudders to keep the ship's roll within a 3-degree envelope. The carrier is also equipped with a COGITE (*compensation de gîte*) system designed to compensate for heel, comprising twelve wagons on transverse rails located on the 2nd Gallery Deck with a total weight of 240 tonnes; the wagons are moved from side to side by cables powered by winches. These two systems, when acting together, ensure that flying operations can take place up to Sea State 6.

## PROTECTION

The internal box armour of *Clemenceau* was abandoned in favour of tight compartmentation. The double hull was reinforced by additional watertight compartments at the waterline (*dispositif Poseidon*), while protective bulkheads to the sides of the nuclear reactors were designed to resist anti-ship missiles. The hull is divided into no fewer than twenty watertight sections, designated A–T, and there are 2,600 compartments excluding the island.

The nine decks in the hull are as follows: Flight Deck, 2nd Gallery, 1st Gallery, Hangar Deck, First Deck, Main Deck, Platform Deck, plus a Hold on two levels. The island has seven levels; the bridge and aviation platform are on the fourth.

## ARMAMENT

Although it was assumed that the carrier would always be accompanied in a conflict zone by an air defence escort armed with long-range surface-to-air missiles, *Charles de Gaulle* was equipped with a full range of self-defence systems.

The SAAM medium-range air defence system is based around the Aster 15 missile, which has a theoretical range of 30,000 metres. Similar in conception to the US Navy's Standard, the Aster 15 missiles are fired from one of two blocks of sixteen Sylver 43 vertical launch cells, located *en echelon* to starboard forward and to port aft – an identical disposition to the launchers for Crotale on *Clemenceau* and *Foch* as modernised in 1986–88.

Three-dimensional air surveillance for the Aster missile was initially provided by the DRBJ 11B radar (replaced in 2018 by the SMART-S Mk II), and missile guidance by Arabel. The DRBJ 11 electronically scanned radar used a circular planar antenna covered by 1,000–1,500 phase shifters, which steered the beam in elevation (over a 60-degree angle) and bearing. The antenna was inclined at a 15-degree angle and rotated inside a protective radome; range was about 100nm. The Arabel multifunction radar has a planar antenna inclined at 30 degrees rotating at 60rpm, likewise within a radome. The beam is 2 degrees wide and can scan up to 70 degrees in elevation, and the transmitter can hop frequencies over 10 per cent of its frequency range. A lens antenna is used to steer the beam, a technology that has reduced the number of phase shifters to 100. Arabel is essentially a shorter-range, higher-data-rate version of DRBJ 11.

For point defence against low-flying anti-ship missiles there are two Sadral missile launchers, each with six Mistral missiles, which have a range of 6,000 metres. Eight 20mm F 2 guns were originally to have been embarked, but they were never mounted. Fire control for these close-range systems is provided by two small C 2A Vigy 105 EOD electro-optical target indication directors equipped with an infrared camera,

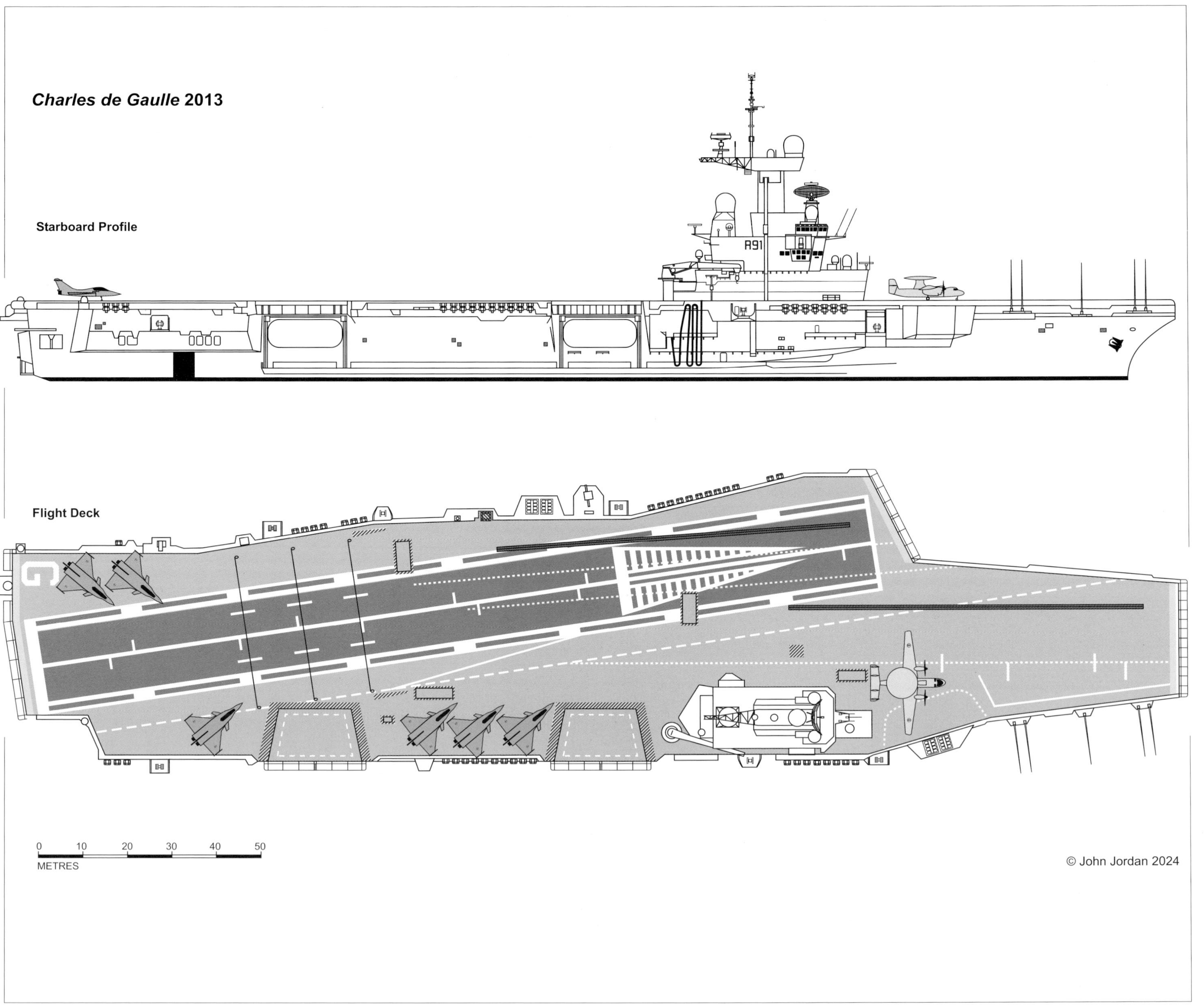

Charles de Gaulle 2013
Starboard Profile
R91
Flight Deck
0 10 20 30 40 50
METRES
© John Jordan 2024

Above: *Charles de Gaulle* in the Gulf of Aden on 3 February 2015, with Rafale and Super Etendard aircraft on board. *(ARDHAN collection)*

a TV camera and a laser rangefinder, backed up by a TDS 90 light TI director (DLO).

## RADAR AND ELECTRONIC COUNTERMEASURES

*Charles de Gaulle* has the standard outfit of modern French surveillance and navigation radars. The antenna for the DRBV 26D air surveillance radar is mounted on a pylon atop the bridge, a DRBV 15C radar provides target indication, and there are antennae for the DRBN 34 navigation radar at the forward and after ends of the bridge (see drawing). DRBV 26 is capable of detection of an aircraft up to 160nm from the carrier.

For the detection of hostile radar emissions the ship is equipped with ARBR 21A; ARBG 2B Maigret direction finding equipment can intercept and monitor radio transmissions, while infrared emissions are detected by the DIBV 2A Vampir system.

Provision for electronic countermeasures (ECM) is exceptionally complete. ARBB 33 jammers are mounted on either side of the island, and these are allied to no fewer than four Sagaie AMBL 2B NG decoy launchers, which are disposed below flight level on either side of the ship. The Sagaie (*système d'autodéfense pour la guerre antimissile infrarouge et électromagnétique*) launcher comprises ten tubes each

**Charles de Gaulle: Electronics Outfit [as completed]**

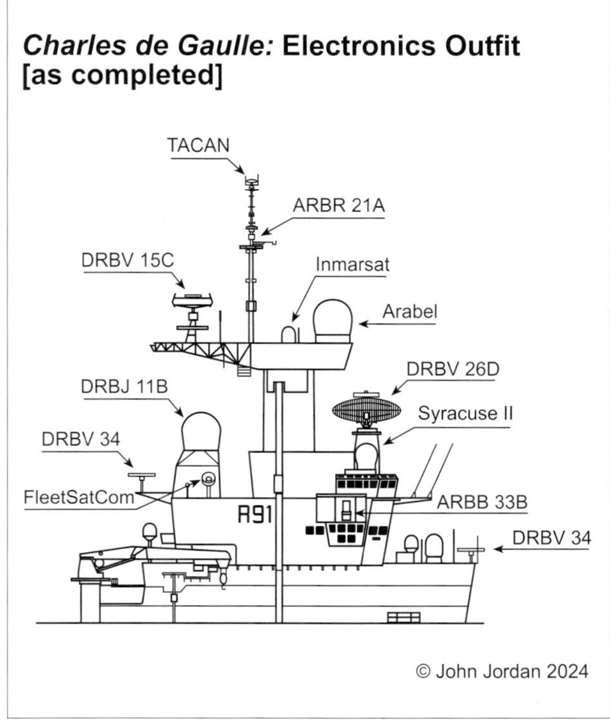

CHARLES DE GAULLE

A starboard-side view of *Charles de Gaulle* on 16 December 2016 showing the layout of the island. *(US Navy)*

**Right:** Super Etendard and Rafale aircraft on *Charles de Gaulle* during a visit to Lisbon on 30 March 2010. *(ARDHAN collection)*

capable of firing a 45kg, 170mm-diameter rocket dispensing either chaff (REM) or infrared (RIR) decoys. The tubes can be elevated and the launcher trained to create a false target up to 3,000 metres from the ship.

No sonar was fitted, but *Charles de Gaulle* is fitted with an ALTO torpedo detection system, a SLAT torpedo decoy launcher allied to a linear towed array (ALR), and the US Navy's Nixie electro-acoustic device.

## COMMAND, CONTROL & COMMUNICATIONS

Unlike her two predecessors, *Charles de Gaulle* was equipped with an advanced suite of digital command and control systems from the outset.

The Combat System (*système de combat* or SDC) comprises two interlinked systems to assist the command in its decision-making: one for the naval force and the other for the ship itself. The central element is the SENIT 8/05 tactical data system, which was derived from the SENIT 6 fitted in the air defence frigates of the *Cassard* class. The initial installation comprised four computers allied to twenty-five consoles. It is operated from the Operations Centre (CO), which has thirty-eight work stations (of which twenty-two are SENIT consoles). It is organised into five modules: surveillance, command & control, self-defence, air operations, and monitoring of emissions.

For command of a naval force there was initially AIDCOMER (*aide au commandement à la mer*), a French-developed system that was nevertheless compatible with NATO operations. Tactical data

**Right:** A Grumman E-2C Hawkeye AEW aircraft at Lann-Bihoué on 18 June 2000. *(Jean Moulin)*

## Table 2: **CHARACTERISTICS**

| | |
|---|---|
| Displacement: | 37,585 tonnes standard<br>42,500 tonnes deep load |
| Dimensions: | |
| length | 238m pp; 261.5m oa |
| beam | 31.50m wl |
| mean draught | 10.50m deep load |
| Aviation: | |
| flight deck | 261.5m |
| width of deck | 64.36 max |
| height above wl | 17.20m |
| angled deck | 203m x 20m (8°30′) |
| hangar | 138m x 29m x 6.10m |
| lifts (LxW) | 21m x 12m (36 tonnes) |
| catapults | two C13-3 75-metre (25-tonne aircraft) |
| arrester cables | three Mk 7 Mod 3 at 13m intervals |
| cranes | one fixed (37 tonnes), one mobile |
| Machinery: | |
| steam supply | two K15 nuclear reactors, each 150MW |
| engines | two-shaft geared turbines (HP + LP)<br>two turbo-alternators |
| horsepower | 83,000cv |
| propellers | two 4-bladed, 5.9m diameter |
| speed | 27 knots max (25kts cruising) |
| electricity | four turbo-alternators, each 4000kW<br>four diesel alternators, each 1,100kW<br>two emergency gas turbines, each 500kW |
| Armament: | |
| missiles | two SAAM systems for Aster 15 SAMs (2 x XVI)<br>two SADRAL for Mistral SAMs (2 x VI) |
| aircraft | forty |
| Electronics: | |
| air search | DRBV 26D (D band) |
| target designation | DRBV 15C (E/F band) |
| 3-D air surveillance | DRBJ 11B (E/F band) |
| fire control | Arabel (I/J band)<br>2 x DIBC 2A Vigy 105 EOD<br>TDS 90 DLO |
| navigation | 2 x DRBN 34 |
| ESM | ARBR 21A, ARBG 2B Maigret<br>DIBV 2A Vampir |
| ECM | 2 x ARBB 33B, 4 x Sagaie AMBL 2B NG<br>SLAT, Alto, Nixie |
| Satcom | Syracuse II, Inmarsat, Fleetsatcom |
| Complement: | |
| incl air group | 1,950: 177 officers, 890 POs, 883 men |
| excl air group | 1,250 |
| flag staff | +100 |

## Table 3: **EMBARKED AIRCRAFT**

**Dassault Rafale**

Derived from ACT/ACM programme begun 1976. Prototype ACX (> Rafale A) made approaches to *Clemenceau* without touching down 1987. Four development aircraft included M01/02 single-seat fighter for Navy. M01 first flight 19 Dec 1991. M01/02 trials aboard *Foch* Apr 1993 to Feb 1998. First production aircraft M1 flew 1 Jul 1999. Nine of first 10 F1 interceptors (M1–10) joined 12F 2000–02. In service 21 Jun 2004. Cocooned 2008 and upgraded to F3 standard; replaced in 12F by F2 variant M11–26). First in service 19 May 2006; adapted to fire ASMs. F3 variant operational 2009 onwards. Total of forty-six delivered.

Characteristics:

| | |
|---|---|
| Type: | single-seat multirole fighter |
| Weight: | 10,196kg light, 14,000kg fully loaded |
| Dimensions: | 15.27m(L) x 10.86m(S) x 5.34m(H) |
| Performance: | powered by 2 x Snecma M88 turbofans with afterburner, each 50.04/75kN; 1912km/h (Mach 1.8) at high altitude; 1850km radius |
| Armament: | 1x 30mm cannon, 4–6 x Mica IR/EM AAMs,<br>SCALP EG cruise missiles,<br>ASMP-A nuclear missile |
| Electronics: | Thales RBE2-AA AESA radar |

Can be equipped with AREOS reconnaissance pod.

| | |
|---|---|
| Flotille 11F | 2011– |
| Flotille 12F | 2000– |
| Flotille 17F | 2016– |

**Grumman E-2C Hawkeye**

Airborne Early Warning (AEW) aircraft in service with US Navy. French Navy purchased three, delivered Dec 1998, Mar 1999 and Feb 2004 specifically to operate from *Charles de Gaulle*. Initially E-2C variant, but updated to NP2000 standard 2006–07.

Characteristics:

| | |
|---|---|
| Type: | all-weather AEW; crew of five |
| Weight: | 17,091kg light, 23,810kg fully loaded |
| Dimensions: | 17.56m(L) x 24.58m(S) x 5.58m(H) |
| Performance: | powered by 2 x Allison/RR T56-A-427 turboprop engines, each 5100hp; 650km/h; six hours endurance |
| Electronics: | AN/APS-145 radar |

| | |
|---|---|
| Flotille 4F | 2000– |

transfer was ensured by NATO Links 11 and 16. Other transmissions use the standard HF, VHF and UHF frequencies.

*Charles de Gaulle* had the now-standard outfit of satellite communications of Syracuse, Inmarsat, and the US Navy's FleetSatCom.

## AIR GROUP

The provision of an air group capable of undertaking a range of missions was problematic from the outset. The Navy was inclined towards the purchase of US Navy aircraft such as the F-18 Hornet and E-2C Hawkeye, but there was political pressure for a solution that would support the French aviation industry, and although three Hawkeyes were purchased direct from Grumman, the multirole, high-performance fighter to be embarked had to be developed from a land-based model, the Dassault Rafale. Development was prolonged and the purchase of sufficient aircraft had to be spread over a number of years, which meant that the Super Etendard had to be upgraded to S3, then S4 and finally, between 2007 and 2009, to S5 standard (thirty-five aircraft) to perform the strike and reconnaissance missions.

The first nine production Rafale fighters (F1 variant) joined Squadron 12F in 2000–2002 and entered service in 2004. They were withdrawn in 2008, and when funding became available were upgraded to F3 standard. In the interim they were replaced in 12 F by an F2 strike fighter variant capable of firing air-to-ground missiles, which entered service in May 2006. The F3 variant was operational from 2009 onwards, and by the middle of the next decade the Rafale had taken on all the former roles of the Super Etendard, which was retired from service in 2016.

**Above and right:** Bow and stern quarter views of *Charles de Gaulle* taken on 15 April 2019, when she operated in the Red Sea in company with the US Navy carrier *John C Stennis* (CVN-74). Note the replacement of the DRBJ 11 radar by the SMART-S Mk II. *(US Navy)*

CHAPTER 10

# EPILOGUE

THE COMPLETION OF *CHARLES DE GAULLE* does not mark the end of the story. The *Marine Nationale* continued to push for the construction of a second carrier to ensure that one of the two units would always be in commission and available to deploy. In 1991, the Navy still hoped for the order of a ship identical to *Charles de Gaulle*, to be in service by 2004, the date *Foch* was due to decommission. In 1993 it was envisaged that this second carrier would be laid down in 1997, but a decision was postponed first to 1995, then to 1997. It was now hoped to keep *Foch* in service until 2006, but in 1997 the decision was again postponed until 2001, with a possible abandonment of nuclear propulsion to reduce costings. At the end of 1999 it was decided to delay once again until 2003, and to investigate the possibility of a joint project with the British, whose CVF design would eventually result in HMS *Queen Elizabeth*. However, on 11 July 2001 the Minister of Defence announced that *Foch* would not be replaced, and that the 2003–08 programme would prioritise the construction of new frigates.

Despite the above, on 6 September of the following year President Jacques Chirac announced that a second carrier would feature in the 2003–08 programme; the ship would be ordered in 2005 and would enter service in 2014 – an ambitious hope given the delays experienced with *Charles de Gaulle*. Three possible iterations were mooted:

- a sister of *Charles de Gaulle*
- a new type of carrier with conventional propulsion machinery
- a joint Franco-British project for a conventional carrier.

On 13 February 2004, the President announced his decision to abandon nuclear propulsion. The ship, to be ordered as PA 2 under the 2003–08 programme, was to be a variant of the British CVF project with catapults and arrester wires (CATOBAR); there would otherwise be 80 per cent commonality between the two designs. The ship was to be ordered in December 2006 from Saint-Nazaire and fitted out at Brest. A bilateral agreement was signed with the UK on 6 March 2006. The order was due to be placed in 2008; the ship would be laid down in 2010, launched in 2012 and in service in 2015. An order for the catapults was placed on 4 May 2007, but on 27 May 2008 the new President of the Republic, Nicolas Sarkozy, put the decision on hold. Co-operation with the British was suspended on 21 June, and the order for the catapults suspended in March of the following year. PA 2 had not officially been abandoned, but the contract with the British was terminated, and the *Marine Nationale* again considered nuclear propulsion.

**Above:** Artist's impression of the joint project with Britain published in 2007. Unlike the Royal Navy's *Queen Elizabeth* and *Prince of Wales*, which were designed to operate the advanced V/STOL F-35B multirole fighter, the French variant would have had conventional catapults and arrester wires.

Studies for a carrier of new design resumed in earnest in 2019. The project was christened PA-Ng, the *Porte-Avions Nouvelle Génération*, and the ship was to replace *Charles de Gaulle* when she reached the end of her service life around 2038. Construction of the carrier, which was to have an overall length of around 300 metres and a displacement of 75,000 tonnes, was authorised by President Emmanuel Macron in December 2020.

In configuration the PA-Ng closely resembles contemporary US Navy carriers, of which the design is a reduced version. Artist's impressions show a broad flight deck equipped with two or three catapults, and with two side lifts to starboard forward of a short island. Like her predecessor the ship will have nuclear propulsion; steam will be supplied by two K22 220MW nuclear reactors, preliminary design work for which was completed in 2023. The catapults and arrester cables will be of the advanced US EMALS (Electromagnetic Aircraft Launch System) and AAG (Advanced Arresting Gear) types, the sale of which was authorised by the US State Department in 2021; estimated cost for these items alone is US $1.3 billion.

The new carrier is too large to be built in any of the state dockyards, so the hull will be ordered from Chantiers de l'Atlantique of Saint-Nazaire, then fitted out at Brest. She is due to be laid down in late 2025 or early 2026, with sea trials from 2036.

**Right:** Two artist's impressions of PANG dating from 2022. In the first, the island superstructure is topped by a distinctive cone structure similar to that of the former USS *Enterprise* (CVN-65). This appears to have been superseded by a more conventional island with a broadly rectangular configuration. In the second image, note the third catapult forward, to starboard. The aircraft depicted is the SCAF next-generation multirole fighter under development. The current E-2C model of Hawkeye will be replaced by the more advanced E-2D, three of which are to be delivered from 2029. *(Naval Group).*

# SOURCES

## PUBLICATIONS


Alhéritière, Jacques: *L'engagement de l'aviation embarquée en Indochine (1947–1954)*, ARDHAN (2016).

Bail, René:
*L'aventure Corsair* (1990)
*La légende des Corsair*, éditions Larivière (2005).

Barjot, VA Pierre:
*Vers la Marine de l'âge atomique*, Amiot-Dumont (Paris, 1955)
*Histoire de la guerre aéro-navale*, Flammarion (Paris, 1961).

Bruneau, Jean-Baptiste: *La Marine de Vichy aux Antilles juin 1940–juillet 1943*, Rivages des Xantons (2014).

Centre d'études d'histoire de la Défense:
*La France face aux problèmes d'armement 1945–1950*, Editions complexes (1996)
*La France dans l'opération de Suez de 1956*, ADDIM (1997).

Conq, Joseph: *Pilote de chasse et officier d'appontage (Marine 1937–1974)*, ARDHAN (2014).

Couteau-Bégarie, Hervé:
*Le problème du porte-avions*, Economica (1990)
*Le meilleur des ambassadeurs: théorie et pratique de la diplomatie navale*, Economica (2010).

Croulebois, Georges: *Pont libre*, Editions les 7 vents (1993).

Dousset, Francis: *Les porte-avions français des origines (1911) à nos jours*, Editions de la Cité (Brest =, 1978).

Escoubet, Eric:
*Le Super Frelon SA 321, une épopée de 45 ans dans l'Aéronautique navale 1965–2010*, ARDHAN (2013)
*Les formations d'hélicoptères de l'Aéronautique navale*, Vols 1 & 2 ARDHAN (2017–18).

Friedman, Norman:
*Carrier Air Power*, Conway Maritime Press (London, 1981)
*British Carrier Aviation*, Conway Maritime Press (London, 1988).

Gall, Jean-Marie:
*Le SNCASE Aquilon*, Lela Presse (1999)
*Les Crusader français en action*, Lela Presse (2003)
*La saga Etendard*, Vols 1 & 2, Lela Presse (2009).

Heger, Michel: *Une ancre et des ailes*, Editions Ouest-France (1989).

Hobbs, David:
*A Century of Carrier Aviation*, Seaforth Publishing (Barnsley, 2009)
*British Aircraft Carriers*, Seaforth Publishing (Barnsley, 2013).

Hone, Thomas C; Friedman, Norman; Mandeles, Mark D: *American & British Aircraft Carrier Development 1919–1941*, US Naval Institute Press (Annapolis, 1999).

Jordan, John:
'*The* Aircraft Transport *Commandant Teste*', *Warship 2002–2003*, Conway (London, 2003)
'PA16: France's Carrier Project of 1938', *Warship 2010*, Conway (London, 2010)
'From Battleship to Carrier: *Béarn*', *Warship 2020*, Osprey (Oxford, 2020)
'*Clemenceau* and *Foch*: France's First Modern Aircraft Carriers', *Warship 2023*, Osprey (Oxford, 2023)
*Warships After Washington*, Seaforth Publishing (Barnsley, 2011)
*Warships After London*, Seaforth Publishing (Barnsley, 2020).

Josa, Ramon: *Marin & pilote: servir en mer et dans les airs*, Editions JPO (2018).

Klotz, VAE Bernard: *Enfer au paradis: trois campagnes sur Hellcat Indochine (1952–1953–1954)*, ARDHAN (2005).

Lemaire, CV André: *Haute et Claire! Marine et Aviation 1943–1980*, ARDHAN (2014).

*Le porte-avions Charles de Gaulle*, Vols I, II & III, Editions SPE Barthelemy (2000, 2003, 2005).

*Les Flottes de combat*, 1914–2018.

Masson, M: *La crise de Suez novembre 1956–avril 1957*, Service historique de la Marine, (Paris, 1966).

Morareau, Lucien:
*Les aéronefs de l'Aviation maritime (1910–1942)*, ARDHAN (2002)
*Mémorial de l'Aéronautique navale (1910–2010)*, ARDHAN (2010).

Mordal, Jaques, *Marine Indochine*, Amiot-Dumont (Paris, 1953).

Moulin, Jean; Morareau, Lucien; Picard, Claude: *Le Béarn et le Commandant Teste*, Marines Edition (Bourg en Bresse, 1996).

Moulin, Jean:
*Les porte-avions Dixmude & Arromanches*, Marines éditions (1998)
*Les porte-avions La Fayette & Bois Belleau*, Marines éditions (2000)
*Les porte-avions Clemenceau & Foch*, Marines Editions (Rennes, 2006)
*Les porte-avions français*, Marines éditions (2008)
*Tous les porte-aéronefs en France*, Editions Lela Presse (Le Vigen, 2020).

Oudot de Sainville, Admiral Alain: *Vol au vent marin: un regard sur l'histoire de l'Aéronautique navale*, ARDHAN (2017).

Paringaux, Alexandre: *Le porte-avions Foch*, Editions du Zéphyr (2000).

Piart, Yannick: *La pointe du diamant*, Nimrod (2017).

Quérel Bruylant, Philippe: *Vers une Marine atomique, la Marine française (1945–1958)*, LGDJ (1997).

Razoux, Pierre: *La guerre Iran–Irak, première guerre du Golfe 1980–1988*, Perrin (2013).

Robin, Henri; Feuilloy, Robert: *L'Aéronautique navale en Indochine 1927–1956*, ARDHAN (2007).

Saibène, Marc: *Toulon et la Marine du sabordage à la Libération*, Marines éditions (2002).

Service d'information et de relations publique de la Marine:
*Marine et guerre du Golfe*, ADDIM (1992)
*Le Clemenceau et le Foch*, ADDIM (1993).

Thuille, Jean-Louis: *Cher porte-avions: un récit entre ciel et mer*, Editions Jean-Marie Bordessoules (1999).

Touzet, Christophe: *Bréguet 1050 Alizé*, self-published (2017).

Vercken, VA Roger:
*Au-delà du pont d'envol*, Alerion (1995)
*Sur les traces du tigre ou mes années Clemenceau*, ARDHAN (1997)
*Histoire succincte de l'Aéronautique navale (1910–1998)*, ARDHAN (1998).

Verdier, CV Armand: *Des ailes, des raquettes et du ciel, la flottille 3F et l'Arromanches en Indochine (1951–1952)*, ARDHAN (2004).

Vulliez, CV (Ret) Albert: *Aéronavale*, Amiot-Dumont (Paris, 1955).

## PERIODICALS

*Marine Nationale*
*La Revue Maritime*
*Cols Bleus*
*Marines & Forces Navales*
*Navires & Histoire*
*Los!*

## ARCHIVES

Plans and other documentation from the Centre d'Archives de l'Armement et du Personnel Civil (CAAPC), Châtellerault, which forms part of the Service Historique de la Défense (SHD).

## WEBSITES

Net-Marine (www.netmarine.net)
Mer et Marine (www.meretmarine.com)
La Marine Nationale (www.defense.gouv.fr/marine)

Many of the photographs in this book come from the collection of the Association pour la Recherche de Documentation sur l'Aéronautique Navale (ARDHAN), an association formed to honour former French naval aviators and to preserve documentation related to the naval air arm.

# INDEX

## NOTE ABOUT THE INDEX

The main body of the index consists predominantly of names of ships and people. For ships, the type of vessel, together with nationality for non-French vessels, are given are in parentheses. Due to the broad scope of the historical section, the only place names included in the index are major ports and those associated with significant actions or campaigns. With regard to French naval officers, only those of flag officers and prominent figures in the development of naval aviation feature in the index. There are 'thematic' entries for the following: **aircraft**, **formations**, **guns**, **missiles** and **radars**. Sections of the book that focus on a particular system, or on a particular aspect of a ship (or class of ship) are in **bold** type; *italics* are used for photographs.